# Casenote™ Legal Briefs

---

# PROPERTY

---

Keyed to Courses Using

**Cribbet, Findley, Smith, and Dzienkowski's**
**Property: Cases and Materials**

Ninth Edition

## Wolters Kluwer
### Law & Business

AUSTIN   BOSTON   CHICAGO   NEW YORK   THE NETHERLANDS

This publication is designed to provide accurate and authoritative information
in regard to the subject matter covered. It is sold with the understanding that the
publisher is not engaged in rendering legal, accounting, or other professional
services. If legal advice or other expert assistance is required, the services of a
competent professional person should be sought.

> — From a Declaration of Principles adopted jointly
> by a Committee of the American Bar Association
> and a Committee of Publishers and Associates

To contact Customer Care, e-mail customer.care@aspenpublishers.com,
call 1-800-234-1660, fax 1-800-901-9075, or mail correspondence to:

Aspen Publishers
Attn: Order Department
P.O. Box 990
Frederick, MD 21705

Printed in the United States of America.

1 2 3 4 5 6 7 8 9 0

ISBN 978-0-7355-7179-2

## About Wolters Kluwer Law & Business

Wolters Kluwer Law & Business is a leading provider of research information and workflow solutions in key specialty areas. The strengths of the individual brands of Aspen Publishers, CCH, Kluwer Law International and Loislaw are aligned within Wolters Kluwer Law & Business to provide comprehensive, in-depth solutions and expert-authored content for the legal, professional and education markets.

**CCH** was founded in 1913 and has served more than four generations of business professionals and their clients. The CCH products in the Wolters Kluwer Law & Business group are highly regarded electronic and print resources for legal, securities, antitrust and trade regulation, government contracting, banking, pension, payroll, employment and labor, and health-care reimbursement and compliance professionals.

**Aspen Publishers** is a leading information provider for attorneys, business professionals and law students. Written by preeminent authorities, Aspen products offer analytical and practical information in a range of specialty practice areas from securities law and intellectual property to mergers and acquisitions and pension/benefits. Aspen's trusted legal education resources provide professors and students with high-quality, up-to-date and effective resources for successful instruction and study in all areas of the law.

**Kluwer Law International** supplies the global business community with comprehensive English-language international legal information. Legal practitioners, corporate counsel and business executives around the world rely on the Kluwer Law International journals, loose-leafs, books and electronic products for authoritative information in many areas of international legal practice.

**Loislaw** is a premier provider of digitized legal content to small law firm practitioners of various specializations. Loislaw provides attorneys with the ability to quickly and efficiently find the necessary legal information they need, when and where they need it, by facilitating access to primary law as well as state-specific law, records, forms and treatises.

Wolters Kluwer Law & Business, a unit of Wolters Kluwer, is headquartered in New York and Riverwoods, Illinois. Wolters Kluwer is a leading multinational publisher and information services company.

# Format for the Casenote Legal Brief

**Nature of Case:** This section identifies the form of action (e.g., breach of contract, negligence, battery), the type of proceeding (e.g., demurrer, appeal from trial court's jury instructions) or the relief sought (e.g., damages, injunction, criminal sanctions).

**Fact Summary:** This is included to refresh your memory and can be used as a quick reminder of the facts.

**Rule of Law:** Summarizes the general principle of law that the case illustrates. It may be used for instant recall of the court's holding and for classroom discussion or home review.

**Facts:** This section contains all relevant facts of the case, including the contentions of the parties and the lower court holdings. It is written in a logical order to give the student a clear understanding of the case. The plaintiff and defendant are identified by their proper names throughout and are always labeled with a (P) or (D).

## Palsgraf v. Long Island R.R. Co.

Injured bystander (P) v. Railroad company (D)

N.Y. Ct. App., 248 N.Y. 339, 162 N.E. 99 (1928).

**NATURE OF CASE:** Appeal from judgment affirming verdict for plaintiff seeking damages for personal injury.

**FACT SUMMARY:** Helen Palsgraf (P) was injured on R.R.'s (D) train platform when R.R.'s (D) guard helped a passenger aboard a moving train, causing his package to fall on the tracks. The package contained fireworks which exploded, creating a shock that tipped a scale onto Palsgraf (P).

### 🏛 RULE OF LAW
The risk reasonably to be perceived defines the duty to be obeyed.

**FACTS:** Helen Palsgraf (P) purchased a ticket to Rockaway Beach from R.R. (D) and was waiting on the train platform. As she waited, two men ran to catch a train that was pulling out from the platform. The first man jumped aboard, but the second man, who appeared as if he might fall, was helped aboard by the guard on the train who had kept the door open so they could jump aboard. A guard on the platform also helped push him onto the train. The man was carrying a package wrapped in newspaper. In the process, the man dropped his package, which fell on the tracks. The package contained fireworks and exploded. The shock of the explosion was apparently of great enough strength to tip over some scales at the other end of the platform, which fell on Palsgraf (P) and injured her. A jury awarded her damages, and R.R. (D) appealed.

**ISSUE:** Does the risk reasonably to be perceived define the duty to be obeyed?

**HOLDING AND DECISION:** (Cardozo, C.J.) Yes. The risk reasonably to be perceived defines the duty to be obeyed. If there is no foreseeable hazard to the injured party as the result of a seemingly innocent act, the act does not become a tort because it happened to be a wrong as to another. If the wrong was not willful, the plaintiff must show that the act as to her had such great and apparent possibilities of danger as to entitle her to protection. Negligence in the abstract is not enough upon which to base liability. Negligence is a relative concept, evolving out of the common law doctrine of trespass on the case. To establish liability, the defendant must owe a legal duty of reasonable care to the injured party. A cause of action in tort will lie where harm,

though unintended, could have been averted or avoided by observance of such a duty. The scope of the duty is limited by the range of danger that a reasonable person could foresee. In this case, there was nothing to suggest from the appearance of the parcel or otherwise that the parcel contained fireworks. The guard could not reasonably have had any warning of a threat to Palsgraf (P), and R.R. (D) therefore cannot be held liable. Judgment is reversed in favor of R.R. (D).

**DISSENT:** (Andrews, J.) The concept that there is no negligence unless R.R. (D) owes a legal duty to take care as to Palsgraf (P) herself is too narrow. Everyone owes to the world at large the duty of refraining from those acts that may unreasonably threaten the safety of others. If the guard's action was negligent as to those nearby, it was also negligent as to those outside what might be termed the "danger zone." For Palsgraf (P) to recover, R.R.'s (D) negligence must have been the proximate cause of her injury, a question of fact for the jury.

### ▶ ANALYSIS

The majority defined the limit of the defendant's liability in terms of the danger that a reasonable person in defendant's situation would have perceived. The dissent argued that the limitation should not be placed on liability, but rather on damages. Judge Andrews suggested that only injuries that would not have happened but for R.R.'s (D) negligence should be compensable. Both the majority and dissent recognized the policy-driven need to limit liability for negligent acts, seeking, in the words of Judge Andrews, to define a framework "that will be practical and in keeping with the general understanding of mankind." The Restatement (Second) of Torts has accepted Judge Cardozo's view.

━━

### Quicknotes

**FORESEEABILITY** A reasonable expectation that change is the probable result of certain acts or omissions

**NEGLIGENCE** Conduct falling below the standard of care that a reasonable person would demonstrate under similar conditions.

**PROXIMATE CAUSE** The natural sequence of events without which an injury would not have been sustained.

━━

**Party ID:** Quick identification of the relationship between the parties.

**Concurrence/Dissent:** All concurrences and dissents are briefed whenever they are included by the casebook editor.

**Analysis:** This last paragraph gives you a broad understanding of where the case "fits in" with other cases in the section of the book and with the entire course. It is a hornbook-style discussion indicating whether the case is a majority or minority opinion and comparing the principal case with other cases in the casebook. It may also provide analysis from restatements, uniform codes, and law review articles. The analysis will prove to be invaluable to classroom discussion.

**Issue:** The issue is a concise question that brings out the essence of the opinion as it relates to the section of the casebook in which the case appears. Both substantive and procedural issues are included if relevant to the decision.

**Holding and Decision:** This section offers a clear and in-depth discussion of the rule of the case and the court's rationale. It is written in easy-to-understand language and answers the issue presented by applying the law to the facts of the case. When relevant, it includes a thorough discussion of the exceptions to the case as listed by the court, any major cites to the other cases on point, and the names of the judges who wrote the decisions.

**Quicknotes:** Conveniently defines legal terms found in the case and summarizes the nature of any statutes, codes, or rules referred to in the text.

Aspen Publishers is proud to offer *Casenote Legal Briefs*—continuing thirty years of publishing America's best-selling legal briefs.

*Casenote Legal Briefs* are designed to help you save time when briefing assigned cases. Organized under convenient headings, they show you how to abstract the basic facts and holdings from the text of the actual opinions handed down by the courts. Used as part of a rigorous study regimen, they can help you spend more time analyzing and critiquing points of law than on copying bits and pieces of judicial opinions into your notebook or outline.

*Casenote Legal Briefs* should never be used as a substitute for assigned casebook readings. They work best when read as a follow-up to reviewing the underlying opinions themselves. Students who try to avoid reading and digesting the judicial opinions in their casebooks or online sources will end up shortchanging themselves in the long run. The ability to absorb, critique, and restate the dynamic and complex elements of case law decisions is crucial to your success in law school and beyond. It cannot be developed vicariously.

*Casenote Legal Briefs* represents but one of the many offerings in Aspen's Study Aid Timeline, which includes:

- *Casenote Legal Briefs*
- *Emanuel Law Outlines*
- *Examples & Explanations* Series
- *Introduction to Law* Series
- Emanuel *Law in a Flash* Flashcards
- Emanuel *CrunchTime* Series

Each of these series is designed to provide you with easy-to-understand explanations of complex points of law. Each volume offers guidance on the principles of legal analysis and, consulted regularly, will hone your ability to spot relevant issues. We have titles that will help you prepare for class, prepare for your exams, and enhance your general comprehension of the law along the way.

To find out more about Aspen Study Aid publications, visit us online at *http://lawschool.aspenpublishers.com* or email us at *legaledu@aspenpubl.com*. We'll be happy to assist you.

# Get this Casenote Legal Brief as an AspenLaw Studydesk eBook today!

By returning this form to Aspen Publishers, you will receive a complimentary eBook download of this Casenote Legal Brief in the AspenLaw Studydesk digital format.* Learn more about AspenLaw Studydesk today at *www.AspenLaw.com.*

| Name | Phone ( ) |
|---|---|
| Address | Apt. No. |
| City | State | ZIP Code |
| Law School | Graduation Date |

Cut out the UPC found on the lower left corner of the back cover of this book. Staple the UPC inside this box. Only the original UPC from the book cover will be accepted. (No photocopies or store stickers are allowed.)

**Attach UPC inside this box.**

**Email** (Print legibly or you may not get access!)

**Title of this book** (course subject)

**ISBN of this book** (10- or 13-digit number on the UPC)

**Used with which casebook** (provide author's name)

**Mail the completed form to:**    Aspen Publishers, Inc.
Legal Education Division
130 Turner Street, Bldg 3, 4th Floor
Waltham, MA 02453-8901

* Upon receipt of this completed form, you will be emailed a code for the digital download of this book in AspenLaw Studydesk format. The AspenLaw Studydesk application is available as a 60-day free trial at *www.AspenLaw.com.*

**For a full list of print titles by Aspen Publishers, visit *lawschool.aspenpublishers.com.***
**For a full list of digital eBook titles by Aspen Publishers, visit *www.AspenLaw.com.***

(Make a photocopy of this form and your UPC for your records.)

## A. Decide on a Format and Stick to It

Structure is essential to a good brief. It enables you to arrange systematically the related parts that are scattered throughout most cases, thus making manageable and understandable what might otherwise seem to be an endless and unfathomable sea of information. There are, of course, an unlimited number of formats that can be utilized. However, it is best to find one that suits your needs and stick to it. Consistency breeds both efficiency and the security that when called upon you will know where to look in your brief for the information you are asked to give.

Any format, as long as it presents the essential elements of a case in an organized fashion, can be used. Experience, however, has led *Casenotes* to develop and utilize the following format because of its logical flow and universal applicability.

**NATURE OF CASE:** This is a brief statement of the legal character and procedural status of the case (e.g., "Appeal of a burglary conviction").

There are many different alternatives open to a litigant dissatisfied with a court ruling. The key to determining which one has been used is to discover *who is asking this court for what.*

This first entry in the brief should be kept as *short as possible.* Use the court's terminology if you understand it. But since jurisdictions vary as to the titles of pleadings, the best entry is the one that addresses who wants what in this proceeding, not the one that sounds most like the court's language.

**RULE OF LAW:** A statement of the general principle of law that the case illustrates (e.g., "An acceptance that varies any term of the offer is considered a rejection and counteroffer").

Determining the rule of law of a case is a procedure similar to determining the issue of the case. Avoid being fooled by red herrings; there may be a few rules of law mentioned in the case excerpt, but usually only one is *the* rule with which the casebook editor is concerned. The techniques used to locate the issue, described below, may also be utilized to find the rule of law. Generally, your best guide is simply the chapter heading. It is a clue to the point the casebook editor seeks to make and should be kept in mind when reading every case in the respective section.

**FACTS:** A synopsis of only the essential facts of the case, i.e., those bearing upon or leading up to the issue.

The facts entry should be a short statement of the events and transactions that led one party to initiate legal proceedings against another in the first place. While some cases conveniently state the salient facts at the beginning of the decision, in other instances they will have to be culled from hiding places throughout the text, even from concurring and dissenting opinions. Some of the "facts" will often be in dispute and should be so noted. Conflicting evidence may be briefly pointed up. "Hard" facts must be included. Both must be *relevant* in order to be listed in the facts entry. It is impossible to tell what is relevant until the entire case is read, as the ultimate determination of the rights and liabilities of the parties may turn on something buried deep in the opinion.

Generally, the facts entry should not be longer than three to five *short* sentences.

It is often helpful to identify the role played by a party in a given context. For example, in a construction contract case the identification of a party as the "contractor" or "builder" alleviates the need to tell that that party was the one who was supposed to have built the house.

It is always helpful, and a good general practice, to identify the "plaintiff" and the "defendant." This may seem elementary and uncomplicated, but, especially in view of the creative editing practiced by some casebook editors, it is sometimes a difficult or even impossible task. Bear in mind that the *party presently* seeking something from this court may not be the plaintiff, and that sometimes only the cross-claim of a defendant is treated in the excerpt. Confusing or misaligning the parties can ruin your analysis and understanding of the case.

**ISSUE:** A statement of the general legal question answered by or illustrated in the case. For clarity, the issue is best put in the form of a question capable of a "yes" or "no" answer. In reality, the issue is simply the Rule of Law put in the form of a question (e.g., "May an offer be accepted by performance?").

The major problem presented in discerning what is *the* issue in the case is that an opinion usually purports to raise and answer several questions. However, except for rare cases, only one such question is really the issue in the case. Collateral issues not necessary to the resolution of the matter in controversy are handled by the court by language known as *"obiter dictum"* or merely *"dictum."* While dicta may be included later in the brief, they have no place under the issue heading.

To find the issue, ask *who wants what* and then go on to ask *why did that party succeed or fail in getting it.* Once this is determined, the "why" should be turned into a question.

The complexity of the issues in the cases will vary, but in all cases a single-sentence question should sum up the issue. *In a few cases,* there will be two, or even more rarely, three issues of equal importance to the resolution of the case. Each should be expressed in a single-sentence question.

Since many issues are resolved by a court in coming to a final disposition of a case, the casebook editor will reproduce the portion of the opinion containing the issue or issues most relevant to the area of law under scrutiny. A noted law professor gave this advice: "Close the book; look at the title on the cover." Chances are, if it is Property, you need not concern yourself with whether, for example, the federal government's treatment of the plaintiff's land really raises a federal question sufficient to support jurisdiction on this ground in federal court.

The same rule applies to chapter headings designating sub-areas within the subjects. They tip you off as to what the text is designed to teach. The cases are arranged in a casebook to show a progression or development of the law, so that the preceding cases may also help.

It is also most important to remember to *read the notes and questions* at the end of a case to determine what the editors wanted you to have gleaned from it.

**HOLDING AND DECISION:** This section should succinctly explain the rationale of the court in arriving at its decision. In capsulizing the "reasoning" of the court, it should always include an application of the general rule or rules of law to the specific facts of the case. Hidden justifications come to light in this entry; the reasons for the state of the law, the public policies, the biases and prejudices, those considerations that influence the justices' thinking and, ultimately, the outcome of the case. At the end, there should be a short indication of the disposition or procedural resolution of the case (e.g., "Decision of the trial court for Mr. Smith (P) reversed").

The foregoing format is designed to help you "digest" the reams of case material with which you will be faced in your law school career. Once mastered by practice, it will place at your fingertips the information the authors of your casebooks have sought to impart to you in case-by-case illustration and analysis.

## B. Be as Economical as Possible in Briefing Cases

Once armed with a format that encourages succinctness, it is as important to be economical with regard to the time spent on the actual reading of the case as it is to be economical in the writing of the brief itself. This does not mean "skimming" a case. Rather, it means reading the case with an "eye" trained to recognize into which "section" of your brief a particular passage or line fits and having a system for quickly and precisely marking the case so that the passages fitting any one particular part of

the brief can be easily identified and brought together in a concise and accurate manner when the brief is actually written.

It is of no use to simply repeat everything in the opinion of the court; record only enough information to trigger your recollection of what the court said. Nevertheless, an accurate statement of the "law of the case," i.e., the legal principle applied to the facts, is absolutely essential to class preparation and to learning the law under the case method.

To that end, it is important to develop a "shorthand" that you can use to make margin notations. These notations will tell you at a glance in which section of the brief you will be placing that particular passage or portion of the opinion.

Some students prefer to underline all the salient portions of the opinion (with a pencil or colored underliner marker), making marginal notations as they go along. Others prefer the color-coded method of underlining, utilizing different colors of markers to underline the salient portions of the case, each separate color being used to represent a different section of the brief. For example, blue underlining could be used for passages relating to the rule of law, yellow for those relating to the issue, and green for those relating to the holding and decision, etc. While it has its advocates, the color-coded method can be confusing and time-consuming (all that time spent on changing colored markers). Furthermore, it can interfere with the continuity and concentration many students deem essential to the reading of a case for maximum comprehension. In the end, however, it is a matter of personal preference and style. Just remember, whatever method you use, underlining must be used sparingly or its value is lost.

If you take the marginal notation route, an efficient and easy method is to go along underlining the key portions of the case and placing in the margin alongside them the following "markers" to indicate where a particular passage or line "belongs" in the brief you will write:

N   (NATURE OF CASE)
RL  (RULE OF LAW)
I   (ISSUE)
HL  (HOLDING AND DECISION, relates to the RULE OF LAW behind the decision)
HR  (HOLDING AND DECISION, gives the RATIONALE or reasoning behind the decision)
HA  (HOLDING AND DECISION, APPLIES the general principle(s) of law to the facts of the case to arrive at the decision)

Remember that a particular passage may well contain information necessary to more than one part of your brief, in which case you simply note that in the margin. If you are using the color-coded underlining method instead of margin notation, simply make asterisks or checks in the margin next to the passage in question in the colors that indicate the additional sections of the brief where it might be utilized.

The economy of utilizing "shorthand" in marking cases for briefing can be maintained in the actual brief writing process itself by utilizing "law student shorthand" within the brief. There are many commonly used words and phrases for which abbreviations can be substituted in your briefs (and in your class notes also). You can develop abbreviations that are personal to you and which will save you a lot of time. A reference list of briefing abbreviations can be found on page xii of this book.

## C. Use Both the Briefing Process and the Brief as a Learning Tool

Now that you have a format and the tools for briefing cases efficiently, the most important thing is to make the time spent in briefing profitable to you and to make the most advantageous use of the briefs you create. Of course, the briefs are invaluable for classroom reference when you are called upon to explain or analyze a particular case. However, they are also useful in reviewing for exams. A quick glance at the fact summary should bring the case to mind, and a rereading of the rule of law should enable you to go over the underlying legal concept in your mind, how it was applied in that particular case, and how it might apply in other factual settings.

As to the value to be derived from engaging in the briefing process itself, there is an immediate benefit that arises from being forced to sift through the essential facts and reasoning from the court's opinion and to succinctly express them in your own words in your brief. The process ensures that you understand the case and the point that it illustrates, and that means you will be ready to absorb further analysis and information brought forth in class. It also ensures you will have something to say when called upon in class. The briefing process helps develop a mental agility for getting to the *gist* of a case and for identifying, expounding on, and applying the legal concepts and issues found there. The briefing process is the mental process on which you must rely in taking law school examinations; it is also the mental process upon which a lawyer relies in serving his clients and in making his living.

# Abbreviations for Briefs

| Term | Abbr. | Term | Abbr. |
|---|---|---|---|
| acceptance | acp | offer | O |
| affirmed | aff | offeree | OE |
| answer | ans | offeror | OR |
| assumption of risk | a/r | ordinance | ord |
| attorney | atty | pain and suffering | p/s |
| beyond a reasonable doubt | b/r/d | parol evidence | p/e |
| bona fide purchaser | BFP | plaintiff | P |
| breach of contract | br/k | prima facie | p/f |
| cause of action | c/a | probable cause | p/c |
| common law | c/l | proximate cause | px/c |
| Constitution | Con | real property | r/p |
| constitutional | con | reasonable doubt | r/d |
| contract | K | reasonable man | r/m |
| contributory negligence | c/n | rebuttable presumption | rb/p |
| cross | x | remanded | rem |
| cross-complaint | x/c | res ipsa loquitur | RIL |
| cross-examination | x/ex | respondeat superior | r/s |
| cruel and unusual punishment | c/u/p | Restatement | RS |
| defendant | D | reversed | rev |
| dismissed | dis | Rule Against Perpetuities | RAP |
| double jeopardy | d/j | search and seizure | s/s |
| due process | d/p | search warrant | s/w |
| equal protection | e/p | self-defense | s/d |
| equity | eq | specific performance | s/p |
| evidence | ev | statute of limitations | S/L |
| exclude | exc | statute of frauds | S/F |
| exclusionary rule | exc/r | statute | S |
| felony | f/n | summary judgment | s/j |
| freedom of speech | f/s | tenancy in common | t/c |
| good faith | g/f | tenancy at will | t/w |
| habeas corpus | h/c | tenant | t |
| hearsay | hr | third party | TP |
| husband | H | third party beneficiary | TPB |
| in loco parentis | ILP | transferred intent | TI |
| injunction | inj | unconscionable | uncon |
| inter vivos | I/v | unconstitutional | unconst |
| joint tenancy | j/t | undue influence | u/e |
| judgment | judgt | Uniform Commercial Code | UCC |
| jurisdiction | jur | unilateral | uni |
| last clear chance | LCC | vendee | VE |
| long-arm statute | LAS | vendor | VR |
| majority view | maj | versus | v |
| meeting of minds | MOM | void for vagueness | VFV |
| minority view | min | weight of the evidence | w/e |
| Miranda warnings | Mir/w | weight of authority | w/a |
| Miranda rule | Mir/r | wife | W |
| negligence | neg | with | w/ |
| notice | ntc | within | w/i |
| nuisance | nus | without prejudice | w/o/p |
| obligation | ob | without | w/o |
| obscene | obs | wrongful death | wr/d |

# Table of Cases

# What Is Property?

## Quick Reference Rules of Law

# Kremen v. Cohen Network Solution, Inc.

Domain name owner (P) v. Domain name thief (D)

337 F.3d 1024 (9th Cir. 2003).

**NATURE OF CASE:** Appeal from summary judgment for defendant in action for, inter alia, conversion and conversion by bailee.

**FACT SUMMARY:** Cohen (D) forged a letter that caused Network Solutions, the domain name registrar, to transfer the domain name "sex.com" from its rightful owner, Kremen (P), to Cohen (D). Kremen (P) sued Network Solutions for, inter alia, conversion and conversion by bailee.

## RULE OF LAW
The tort of conversion applies to domain names.

**FACTS:** Kremen (P) registered the domain name sex.com with Network Solutions (D), the domain name registrar. Con man Cohen (D), seeing great potential in that domain name, forged a letter that he sent to Network Solutions (D) indicating that Kremen (P) and his company, Online Classifieds, had decided to abandon the domain name and transfer it to Cohen (D). Although the letter's claim was less than believable, e.g., it claimed that a company called "Online Classifieds" had no Internet connection, Network Solutions (D) accepted the letter at face value and transferred the domain name to Cohen (D), who went on to turn sex.com into a lucrative online porn empire. Kremen (P) sued Cohen (D), but could not collect the $40 million in compensatory damages and $25 million in punitive damages that the court had awarded, as Cohen (D) flagrantly ignored court order after court order and became a fugitive from justice. Although the domain name was returned to Kremen (P), he sought to recover his losses from Network Solutions (D) and sued it for, inter alia, conversion and conversion by bailee. The district court granted summary judgment in favor of Network Solutions (D), finding that the tort of conversion does not apply to intangible property, such as a domain name. The court of appeals granted review.

**ISSUE:** Does the tort of conversion apply to domain names?

**HOLDING AND DECISION:** (Kozinski, J.) Yes. The tort of conversion applies to domain names. To establish the tort of conversion, a plaintiff must establish ownership or right to possession of property, wrongful disposition of the property right, and damages. The threshold issue, therefore, is whether registrants have a property right in their domain names. They do, because a domain name is a well-defined interest, like stock; because ownership is exclusive insofar as a registrant alone decides where those invoking the domain name will be sent on the Internet; because domain names are valued (being bought and sold for millions of dollars sometimes); and because registrants have a legitimate claim to exclusivity—like laying claim to a plot of land. Therefore, Kremen (P) had an intangible property right in his domain name and a jury could have found that Network Solutions (D) wrongfully disposed of that right to Kremen's (P) detriment when it transferred the domain name to Cohen (D). The district court held that intangibles are not subject to conversion. However, almost every jurisdiction has discarded this rigid limitation. Some courts, and the Restatement (Second) of Torts § 242, hold that an intangible is merged in a document when the right to possession of a chattel and the power to acquire such possession is represented by the document, or when an intangible obligation is represented by the document, which is regarded as equivalent to the obligation. Applying this test, the court found no evidence that Kremen's (P) domain name was merged in a document. However, there is no indication whether the "merged with" requirement is a part of California law. A review of California law reveals that it does not follow the Restatement's strict merger requirement, and that, in fact, it rejects a tangibility requirement altogether. Federal cases applying California law take an equally broad view. Even assuming that California retains some minimal vestigial merger requirement, Kremen's (P) domain name falls easily within a class of property that requires only some connection to a document or tangible object—not representation of the owner's intangible interest in a strict sense. The relevant document is the Domain Name System (DNS), a database that happens to be stored in electronic form. Therefore, Kremen's (P) domain name is protected by California conversion law. There is nothing unfair about holding a company, such as Network Solutions (D), liable for giving away someone else's property even if it was not at fault—"the common law does not stand idle while people give away the property of others." Finally, Kremen's (P) conversion by bailee claim does not state a cause of action independent of his conversion claim. This is not a distinct tort, but is merely the tort of conversion committed by one who is a bailee, so Kremen (P) gains nothing by showing that Network Solutions (D) is a bailee. Reversed and remanded (on the conversion claim).

## ▶ ANALYSIS

The Court of Appeals soundly rejected the district court's concern that allowing a conversion claim for domain names would increase the threat of litigation and stifle the registration system by requiring further regulations by

*Continued on next page.*

Network Solutions (D) and potential increases in fees. The Court of Appeals reasoned that given that Network Solutions' (D) regulations allowed it to hand over a registrant's domain name on the basis of a facially suspect letter, further regulations would be a good idea. It also opined that an increase in fees to increase security would not be regarded as a negative by registrants.

■■■

## Quicknotes

**CONVERSION**  The act of depriving an owner of his property without permission or justification.

**INTER ALIA**  Among other things.

■■■

# Moore v. Regents of the University of California

Patient (P) v. Physician (D) and powers of hospital (D)

Cal. Sup. Ct., 51 Cal. 3d 120, 793 P.2d 479 (1990).

**NATURE OF CASE:** Review of conversion cause of action.

**FACT SUMMARY:** Moore (P), whose cells, unbeknownst to him, had been used in medical research, contended that the cells had been converted.

## 🏛 RULE OF LAW
Unauthorized use of human tissue in medical research does not constitute a conversion.

**FACTS:** Golde (D), a physician associated with UCLA's School of Medicine, treated Moore (P) for a rare form of cancer, hairy-cell leukemia. Golde (D) realized that Moore's (P) tissues had certain unique qualities and commenced research thereon. He later developed certain tissue products whose potential economic value was great. Moore (P) later brought an action alleging that he had not consented to research on his tissues and that the tissues had been converted.

**ISSUE:** Does unauthorized use of human tissue in medical research constitute a conversion?

**HOLDING AND DECISION:** (Panelli, J.) No. Unauthorized use of human tissue in medical research does not constitute a conversion. Conversion is interference with a right of ownership or possession. One's giving up his tissue to a physician clearly has no possessory interest, so the question is whether he retains title thereto. This court concludes that he does not. Laws governing tissues tend to relate to public policy goals, not the general law of personal property. Also, California's Health and Safety Code § 7054.4 requires that human tissue and byproducts be disposed of by internment or incineration, which is certainly inconsistent with retention of title by the donor. In light of this, the rule must be that the donor of tissue does not retain title thereto. Finally, such a rule would increase the risk of liability for researchers and possibly hinder new medical research.

**CONCURRENCE:** (Arabian, J.) Moore (P) would have this court condone selling body tissue for profit, a troubling notion.

**CONCURRENCE AND DISSENT:** (Broussard, J.) If the doctor wrongfully withheld material information as to the intended use of the tissue, he committed a conversion.

**DISSENT:** (Mosk, J.) Research with human tissue that results in significant economic gain for the researcher and none for the patient offends the mores of our society by treating the human body as a commodity, much as was the case with slavery. To allow the researchers alone to profit would be unjust. The patient deserves a fair share for contributing the raw materials.

## ▶ ANALYSIS

As the court here noted in passing, it is often quite hard to apply laws that arose in ancient times to the types of controversies that can arise in the modern era. At common law, conversion was a remedy appropriate when two parties each claimed a chattel, such as a horse. This situation is light-years removed from the issues here, yet the rules of law applied were the same.

■≡■

## Quicknotes

**CONVERSION** The act of depriving an owner of his property without permission or justification.

■≡■

# Attributes of Property

## Quick Reference Rules of Law

# State v. Shack

### State of New Jersey (P) v. Agencies seeking to aid migrant farm workers (D)

N.J. Sup. Ct., 58 N.J. 297, 277 A.2d 369 (1971).

**NATURE OF CASE:** Appeal from a conviction of trespassing.

**FACT SUMMARY:** Tejeras (D) and Shack (D) entered upon private property against the orders of the owner of that property, to aid migrant farm workers employed and housed there.

## 🏛 RULE OF LAW
Real property rights are not absolute; and "necessity, private or public, may justify entry upon the lands of another."

**FACTS:** Tejeras (D) and Shack (D) worked with migrant farm workers. Tejeras (D) was a field worker for the Farm Workers Division of the Southwest Citizens Organization for Poverty Elimination (known as SCOPE), a nonprofit corporation funded by the Office of Economic Opportunity which provided for the "health services of the migrant farm worker." Shack (D) was a staff attorney with the Farm Workers Division of Camden Regional Legal Services, Inc. (known as CRLS), also a nonprofit corporation funded by the Office of Economic Opportunity which provided (along with other services) legal advice for, and representation of, migrant farm workers. Tejeras (D) and Shack (D), pursuant to their roles in SCOPE and CRLS, entered upon private property to aid migrant workers employed and housed there. When both Tejeras (D) and Shack (D) refused to leave the property at the owner's request, they were charged with trespassing under a New Jersey statute which provides that "any person who trespasses on any lands . . . after being forbidden so to trespass by the owner . . . is a disorderly person and shall be punished by a fine of not more than $50." After conviction for trespassing, Tejeras (D) and Shack (D) brought this appeal.

**ISSUE:** Does an owner of real property have the absolute right to exclude all others from that property?

**HOLDING AND DECISION:** (Weintraub, C.J.) No. Real property rights are not absolute; and "necessity, private or public, may justify entry upon the lands of another." This rule is based upon the basic rationale that "property rights serve human values. They are recognized to that end and are limited by it." Here, a central concern is the welfare of the migrant farm workers—a highly disadvantaged segment of society. Migrant farm workers, in general, are "outside of the mainstream of the communities in which they are housed and are unaware of their rights and opportunities, and of the services available to them." As such, here, the "necessity" of effective communication of legal rights and of providing medical services for the migrant farm workers justifies entry upon the private property. Of course, the owner of such property has the right to pursue his farming activities without interference, but, here, there is no legitimate need for the owner to exclude those attempting to assist the migrant farm workers. Furthermore, the migrant farm worker must be allowed to receive visitors of his choice, so long as there is no behavior harmful to others, and members of the press may not be denied access to any farm worker who wishes to see them. In any of these situations, since no possessory right of the farmer-employer-landowner has been invaded (i.e., since he has no right to exclude such persons), there can be no trespassing. Reversed and remanded.

## ▶ ANALYSIS

Generally, the right to exclusive possession is considered "the oldest, most widely recognized right of private property in land." This case, though, illustrates the central limitation on the right to possession or use of private property—i.e., it may not be used to harm others. Here, the exclusion of Tejeras (D) and Shack (D) was, therefore, invalid because it would harm a very disadvantaged segment of society (the farm workers). Note, that under this principle, an owner of property, also, has no right to maintain a nuisance, to violate a building code, or to violate any "police power" laws (i.e., laws for the general public welfare).

■═■

# Intel Corporation v. Hamidi

## Employer (P) v. Former employee (D)

Cal. Sup. Ct., 71 P.3d 296 (2003).

**NATURE OF CASE:** Appeal from an injunction granted in an action for trespass to chattels.

**FACT SUMMARY:** A former employee mass-mailed emails that were critical of his former employer to thousands of the former employer's current employees at their email addresses on the employer's email system.

## 🏛 RULE OF LAW
Trespass to chattels does not encompass an electronic communication that neither damages a recipient computer system nor impairs its functioning.

**FACTS:** Hamidi (D), a former employee of Intel Corporation (P), formed an organization named Former and Current Employees of Intel (FACE-Intel) (D) to disseminate information and views critical of Intel's (P) employment and personnel policies and practices. Over a 21-month period, Hamidi (D), on behalf of FACE-Intel (D), sent six mass emails that criticized Intel (P) and invited recipients to go to FACE-Intel's (D) Web site; these emails were sent to as many as 35,000 employee addresses on Intel's (P) electronic mail system. Recipients could request to be removed from FACE-Intel's (D) mailing list. In sending the mass mailing, Hamidi (D) did not breach Intel's (P) computer security. Despite Intel's (P) request that the e-mails cease, Hamidi (D) continued his mailings. Intel (P) sued Hamidi (D) and FACE-Intel (D) for trespass to chattels. The trial court granted summary judgment against Hamidi (D), permanently enjoining him from sending unsolicited email to addresses on Intel's (P) computer system. The intermediate appellate court affirmed, and the supreme court granted review.

**ISSUE:** Does trespass to chattels encompass an electronic communication that neither damages a recipient computer system nor impairs its functioning?

**HOLDING AND DECISION:** (Werdegar, J.) No. Trespass to chattels does not encompass an electronic communication that neither damages a recipient computer system nor impairs its functioning. Such an electronic communication does not constitute actionable trespass to personal property because it does not interfere with the possessor's use or possession of, or any other protected interest in, the personal property itself. Any consequential damages, such as loss of productivity, are not an injury to the company's interest in its computers. To prevail on this particular claim, Intel (P) would have to prove injury to its computer systems—such as where the quantity of unwanted e-mail overloads a system. Moreover, the common-law basis of this decision should not be disturbed by extending our common law to encompass communications such as

Hamidi's (D). Given the great uncertainty in this area of the law at this time, establishing any such new rule would simply be rash. Reversed.

**CONCURRENCE:** (Kennard, J.) Hamidi (D) used Intel's (P) computer equipment to communicate with third parties (Intel's (P) current employees) who had permission to use Intel's (P) computers and who did not object to the communications. Under such circumstances, trespass to chattels will lie only if the communications somehow damage Intel's (P) equipment or significantly interfere with Intel's (P) ability to use the equipment. Theories such as defamation and wrongful interference with business interests, however, might provide Intel (P) an effective basis for relief.

**DISSENT:** (Brown, J.) Intel (P) invested in its computer system, not to serve as a public forum for expression of ideas, but to improve its own corporate productivity. Contrary to today's decision, Intel (P) is not complaining about the contents of Hamidi's (D) messages; it is complaining about his using Intel's (P) equipment to disseminate his messages. That actual basis for Intel's (P) complaint is sound because the company may exclude email on its systems for any reason, even for a message's unwanted content. Hamidi's (D) e-mails caused no equipment injury here only because Intel (P) had the business acumen and foresight to buy enough storage capacity to prevent such a volume of messages from slowing down the company's computer system. Today's decision, then, effectively punishes Intel (P) for its insightful preemptive business practices. This decision might even have the unexpected consequence of limiting the liberty of ideas because our notions of property rights to objects and property rights to ideas and expressions have long been interrelated.

**DISSENT:** (Mosk, J.) Hamidi's (D) emails are not analogous to speech in a public commons area such as the Internet. He was able to publish his speech at all only by misappropriating Intel's (P) computer system, and he did so against Intel's (P) wishes. Traditionally, harm has been required for a trespass to chattels because the injured party has been presumed to have recourse to self-help. But as Intel's (P) extensive efforts at self-help in this case demonstrate, the self-help rationale in the law of trespass to chattels no longer applies in the computer age.

---

## ▶ ANALYSIS

The majority emphasized that its decision did not rest on any special consideration for e-mail communications; such communications, the Court noted, could cause legally

*Continued on next page.*

cognizable injury under other legal theories, such as defamation and intentional infliction of emotional distress. As the majority opinion makes clear, however, for conduct to amount to trespass to chattels, there must be injury to the chattel itself or to some right in that property.

■━■

## Quicknotes

**TRESPASS TO CHATTELS** Action for damages sustained as a result of defendant's unlawful interference with plaintiff's personal property.

■━■

# Jones v. Alfred H. Mayer Co.

Negro home buyer (P) v. Seller (D)

392 U.S. 409 (1968).

**NATURE OF CASE:** On writ of certiorari in an action for injunctive relief.

**FACT SUMMARY:** Mayer (D) refused to sell a home to Jones (P) allegedly for the sole reason that Jones (P) was a Negro.

## RULE OF LAW

(1) The Act of Congress, 42 U.S.C.A. § 1982, bars all racial discrimination, private as well as public, in the sale or rental of property.
(2) That statute, thus construed, is a valid exercise of the power of Congress to enforce the Thirteenth Amendment.

**FACTS:** The Joneses (P) filed a complaint in the federal district court alleging that Mayer (D) had refused to sell them a home for the sole reason that Joseph Jones (P) was a Negro. They sought an injunction under an Act of Congress, 42 U.S.C.A. § 1982, which provides that all citizens shall enjoy the same right in every state, as is enjoyed by the citizens thereof, to hold and convey property. The district court dismissed the complaint. The court of appeals affirmed, concluding that § 1982 applied only to state—not private—action. The U.S. Supreme Court granted certiorari. Mayer (D) pointed out that § 1982 was originally part of § 1 of the 1866 Civil Rights Act and, as such, was intended to forbid only discriminatory governmental action—not private action. Also, Mayer (D) claimed, Congress lacked the power under the Constitution to prohibit private racial discrimination in the sale and rental of property.

**ISSUE:**
(1) Does the Act of Congress, 42 U.S.C.A. § 1982, bar all racial discrimination, private as well as public, in the sale or rental of property?
(2) Is § 1982, thus construed, a valid exercise of the power of Congress to enforce the Thirteenth Amendment?

**HOLDING AND DECISION:** (Stewart, J.)
(1) Yes. The Act of Congress, 42 U.S.C.A. § 1982, bars all racial discrimination, private as well as public, in the sale or rental of property. Although in 1948, this Court, in Hurt v. Hodge, applied § 1982 to forbid private racially discriminatory housing covenants, still, that case did not reach the instant issue, but rather involved governmental action since those wrongful covenants had been enforced by the courts. However, we believe that the plain language of § 1982 forbids private action since it prohibits denying to any citizen "the same right" to purchase and lease property "as is enjoyed by white citizens." But to exclude Negroes from property on the public market is clearly a denial of such rights. Next, as Mayer (D) noted, § 1982, in its original form, was part of § 1 of the 1866 Civil Rights Act. But we note that, although § 2 of that Act provided fines and prison for those violating § 1, it was nevertheless drafted so as to exempt private violations from these penalties. This would have been nonsensical if § 1 dealt only with governmental violations.
(2) Yes. Section 1982, thus construed, is a valid exercise of the power of Congress to enforce the Thirteenth Amendment. The amendment not only eliminates badges of slavery but also grants Congress the power to enforce the article by appropriate legislation. This includes legislation reaching the conduct of private individuals. Reversed.

## ANALYSIS

The "Badges of Slavery" theory is limited to congressional regulation. That is to say, the Supreme Court has not held that the Thirteenth Amendment forbids, of its own force, all private racial discrimination. Thus, in the absence of a congressional law, private racial discrimination is not reached by the Thirteenth Amendment. Additionally, Congress's power to prohibit private racial discrimination is probably limited, at some point, by a right of privacy.

## Quicknotes

**42 U.S.C. § 1982** "All citizens of the United States shall have the same right in every State and Territory, as is enjoyed by white citizens thereof to inherit, purchase, lease, sell, hold, and convey real and personal property."

**CERTIORARI** A discretionary writ issued by a superior court to an inferior court in order to review the lower court's decisions; the Supreme Court's writ ordering such review.

# Objects and Classifications of Property

## *Quick Reference Rules of Law*

# Edwards v. Sims

Cave discoverer (P) v. Judge (D)

Ky. Ct. of App., 232 Ky. 791, 24 S.W.2d 619 (1929).

**NATURE OF CASE:** Petition for a writ of prohibition.

**FACT SUMMARY:** Judge Sims (D) ordered a survey of Edwards's (P) cave for the purpose of determining whether or not it extended underneath property owned by Lee.

## 🏛 RULE OF LAW
Although the owner of real property also owns the space and resources above and beneath his land, a court of equity may require a cave owner to submit to a survey for the purpose of ascertaining whether or not his cave extends beyond the boundaries of his property.

**FACTS:** In a circuit court action, Edwards (P) was sued by a neighbor who claimed that Edwards's (P) cave extended beneath the neighbor's property. Judge Sims (D) issued an order directing a survey of Edwards's (P) cave for the purpose of determining whether or not it did, in fact, run underneath the property of Lee, the neighbor. Edwards (P) appealed from the order directing the survey to be made, but since that order was of an interlocutory nature, the appeal was dismissed. Edwards (P) then sought a writ of prohibition preventing Judge Sims (D) from enforcing the order. In his petition, Edwards (P) alleged that Judge Sims (D) had been without jurisdiction to issue the order, that great and irreparable injury would result from its implementation, and that a subsequent appeal from the order would be too late to afford Edwards (P) an adequate remedy.

**ISSUE:** May a court order a privately owned cave to be surveyed for the purpose of determining whether or not it extends beneath the property of an adjacent landowner?

**HOLDING AND DECISION:** (Stanley, J.) Yes. Although the owner of real property also owns the space and resources above and beneath his land, a court of equity may require a cave owner to submit to a survey for the purpose of ascertaining whether or not his cave extends beyond the boundaries of his property. In analogous cases involving mines, courts have concluded that such surveys and inspections can be ordered. The right of a landowner to enjoy undisturbed possession of the subsurface must occasionally be subjected to such intrusions as may be necessary to secure certain rights of his neighbors. In this case, Lee presented a bona fide claim which entitled him to a survey of Edwards's (P) cave, and Edwards (P) was afforded an opportunity to be heard in opposition to Lee's claim. In view of these circumstances, implementation of Judge Sims's (D) order should not be prohibited and the writ of prohibition is therefore denied.

**DISSENT:** (Logan, J.) The rule which should control this case is that a landowner is also the owner of anything lying beneath the surface which he is able to use for his pleasure or profit and which he is able to subject to his dominion or control. Since the entrance to the cave is located on Edwards's (P) property, Lee cannot hope to control any part of the cave or to use it for his pleasure or profit. Edwards (P) has developed the cave into a popular commercial attraction, and it would be unjust to permit the value of his property to be reduced or interfered with at the urging of Lee, who cannot hope to gain anything which will confer a benefit upon him. Therefore, the writ of prohibition should issue.

## ▶ ANALYSIS

According to the common law rule, a property owner also enjoys ownership of the airspace located above his land and the subsurface beneath it. In theory, he owns from the core of the earth to the furthest reaches of the heavens. Most litigation involving subsurface ownership relates to disputes concerning mineral rights. Where solid minerals are involved, the common law rule is generally adequate. In the case of volatile materials, sometimes referred to as "fugitive" minerals, different problems obviously arise. Some courts hold that a landowner also owns all oil and gas beneath his property. Other courts, preferring a rule which is of little practical difference, allow the landowner an exclusive right to possess the oil and gas beneath his property, but deny him ownership of these resources. Almost all jurisdictions also recognize the "rule of capture" which permits a landowner to retain any oil or gas which he has tapped through drills or wells located on his own property, notwithstanding that these resources may have been drawn in part from beneath the land of his neighbors.

■≡■

## Quicknotes

**COURT OF EQUITY** A court that determines matters before it consistent with principles of fairness and not in strict compliance with rules of law.

**INTERLOCUTORY (ORDER)** An order entered by the court determining an issue that does not resolve the disposition of the case, but is essential to a proper adjudication of the action.

**WRIT OF PROHIBITION** A writ issued by a superior court prohibiting a lower court from exceeding its jurisdiction or from usurping jurisdiction beyond that authorized by law.

■≡■

# CHAPTER 4

# Role of Property in Society

## *Quick Reference Rules of Law*

# Johnson v. McIntosh

### Claimer of title (P) v. Unidentified party (D)

21 U.S. (8 Wheat.) 543 (1823).

**NATURE OF CASE:** Appeal in an action to determine title to land.

**FACT SUMMARY:** Johnson (P) claimed valid title to land granted him by the chiefs of certain Indian tribes.

## 🏛 RULE OF LAW
The discovery of the Indian-occupied lands of this nation vested absolute title in the discoverers, and rendered the Indian inhabitants themselves incapable of transferring absolute title to others.

**FACTS:** Johnson (P) claimed valid title to land by reason of two grants, purportedly made in 1773 and 1775, respectively, by the chiefs of certain Indian tribes. The proofs showed that the chiefs executing the conveyances had the authority to do so, and that the tribes were in rightful possession of the lands they sold. Nevertheless, the trial court denied the power of the Indians to convey such lands since, although they had retained title to the land's occupancy, they nevertheless remained incapable of transferring absolute title to others. Johnson (P) appealed.

**ISSUE:** Do the Indian tribes have the power of conveying absolute title of their lands to others?

**HOLDING AND DECISION:** (Marshall, C.J.) No. The discovery of the Indian-occupied lands of this nation vested absolute title in the discoverers; and while the Indian inhabitants retained title of occupancy, they were nevertheless incapable of transferring absolute title to others. As the result, this title claimed by Johnson (P) cannot be recognized by the U.S. courts. The very history of America, from its discovery to the present, demonstrates this principle. For example, when the English discoverers first acquired territory on this continent, they assumed title to the lands despite their admitted possession by the natives. While still under Indian occupation, these lands and waters were conveyed to others by the English monarch. These extensive grants cannot be regarded as nullities. That this principle has been ever recognized is seen in the history of wars, negotiations, and treaties. In fact, all the nations of Europe who have acquired territory on this continent have recognized the principle. The validity of these titles has never been questioned by the courts. Finally, an absolute title cannot exist at the same time in different governments over the same land. It would be incompatible to vest absolute title in the Indians as a distinct nation and country. Therefore, they are regarded as merely occupants to be protected while at peace, but to be deemed incapable of transferring absolute title to others. Affirmed.

## ▶ ANALYSIS

As reflected in the case of *Tee-Hit-Ton Indians v. United States*, 348 U.S. 272 (1955), the courts have generally followed the principal case and denied Indian land titles. However, Congress has followed a fairly consistent policy of making voluntary payments to the Indians. See Cohen, Original Indian Title, 32 Minn. L. Rev. 28 (1947). In his conclusion, Mr. Cohen said that: "The notion that America was stolen from the Indians is one of the myths by which we Americans are prone to hide our real virtues and make our idealism look as hard-boiled as possible." The story, nevertheless, is not pleasant.

■══■

## Quicknotes

**ABSOLUTE TITLE** Exclusive title to land.

■══■

# Shelley v. Kraemer

Negro buyers (D) v. Neighboring owners (P)

334 U.S. 1 (1948).

**NATURE OF CASE:** On writ of certiorari in action to enjoin a sale of property.

**FACT SUMMARY:** The Kraemers (P) sought to oust the Shelleys (D), Negroes, from their recently purchased property on the grounds that it was subject to a racially restrictive covenant.

## 🏛 RULE OF LAW
The Equal Protection Clause of the Fourteenth Amendment prohibits judicial enforcement by state courts of restrictive covenants based on race or color.

**FACTS:** In 1945, the Shelleys (D), Negroes, purchased property which, unknown to them, was subject to a racially restrictive covenant signed in 1911 for a 50-year period by the majority of property owners on the block. The Kraemers (P), also owners of property subject to the covenant, sued in the state court to restrain the Shelleys (D) from taking possession and to revest the title in others. The state court denied relief on the grounds that the covenant had never been finalized. However, the Missouri Supreme Court reversed. The U.S. Supreme Court granted the Shelleys (D) certiorari. They argued that the Equal Protection Clause of the Fourteenth Amendment prevented the judicial enforcement by state courts of racially restrictive covenants.

**ISSUE:** Does the Equal Protection Clause of the Fourteenth Amendment prohibit judicial enforcement by state courts of racially restrictive covenants?

**HOLDING AND DECISION:** (Vinson, C.J.) Yes. The Equal Protection Clause of the Fourteenth Amendment prohibits judicial enforcement by state courts of racially restrictive covenants. Equality in the enjoyment of property rights was clearly among the civil rights intended to be protected from discriminatory state action by the framers of the Fourteenth Amendment. And although past cases have struck down such discrimination when enacted by state legislatures or city councils, it may not be said that such discrimination, as in the instant case, may escape on the grounds that it was only an agreement between private individuals. Indeed, were it no more than that, no violation would exist. However, in this case state action is clearly present by reason of the active intervention of the state court to enforce the covenant. As early as 1880, in *Ex Parte Virginia*, this Court found state action in violation of the Fourteenth Amendment when a state judge restricted jury service to whites. Nor is the Amendment ineffective simply because this action was taken according to the state's common law policy. We hold that in granting judicial enforcement of these restrictive covenants, the state has denied the Shelleys (D) equal protection of the laws. Reversed.

## ▶ *ANALYSIS*

In the 1961 case of *Burton v. Wilmington Parking Authority*, a state agency had built and owned a parking garage, and rented space in the garage to a private restaurant. The Supreme Court held that the restaurant's exclusion of blacks from service amounted to state action under the Fourteenth Amendment. The test announced was that of significant state involvement in private discrimination.

■▬■

## *Quicknotes*

**CERTIORARI** A discretionary writ issued by a superior court to an inferior court in order to review the lower court's decisions; the Supreme Court's writ ordering such review.

**EQUAL PROTECTION CLAUSE** A constitutional provision that each person be guaranteed the same protection of the laws enjoyed by other persons in like circumstances.

■▬■

# Finding

## *Quick Reference Rules of Law*

# Goddard v. Winchell

Landowner (P) v. Buyer of aerolite (D)

Iowa Sup. Ct., 86 Iowa 71, 52 N.W. 1124 (1892).

**NATURE OF CASE:** Appeal in an action in replevin.

**FACT SUMMARY:** Winchell (D) claimed ownership by reason of purchasing an aerolite found on Goddard's (P) land by Hoagland.

## 🏛 RULE OF LAW
Natural deposits, such as mineral or vegetable matter, which have been brought to the soil by natural forces, are not to be regarded as "unclaimed movables"; but, rather, belong to the owner of the soil wherein they are found.

**FACTS:** A 66-pound aerolite fell from the skies and imbedded itself beneath the soil of prairie land belonging to Goddard (P). Hoagland saw the aerolite fall, dug it out of the ground, and claimed it as his property. Hoagland sold the aerolite to Winchell (D) for $105. Goddard (P) brought this action in replevin to recover the aerolite. Goddard (P) claimed that the aerolite, being part of the soil by nature's action, belonged to the soil as part of the realty which Goddard (P) owned. However, Winchell (D) claimed "title by occupancy" which is the taking possession of those things belonging to nobody. The court ruled for Goddard (P). Winchell (D) appealed.

**ISSUE:** Are mineral or vegetable deposits, which are brought into the soil by nature's forces, to be regarded as unclaimed "movables" to become the property of whoever finds them?

**HOLDING AND DECISION:** (Granger, J.) No. Natural deposits, such as mineral and vegetable matter, which have been brought to the soil by nature's forces are not to be regarded as unclaimed "movables" to become the property of whoever finds them. On the contrary, they belong to the owner of the soil where they are found. But the aerolite in question came to the earth through natural causes. It was one of nature's deposits—a stone, or "ball of metallic iron," composed of those elements normally found in the soil. Its only peculiarity is the manner in which it came to the soil, i.e., it "fell from the heavens." We are familiar with the doctrine of accretion whereby riparian owners gain or lose land by the forces of wind and water. Such principle applies here. In fact, according to scientists, about 600 to 900 such stones fall annually to the earth. Their ownership is governed by the same rules applying to the deposit of boulders or stones on our prairies by glacier action. The fact that the aerolite has scientific value makes this principle no less applicable. Affirmed.

## ▶ ANALYSIS

O is a riparian owner, with land adjacent to a riverbed owned by the state. As the above case indicates, if gradual deposits of soil on O's land by the currents and waves of the river occur, O acquires title to these accretions. Also, gradual losses by erosion will cause shrinkage of his land. However, sudden (avulsive) changes usually do not have the same consequences. Suppose that the river gradually encroaches upon O's land as a consequence of subsidence of O's land due to extensive pumping of water from wells in the area. It was held that O's title to his land was not affected by this kind of encroachment by the river.

■═■

## Quicknotes

**REPLEVIN** An action to recover personal property wrongfully taken.

■═■

# Eads v. Brazelton

Lead salvager (D) v. Previous finder (P)

Ark. Sup. Ct., 22 Ark. 499 (1861).

**NATURE OF CASE:** Appeal in action for damages and injunctive relief.

**FACT SUMMARY:** Brazelton (P) located and marked a sunken ship; but before he was able to salvage it, Eads (D) and Nelson (D) did so.

## 🏛 RULE OF LAW
In order to obtain legal rights to the possession of lost, abandoned, or ownerless property, the finder must take such intentional acts of possession as are reasonable and possible under the circumstances.

**FACTS:** In 1827, the steamboat America sank in the Mississippi River carrying a large quantity of lead. In December 1854, Brazelton (P) located the sunken boat and intended to salvage the lead. He marked the spot by tracing lines, marked on trees, from various points on the river so that the intersection of these lines converged on the site. In January 1855, Brazelton (P) moved his diving boat to the vicinity of the wreck and marked the actual wreck with a weighted buoy. He intended to move the boat directly over the wreck on the following day. The buoy was admittedly only a guide, not a permanent fixture. However, Brazelton (P) was then called to other business and left the site without doing anything further. In September 1855, Eads (D) and Nelson (D) began salvaging the lead from the wreck. Brazelton (P), arguing that his acts amounted to possession of the lead, obtained an injunction against Eads's (D) and Nelson's (D) further salvaging the lead and damages for the lead already taken by them. Eads (D) and Nelson (D) appealed.

**ISSUE:** In order to obtain legal rights to the possession of lost, abandoned or ownerless property, must the finder take such intentional acts of possession as are reasonable and possible under the circumstances?

**HOLDING AND DECISION:** (Fairchild, J.) Yes. In order to obtain legal rights to the possession of lost, abandoned or ownerless property, the finder must take such intentional acts of possession as are reasonable and possible under the circumstances. It is clear that, its owners had, in fact, abandoned the cargo of the American. But did Brazelton (P) take the acts necessary for his claimed possession to be recognized? We think not. Although he need not manually possess the lead cargo, nevertheless, he must have taken whatever possession the circumstances permitted. But merely marking nearby trees and affixing buoys were not acts of possession, but merely signs of intention to possess. Placing his boat over the wreck along with the means of raising its salvage would have been the expected means of obtaining legal rights. Reversed.

## ⯈ ANALYSIS

A different result might have been reached had Brazelton (P) returned the following day and found his buoys and markers destroyed and himself unable thereby to locate the wreck. For example, in *Keeble v. Hickeringill,* 103 Eng. Rep. 1127 (K.B. 1706), the defendant, intending to deprive the plaintiff of the opportunity of capturing wild ducks, frightened them away from the plaintiff's possession by shooting guns. The court found him liable for hindering the plaintiff in his trade or livelihood.

■══■

### Quicknotes

**INJUNCTION** A court order requiring a person to do, or prohibiting that person from doing, a specific act.

**INJUNCTIVE RELIEF** A court order issued as a remedy, requiring a person to do, or prohibiting that person from doing, a specific act.

■══■

# Popov v. Hayashi

Baseball fan (P) v. Baseball fan (D)

Cal. Super. Ct., No. 400545, WL 31833731 (2002).

## NATURE OF CASE:
Action for conversion, trespass to chattels, injunctive relief and constructive trust.

## FACT SUMMARY:
Both Popov (P) and Hayashi (D) intended to establish and maintain control over a baseball that gave Barry Bonds his 73rd home run in 2001, but just as Popov (P) was getting it in his glove, a crowd engulfed him, and brought him to the ground. Hayashi (D), who was near Popov (P) and who also was brought to the ground by the crowd, found the ball and pocketed it. Popov (P) claimed he had established sufficient possession of the ball to gain title to it and brought suit to compel Hayashi (D) to return the ball to him.

## RULE OF LAW
Where an actor undertakes significant but incomplete steps to achieve possession of a piece of abandoned personal property and the effort is interrupted by the unlawful acts of others, the actor has a legally cognizable pre-possessory interest in the property sufficient to support a claim of conversion.

## FACTS:
Barry Bonds, a professional baseball player, hit a record-setting 73rd home run on October 7, 2001. On that day, Popov (P) and Hayashi (D) and many others had positioned themselves in an area of the stadium where Bonds hit the greatest number of home runs in the hopes of catching a record-setting ball (so they brought their baseball gloves with them). The ball hit by Bonds initially landed in Popov's (P) glove, but it was not clear whether the ball was secure there, as Popov (P) may have lost his balance while reaching for the ball. However, even as the ball was going into his glove, a crowd engulfed him and he was tackled and brought to the ground, with people hitting and grabbing him. Hayashi (D), who had been near Popov (P), was also forced by the crowd to the ground, where he saw the ball. He pocketed it and revealed it only when a camera was trained on him, presumably because he wanted proof that he was the owner of the ball. Popov (P), seeing the ball, grabbed for it, believing it to be his, but Hayashi (D) refused to give it to him. Popov (P) then brought suit for conversion, trespass to chattels, injunctive relief, and constructive trust.

## ISSUE:
Where an actor undertakes significant but incomplete steps to achieve possession of a piece of abandoned personal property and the effort is interrupted by the unlawful acts of others, does the actor have a legally cognizable pre-possessory interest in the property sufficient to support a claim of conversion?

## HOLDING AND DECISION:
(McCarthy, J.) Yes. Where an actor undertakes significant but incomplete steps to achieve possession of a piece of abandoned personal property and the effort is interrupted by the unlawful acts of others, the actor has a legally cognizable pre-possessory interest in the property sufficient to support a claim of conversion. As an initial matter, there was no trespass to chattels—which requires injury to the chattel—because the ball itself was not damaged and because Popov (P) did not claim that Hayashi (D) interfered with his use and enjoyment of the ball. If there was a wrong at all, it was conversion, which is the wrongful exercise of dominion over the personal property of another. One who has neither title nor possession, nor any right to possession, may not assert a conversion claim. The key issue, therefore, is whether Popov (P) achieved possession or the right to it. "Possession," however, does not have one meaning; the meaning varies depending on the context in which it is used. Some guidelines, however, do exist, e.g., that possession requires both physical control over an item and an intent to control it and exclude others from it. Here, Popov (P) clearly had the requisite intent, so the issue is whether he had exclusive dominion and control over the ball. Possession in this context is based on custom and what is physically possible. Here, "not only is it physically possible for a person to acquire unequivocal dominion and control of an abandoned baseball, but fans generally expect a claimant to have accomplished as much." Because Popov (P) did not establish by a preponderance of the evidence that he would have retained control of the ball after all momentum ceased and after any incidental contact with other people or objects, he did not achieve full possession. This conclusion does not resolve the case, however, because Popov (P) was attacked illegally by the crowd, and because, therefore, it is unknown whether he would have retained control over the ball absent the crowd's actions. Because Popov (P) has a legally protected pre-possessory interest in the ball, he may advance a legitimate claim to the ball. Hayashi (D), too, was a victim of the crowd's illegal activity, but was able to extricate himself from the crowd. Although Hayashi (D) exercised complete dominion and control over the ball, the ball was encumbered by the qualified pre-possessory interest of Popov (P). Thus, awarding the ball to either of the two parties is unfair to the other. Both have a superior claim to the ball as against all the world, but not against each other; they are equally entitled to the ball. Because the court sits in equity, it may

*Continued on next page.*

devise an equitable solution to this problem. Here, that solution is equitable division, whereby both Popov (P) and Hayashi (D) have an equal and undivided interest in the ball. Accordingly, Popov's (P) conversion claim is sustained only as to his equal and undivided interest.

## ▶ *ANALYSIS*

The parties agreed that before Bonds hit the ball, it belonged to Major League Baseball, but that at the time it was hit, it became intentionally abandoned property. Also, to effectuate its decision, the court ordered the sale of the ball, with the proceeds being equally split between the two men. The ball ultimately sold for $450,000—Hayashi (D) estimated that his share would only cover his legal fees.

■══■

## *Quicknotes*

**CONVERSION**   The act of depriving an owner of his property without permission or justification.

■══■

# Armory v. Delamirie

Jewel finder (P) v. Goldsmith (D)

King's Bench, 1 Sess. Cas. 505 (1722).

**NATURE OF CASE:** Action in trover to recover the value of personal property.

**FACT SUMMARY:** Armory (P) found a jewel which he took to Delamirie (D), a goldsmith, for appraisal, but Delamirie's (D) apprentice removed the stones which Delamirie (D) refused to return.

## 🏛 RULE OF LAW
A finder of chattel has title superior to all but the rightful owner upon which he may maintain an action at law or in equity.

**FACTS:** Armory (P), a chimney sweeper's boy, found a jewel which he took to Delamirie's (D) goldsmith shop to learn what it was. Delamirie's (D) apprentice, under the pretense of weighing the jewel, removed the stones from the setting and told his master the value. Delamirie (D) offered Armory (P) three halfpence for the stones, but he refused. Delamirie (D) returned the setting without the stones.

**ISSUE:** Could Armory (P), who lacked legal title to the chattel, maintain an action to recover its value?

**HOLDING AND DECISION:** [Judge not stated in casebook excerpt.] Yes. The finder of lost property, although he does not acquire absolute ownership, does acquire title superior to everyone else except the rightful owner. Such title is a sufficient property interest in the finder upon which he may maintain an action against anyone (except the rightful owner) who violates that interest. Additionally, Delamirie (D) was liable as he was responsible for the actions of his apprentice. As for the measure of damages, if Delamirie (D) did not show the stones were not of the finest value, their value would be so determined.

## ▶ ANALYSIS

As to ownership, the finder is in a position similar to that of a bailee. The finder does not obtain absolute ownership, but does have the right of ownership against everybody except the true owner. Here, the chattel, the jewel, was subsequently converted against the finder. Yet the finder, if he should subsequently lose the chattel, may reclaim it from a subsequent finder. The finder has a choice of remedies. He may recover the chattel in specie if it is still in the converter's possession, or he may recover full value from the wrongdoer. Notice that an action in trover, which is an action at law, is to recover the value of the chattel. If it is desired to have the item returned, an action in replevin must be brought in equity.

## Quicknotes

**REPLEVIN** An action to recover personal property wrongfully taken.

**TROVER** An action for damages resulting from the unlawful conversion of, or to recover possession of, personal property.

# Bridges v. Hawkesworth

Banknote finder (P) v. Store owner (D)

Queen's Bench, 21 L.J. Q.B. 75 (1851).

**NATURE OF CASE:** Action to recover goods.

**FACT SUMMARY:** Bridges (P) found bank notes in Hawkesworth's (D) store, and when there was no claimant, Hawkesworth (D) asserted ownership of the bank notes.

## 🏛 RULE OF LAW
The finder of a lost article, no matter where found, is entitled to its possession as against all persons except for the rightful owner of the article.

**FACTS:** Bridges (P) was a traveling salesman for a large firm. Hawkesworth (D) owned a store and had dealings with Bridges' (P) firm. Bridges (P) went to the store to do business. As he was leaving the store, Bridges (P) noted a parcel lying on the shop floor. It contained bank notes. The owner of the notes was unknown. Bridges (P) requested Hawkesworth (D) to keep the notes in order to deliver them to the true owner. Three years later, after no one had appeared to claim the bank notes, Bridges (P) asked for the notes to be returned to him but Hawkesworth (D) asserted his own right to keep them.

**ISSUE:** Does the location where a lost article was found alter the rule that the finder is entitled to it as against all but the true owner?

**HOLDING AND DECISION:** (Patteson, J.) No. The fact that the notes were found by Bridges (P) in Hawkesworth's (D) shop does not give Hawkesworth (D) a greater right to the lost articles than the finder. If Hawkesworth (D) were to have a prior right, that right would have had to come into existence prior to the finding of the notes by Bridges (P), because that finding could not give Hawkesworth (D) any right. Hawkesworth (D) never had custody of the notes, nor were they within the protection of his house because they had not been intentionally deposited there. There are no circumstances to take this case out of the general rule that the finder of a lost article has paramount title over all but the real owner of the property. Reversed.

## ▶ ANALYSIS

The finder of lost goods does not gain title to the found property, but he has a right to possession of the property against everyone except the true owner. He does not become the owner, but is, instead, the bailee of the property for the owner. Bailment is a situation where the owner of goods, the bailor, delivers the property to the bailee, in trust, for the bailee to keep the goods or dispose of them under the direction of the true owner. Although the lost property situation does not, of course, involve an express bailment agreement between the owner and the finder, this fiction is used to give the finder the right to possession with the duty to preserve the property for the true owner. The finder will be guilty of conversion if he appropriates the chattel to his own use with knowledge of who the true owner is, or if the finder is reasonably able to discover the true owner's identity and fails to do so. The weight of authority holds that when, as in this case, a person finds a chattel on the property of another, he is entitled to the chattel unless he is a trespasser when he makes the find.

■══■

## Quicknotes

**BAILMENT** The delivery of property to be held in trust for a particular purpose, following the satisfaction of which the property is either to be returned or disposed of as specified.

**CHATTEL** An article of personal property, as distinguished from real property; a thing personal and moveable.

■══■

# South Staffordshire Water Co. v. Sharman

Pool owners (P) v. Pool cleaners (D)

Queen's Bench, 2 Q.B. 44 (1896).

**NATURE OF CASE:** Action in detinue for recovery of goods.

**FACT SUMMARY:** The owner of land hired Sharman (D) to clean out a pond, and Sharman (D) found two gold rings in the pond to which he asserted ownership.

## 🏛 RULE OF LAW
The possession of land carries with it the possession of everything which is attached to it or under it, and carries with it the right of ownership of anything found there in the absence of a superior claim of ownership.

**FACTS:** South Staffordshire Water Company (P) owned land which was covered by water, the Minster Pool. Sharman (D), along with others, was hired to clean out the pool. Sharman (D) found two gold rings in the mud which was at the bottom of the pool. South Staffordshire (P) demanded the rings, but Sharman (D) gave them to the police. After no one claimed the rings, the police handed them to Sharman (D) who asserted ownership over them. There was no special contract which provided that the workers were to give up anything found to South Staffordshire (P).

**ISSUE:** Does the possession of land carry with it the right to ownership of all articles found on or under the land?

**HOLDING AND DECISION:** (Lord Russell, C.J.) Yes. It makes no difference that the possessor of the land was unaware of the rings' existence or that someone else found the rings. South Staffordshire (P) had actual control over the land and anything on it. They could forbid anyone from entering on the land or interfering with it. Where there is, as here, a manifested intent to exercise control over the land and anything on it, then if something is found on the land, whether by an employee or a stranger, it is presumed that the ownership of the article is in the ownership of the land. It can only be defeated by the assertion of a superior title, such as that of the original owner. Reversed.

**CONCURRENCE:** (Wills, J.) A finding to the contrary would encourage dishonesy.

## ▶ ANALYSIS

This case is distinguishable from the *Bridges* case. In *Bridges*, the shop was open to the public, and the finder, as well as all others, was invited in. In the present case, the rings were found on land which was not open to the public and were found by employees who were under the control of South Staffordshire (P). The essential difference is that South Staffordshire (P) manifested control over the land and its content, whereas Hawkesworth, being a public shopkeeper, had not.

■═■

## Quicknotes

**DETINUE** A writ to recover personal property wrongfully taken by another.

■═■

# Hannah v. Peel

### Soldier (P) v. Home owner (D)

King's Bench, 1 K.B. 509 (1945).

**NATURE OF CASE:** Action for recovery of goods or their value.

**FACT SUMMARY:** A soldier stationed at a requisitioned house, which had never been occupied by its owner, found a broach inside the house, and the owner of the house asserted his right to possession.

### 🏛 RULE OF LAW
A lost article which is found lying unattached on the surface of the land is not possessed by the owner of the land unless he had previously manifested a control over it, and is instead possessed by the finder, subject to the rights of the real owner.

**FACTS:** In 1938, a house was conveyed to Peel (D). Peel (D) never occupied the house. The house was requisitioned in 1940 for war use for £250 a year. In 1940, a corporal stationed at the house, Hannah (P), found a cobweb-covered broach on the top of a window frame. He later informed his commanding officer of the find, and then Hannah (P) gave the broach to the police. When the owner was not located, the police delivered the broach to Peel (D), who sold the broach to a wholesaler for £66. Peel (D) never had any knowledge of the existence of the broach until it was found, and had offered Hannah (P) a reward if it were given to Peel (D). Hannah (P) at all times asserted an ownership superior to all but the real owner.

**ISSUE:** Does the owner of land necessarily possess everything which is on the land but not attached to it?

**HOLDING AND DECISION:** (Birkett, J.) No. An owner of land does not necessarily possess everything which is unattached on the surface of the land and which is not possessed by someone else. Peel (D) had never been in possession of the house though he owned it. He had never asserted possession over the broach until it was found by Hannah (P). The court will follow the decision in *Bridges* rather than in *South Staffordshire Water Co.* Judgment for the plaintiff.

### ▶ ANALYSIS

Despite the court's statement, this case is in conformity with the ruling in *South Staffordshire Water Co.* In that case, the finder was an employee or agent of the landowner, the landowner had been in possession of the land, and the lost article was attached to the land by being in the mud and under the water. In the present case, the finder was on the land rightfully and was independent of the owner, the owner had never been in possession of the land, and the broach was unattached to the land. In essence, the court found that the broach had been involuntarily lost, rather than voluntarily misplaced, so the finder would have possession.

■≡■

# McAvoy v. Medina

Wallet finder (P) v. Barber shop owner (D)

Mass. Sup. Jud. Ct., 11 Allen (93 Mass.) 548 (1866).

**NATURE OF CASE:** Action to recover money.

**FACT SUMMARY:** A wallet was inadvertently left at a barber shop, a customer found it, and the barber asserted ownership.

## 🏛 RULE OF LAW
Misplaced goods (items intentionally placed by the owner where they were found and then forgotten or left there) are deemed to be in the bailment of the owner of the property on which they are found for the true owner.

**FACTS:** McAvoy (P) was a customer in Medina's (D) barber shop. McAvoy (P) found a wallet which was lying on a table. McAvoy (P) showed Medina (D) where he found the wallet and told Medina (D) to keep the wallet and the money in it and to give it to the real owner. Medina (D) promised to attempt to find the owner. McAvoy (P) later made three demands for return of the money, but Medina (D) refused. The wallet had been placed on the table by a transient customer of the barber shop, and had been accidentally left there. The true owner was never found.

**ISSUE:** Does the finder of misplaced goods on another's property obtain title to the goods?

**HOLDING AND DECISION:** (Dewey, J.) No. The owner of the premises on which misplaced goods are found is deemed to be the bailee of the goods for the true owner. This wallet was not lost. It had been voluntarily placed upon a table and then accidentally left there. This is different from lost property which had not been voluntarily placed by the owner where it was later found. When goods are misplaced, the finder acquires no original right to the property. Holding the owner of the premises as bailee of the goods is better adapted to secure the rights of the true owner. Exceptions overruled.

## ▶ ANALYSIS

The focus of lost or misplaced property cases is to determine whether it is likely that the true owner can ever be found. Therefore, because the finder was the first in possession, he will have paramount rights. On the other hand, where goods have been voluntarily placed and then forgotten, the true owner is much more likely to be found. As the true owner would be more likely to return to where he remembered placing the article, the owner of the premises will be deemed a bailee for the true owner.

## Quicknotes

**BAILMENT** The delivery of property to be held in trust and which is designated for a particular purpose, following the satisfaction of which the property is either to be returned or disposed of as specified.

■=■

# Schley v. Couch

Landowner (D) v. Workman (P)

Tex. Sup. Ct., 155 Tex. 195, 284 S.W.2d 333 (Tex. 1955).

**NATURE OF CASE:** Action for return of money.

**FACT SUMMARY:** A workman, hired to construct a cement floor in a garage, found $1,000 buried there, but the owner of the land claimed possession of the money.

## 🏛 RULE OF LAW
The possession of buried money should be determined by the rules of lost or misplaced property rather than by the rule of treasure trove.

**FACTS:** Allen built a garage on his land and then sold the land to Adams in 1948. Adams sold the land to Schley (D) in 1952. There was concrete on half of the garage floor. Schley (D) hired Couch (P) to lay concrete on the other half. Because a tractor would not fit, Couch (P) was ordered by the foreman to loosen up the dirt in the garage. Couch's (P) pick struck what turned out to be $1,000 in fresh, well-preserved bills, including two Hawaiian bills issued during World War II. The money had been deliberately buried in glass jars. One prior owner of the land asserted ownership of the money, but he was nonsuited in a prior case. Schley (D) asserted possession of the money, and Couch (P) sued.

**ISSUE:** Should the possession of buried money be determined by the rules of lost or misplaced property rather than by the rule of treasure trove?

**HOLDING AND DECISION:** (Griffin, J.) Yes. The possession of buried money should be determined by the rules of lost or misplaced property rather than by the rule of treasure trove. Under the rule of treasure trove, coin or money concealed in the earth or other private place belongs to the finder and not the owner of land on which it was found. Texas will not follow the rule of treasure trove, but will adjudicate possession of buried money by the usual rules pertaining to lost or misplaced property. If the circumstances indicate that the money was voluntarily placed somewhere and then forgotten, it has been misplaced and the owner of the property will have possession. If the circumstances indicate that the money was involuntarily placed somewhere, then it was lost and the finder has possession. Money buried in glass jars indicates that it was misplaced. If there has been a sufficient lapse of time since it was buried, it could be deemed to be lost. Here, the money was buried during World War II, which is too short a time to be considered lost property. The money therefore will be deemed to be in the bailment of Schley (D). Reversed and judgment of the trial court affirmed.

**CONCURRENCE:** (Calvert, J.) The Court's decision seems unprecedented because apparently no case has deemed property embedded in soil to be mislaid. A fourth rule specifically covers this category of property, but the majority has combined that rule with the rationale of mislaid property.

**CONCURRENCE:** (Wilson, J.) The result is correct, but the Court should adopt a simpler rationale that moves beyond the traditional categories of treasure trove, lost property, and mislaid property. Courts would do better to presume that the landowner has lawful possession until the true owner proves his title to the property.

## ▶ ANALYSIS

Treasure trove refers to gold and silver coins, bars, plate, and valuable objects intentionally hidden or secreted, usually in the earth, but the concept is frequently applied to valuables wherever or however hidden. The owner is usually unknown and not likely to appear. In England, at common law, treasure trove escheated, or belonged, to the Crown. The majority rule in the United States is that treasure trove belongs to the finder, not the owner, of the land on which it was secreted.

■■■

## Quicknotes

**BAILMENT** The delivery of property to be held in trust and which is designated for a particular purpose, following the satisfaction of which the property is either to be returned or disposed of as specified.

■■■

# CHAPTER 6

# Creation of Bailments

## *Quick Reference Rules of Law*

# Allen v. Hyatt Regency-Nashville Hotel

## Car owner (P) v. Hotel (D)

Tenn. Sup. Ct., 668 S.W.2d 286 (1984).

**NATURE OF CASE:** Appeal of judgment in favor of plaintiff in an action for negligent bailment.

**FACT SUMMARY:** Allen's (P) car, parked in the Hyatt Regency (D) parking lot, was stolen.

## 🏛 RULE OF LAW
Enclosed, attended commercial parking garages create bailments for hire and a presumption of negligence if a car is stolen.

**FACTS:** Allen (P) parked his car in a multistory garage at the Hyatt Regency (D). The garage was open to the public, and the single entrance was controlled by a ticket machine. The lone exit was manned by an attendant who checked the ticket only to determine the time parked. The tickets did not identify the vehicle, but did state that the Hyatt Regency (D) assumed no responsibility for theft. Two security guards were on the grounds most of the time. Allen's (P) car was stolen while he was gone, and he filed suit against the Hyatt Regency (D). The trial court ruled that a bailment was created when Allen (P) parked his car in the garage and awarded damages. An appellate court agreed, and the Hyatt Regency (D) appealed.

**ISSUE:** Do enclosed, attended commercial parking garages create bailments for hire and a presumption of negligence if the car is stolen?

**HOLDING AND DECISION:** (Harbison, J.) Yes. Enclosed, attended commercial parking garages create bailments for hire and a presumption of negligence if the car is stolen. The legal relationship between vehicle operators and parking establishments has been the subject of frequent litigation throughout the country. Courts have reached varying conclusions. Tennessee courts have analyzed the situation on a case-by-case basis, seeking to determine whether there is sufficient conduct to create a bailment. Generally, vehicles driven into unattended and open lots will not be considered bailments for hire. However, in the present case the Hyatt Regency (D) garage was enclosed and attended, showing sufficient control and custody. Therefore, a bailment for hire was created when Allen (P) left his car there. When a car is stolen from such a garage, there is a statutory presumption of negligence which must be rebutted by the garage. In the instant case, Hyatt Regency (D) made no effort to rebut the presumption of negligence. Accordingly, the judgment is affirmed.

**DISSENT:** (Drowota, J.) Bailments are created when the garage owner knowingly and voluntarily assumes control, possession, or custody of the vehicle. The Hyatt Regency (D) could not move Allen's (P) car, did not know to whom it belonged, and did not know when it would be reclaimed. Therefore, it certainly did not have sufficient control to create a bailment.

## ▶ ANALYSIS

The statutory presumption of negligence in this case accords with the majority common law rule. When the bailee rebuts the presumption, the bailor must take the burden of persuasion on the negligence issue. In this case, the dissent was correct that the Hyatt Regency (D) ticket system offered no actual opportunity for the attendant to prevent theft.

■═■

## Quicknotes

**BAILMENT** The delivery of property to be held in trust and which is designated for a particular purpose, following the satisfaction of which the property is either to be returned or disposed of as specified.

■═■

# CHAPTER 7

# Unauthorized Possession (Including Adverse Possession)

## Quick Reference Rules of Law

# Anderson v. Gouldberg

Wrongful wood cutter (P) v. Timber converter (D)

Minn. Sup. Ct., 51 Minn. 294, 53 N.W. 636 (1892).

**NATURE OF CASE:** Action to recover pine logs or their value.

**FACT SUMMARY:** Anderson (P), who trespassed on the land of a stranger, cut and removed 93 pine logs without the consent of the owner, and hauled these logs, bearing his initials, to a mill where they were taken by Gouldberg (D). Gouldberg (D) claimed possession on direction of owner and Anderson (P) sued for conversion.

## 🏛 RULE OF LAW
A possessor, even one who has converted the chattels himself, may recover for their conversion by a third party. His claim to title is superior to the whole world but for the true owner.

**FACTS:** Anderson (P), who trespassed on the land of a stranger, cut and removed 93 pine logs without the consent of the owner and hauled these logs, bearing his initials, to a mill where they were taken by Gouldberg (D). Gouldberg (D) claimed possession on direction of owner and Anderson (P) sued for conversion.

**ISSUE:** May a converter, in possession of goods, assert a superior claim of title over the conversion of the same goods by a third party?

**HOLDING AND DECISION:** (Mitchell, J.) Yes. Possession is good title against all the world except the true owner. One who takes property from the possession of another can only rebut the presumption of possession as title by showing a superior title in himself, or in some way connecting himself with one who has. The rule applies whether possession is by finding, bailment, or by mere tort. Any other rule would lead to an endless series of unlawful seizures and reprisals. Affirmed.

## ▌ ANALYSIS

Gouldberg (D) should not be permitted to raise the question of title in Anderson's (P) claim as the law seeks to protect the goods when not in the possession of the rightful owner. Otherwise, successive conversions of the same goods will be encouraged. Any other course would lead to multiple breaches of the peace and lack of property protection.

■■■

## Quicknotes

**CHATTEL** An article of personal property, as distinguished from real property; a thing personal and moveable.

**TITLE** The right of possession over property.

**TRESPASS** Unlawful interference with, or damage to, the real or personal property of another.

■■■

# Russell v. Hill

## Wood cutter (P) v. Timber converter (D)

N.C. Sup. Ct., 125 N.C. 470, 34 S.E. 640 (1899).

**NATURE OF CASE:** Appeal in an action in trover for cut timber.

**FACT SUMMARY:** The trial court held that Russell (P) was not entitled to trover for logs wrongfully taken from him by Hill (D), since the party from whom Russell (P) purchased the logs also lacked title or right of possession.

## 🏛 RULE OF LAW
Before a plaintiff can recover in an action in trover, he must show either title and possession or the right to possession.

**FACTS:** Busbee received, and duly registered title to, a grant of land from the state. Unaware of this title, Mrs. McCoy subsequently also received a state grant for these same lands. She then sold Russell (P) some timber on these lands. Russell (P) cut the timber and, while he was in the process of floating the logs to a furniture company for sale, Hill (D) wrongfully took them and sold them himself to that same company for $686.84. The company then became insolvent. Russell (P) sued Hill (D). The trial court ruled that he could not recover since: (1) Mrs. McCoy was neither the logs' owner nor even in adverse possession of them; and (2) the action, being in the nature of trover, required that Russell (P) show that he had both title and possession, or the right to possession. Russell (P) appealed.

**ISSUE:** Before a plaintiff can recover in an action in trover, must he show both title and possession, or the right to possession?

**HOLDING AND DECISION:** (Montgomery, J.) Yes. Before a plaintiff can recover in an action in trover, he must show either title and possession, or right to possession. All cases are in accord on this point. Even though a defendant may be wrongful, a plaintiff cannot recover if his own lack of title is proven. One of the characteristic distinctions between trover and trespass is that, although trespass may be maintained on possession, trover requires property and the right to possession. Trover is to personalty what ejectment is to realty. That is, title is indispensable. While it is true that property may be presumed from possession, this is a rebuttable presumption which, since the deed shows title in Busbee, is here rebutted. Finally, satisfaction of judgment would require us to vest title in Hill (D). This clearly cannot be done since title remains in Busbee. Affirmed.

## ▶ *ANALYSIS*

A related issue arises as to whether payment by a wrong-doer to a bailee is binding upon the bailor. In *The Winkfield*

(1902) P. 42 (C.A.), the Postmaster General, as bailee of mail lost in a collision of ships at sea, was allowed to recover for those owners not filing claims. The court held that, as between a bailee and a stranger, possession gives title; and that the wrongdoer, having paid full damages to the bailee, was thus provided with a defense against the bailor's action.

■■■

## *Quicknotes*

**TROVER** An action for damages resulting from the unlawful conversion of, or to recover possession of, personal property.

■■■

# Chapin v. Freeland

## Buyer of counters (P) v. Original owner (D)

Mass. Sup. Jud. Ct., 142 Mass. 383, 8 N.E. 128 (1886).

**NATURE OF CASE:** A bill of exceptions in an action to replevy store counters.

**FACT SUMMARY:** Freeland (D) took her display counters from Chapin (P) despite the fact that Chapin (P) had purchased them from parties holding them in valid adverse possession.

## 🏛 RULE OF LAW
The purchaser of an item from a vendor who held valid title to it by adverse possession has as valid a claim to the item as did his vendor.

**FACTS:** In 1867, the two counters, whose ownership is here contested, belonged to Freeland (D). However, in that same year they were installed by Warner in his shop and nailed to the floor. In 1871, Warner mortgaged the shop to DeWitt. In 1879, DeWitt's executors foreclosed and sold the premises to Chapin (P). Then, in 1881, Freeland (D) took the counters back from Chapin's (P) possession. Accordingly, Chapin (P) sued in replevin. However, the trial court found for Freeland (D) on the following theory: even though the statutory time for adverse possession had run in favor of either Warner or DeWitt, nevertheless, this did not either prevent Freeland (D) from taking the counters, nor entitle Chapin (P) to sue Freeland (D) in replevin since Freeland (D) was the original owner. Chapin (P) sought a bill of exceptions, arguing that his claim was as valid as was the claim of his vendors who were legally adverse possessors.

**ISSUE:** Does the purchaser of an item from a vendor who held valid title to it by adverse possession have as valid a claim to the item as did his vendor?

**HOLDING AND DECISION:** (Holmes, J.) Yes. The purchaser of an item from a vendor who held valid title to it by adverse possession has as valid a claim to the item as did his vendor. Therefore, just as Freeland (D) could not have taken direct action in replevin against Warner or DeWitt, neither can she indirectly take the counters from Chapin (P) by her own hand. Since Freeland's (D) title could not sustain a declaration of her ownership were she to have sued for it in court, neither will she be able to defend her title by this plea of original ownership. Exceptions sustained.

**DISSENT:** (Field, J.) There is no statute and no law prohibiting the owner of personal chattels from peaceably taking possession of them wherever he finds them. There is nothing in our law holding that the possession of chattels for the statutory period of limitations for personal actions thereby creates title.

## ▌ANALYSIS

Acquisition of title by adverse possession has been an issue in a vast number of cases involving land, but has rarely been raised in cases involving chattels. Its justification—especially in land use—is the policy of protecting the parties' expectations as to the sale of property, and of clearing title of old, stale claims. It has further roots in the recognition of the fact that one in possession has many of the rights of ownership.

■━■

## *Quicknotes*

**ADVERSE POSSESSION** A means of acquiring title to real property by remaining in actual, open, continuous, exclusive possession of property for the statutory period.

**REPLEVIN** An action to recover personal property wrongfully taken.

■━■

# O'Keeffe v. Snyder

## Artist (P) v. Adverse possessor (D)

N.J. Sup. Ct., 83 N.J. 478, 416 A.2d 862 (1980).

**NATURE OF CASE:** Appeal from order granting summary judgment in action for replevin.

**FACT SUMMARY:** O'Keeffe (P), who maintained that in 1946 several of her paintings were stolen from a gallery, sued Snyder (D) in 1976, claiming that he had illegal possession of them, and further that this was the first opportunity she had to sue.

## 🏛 RULE OF LAW
The discovery rule provides that in an appropriate case a cause of action will not accrue until the injured party discovers, or by reasonable diligence should have discovered, facts which form the basis of a cause of action.

**FACTS:** In 1946, Alfred Steiglitz arranged an art exhibition which included an O'Keeffe painting. Later, O'Keeffe (P) discovered the painting had been stolen, along with several other of her paintings. O'Keeffe (P) did not report them missing to the police nor did she report the theft to the Art Dealers Association of America until 1972. In 1975, O'Keefe learned that the paintings were in a New York gallery, and in 1976, she discovered that Ulrich A. Frank had sold them to Barry Snyder (D) of the Princeton Gallery of Fine Art. Frank maintained that his family had continuous possession of the paintings for over 30 years prior to the sale to Snyder (D). O'Keeffe (P) sued Synder (D) after his refusal to return the pictures to her. The trial court granted summary judgment for Snyder (D) on the grounds that O'Keeffe's (P) action was barred by the statute of limitations and that title had vested in Frank by adverse possession, and O'Keeffe (P) appealed.

**ISSUE:** Does the discovery rule provide that in an appropriate case a cause of action will not accrue until the injured party discovers, or by reasonable diligence should have discovered, facts which form the basis of a cause of action?

**HOLDING AND DECISION:** (Pollock, J.) Yes. The operative fact that divests the original owner of title to either personal or real property is the expiration of the period of limitations. In the past, adverse possession has described the conduct that will vest title of a chattel at the end of a statutory period. The discovery rule, which holds that a cause of action will not accrue until the injured party discovers, or reasonably should have discovered, facts which form the basis of a cause of action, is a principle of equity designed to mitigate unjust results. Under the discovery rule, the burden is on the owner to establish facts that would justify deferring the beginning of the period of limitations; while under adverse possession, the burden is on the possessor to prove the elements of adverse possession. Here, O'Keeffe (P) should be given an opportunity to demonstrate if once having discovered the paintings were stolen, she acted with due diligence to discover the identity of the possessor of the paintings. The discovery rule becomes a vehicle for transporting equitable considerations into the statute of limitations and will assist artists in recovering stolen work. Reversed and remanded.

## ▶ ANALYSIS

Prior to *O'Keeffe v. Snyder*, there have been only two cases that had applied adverse possession to chattels in New Jersey. In *O'Keeffe*, the court overruled those two cases and held for the first time that adverse possession does not apply to chattels, while stating that real property will still be subject to the doctrine. In *O'Keeffe*, the court opined that the requirements of open, notorious, and visible possession were too difficult to be applied to chattels, especially artwork which can be easily hidden.

■══■

## Quicknotes

**DUE DILIGENCE** The standard of care as would be taken by a reasonable person in accordance with the attendant facts and circumstances.

**REPLEVIN** An action to recover personal property wrongfully taken.

■══■

# Marengo Cave Co. v. Ross

Tour company (D) v. Landowner (P)

Ind. Sup. Ct., 212 Ind. 624, 10 N.E.2d 917 (1937).

**NATURE OF CASE:** Action to quiet title to that portion of a subterranean cave extending under plaintiff's land.

**FACT SUMMARY:** Marengo Cave Co. (D) conducted tours of a subterranean cave which extended under a portion of Ross's (P) land.

## 🏛 RULE OF LAW
Before the adverse possession period begins to run against subsurface land, the true owner must have knowledge of the trespass.

**FACTS:** Marengo Cave Co. (D) and its predecessors in interest owned and operated a cave tour. The cave was approximately 700 feet below the surface of the land. Both Marengo Cave Co. (D) and Ross (P) thought that the entire cave was on Marengo's (D) land. In actuality, a portion of the cave extended under Ross's (P) property. After some 40 years of use, Ross (P) became aware that a portion of the cave was under his land. Ross (P) brought suit to quiet title to that portion of the cave and a survey was ordered by the court. Marengo Cave Co. (D) defended on the basis that it had acquired title to the entire cave through adverse possession. The trial court found that the possession was not open and notorious as to Ross (P) and quieted title in him. Marengo Cave Co. (D) appealed on the basis that Ross (P) knew of the cave and had even visited it himself. It was Ross's (P) responsibility to determine whether any portion of the cave was on his land and, having failed to do so, Marengo Cave Co. (D) should acquire title through adverse possession.

**ISSUE:** Will adverse possession begin to run, as to subsurface land use, prior to the owner's learning of the trespass?

**HOLDING AND DECISION:** (Roll, J.) No. The requirement that possession be "open and notorious" is only satisfied where the owner has actual or constructive notice of the possession. On the land's surface, this is satisfied by ownership claims and open and continuous use. With respect to subsurface uses, an owner cannot determine, on his own, whether a trespass is taking place. He must hire an expert to survey the subsurface land in order to establish boundaries. Prior to the period for adverse possession to run, the true owner must actually be aware of the trespass. It is stipulated here that both Ross (P) and Marengo Cave Co. (D) thought the cave was solely on Marengo Cave Co.'s (D) land. The cave was not separately taxed, nor was it assessed against either's property. Actual knowledge of the cave's existence does not equal knowledge that part of it is on his property. Finally, secret trespasses will not start the statute running. The adverse possessor must, through his actions, apprise the owner of his own claim to the land. The decision of the trial court is sustained.

## ▶ ANALYSIS

Where the mineral rights have been previously severed from the surface estate, the surface owner may not complain of the adverse possession of the subsurface. Also, the knowledge of the surface owner of a trespass to the subterranean land will not be imputed to the owner of the severed mineral estate unless there is an agency or fiduciary relationship between the two.

■■■

## Quicknotes

**ADVERSE POSSESSION** A means of acquiring title to real property by remaining in actual, open, continuous, exclusive possession of the property for the statutory period.

**CONSTRUCTIVE NOTICE** Knowledge of a fact that is imputed to an individual who was under a duty to inquire and who could have learned of the fact through the exercise of reasonable prudence.

**QUIET TITLE** Equitable action to resolve conflicting claims to an interest in real property.

■■■

# Howard v. Kunto

## Owner of land (P) v. Grantee (D)

Wash. Ct. App., 3 Wash. App., 477 P.2d 210 (1970).

**NATURE OF CASE:** Appeal from action granting a decree quieting title to real property.

**FACT SUMMARY:** Due to a mistake in the survey, a summer cottage was constructed on the land of another.

### 🏛 RULE OF LAW
Part-time residency alone does not destroy the continuity of possession required to establish title by adverse possession if such residency is similar in nature to owners of like property.

**FACTS:** Due to a surveying error, Kunto's (D) grantor built a summer cottage on property located outside the boundaries of his land. The error was discovered some 30 years later. Howard (P), the owner of the land on which the cottage was built, sued. Kunto (D) attempted to establish adverse possession through "tacking" since he hadn't been in possession for the statutory period. "Tacking" is the use of your predecessor's possession to meet the continuous possession requirement for adverse possession. The trial court permitted the tacking and held that there was sufficient privity between Kunto (D) and his predecessor in title, even though the deed did not contain the disputed property. It quieted title in favor of Kunto (D) and Howard (P) appealed.

**ISSUE:** Is tacking permitted where land is only used during a portion of the year and the deed of title does not contain the disputed property?

**HOLDING AND DECISION:** (Pearson, J.) Yes. Tacking, per statute, requires a "claim of right." Mere "squatting" is not sufficient to establish title by adverse possession. There must be privity between the "grantor" and "grantee" to establish privity. While the deed transferring the property does not contain any of the land in question, two factors require this court to find that privity existed to a sufficient extent as to allow tacking. First, Kunto (D) and his grantors acted in good faith, and, merely because of a surveying error, they cannot be considered squatters. Secondly, public policy favors early certainty as to the location of land ownership. The next question involves the fact that the land was only occupied during a portion of each year. To constitute adverse possession, the occupation must be actual, uninterrupted, open, notorious, hostile, and exclusive, and under a claim of right made in good faith. It has become firmly established that the requisite possession is only to the extent that ordinarily marks the conduct of owners in general who hold similar property. Since this property and other similarly situated property are used as summer residences, partial occupation during the summer months satisfies this requirement. Reversed with directions for the defendants.

## ▶ ANALYSIS

If possession is interrupted for any reason, the statute of limitations starts to run all over again. Since all presumptions are made in favor of the real owner, even a short break in possession is held to destroy the adverse possessor's claim to the property.

■■■

## Quicknotes

**ADVERSE POSSESSION** A means of acquiring title to real property by remaining in actual, open, continuous, exclusive possession of property for the statutory period.

**STATUTE OF LIMITATIONS** A law prescribing the period in which a legal action may be commenced.

**TACKING** The attachment of periods of adverse possession by different adverse possessors in order to fulfill the requirement of continuous possession for the period proscribed by statute.

■■■

# Improving Another's Property by Mistake (Accession)

## Quick Reference Rules of Law

# Wetherbee v. Green

Hoop maker (D) v. Land owner (P)

Mich. Sup. Ct., 22 Mich. 311, 7 Am. Rep. 653 (1871).

**NATURE OF CASE:** To replevy timber converted into hoops.

**FACT SUMMARY:** Acting in good faith and under apparent lawful permission, Wetherbee (D) cut timber on Green's (P) land and manufactured it into valuable hoops.

## 🏛 RULE OF LAW
When a party, acting in good faith and relying upon apparent lawful permission, takes property from another and, by expenditure of money and labor, transforms it into a much more valuable article, then the true owner is entitled to no more damages than the property's original unchanged value.

**FACTS:** Wetherbee (D) cut timber on Green's (P) land and, by the substantial expenditure of his money and labor, he converted the timber into hoops. When Green (P) replevied these hoops, Wetherbee (D) argued that such replevin could not be maintained because he: (1) had cut the timber in good faith in reliance upon the permission of parties whom he reasonably believed owned the timber; and (2) had, at substantial cost and labor, converted the timber into hoops immensely more valuable than it was in its natural state. However, the trial court refused Wetherbee's (D) offer of evidence that, while the standing timber was worth $25, the hoops were worth nearly $700. The jury ruled for Green (P). Wetherbee (D) appealed, arguing that, under such circumstances, Green (P) was entitled only to the value of the timber before its conversion.

**ISSUE:** When a party, acting in good faith and reasonable reliance on an apparent right, takes property from another and, by expenditure of money and labor, transforms it into a much more valuable article, is the true owner entitled to no more in damages than the property's original unchanged value?

**HOLDING AND DECISION:** (Cooley, J.) Yes. When a party, acting in good faith and reasonable reliance on apparent lawful permission, takes property from another and, by expenditure of money and labor, transforms it into a much more valuable article, then the true owner is entitled to no more damages than the property's original unchanged value. To hold otherwise would too severely punish an unintentional and involuntary wrongdoer and compensate the owner beyond all reason and justice. The question of motive is essential. Some cases never allow such "title by accession" to be acquired by a willful trespasser. However, even in innocent misappropriation, the materials can be reclaimed unless, as here, they have undergone such a radical change that their original character has been lost or greatly enhanced. For example, it is clear that wood made into a church organ or a house cannot be reclaimed. Accordingly, it was an error to deny the jury this evidence and to instruct them accordingly. Reversed for a new trial.

## ▶ ANALYSIS

According to *Somers v. Kane*, 168 Minn. 420 (1926), when a party negligently or in bad faith has commingled his goods with those of another, he may, nevertheless, recover their relative amount and value if it can be determined with approximate correctness. There, the plaintiff had mingled his logs with those of the defendant. The court held that the law intended compensation for the wrong done, but not a penalty.

■■■

## Quicknotes

**ACCESSION** The addition of value to an existing good, typically through labor or the addition of new goods.

**AMELIORATIVE WASTE** An unauthorized change in a physical structure which, though technically "waste," in fact increases the value of the land.

**REPLEVIN** An action to recover personal property wrongfully taken.

■■■

# Isle Royal Mining Co. v. Hertin

Land owner (D) v. Wood pile maker (P)

Mich. Sup. Ct., 37 Mich. 332, 26 Am. Rep. 520 (1877).

**NATURE OF CASE:** Appeal from jury verdict awarding damages in quantum meruit.

**FACT SUMMARY:** Hertin (P) mistakenly cut timber on property belonging to Isle Royal Mining Co. (D), and then sought the value of his labor when Isle Royal (D) reclaimed the wood.

## 🏛 RULE OF LAW
The value of labor is not recoverable for a person who inadvertently exploits the property resources of another.

**FACTS:** Hertin (P) and Isle Royal Mining Co. (D) were owners of adjacent timberland. Hertin (P) felled trees he believed to be on his property but which actually belonged to Isle Royal (D). He piled the wood into cords. Isle Royal (D) retook possession of the wood. Hertin (P) sued to recover the value of his labor. The jury awarded damages to Hertin (P), and Isle Royale (D) appealed.

**ISSUE:** Is the value of labor recoverable when a person inadvertently exploits the property of another?

**HOLDING AND DECISION:** (Cooley, C.J.) No. The value of labor is not recoverable for a person who inadvertently exploits the property resources of another. The law requires persons to properly assess the extent of their own property. A person who fails to do so must bear the responsibility for the mistake. One may inadvertently trespass and nonetheless be civilly liable in trespass. Similarly, affirmative rights cannot be established in the unlawful use of another's property. One using another's property deprives the owner of that property, if only temporarily, and this offense does not create any rights in the offender. To hold otherwise would be to reward the negligent and blundering and to penalize the careful, a result this court will not countenance. Reversed.

## ▶ ANALYSIS

This case should be compared to contract law. There, one who performs services for another may recover the value of his services, even if the services were not a part of any contract between the parties. This is known in contract law as quasi-contractual or quantum meruit damages.

■■■

## Quicknotes

**QUANTUM MERUIT** Equitable doctrine allowing recovery for labor and materials provided by one party, even though no contract was entered into, in order to avoid unjust enrichment by the benefited party.

■■■

# Hardy v. Burroughs

Home builder (P) v. Land owner (D)

Mich. Sup. Ct., 251 Mich. 578, 232 N.W. 200 (1930).

**NATURE OF CASE:** Appeal of the denial of a motion to suppress an equitable complaint.

**FACT SUMMARY:** The Hardys (P) mistakenly constructed a house on the Burroughses' (D) property.

## 🏛 RULE OF LAW
The fact that an innocent property owner seeks no relief for improvements mistakenly made in good faith on his land by a builder, does not thereby prevent the builder himself from suing in equity for the value of the improvements.

**FACTS:** The Hardys (P), by a good-faith mistake, constructed a house valued at $1,250 on the Burroughses' (D) lot. However, the Burroughses (D) refused to make any adjustments with the Hardys (P) despite the fact that they benefited by the mistake. Admittedly, however, there was no fraud on the Burroughses' (D) part such as their standing by and permitting the Hardys' (P) mistake. The Hardys (P) brought this suit in equity for the value of the improvements made. The Burroughses (D) argued that they (D) were doing no more than enjoying their own land, and that the house on it was theirs through no fraud or act of their own but solely by operation of law. They claimed that the only way they could be required to compensate the Hardys (P) would have been if the Burroughses (D) themselves had been plaintiffs in equity and, thus, been required to do equity. The trial court denied the Burroughses' (D) motion to dismiss the complaint. The Burroughses (D) appealed.

**ISSUE:** Does the fact that an innocent property owner seeks no relief for improvements mistakenly made in good faith on his land by a builder thereby prevent the builder himself from suing in equity for the value of the improvements?

**HOLDING AND DECISION:** (Clark, J.) No. The fact that an innocent property owner seeks no relief for improvements mistakenly made in good faith on his land by a builder does not thereby prevent the builder himself from suing in equity for the value of the improvements. Concededly: (1) there can be no recovery at law; (2) were the Burroughs (D) the plaintiffs, the equity would also grant the Hardys (P) relief under the maxim "he who seeks equity must do equity"; and (3) relief would be granted were the Burroughses (D) guilty of fraud. However, none of these elements are present. Furthermore, some authorities would clearly not allow relief for the reasons already stated. Nevertheless, we follow the above-stated rule since to do otherwise would not be equitable. Affirmed.

## ▌ ANALYSIS

Although the case of *Somerville v. Jacobs*, 153 W. Va. 613 (1969), followed *Hardy v. Burroughs*, in a dissenting opinion the judge observed that this decision amounted to the condemnation of private property by private parties for private use. "It clearly is the accepted law that as between two parties in the circumstances of this case he who made the mistake must suffer the hardship rather than he who was without fault."

■■■

## Quicknotes

**EQUITABLE** Just; fair.

**MOTION TO DISMISS** Motion to terminate an action based on the adequacy of the pleadings, improper service or venue, etc.

■■■

# CHAPTER 9

# Bona Fide Purchase

## *Quick Reference Rules of Law*

# Porter v. Wertz

## Painting owner (P) v. Bailee (D) and Purchaser (D)

N.Y. Sup. Ct., App. Div., 68 A.D.2d 141, 416 N.Y.S.2d 254 (1979), *aff'd*, 439 N.Y.S.2d, 421 N.E.2d 500 (1981).

**NATURE OF CASE:** Appeal from order denying recovery of possession.

**FACT SUMMARY:** Porter (P) lent a painting to Wertz (D), who fraudulently held himself out as an art dealer and then sold it without authorization.

## 🏛 RULE OF LAW
Granting possession of a chattel to another who disposes of it without authority does not estop the true owner from recovering the chattel.

**FACTS:** Porter (P) owned certain art works, including a painting by Utrillo. He lent the painting to Wertz (D), who held himself out as a dealer/collector, so that Wertz (D) could see how the painting looked in his house. Porter's (P) understanding was that Wertz (D) would buy it or return it. This agreement was later reduced to writing. Unbeknownst to Porter (P), Wertz (D) was approached by Feigin (D), an art dealer/broker. Feigin (D) had a client interested in the Utrillo painting. Wertz (D) delivered the painting to Feigin (D), who collected a fee upon sale. Porter (P) later sued Wertz (D) and Feigin (D) to recover the painting or its value, $30,000. The trial court denied recovery on equitable estoppel grounds, and Porter (P) appealed.

**ISSUE:** Does granting possession of a chattel to another who disposes of it without authority estop the true owner from recovering the chattel?

**HOLDING AND DECISION:** (Birns, J.) No. Granting possession of a chattel to another who disposes of it without authority does not estop the true owner from recovering the chattel. As a general matter, if one entrusts an item of personal property to one who deals in that type of property, one is estopped to deny authority to sell against a purchaser. However, good faith is required for this to be operative; possession without implied authority does not create an estoppel. Here, Feigin (D) made no effort to discover the owner of the painting, apparently considering this a bothersome detail. Estoppel is not designed to cover those who engage in sharp practice. Reversed.

## ▶ *ANALYSIS*

The common law created equitable estoppel in one who transfers a chattel to a dealer who then undertakes to deal the chattel. The U.C.C. codified this rule. It is found in § 2-403 of the code.

# Sheridan Suzuki, Inc. v. Caruso Auto Sales

Motorcycle seller (P) v. Motorcycle reseller (D)

N.Y. Sup. Ct., 110 Misc. 2d 823, 442 N.Y.S.2d 957 (1981).

**NATURE OF CASE:** Appeal from preliminary order in action to recover property.

**FACT SUMMARY:** Suzuki (P) sold a motorcycle to Ronald Bouton whereupon Bouton immediately resold the motorcycle to Caruso (D), having given Suzuki (P) a check that was subsequently dishonored.

## 🏛 RULE OF LAW
A bona fide purchaser for value cannot receive good title from a person with voidable title under the U.C.C. when such title has not yet been perfected as required by statute.

**FACTS:** Suzuki (P) sold a motorcycle to Ronald Bouton in exchange for a check incident to the sale. Suzuki (P) gave Bouton possession of the motorcycle, a signed bill of sale, and a registration, and filed an application for an original Certificate of Title. The day after the purchase, Bouton (D) sold the motorcycle to Caruso (D) for less money than the original purchase price. Bouton gave Caruso (D) possession of the motorcycle and agreed to transfer to Caruso (D) the Certificate of Title upon receipt. Bouton (D) absconded, and the Certificate of Title was never issued as a result of the bad check Bouton had given Suzuki (P). After Bouton's (D) check was dishonored, Suzuki (P) sued Caruso (D) to obtain possession of the motorcycle. The trial court entered an order for Suzuki (P). Caruso (D) appealed.

**ISSUE:** Can a bona fide purchaser for value receive good title from a person with voidable title under the U.C.C. when said title has not yet been perfected pursuant to a state statute?

**HOLDING AND DECISION:** (Sedita, J.) No. If a voidable title has never been perfected as required by statute, then title cannot successfully be passed on to a bona fide purchaser for value. While a bona fide purchaser for value can receive good title from one with a "voidable" title under U.C.C., if there exists an additional statutory requirement of title being perfected prior to the passing of ownership, then that must be complied with. Here, since Bouton (D) never received the Certificate of Title which would have perfected his voidable title as required by New York statute, he could not successfully pass title to a bona fide purchaser for value. Consequently, Caruso (D) never acquired any legal title or right to the vehicle. Affirmed.

## ▌ *ANALYSIS*

When one buys in good faith and in the regular course of commerce, he is now assured by the U.C.C. of broad protection against prior claims of ownership and defenses with respect to negotiable instruments, documents of title, and investment securities. The code's inclusion of § 2-403, granting a measure of negotiability to goods in the commercial setting, by protecting a bona fide purchaser for value, has been the most dramatic step.

■■■

## *Quicknotes*

**"VOIDABLE" TITLE** Where a true owner initially intends to clothe another with a title, but because of the other's wrongful action, is able to avoid the transaction and reclaim the title.

■■■

# Transfers of Ownership by Gift

## Quick Reference Rules of Law

# In re Cohn

## Executors of the state (P) v. Widow (D)

N.Y. Sup. Ct., App. Div., 187 App. Div. 392, 176 N.Y.S. 225 (1919).

**NATURE OF CASE:** Appeal from a finding of validity of a gift.

**FACT SUMMARY:** The decedent delivered to his wife a writing stating that he gave her that day shares of stock as a birthday present, but he died before he could make actual delivery of the stock certificates.

## 🏛 RULE OF LAW
The requirement that for a gift to be valid it must be delivered is satisfied by the delivery by the donor of an instrument of gift to the donee.

**FACTS:** The decedent, in a dated and signed writing which he handed to his wife, stated: "I give this day to my wife, Sara K. Cohn, as a present for her (46) forty-sixth birthday (500) five hundred shares of American Tobacco Company common stock." The decedent died six days later without making actual delivery of the stock certificates to his wife. The certificates were in the name of his business firm which had been dissolved shortly before his wife's birthday by the death of one of the partners. The decedent said that he would give his wife the certificates as soon as they were available to him. A question arose as to the validity of the gift. The trial court found that the gift was valid and this appeal followed.

**ISSUE:** Is the requirement that for a gift to be valid it must be delivered, satisfied by the delivery by the donor of an instrument of gift to the donee?

**HOLDING AND DECISION:** (Shearn, J.) Yes. The requirement that for a gift to be valid it must be delivered is satisfied by the delivery by the donor of an instrument of gift to the donee. First, there was here a present gift because the decedent stated "I give this day," and actual possession was not given only because decedent had to wait until he could get the certificates. The circumstances afforded a reasonable and satisfactory excuse for not making actual delivery of the certificates at the time the gift was made. The rule requiring actual delivery to effect a valid gift is not inflexible. "The necessity of delivery where gifts resting in parol are asserted against the estates of decedents is obvious; but it is equally plain that there is no such impelling necessity when the gift is established by the execution and delivery of an instrument of gift." Furthermore, there was present, as evidenced by the writing, not only an intention to then give, but also to then deliver the thing given. Affirmed.

**DISSENT:** (Page, J.) The delivery of the writing accompanied by a statement that the stock certificates would be given when the decedent could get hold of them showed an intention to make a future gift. Further, the writing did not have such effect as to transfer right of possession, and, additionally, there was nothing preventing decedent from making an actual delivery of the certificates.

## ▶ ANALYSIS

Much confusion exists as to what type of a writing will serve as a vehicle for a gift and under what circumstances. There appears to be no problem where the writing is under seal. Also, where the writing is formal in every sense except that it lacks a seal, it should be effective in those states that no longer require writings to be under seal. The real difficulty arises with writings of varying degrees of formality, such as correspondence. There, the cases are in conflict.

■=■

## Quicknotes

**GIFT** A transfer of property to another person that is voluntary and which lacks consideration.

**PAROL EVIDENCE RULE** Doctrine precluding parties to an agreement from introducing evidence of prior or contemporaneous agreements in order to repudiate or alter the terms of a written contract.

■=■

# Gruen v. Gruen

## Son (P) v. Stepmother (D)

N.Y. Ct. App., 68 N.Y.2d 48, 496 N.E.2d 869 (1986).

**NATURE OF CASE:** Appeal from an enforcement of an inter vivos gift.

**FACT SUMMARY:** Gruen (D) contended her husband could not make a valid inter vivos gift to his son and still retain present exclusive possession of the property for his life.

### 🏛 RULE OF LAW
A valid inter vivos gift of chattel may be made where the donor reserves a life estate and the donee never has physical possession until the donor's death.

**FACTS:** Gruen (P) received a letter from his father indicating the latter wished to make a gift of a painting, but that he wished to use it for his life. Gruen (P) never took possession of the painting. After his father's death, he requested the painting from his stepmother, who refused. Gruen (P) sued, contending a valid inter vivos gift had been made. His stepmother defended, contending no valid gift could be made if the donor retained a life estate and no physical delivery was made during life. The trial court held against Gruen (P), while the appellate court reversed. Gruen (D) appealed.

**ISSUE:** May a valid inter vivos gift of chattel be made where the donor reserves a life estate and the donee does not take physical possession?

**HOLDING AND DECISION:** (Simons, J.) Yes. A valid inter vivos gift of chattel may be made where the donor reserves a life estate and the donee never takes physical possession until after the donor's death. In this case, donative intent was established constructively through the document of transfer, the letter. Acceptance is implied because the painting had value. Thus, a valid gift was made. Affirmed.

### ▶ ANALYSIS

Various estates in chattel can be created just as various estates in land are. The property in this case happened to be personal rather than real, yet the creation of a remainder interest was valid. It is clear the elder Gruen intended to make a current transfer of such interest, while retaining a possessory interest.

■═■

## Quicknotes

**GIFT** A transfer of property to another person that is voluntary and which lacks consideration.

**INTER VIVOS** Between living persons.

**LIFE ESTATE** An interest in land measured by the life of the tenant or a third party.

■═■

# Lindh v. Surman

Ex-fiancé (P) v. Ex-fiancée (D)

Pa. Sup. Ct., 560 Pa. 1, 742 A.2d 643 (1999).

**NATURE OF CASE:** Complaint for recovery of a ring or its equivalent value.

**FACT SUMMARY:** When Lindh (P) called off his proposal of marriage to Surman (D) she refused to return the engagement ring.

## 🏛 RULE OF LAW
The donor of an engagement ring is entitled to its return even if the donor broke the engagement.

**FACTS:** Lindh (P) proposed marriage to Surman (D) and gave her an engagement ring worth $17,000. When he called off the engagement, she refused to return the ring. He filed a two-count complaint, seeking recovery of the ring or a judgment for its equivalent value. He received a judgment for $21,200 and the Supreme Court affirmed. Surman (D) appealed.

**ISSUE:** Is the donor of an engagement ring entitled to its return even if the donor broke the engagement?

**HOLDING AND DECISION:** (Newman, J.) Yes. The donor of an engagement ring is entitled to its return even if the donor broke the engagement. The giving of an engagement gift has an implied condition that the marriage must occur in order to vest title in the donee; mere acceptance of the marriage proposal is not the implied condition for the gift. The no-fault principle is the best rule, requiring no investigation into the motives or reasons for the cessation of the engagement and requiring the return of the ring upon the mere nonoccurrence of the marriage. Affirmed.

**DISSENT:** (Cappy, J.) There is no difference in the sordidness of the court's daily cases and any fact pattern in which a person broke an engagement and why.

**DISSENT:** (Castille, J.) Gifts made in the hope of marriage are not recoverable in the absence of fraud.

## ▶ ANALYSIS

The court here rejects the fault-based rule, which requires an inquiry into the motives for the breaking of the engagement on the basis that it would offend our senses of "equity." The court also rejects the modified no-fault rule, which requires the return of the ring in all cases where the donor breaks the engagement.

■■■■

## Quicknotes

**EQUITABLE** Just; fair.

**GIFT** A transfer of property to another person that is voluntary and which lacks consideration.

**TITLE** The right of possession over property.

**VESTING** The attaining of the right to pension or other employer-contribution benefits when the employee satisfies the minimum requirements necessary in order to be entitled to the receipt of such benefits in the future.

■■■■

# Foster v. Reiss

## Unidentified party (P) v. Surviving husband (D)

N.J. Sup. Ct., 18 N.J. 41, 112 A.2d 553, 48 A.L.R.2d 1391 (1955).

**NATURE OF CASE:** Action to recover possession of personal property.

**FACT SUMMARY:** In contemplation of death, the decedent wrote out a paper making a gift of personal property to her husband and later she died; the paper was given to the husband but the property was never actually delivered to him.

## RULE OF LAW
To constitute a valid gift causa mortis, the gift must be made in contemplation of the donor's imminent death, the donor must die of that sickness or peril, there must be a present intent to transfer ownership, and there must be a delivery of the property to the donee.

**FACTS:** Ethel and Adam Reiss (D) were married in 1940. Ethel Reiss executed a will leaving one dollar to Adam Reiss (D) and the rest to her children. After a short separation, the two reconciled and cohabited. In 1951, Ethel Reiss entered a hospital for major surgery. Just prior to going to the operating room, she wrote a note to her husband. The note told Adam Reiss (D) where certain money was hidden and to give that money to her daughter. The note also gave to Adam Reiss (D) some cash, a bank book, and a book of building loan stock. The note told where her will was and told Adam Reiss (D) to live a good life because she could no longer be with him. Ethel Reiss told a friend to give the note to Adam Reiss (D) and the note was given to him during Ethel's surgery. He went home, found the items, and took possession of those which had been given to him. Ethel never regained rational consciousness and died nine days after the operation, never having revoked the gift. Ethel's personal representatives, and her trustee, brought suit against Adam Reiss (D) to regain possession of the property given to him.

**ISSUE:** Was there an actual, unequivocal, and complete delivery during the donor's lifetime which wholly divested the decedent of the possession, dominion and control of the property?

**HOLDING AND DECISION:** (Vanderbilt, C.J.) No. The test for delivery is that the transfer, in conjunction with donative intent, must completely strip the donor of dominion of the thing given. Here there was no delivery by the donor, which requires an affirmative act on her part and not the mere taking of possession of the property by the donee. Delivery is the only safeguard which differentiates a gift causa mortis from a legacy in a will. The writing merely indicated the donor's unequivocal intent, but it does not satisfy the separate and distinct requirement of delivery. The fact that the donee took possession of the property does not make delivery unnecessary. The decedent was required to make an actual delivery of the goods, because there are no circumstances present which would allow for a constructive delivery. Gifts causa mortis are not favored by the law because they avoid the safeguards of the Statute of Wills, and, therefore, the requirements are to be strictly complied with. The gift was invalid. Appellate Division judgment reversed and Chancery Division judgment reinstated.

**DISSENT:** (Jacobs, J.) The donor expressly intended to give Adam Reiss (D) a gift, and gave him a note which both expressed this intent and told him where the property was to be found. The donee took possession of the goods and retained them. The intention of the donor should not be thwarted by a narrow construction of sufficient delivery. Once intent is established, delivery is secondary and evidentiary.

## ANALYSIS

A gift causa mortis becomes absolute on the donor's death from the anticipated peril, with the donee surviving, and without the donor having revoked the gift. The gift is revocable by the donor until the death of the donor, and it is automatically revoked on the donor's recovery. The gift causa mortis allows gifts which are basically testamentary in character from having to comply with the Statute of Wills, such as being signed, dated, and attested by two witnesses. The urge to protect the Statute of Wills leads this court to treat intent and delivery as separate requirements and to require a strict compliance with each.

■=■

## Quicknotes

**ACTUAL DELIVERY** The transfer of title or possession of property.

**CONSTRUCTIVE DELIVERY** The transfer of title or possession of property by means other than actual delivery indicative of the parties' intent to effect a transfer.

**STATUTE OF WILLS** An English law stating the requirements for a valid testamentary disposition.

■=■

# Scherer v. Hyland

Surviving lover (P) v. Administrator of the estate (D)

N.J. Sup. Ct., 75 N.J. 127, 380 A.2d 698 (1977).

**NATURE OF CASE:** Appeal from the finding of a valid gift.

**FACT SUMMARY:** Wagner left a suicide note and an endorsed check on the table of an apartment she shared with Scherer (P).

## 🏛 RULE OF LAW
Where there is unequivocal proof that the decedent has done everything possible to effectuate delivery of a gift causa mortis, it will be upheld.

**FACTS:** Wagner was living with Scherer (P). Wagner was severely injured in an automobile accident. Scherer (P) took over her care and paid all of their bills. Wagner became depressed and attempted suicide. The attempt failed. Wagner received a settlement check on the accident. She called Scherer (P) to tell him it had arrived. Wagner endorsed the check and left it on the table. Wagner left a suicide note and a note bequeathing Scherer (P) the check. Wagner then locked up the apartment, went up to the roof, and jumped to her death. The Administrator of her estate, Hyland (D), refused Scherer's (P) request for the check. Hyland (D) alleged that there had been no delivery, that the purported will was invalid, and that suicides cannot give a valid gift causa mortis.

**ISSUE:** Where the decedent has done everything within her power to effectuate constructive delivery of a gift causa mortis, is it valid?

**HOLDING AND DECISION:** (Per curiam) Yes. There is no public policy against a gift causa mortis. If there has been delivery, death was imminent and the decedent died within a short time of the gift in the expected manner, a valid gift causa mortis has been made. The delivery requirement is evidentiary in nature to prevent fraud and to guarantee that a present gift was intended. Constructive delivery will validate the gift where the decedent has done everything reasonably necessary under the circumstances to effectuate delivery. Here, Wagner endorsed the check, left it where Scherer (P) was certain to see it, informed him it had arrived, and locked the apartment when she left. The note and all of the factors surrounding the situation are sufficient to guarantee the authenticity of the gift and that Wagner's actions indicated that she had done everything possible to complete delivery. We further hold that suicides may give a valid gift causa mortis. Judgment for Scherer (P) is affirmed.

## ▶ ANALYSIS

In *Gordon v. Barr*, 13 Cal. 2d 596, the court stated that there must be unequivocal proof of a deliberate and well-considered donative intent on the part of the donor. However, many courts have been inclined to overlook the technical requirements of delivery in favor of a finding of constructive or symbolic delivery. To uphold such delivery, there must be a clear intent to presently part with some substantive incident of ownership.

■═■

## Quicknotes

**CONSTRUCTIVE DELIVERY** The transfer of title or possession of property by means other than actual delivery indicative of the parties' intent to effect a transfer.

**GIFT CAUSAS MORTIS** A gift made contingent on the donor's anticipated death.

■═■

# CHAPTER 11

# A Brief Look at the Historical Development of Estates Doctrine

## *Quick Reference Rules of Law*

# In re O'Connor's Estate

## County of probate (P) v. Nebraska (D)

Neb. Sup. Ct., 252 N.W. 826 (1934).

**NATURE OF CASE:** Appeal in an inheritance tax action.

**FACT SUMMARY:** Adams County (P) claimed that the State of Nebraska (D) was liable for the inheritance tax for O'Connor's estate which had escheated to the State (D).

## 🏛 RULE OF LAW
The escheat of property to the state constitutes a transfer by reversion, not by succession, and, therefore, the state is not liable for the payment of inheritance tax.

**FACTS:** The estate of John O'Connor escheated to the State of Nebraska (D) for want of heirs or any other testamentary disposition. However, Adams County (P) successfully sued the State (D) for the inheritance taxes on the property. The State (D) appealed, arguing that, since escheat amounted to a passage of property by reversion, and not by succession, no tax liability was thereby created.

**ISSUE:** Does the escheat of property to the state constitute a transfer by reversion, not by succession, and thereby create no tax liability on the part of the state?

**HOLDING AND DECISION:** (Yeager, J.) Yes. The escheat of property to the state constitutes a transfer by reversion, not by succession, and therefore, the state is not liable for the payment of inheritance tax. Clearly, the theory of the law of escheat in the United States is that the state was originally the proprietor of all real property and will also ultimately be its last proprietor. Therefore, what we commonly term ownership in the individual is in reality but a tenancy whose continuance is contingent upon the legally recognized rights of tenure, transfer, and of succession in use and occupancy. When this tenure expires, or is exhausted due to the death of the property holder without a will, heirs, or other arrangements for its succession, then the real estate merely reverts back to its original proprietor, that is, it escheats to the state. Clearly, the inheritance tax laws never intended to tax such a reversion. Reversed and dismissed.

## ▶ ANALYSIS

A contrary result was reached in *In re Estate of O'Brine*, 37 N.Y.2d 81 (1975). The court held that the United States (through the Veterans Administration) was entitled only to those funds of an incompetent veteran that escheated, after deduction of New York estate taxes. However, three judges dissented, remarking that "courts of other jurisdictions, when faced with similar situations, have held that the entirety of the funds is returnable, without being diminished by state-imposed taxation, under the theory that the United States has retained a reversionary interest."

■=■

## Quicknotes

**ESCHEAT** The transfer of property to the state because its owner died with no one legally entitled to claim it.

**REVERSION** An interest retained by a grantor of property in the land transferred, which is created when the owner conveys less of an interest than he or she owns and which returns to the grantor upon the termination of the conveyed estate.

**SUCCESSION** The scheme pursuant to which property is distributed in the absence of a valid will or of a disposition of particular property.

■=■

# CHAPTER 12

# Freehold Estates

## Quick Reference Rules of Law

*Fee Tail - The owner of land in fee tail is required to
pass that land onto their children — passes
automatically by law. The children have no
transferable interest. The future interest is
either a "reversion" or "remainder" (3P).*

*Fee Simple determinable =*

# Cole v. Steinlauf

Buyer of real property (D) v. Seller (D)

Conn. Sup. Ct. of Errors, 136 A.2d 744 (1957).

**NATURE OF CASE:** Appeal from defense verdict in action seeking recovery of a purchase deposit.

**FACT SUMMARY:** Cole (P) contended that Steinlauf's (D) title to property was clouded because a conveyance in the chain of title had not included the grantee's heirs in the conveyance.

## 🏛 RULE OF LAW
A conveyance that omits the word "heirs" does not express an intention to grant a fee simple estate with sufficient certainty to create a marketable title.

**FACTS:** Cole (P) contracted to purchase certain real estate from Steinlauf (D), provided he could convey unclouded title. Cole (P) paid $420 as a deposit. A title search revealed that a deed in 1945 to Steinlauf's (D) predecessor in title ran to the grantee and his assigns, but did not mention the grantee's heirs. Cole (P), contending that this clouded title, demanded a refund of his deposit. Steinlauf (D) refused. Cole (P) sued to recover his deposit. The trial court found in favor of Steinlauf (D), concluding that the 1945 deed conveyed a fee simple absolute, and Cole (P) appealed.

**ISSUE:** Does the failure of a conveyance to include the word "heirs" express an intention to grant fee simple estate with sufficient certainty to create a marketable title?

**HOLDING AND DECISION:** (Wynne, C.J.) No. A conveyance that omits the word "heirs" does not express an intention to grant a fee simple estate with sufficient certainty to create a marketable title. At common law, to convey title in fee simple, a grant must include words of inheritance—i.e., to the grantee "and his heirs." The failure to include the heirs creates a life estate only. If it can be shown that a conveyance omitting the word "heirs" was intended to convey fee simple, the common law presumption can be overcome. Here, however, there is no evidence of the parties' intentions in the prior conveyance. Since the prior conveyance was questionable, Cole (P) is justified in refusing to take a chance on an unmarketable title. Reversed and remanded.

**CONCURRENCE:** (Baldwin, J.) The issue of whether the prior parties intended a fee simple conveyance can be determined in equity, but that issue need not be decided here.

## ▶ ANALYSIS

The requirement of the word "heirs" in a fee simple conveyance is a relic from the English feudal system, which emphasized dynastic family concepts. Courts tend to give less and less deference to the requirement with the passage of time. It has been criticized as defeating the intent of the grantor and as a hangover lacking a modern justification. Wills and trust are not subject to the rule.

---

## Quicknotes

**FEE SIMPLE ABSOLUTE** An estate that will last in perpetuity.

# Lewis v. Searles

Niece (P) v. Competing heirs (D)

Mo. Sup. Ct., 452 S.W.2d 153 (1970).

**NATURE OF CASE:** Action for declaratory judgment to quiet title and construe a will.

**FACT SUMMARY:** A testatrix bequeathed her property to Lewis (P) for as long as she remained unmarried, and if she married, the property was to go to named heirs; Lewis (P) claimed that the will gave her a fee simple determinable rather than a life estate.

## 🏛 RULE OF LAW
The law will hold all devises as being in fee simple if no intent is expressed to create a life estate only, and also no further devise is made to take effect after the death of the devisee.

**FACTS:** Letitia Lewis died in 1926 and left a will which devised all of her real and personal property to Hattie Lewis (P) for so long as Hattie Lewis (P) remained unmarried. In the event that Lewis (P) were to marry, then Lewis (P) would receive one-third of the property, and a third would go to each of two other heirs, La Forge and James Lewis. Both of these heirs died leaving children, one of which is Searles (D). Lewis (P) remained unmarried, and when she was 95, she instituted this action to have the court declare that the will left her a fee simple determinable which could end only if she married. Searles (D) and the other heirs argued that the will gave Lewis (P) and each of the other two heirs title in fee simple to an undivided third of the estate subject to Lewis's (P) life estate.

**ISSUE:** In a will, if there is no expressed intent to create a life estate only, and if no further devise is made to take effect after the death of the devisee, will the law presume that the testatrix manifested an intent to create a fee simple?

**HOLDING AND DECISION:** (Eager, Spec. Commr.) Yes. There exist several factors, all of which indicate that the devisee was to take a fee simple determinable rather than a life estate. First, no intention appears to indicate the conveyance of only a life estate. Second, no further devise is made to take effect after the death of Lewis (P). Third, if Lewis (P) were to marry, she would be immediately given an undivided third of the property in fee. Fourth, it is not stated whether the heirs had to survive Lewis (P) in order to receive a third if Lewis (P) were to marry. Fifth, if it were only a life estate, there could be a partial intestacy if she married because there was no gift or limitation over upon Lewis's (P) death. The law presumes a fee unless there are words in a subsequent and limiting clause which clearly and decisively indicate an intent to devise less than a fee. The words of the will when considered as a whole evinced an intent to pass the maximum estate possible consistent with the limitation on marriage. There are no express words to the contrary present in the will. The fact that the gift to the heirs would come about only by a marriage indicates that this was not meant to be a gift on Lewis's (P) death and, therefore, Lewis (P) had a fee simple determinable, not a life estate. Reversed.

## ▶ ANALYSIS

A fee simple determinable is an estate which automatically terminates on the happening of a stated event and reverts back to the grantor or to whomever the grantor appoints. At common law, this possibility of reverter could not be devised or alienated, but modern law allows it. The basic rule is that a provision in restraint of marriage is void as being against public policy. But there are exceptions, such as where the grantor wishes to provide support to a devisee while single, or in many other situations where the restraint is imposed for legitimate purposes and not out of caprice. The court construed the will such that the testatrix merely wished to support Lewis (P) while she was single, and did not wish to restrain marriage.

■==■

## Quicknotes

**DEVISEE** A person upon whom a gift of real or personal property is conferred by means of a testamentary instrument.

**INTESTACY** To die without leaving a valid testamentary instrument.

**TESTATRIX** A woman who makes a will.

■==■

# Moore v. Phillips

Daughter (P) v. Mother's executor (D)

Kan. Ct. App., 627 P.2d 831 (1981).

**NATURE OF CASE:** Appeal from award of damages for waste.

**FACT SUMMARY:** Dorothy Moore (P) and her son sued as remaindermen to recover damages for the deterioration of a farmhouse resulting from neglect by the life tenant, Moore's (P) mother.

## 🏛 RULE OF LAW
Laches is an equitable defense and will not bar recovery for permissive waste from mere lapse of time nor where there is a reasonable excuse for non-action of a party in making inquiry as to his rights and asserting them.

**FACTS:** Leslie Brannan died in 1962, and by will left his wife, Ada Brannan, a life estate in farmland containing a farmhouse, with remainder interests to Dorothy Moore (P) and Kent Reinhardt. Ada Brannan resided in the farmhouse until 1964, then rented it out until 1965, whereupon the house subsequently became unoccupied. From 1969 through 1971, the house was leased to the remaindermen, but they did not live there, but from time to time they would inspect the premises. In 1976, Ada Brannan died leaving her property to others because she and her daughter, Moore (P), had been estranged since 1964. After Ada Brannan's death in 1976, Moore (P) sued her mother's executor, Phillips (D), on the theory of waste to recover damages for the deterioration of the farmhouse. Phillips (D) raised laches and estoppel as affirmative defenses, which the trial court sustained, but on appeal was reversed. Phillips (D) appealed.

**ISSUE:** Will laches be a bar to recovery in an action for permissive waste, when there was a reasonable excuse for not bringing the action earlier?

**HOLDING AND DECISION:** (Prager, J.) No. Permissive waste is the failure of the tenant to exercise the ordinary care of a prudent man for the preservation and protection of the estate. Where the right of action of the remaindermen is based upon permissive waste, as in this case, it is generally held that the statute of limitations does not commence to run in favor of the tenant until the expiration of the tenancy. Laches is not merely delay, but delay that works a disadvantage to another, and may be used in actions at law as well as in equitable proceedings. A mere lapse of time will not bar recovery where there is a reasonable excuse for non-action of a party in making inquiry as to his rights or in asserting them. Here, the evidence is clear that the life tenant, as a quasi-trustee, did not keep the property in reasonable repair, as was her responsibility. Furthermore, it was Moore's (P) position that she did not file an action against her elderly mother which would have aggravated her. Even though Moore (P) was estranged from her mother, the law should not require her to sue her mother during her lifetime under these circumstances. Affirmed.

## ▶ ANALYSIS

Waste may take on a variety of forms, voluntary, permissive, or ameliorating. While permissive waste was discussed above, voluntary waste occurs during the commission of some deliberate or voluntary destructive act while ameliorating waste occurs when there has been any material change in the nature of the property even though the change enhances the value of the property.

◼▬◼

## Quicknotes

**LACHES** An equitable defense against the enforcement of rights that have been neglected for a long period of time.

**PERMISSIVE WASTE** The mistreatment of another's property by someone in lawful possession by the failure to make ordinary repairs or maintenance.

◼▬◼

*[handwritten note: The delay must be a detriment to someone else in order for laches to apply.]*

# Oldfield v. Stoeco Homes, Inc.

City resident (P) v. Land developer (D)

N.J. Sup. Ct., 139 A.2d 291 (1958).

**NATURE OF CASE:** Action to have extensions on the time of performance of the provisions of deeds declared invalid.

**FACT SUMMARY:** A city deeded land to a land developer in fee simple with the possibility of reverter clearly stated, but also with the right for the city to modify the provisions of the deed, which indicates a power of termination.

## 🏛 RULE OF LAW
If the language of an instrument does not clearly indicate the parties' intent as to whether a fee simple determinable or a fee simple subject to condition subsequent is intended, then the surrounding circumstances and the deed as a whole will be considered to determine intent.

**FACTS:** Ocean City owned a large tract of undeveloped, swampy land. In order to have this land developed, it was sold to Stoeco (D) in 1951. The deed provided that Stoeco (D) had one year to fill and level both the land that it bought and also land still owned by Ocean City. Ocean City reserved the right to modify or change any restriction or condition in the deed. The deed also stated that a failure to comply with the covenants or conditions of the deed would automatically cause title to all lands to revert to Ocean City. Because of unfavorable dredging conditions, Stoeco (D) was unable to complete the task within a year. In 1953, and again in 1954, the city council gave extensions on the agreement until 1958. Oldfield (P) and other residents and taxpayers sued Stoeco (D), claiming that the estate conveyed was a fee simple determinable which had automatically terminated when Stoeco (D) failed to perform within a year.

**ISSUE:** Does the provision in the deed calling for the estate to automatically terminate and revert back to the grantor conclusively establish that the estate granted was a fee simple determinable?

**HOLDING AND DECISION:** (Burling, J.) No. The language of automatic reverter in the deed does not indicate beyond reasonable doubt that the estate created was a fee simple determinable. In addition to the language of automatic reverter, there is language which denominated the restriction as a condition. Also, the city's reserved power to modify the one-year restriction indicates a condition subsequent. The language is ambiguous as to what was meant, so the surrounding circumstances will be considered. There is no indication that time was so essential to the agreement as to indicate an intent to foreclose. The city was to get not only the benefit of the one-year limitation, but also the benefit of its own land being filled in and graded. Finally, the right to modify the restriction clearly goes against any intent to have an automatic foreclosure. A fee simple subject to condition subsequent is the only interpretation consistent with the intent and acts of the parties. Affirmed.

## ▶ ANALYSIS

A fee simple subject to condition subsequent is created when there is a provision giving the grantor the power to terminate the estate upon the happening of a specified event. The grantor retains the right to re-enter the land and to exercise a power to terminate the estate. The estate does not automatically end, but the grantor must take affirmative steps to terminate it. Waiver and estoppel are defenses. Certain key phrases indicate a condition subsequent: upon condition that, provided that, but if, and if it happens that. Key phrases indicating a fee simple determinable include "during," "until," and "so long as." When there is doubt, the courts will construe it as a covenant rather than a condition, and as a condition rather than an automatic termination.

■■■

## Quicknotes

**CONDITION SUBSEQUENT** Potential future occurrence that extinguishes a party's obligation to perform pursuant to the contract.

**FEE SIMPLE DETERMINABLE** A fee simple interest in property that may last forever or until the happening of a specified event.

**POSSIBILITY OF REVERTER** A type of reversionary interest referring to an interest in land that remains in the grantor until the happening of a condition precedent.

■■■

# Roberts v. Rhodes

Reversionary interest holder (P) v. Present holder (D)

Kan. Sup. Ct., 643 P.2d 116 (1982).

**NATURE OF CASE:** Appeal from judgment in action involving title to land.

**FACT SUMMARY:** Roberts (P) sued Rhodes (D) claiming title to land by deed from heirs of the original grantors and by revision, since the land was no longer being used for its original purpose.

## 🏛 RULE OF LAW
The general rule is well settled that the mere expression that property is to be used for a particular purpose will not in and of itself suffice to turn a fee simple into a determinable fee, as forfeitures are not favored in the law.

**FACTS:** Title to two small adjacent tracts of land were deeded to a school more than 70 years ago, with a provision in the deed stating that the land was to be used only for school or cemetery purposes. The school district sold the land in 1971, and Rhodes (D) acquired the land by mesne conveyances from the school district. Roberts (P) claimed title to these tracts by deed from the original heirs of the original grantors and by reversion as the land was no longer being used for school purposes. The trial court held that since the land was not being used for its original purpose, it should revert back to the heirs. On appeal, the lower court decision was reversed with the court of appeals holding that the deeds conveyed fee simple title to the school district. Roberts (P) appealed.

**ISSUE:** Will the mere expression that property is to be used for a particular purpose suffice to turn a fee simple into a determinable fee?

**HOLDING AND DECISION:** (Fromme, J.) No. As a general rule, the mere statement of the purposes of a conveyance will not limit the extent of the grant. Although the purpose of the deeds is disclosed, words by which the purpose is declared will not without more, suffice to limit the estate granted. An estate in fee simple determinable is created by any limitation which creates a fee simple estate and provides that the estate shall automatically expire upon the occurrence of any stated events. In this case, neither deed made provision for the estate to revert or terminate on the occurrence of any stated events. In the absence of an intent to limit the title shown in the conveyance, either expressly or by necessary implication, the grantors pass all the interest they own in the real estate. Affirmed.

interest to automatically expire upon occurrence of a stated event. Words which are sufficient to express such automatic expiration include "until," "so long as," and "during." The courts will strictly construe the language found in deeds and will attempt to avoid forfeitures.

■═■

## Quicknotes

**INTERVENING MESNE CONVEYANCE** An intermediate conveyance, one occupying an intermediate position between the first grantee and the present holder.

■═■

## ▶ ANALYSIS

Courts have in some cases recognized a special limitation on the interest conveyed which may cause the created

# Johnson v. City of Wheat Ridge

Heir of the grantor (P) v. City of Wheat Ridge (D)

Colo. Ct. App., 532 P.2d 985 (1975).

**NATURE OF CASE:** Appeal in a quiet title action.

**FACT SUMMARY:** When the City of Wheat Ridge (D) failed to fulfill one of the conditions subsequent to a land grant, Paul Johnson (P), the heir of the grantor, sought to quiet title to the land in himself.

## 🏛 RULE OF LAW
A breach of a condition subsequent does not cause a land grant title to revert automatically to the grantor or his heirs; and the applicable statute of limitations governs any judicial action to enforce a resulting power to terminate the original grant.

**FACTS:** At an advanced age, Judge Samuel Johnson conveyed two parcels of land as a gift for use as a public park. The larger parcel contained several conditions subsequent which, if not met within certain time limits, would terminate the estate in the grantee (D) and entitle the grantor or his estate to re-enter and take the property. The property eventually went to the City of Wheat Ridge (D). The City (D) complied with all the conditions within the time limits except one, i.e., the installation of a public water supply and lavatory. Paul Johnson (P), the heir of Judge Johnson, sought to quiet title in himself. He also alleged undue influence on Judge Johnson in making the grant. The trial court ruled for the City (D), finding: (1) no undue influence; (2) laches; (3) that the breach did not cause automatic reversion; and (4) that the action was brought outside the statute of limitations. Paul Johnson (P) appealed.

**ISSUE:** Does a breach of a condition subsequent automatically cause a land grant title to revert to the grantor or his heirs regardless of the applicable statute of limitations for bringing an action on the breach?

**HOLDING AND DECISION:** (Enoch, J.) No. A breach of a condition subsequent does not cause a land grant title to revert automatically to the grantor or his heirs; and the applicable statute of limitations governs any judicial action brought to enforce a resulting power to terminate the original grant. But the applicable statute here required a suit to be maintained within one year of the alleged violation. Johnson's (P) action is barred by this statute. Affirmed.

## ▌ ANALYSIS

Most states have such statutes of limitations, barring powers of termination or possibilities of reverter unless the action is brought within a certain gross period of years following the condition's breach. A different type of statute will bar enforcement after a flat number of years from the creation of a defeasible fee (typically 40 years).

## Quicknotes

**ACTION TO QUIET TITLE** Equitable action to resolve conflicting claims to an interest in real property.

**UNDUE INFLUENCE** Improper influence that deprives the individual freedom of choice or substitutes another's choice for the person's own choice.

# Leeco Gas & Oil Company v. County of Nueces

Donor of land (P) v. Donee of land (D)

Tex. Sup. Ct., 736 S.W.2d 629 (1987).

**NATURE OF CASE:** Appeal from award of nominal damages.

**FACT SUMMARY:** Leeco Gas & Oil Company (P) deeded parkland to the County of Nueces (D) but retained a reversionary interest, and the County (D) condemned the interest.

## 🏛 RULE OF LAW
If the grantor of a gift deed to a government entity retains a reversionary interest, and the interest is then condemned, the grantor must receive as compensation the amount by which the value of the unrestricted fee exceeds the value of the restricted fee.

**FACTS:** In 1960, Leeco Gas & Oil Company (P) deeded 50 acres of land to the County of Nueces (D). Leeco (P) retained a reversionary interest in the property. County (D) would keep the property only so long as it was actively maintained by the County (D) as a park. In 1983, County (D) started condemnation proceedings against Leeco (P) for his reversionary interest. The County Commissioners awarded Leeco (P) $10,000 for his interest. Leeco (P) appealed. The trial court awarded Leeco (P) $10 in nominal damages, even though experts testified the property was worth between $3,000,000 and $5,000,000. Leeco (P) appealed.

**ISSUE:** If the grantor of a gift deed to a government entity retains a reversionary interest, and the interest is then condemned, should the grantor receive as compensation the amount by which the value of the unrestricted fee exceeds the value of the restricted fee?

**HOLDING AND DECISION:** (Gonzalez, J.) Yes. If the grantor of a gift deed to a government entity retains a reversionary interest, and the interest is then condemned, the grantor should receive as compensation the amount by which the value of the unrestricted fee exceeds the value of the restricted fee. A mere possibility of reverter has no ascertainable value when the event upon which the estate in fee simple is to end is not probable within a short time. Here, the County (D) was developing various plans to use the land as income producing property. This was not a case of condemning a speculative or remote possibility of a reversion. Therefore, Leeco (P) was entitled to more than nominal damages. Ten dollars compensation for a multi-million dollar property is not adequate compensation as a matter of law. To allow a governmental entity to condemn the grantor's reversionary interest by paying only nominal damages would have a negative impact on future gifts of real property to charities and governmental entities. Reversed and remanded.

**CONCURRENCE:** (Campbell, J.) In future cases, I would hold that implementation of condemnation proceedings by the grantee government entity should terminate the gift, and the land should revert to the grantor in fee absolute.

## ▶ ANALYSIS

The Restatement (Second) of Property 53, Comment b, states that if, viewed from the time of the commencement of an eminent domain proceeding . . . the event upon which a possessory estate in fee simple defeasible is to end is an event the occurrence of which, within a reasonably short period of time is not possible . . . the future interest has no ascertainable value." The court in the principal case ruled that Leeco's (P) reversionary interest had ascertainable value since the County (D) was developing various plans to use the land as income producing property.

### Quicknotes

**CONDEMNATION** The taking of private property for public use so long as just compensation is paid therefor.

**POSSIBILITY OF REVERTER** A type of reversionary interest referring to an interest in land that remains in the grantor until the happening of a condition precedent.

# Caccamo v. Banning

Childless grantee (P) v. Property buyer (D)

Del. Sup. Ct., 75 A.2d 222 (1950).

**NATURE OF CASE:** Action to enforce a land sale contract.

**FACT SUMMARY:** After converting her fee tail estate into one in fee simple, Anna Caccamo (P) sold the estate to Banning (D) who then declined to make payment, claiming it was an unmarketable title.

## 🏛 RULE OF LAW
When a bequest of property contains an alternative testamentary scheme to become effective should the original heir "die without leaving lawful issue," a fee tail estate is thereby created.

**FACTS:** Potter, deceased, left a will devising real estate to his wife (now also deceased). Upon the wife's death, the will provided that the real estate should go to Potter's granddaughter, Anna Caccamo (P), "in fee simple and absolutely forever." However, the will also provided that should Anna "die without leaving lawful issue of her body," then other relatives should take. Anna (P) married Carmen Caccamo. While still childless, Anna (P), pursuant to the statute, attempted to bar the fee tail and convert it into a fee simple absolute by conveying away her interest and then having it reconveyed back to her. She later sold the property to Banning (D). However, Banning (D) refused to accept or pay for the deed. Banning (D) argued that the title was unmarketable since the above-quoted words of the testator did not create a fee tail in Anna (P), but rather a fee simple estate conditioned on definite failure of issue to be determined at Anna's (P) death. Anna (P) sued to enforce the land sale contract.

**ISSUE:** When a bequest of property contains an alternative testamentary scheme to become effective should the original heir "die without leaving lawful issue," is a fee tail thereby created?

**HOLDING AND DECISION:** (Wolcott, J.) Yes. When a bequest of property contains an alternative testamentary scheme to become effective should the original heir "die without leaving lawful issue," a fee tail estate is thereby created. It is well settled that at common law a gift to "A" for life and, upon his death to the heirs of his body or his issue, was a gift of a fee tail. Also, in *Roach v. Martin's Lessee*, a gift to "A" and her heirs forever, "except she should die without heir born of her own body," with a remainder in that event over to "B," was held to create an estate tail in "A" with a vested remainder in "B." The instant estate falls within this rule since there is no evidence that Potter had any different intention. Judgment for Caccamo (P).

## ▶ ANALYSIS

Today, most jurisdictions have statutes converting fee tail estates into fee simple estates. Some statutes provide that language which would have created a fee tail at common law now creates a fee simple. Other statutes provide that the fee tail may be converted into a fee simple by the tenant in tail's making an inter vivos conveyance of a fee simple. Some regard it as creating a life estate with a remainder in fee simple to the first generation of issue.

━▄━■

## Quicknotes

**FEE TAIL** A limitation in either a deed or will limiting succession of property to a grantee and the heirs of his body.

**ISSUE** A fact or question that is disputed between two or more parties.

━▄━■

# Future Interests

## Quick Reference Rules of Law

# Kost v. Foster

Bankrupt son (P) v. Buyer of son's interest (D)

Ill. Sup. Ct., 406 Ill. 565, 94 N.E.2d 302 (1950).

**NATURE OF CASE:** Action for partition of land.

**FACT SUMMARY:** A testator created a life estate in his son with remainder to the son's children; before the life estate ended, one of the children was declared bankrupt and his remainder was sold to his creditor.

## RULE OF LAW
The main difference between a vested and contingent remainder is that in a vested remainder there is the present capacity to take possession with the certainty that the event on which the vacancy depends will happen, and not that the possession will become vacant or that the event will occur during the lifetime of the remainderman.

**FACTS:** In 1897, John Kost executed a deed to his son, Ross Kost. Ross was given a life estate and at his death the remainder was to go to Ross Kost's children. Ross Kost had eight children, only one of whom died before suit. Five were born prior to the creation of the life estate. In 1936, while Ross Kost was still alive, Oscar Kost (P), Ross Kost's son, was declared a bankrupt. The trustee in bankruptcy sold and conveyed Oscar Kost's (P) interest in the land to Foster (D). In 1949, Ross Kost died, and Oscar Kost (P) and the other children brought suit to have the conveyance to Foster (D) set aside because Oscar Kost's (P) interest was merely a contingent remainder. Foster (D) asserted that Oscar Kost (P) had a vested remainder which could be conveyed.

**ISSUE:** Was the interest of Oscar Kost (P) a vested remainder at the time of the purported sale by the trustee in bankruptcy to Foster (D)?

**HOLDING AND DECISION:** (Daily, J.) Yes. To be a vested remainder, there must be an ascertained person who is ready to take and who has a present right of future enjoyment which is not dependent on any uncertain event or contingency. In a contingent remainder the right to take is itself uncertain. The focus is not the actual enjoyment, for all remainders may not be enjoyed if the remainderman dies prior to the termination of the prior freehold estate. If there are words which would condition the person's right to take, then it is contingent. If there are words which merely make the right subject to divestment or diminution, but the right itself is certain, then it is vested. When the remainders were created, each of Ross Kost's children then living had a vested remainder subject to partial divestment if more children were born or total divestment if the child should die without himself having children. The living children had remainders which were vested because they

had the right to eventual possession, although the quantity that they would take was not yet ascertained. When the deed says that the remaindermen will take after the death of the life tenant, that refers to possession, not the eventual right to possession they already had. Affirmed.

## ANALYSIS

A future interest is an estate which will or may become possessory at some future time. A remainder is a future interest created in favor of a transferee which can become a present possessory estate only on the natural expiration of a prior freehold estate created in the same conveyance. A vested remainder is a remainder limited to a person in existence and ascertained who has the right to immediate possession when the preceding estate ends. A contingent remainder is a remainder which is subject to a condition precedent, or is created in favor of an unborn person, or is in favor of an unascertained person. At common law, a contingent remainder had to vest prior to the termination of the preceding freehold estate or it was destroyed. This rule of destructibility has generally been abolished.

---

## Quicknotes

**ASCERTAINED PERSON** Person who is either known or capable of being identified.

**REMAINDERMAN** A person who has an interest in property to commence upon the termination of a present possessory interest.

# Abo Petroleum Corporation v. Amstutz

Buyers of parents' interest (P) v. Children's interest (D)

N.M. Sup. Ct., 93 N.M. 332, 600 P.2d 278 (1979).

**NATURE OF CASE:** Appeal from summary judgment in action to quiet title.

**FACT SUMMARY:** Abo Petroleum Corporation (P) sued the children of Beulah Jones and Ruby Jones to quiet title to certain property that became an issue when Beulah and Ruby Jones attempted to deed the property that their children alleged was theirs as a result of a reversionary interest.

## 🏛 RULE OF LAW
The doctrine of destructibility of contingent remainders is a relic of the feudal past and since its complexity, confusion, unpredictability, and frustration are the demonstrated consequences of adherence to the doctrine, it is no longer applicable.

**FACTS:** In 1908, James and Amanda Turknett, the parents of Beulah and Ruby, owned in fee simple certain property to which they conveyed life estates in two separate parcels, one to each daughter. Each deed stated that the property would remain the daughter's during her life and upon death would revert to her children, and if no children existed would become the property of the daughter's estate. In 1911 and 1916, the parents executed other deeds covering the same land as the 1908 deed, which purported to convey absolute title to the daughters. Subsequent to the execution of these deeds, the daughters, Beulah and Ruby, attempted to convey fee simple interests in the property to the predecessors of Abo Petroleum Corporation (P). The children of Beulah and Ruby contend that the 1908 deeds gave their parents life estates in the property and that Beulah and Ruby could only have conveyed life estates to Abo Petroleum's (P) predecessors. Abo Petroleum (P) argued that by the subsequent conveyances to the daughters, the parents' reversionary interest merged with the daughters' life estates, destroying the contingent remainders in each daughter's children and giving the daughters fee simple title to the property, pursuant to the doctrine of destructibility of contingent remainders. The trial court granted Abo Petroleum's (P) motion for summary judgment. The children appealed.

**ISSUE:** Is the doctrine of destructibility of contingent remainders, due to its complexity, confusion, unpredictability, and frustration, no longer applicable?

**HOLDING AND DECISION:** (Payne, J.) Yes. The doctrine of destructibility of contingent remainders has been almost universally regarded to be obsolete by legislatures, courts, and legal writings, and has been renounced by virtually all jurisdictions in the United States.

The rule originated in England in the sixteenth century and developed so that if the prior estate terminated before the occurrence of the contingency, the contingent remainder was destroyed for lack of supporting estate, i.e., when the supporting life estate merged with the reversionary interest. This doctrine is based on history, not reason. The conveyances of the property to the daughters did not destroy the contingent remainders in the daughters' children. The daughters acquired no more interest in the property by virtue of the latter deeds than they had been granted in the original deeds. Any conveyance by them could only transfer a fee simple. Reversed and remanded.

## ▶ ANALYSIS

At common law there were three ways by which a contingent remainder could be destroyed: (1) by the condition precedent failing to happen which permitted the contingent remainder to vest at or before the termination of the particular estate, (2) by merger, and (3) by forfeiture. Only a few of the states now permit a contingent remainder to be destroyed as at common law, while the destructibility rule has been abolished in the other jurisdictions. England abandoned the doctrine over a century ago, long before American courts had decided to do away with it.

■■■

### Quicknotes

**DOCTRINE OF DESTRUCTIBILITY OF CONTINGENT REMAINDERS** Rule that contingent remainders that do not vest upon or before the termination of the preceding estate are void in violation of the Rule Against Perpetuities.

■■■

# Sybert v. Sybert

Two brothers-in-law (P) v. Widow of third brother (D)

Tx. Sup. Ct., 152 Tex. 106, 254 S.W.2d 999 (1953).

**NATURE OF CASE:** Action to construe a will.

**FACT SUMMARY:** A testator left his land to his wife for life, then to his son for life, and, on his son's death, to the heirs of his body; the son's wife claimed that this created a fee simple in the son under the Rule in Shelley's Case.

## 🏛 RULE OF LAW
At common law, where by an instrument of conveyance a freehold estate was given to a person, and in the same instrument a remainder was limited to the heirs or the heirs of the body of the person, and both the freehold estate and the remainder were either both legal or both equitable, then the recipient took both the freehold estate and the remainder together as his own.

**FACTS:** The testator died in 1942 and left his property to his wife for life, and then to his son Fred for life, and after the son's death, to vest in fee simple in the heirs of Fred's body. Fred Sybert, the son, died childless and intestate, survived by his wife Eunice Sybert (D). Fred Sybert's brothers (P) brought suit, contending that the will vested a life estate only in Fred, and so they would take his land under their father's will. Eunice Sybert (D) contended that the Rule in Shelley's Case operated to vest a fee simple in Fred, so that she would take as an intestate heir.

**ISSUE:** At common law, whereby an instrument of conveyance a freehold estate was given to a person, and in the same instrument a remainder was limited to the heirs or the heirs of the body of the person, and both the freehold estate and the remainder were either both legal or both equitable, does the recipient take both the freehold estate and the remainder together as his own?

**HOLDING AND DECISION:** (Hickman, C.J.) Yes. When the testator used the words "heirs of his body," he used them as words of limitation, meaning that the words were used to mean the heirs, the technical words of inheritance. There is no evidence from the words of the will that the testator intended those words to be words of purchase, which would make the Rule in Shelley's Case inapplicable, giving Fred only a life estate. The Rule in Shelley's Case is a positive rule of law in Texas and cannot be construed away or abrogated by the courts. The use of the technical words "heirs of his body" clearly indicate that the testator meant to give a contingent remainder to the son's children. The Rule in Shelley's case operates to convert that into a remainder in the son. Affirmed.

**CONCURRENCE:** (Griffin, J.) The Rule should be abolished by the legislature because, as here, it is usually the testator's intent to create a life estate with a remainder to the heirs, and this intent should be respected.

## ▶ ANALYSIS

The Rule in Shelley's Case can be best understood by various examples. Where the situation is: O to A for life, then to B for life, then to the heirs of B, then the Rule operates to change the contingent remainder in fee simple in B's heirs to a vested remainder in B; because B would then have both the life estate and the remainder in fee, the law of merger causes a coalescence so that B would have a present estate in fee simple. Where the situation is O to A for life, then to B for life, then to the heirs of A, this rule operates to give A the remainder; however, there is no merger because of the intervening vested remainder in B. Where O to A for life then one day after A's death to the heirs of A, the Rule does not operate because A's heir's interest is not a remainder but an executory interest. Also, if the remainder is given to A's "issue," and not to his "heirs," then the Rule does not operate because the Rule requires the use of technical words of inheritance, "heirs" or "heirs of the body." This Rule has been abolished in most jurisdictions.

■■■

## Quicknotes

**WORDS OF LIMITATION** Words that describe the duration of the estate conveyed.

**WORDS OF PURCHASE** Words that describe who is granted the property.

■■■

# Braswell v. Braswell

### Devisee of deceased (P) v. Brothers of deceased (D)

Va. Sup. Ct. App., 195 Va. 971, 81 S.E.2d 560 (1954).

**NATURE OF CASE:** Action to partition land.

**FACT SUMMARY:** The grantor provided a life estate to his son and on the son's death to the son's heirs, but if the son had no heirs then it shall revert back to the grantor. The son died without issue, and the son's devisee claimed the land as did the heirs of the grantor.

## 🏛 RULE OF LAW
The common-law Doctrine of Worthier Title provided that an inter vivos conveyance for life, with remainder to the heirs or next of kin of the conveyor, is ineffective to create a remainder, but, instead, the conveyor retains a reversion which will pass by operation of law upon his death, unless he had otherwise disposed of it.

**FACTS:** In 1903, James Braswell made an inter vivos conveyance of land to his son Nathaniel. Nathaniel was given a life estate with a remainder in the son's heirs. The deed further provided that if Nathaniel, the son, should die leaving no lawful heir from his body, then the land shall revert back to the grantor or his lawful heirs. The grantor died intestate, leaving three sons as his sole heirs at law, S.I.J.I. (D), W.H. (D), and Nathaniel. Nathaniel Braswell then died without issue but by will devised his real property to Charles Braswell (P).

**ISSUE:** Was the limitation in the deed to the grantor's heirs void under the Doctrine of Worthier Title?

**HOLDING AND DECISION:** (Smith, J.) Yes. Where there is a grant to one for life, with remainder to the heirs of the grantor, there is no remainder because the limitation continues in the grantor as a reversion, which does not devolve upon his heirs as purchasers but as successors. The Doctrine of Worthier Title is a rule of construction which creates a presumption in favor of reversion which may be rebutted by an indication of the grantor's contrary intent from the deed. The words of the deed do not clearly express an intent that the heirs who were to take after the son's life estate were to be determined at that time rather than at the grantor's death. The clear intent was that if the life tenant, the son, were to die without issue, then land should revert and pass to the grantor's heirs as if no conveyance had been made. Therefore, the land reverted back to the grantor's heirs when the son died. Each of the three sons received one-third, and the son's one-third was devised to Charles Braswell (P). The contrary interpretation, that the land was to revert to the grantor's heirs living at the son's death, and, thus, one-half would go to each of the other son's heirs and none to Charles Braswell (P), is rejected. Affirmed.

## ▶ ANALYSIS

At common law, where the heirs of a testator would take the same interest in real property by succession as they would by devise, the limitation in the devise was void under the Doctrine of Worthier Title and the heirs were held to take by succession. This application of the Doctrine to wills is now obsolete. The application to inter vivos conveyances is still good law, but it is a rule of construction and not a rule of law. It is inapplicable if the grantor manifested an intention to make a present gift to those who will be his heirs, and is inapplicable if the word "heir" is not used, or not used in its technical sense. When applicable, the grantor retains the power to use or transfer the reversion, and it can be reached by the grantor's creditors.

■■■

## Quicknotes

**DEVISEE** A person upon whom a gift of real or personal property is conferred by means of a testamentary instrument.

**DOCTRINE OF WORTHIER TITLE** Rule that property conveyed by a grantor to his heirs does not give rise to a remainder interest in the heirs, but to a reversion in the grantor.

**INTER VIVOS** Between living persons.

■■■

# Stoller v. Doyle

Buyer from the grantee (P) v. Children of the grantee (D)

Ill. Sup. Ct., 257 Ill. 369, 100 N.E. 959 (1913).

**NATURE OF CASE:** Action to quiet title.

**FACT SUMMARY:** A conveyance created a fee simple followed by a contingent interest with a reversion in the grantor; a subsequent grantee argued that when the reversion and the fee merged in one person, the contingent interest was destroyed.

## 🏛 RULE OF LAW
Any interest following a fee and held by a person other than a grantor or grantee is an executory interest, and if it cuts short a prior estate created by the same conveyance and not held by the grantor, it is a shifting executory interest.

**FACTS:** Frank Doyle received a deed to a piece of property that contained several limitations. The limitations at issue stated that should Doyle die before his wife and also leave surviving children, the wife should enjoy a life estate and, at her death, the land would go to the children if any were still living. If at the death of Doyle or his wife, no children survived, the land would revert to the grantor. The deed also stated that Doyle could not convey the land except back to the grantor and he could not mortgage it. After the death of Doyle's wife, the grantor executed a new deed to Doyle purporting to remove all the restrictions contained in the prior deed so as to give Doyle fee simple title. Doyle then, by warranty deed, conveyed the land to Stoller (P). Stoller (P) contracted to sell the land to another but the buyer refused acceptance of the deed on the basis Stoller (P) could not convey merchantable title. Specific performance was refused and at a later action at law, the buyer recovered damages from Stoller (P). In that suit, the court characterized the interest of the children (D) as a contingent remainder that could not be destroyed by the grantor's second deed. Stoller (P) then brought this action against Doyle's children (D) to quiet title claiming that the first deed conveyed a life estate only to Doyle, a contingent life estate to his wife and a contingent remainder in fee to the children (D). The second deed conveyed the grantor's reversion to Doyle and that when the life estate and the reversion were vested in the same person, they merged, as a matter of law, into a fee, thus, destroying the children's remainder.

**ISSUE:** Was the interest reserved to Doyle's children (D) in the first deed an executory interest not subject to destruction?

**HOLDING AND DECISION:** (Cartwright, J.) Yes. The first deed gave Doyle an interest which would last forever unless he died without children or unless he died with a wife and children surviving. As there were no express words used in the deed to cut down the estate, Doyle had a fee subject to a condition subsequent. Any interest which follows a fee and is held by a person other than the grantee or grantor is an executory interest. A contingent remainder cannot follow a fee because a remainder can only exist on the natural expiration of the preceding estate. There can be no natural expiration of a fee, and, thus, there was no contingent remainder. The children (D) had a shifting executory interest which could cut short a prior estate created in the same conveyance. Therefore, the second deed, giving Doyle the reversion and a merger, could not destroy the children's interest because the rule of destructibility of contingent remainders is inapplicable to executory interests. Reversed and remanded.

## ▶ ANALYSIS

An executory interest is a future interest which does not vest in immediate possession upon the natural expiration of the prior estate created by the same conveyance. Any interest which divests a vested remainder or any interest which follows a fee and is held by a third person is an executory interest. Executory interests are not destructible if they have not vested when the preceding estate ends, whereas contingent remainders are destructible in some jurisdictions. While they are still future interests, executory interests are not vested, whereas contingent remainders could still become vested while still a future interest.

■≡■

## Quicknotes

**MERCHANTABLE TITLE** Title that, although not perfect, would be acceptable to a reasonably well-informed buyer exercising ordinary business prudence.

**WARRANTY DEED** A deed that guarantees that the conveyor possesses the title that he purports to convey.

■≡■

# Capitol Federal Savings & Loan Association v. Smith

Black buyer (P) v. Enforcers of restrictive covenant (D)

Colo. Sup. Ct., 136 Colo. 265, 316 P.2d 252 (1957).

**NATURE OF CASE:** Action to quiet title.

**FACT SUMMARY:** Lot owners made an agreement not to sell to blacks with an automatic forfeiture to the other lot owners if one owner violated the covenant; the lot owners argued that this arrangement amounted to a fee simple subject to an executory interest.

## 🏛 RULE OF LAW
When a fee simple is followed by an interest held by a third person, that interest is an executory interest which vests automatically upon the happening of the events specified in the grant of the fee simple.

**FACTS:** The owners of lots in a block in Denver made an agreement that if any one of them were to sell a lot to a black person, that lot would automatically be forfeited to any other lot owner who recorded a claim. Smith (P) was black and bought one of the lots. Capitol Federal Savings & Loan Association (D) then recorded a claim to the forfeited lot. Smith (P) sued to quiet title, arguing that the covenant could not be enforced because it violated the Fourteenth Amendment. Capitol (D) argued that the agreement created an executory interest in their favor and, because an executory interest vests automatically on the sale of the land, there was no judicial enforcement and, thus, no state action, which is required for a violation of the Fourteenth Amendment.

**ISSUE:** Are the courts bound by the mechanistic property law rules when determining the substantive, constitutional rights of individuals?

**HOLDING AND DECISION:** (Knauss, J.) No. Regardless of how the covenant is classified, it is still a racial restriction in violation of the Fourteenth Amendment. Whether the interest is called an executory interest or a future interest, it cannot change the character of what is attempted. An executory interest vests automatically in right upon the termination of the preceding fee estate. But the Supreme Court has made it clear that no discrimination shall be practiced against persons because of their race, and that such a rule is not limited to denying courts the right to judicially enforce restrictive covenants by injunction or by damages. Affirmed.

## ▶ ANALYSIS

This case is used to point out the attributes of an executory interest. Any interest which follows a fee and is held by a third person is an executory interest which vests in right, if not in possession, automatically upon the end of the preceding fee. This case also illustrates the proposition that property law rules relate solely to property law, and not to constitutional law. The court indicated that the reason this case was pursued by Capitol (D) was to establish a definite rule of law that restrictive covenants are illegal in whatever form, and so any title containing such a covenant would be clear and good.

■═■

## *Quicknotes*

**FEE SIMPLE** An estate in land characterized by ownership of the entire property for an unlimited duration and by absolute power over distribution.

**RESTRICTIVE COVENANT** A promise contained in a deed to limit the uses to which the property will be made.

**EXECUTORY INTEREST** A type of future interest in property that vests upon the happening of a contingent event.

■═■

# The City of Klamath Falls v. Bell

### Donees of land (P) v. Descendant of donor (D)

Or. Ct. App., 7 Or. App. 330, 490 P.2d 515 (1971).

**NATURE OF CASE:** Appeal in an action for declaratory judgment to determine the ownership of property.

**FACT SUMMARY:** After receiving a grant of land "as long as" it was used as a library site, the City of Klamath Falls (P) closed the library and sought a declaratory judgment of ownership.

## 🏛 RULE OF LAW
When an executory interest, following a fee simple interest in land, is void under the Rule Against Perpetuities, the grantor's possibility of reverter is, nevertheless, not destroyed despite his attempt to alienate it.

**FACTS:** The Daggett-Schallock corporation conveyed land to the City of Klamath Falls (P) as a gift "as long as" the City (P) used the land for a library. Upon breach of that condition, the deed provided for a gift over and executory interest to Fred Schallock and Floy Daggett or their heirs and assigns. In 1929, the corporation was dissolved and its assets were distributed to its sole shareholders, Fred and Floy. In 1969, the City (P) closed the library and sought this declaratory judgment of ownership as against Fred and Floy's heirs (D) who were joined in this suit. However, these heirs (D) conveyed all their interest to Flitcraft (D). The trial court ruled that the executory interest of Fred and Floy was void under the Rule Against Perpetuities and that the property was vested in the City (P). Flitcraft (D) appealed. She argued that she had acquired the corporation's possibility of reverter since, despite the corporation's attempt to alienate the reverter, it was not in fact destroyed; but, on the contrary, remained one of the corporation's assets which was conveyed to Flitcraft (D) by the heirs (D) of Fred Shallock and Floy Daggett, the sole shareholders.

**ISSUE:** When an executory interest, following a fee simple interest in land, is void under the Rule Against Perpetuities, is the grantor's possibility of reverter destroyed, especially if the grantor had also attempted to alienate it?

**HOLDING AND DECISION:** (Schwab, C.J.) No. When an executory interest, following a fee simple interest in land, is void under the Rule Against Perpetuities, the grantor's possibility of reverter is not destroyed even though he also had attempted to alienate it. The estate which the corporation gave to the City (P) was a fee simple on a special limitation. This is shown by the words "as long as" in the grant. The corporation, by its gift over, also created an executory interest in the donees. But the Rule Against Perpetuities applies to executory interests, and as the trial court properly found, this grant violated the Rule

since the gift over to Fred and Floy, their heirs and assigns, might continue in perpetuity without vesting. Therefore, that gift was void ab initio. However, the Rule does not affect a possibility of reverter and therefore, as we have stated above, this returned the property back to the corporation. But the corporation is now lawfully dissolved and its assets including the possibility of reverter were transferred to Flitcraft (D). Reversed.

## ▶ ANALYSIS

This case demonstrates an important distinction between executory interests and possibilities of reverter and powers of termination. The first of these future interests falls within the Rule Against Perpetuities. The latter two do not. However, even they may be barred by relevant statutes of limitations.

■■■

## Quicknotes

**AB INITIO** From its inception or beginning.

**EXECUTORY INTEREST** A type of future interest in property that vests upon the happening of a contingent event.

**POSSIBILITY OF REVERTER** A type of reversionary interest referring to an interest in land that remains in the grantor until the happening of a condition precedent.

**RULE AGAINST PERPETUITIES** The doctrine that a future interest that is incapable of vesting within 21 years of lives in being at the time it is created is immediately void.

■■■

# Shaver v. Clanton

Lessor (P) v. Lessee (D)

Cal. Ct. App., 31 Cal. Rptr. 2d 595, 26 Cal. App. 4th 568 (1994).

**NATURE OF CASE:** Suit to determine validity of a lease amendment.

**FACT SUMMARY:** Shaver (P) challenged the validity of amendments to a lease.

## 🏛 RULE OF LAW
A lease amendment which provides for perpetual options to renew is not void in violation of the Rule Against Perpetuities.

**FACTS:** Clanton (D) entered into a 10-year lease with Stanley for shopping center space. The lease provided for a renewal option of an additional 10 years. The parties amended the lease twice to extend it for additional five-year periods. Following Stanley's death, his daughter, Shaver (P), challenged the validity of the leases. The trial court rejected the validity of the second amendment as in violation of the Rule Against Perpetuities. Clanton (D) appealed.

**ISSUE:** Is a lease amendment which provides for perpetual options to renew void in violation of the Rule Against Perpetuities?

**HOLDING AND DECISION:** (Soneshine, J.) No. A lease amendment which provides for perpetual options to renew is not void in violation of the Rule Against Perpetuities. Commercial, nondonative transaction such as options to renew, rights of first refusal, and commercial leases are exempt from the provisions of the California Uniform Statutory Rule against Perpetuities, but if they involve a lease or grant of a city or town lot, they are limited to 99 years. The amendment is valid and gives the Clantons (D) a series of five-year options to renew their lease on the terms stated in the lease amendment. The total term of the lease is limited to 99 years from its effective date.

## ▶ ANALYSIS

The Rule Against Perpetuities provides that: "No interest is good unless it must vest, if at all, not later than 21 years after some life in being at the creation of the interest." Almost half the states have adopted the Uniform Rule, which preempts the Common Law Rule. It explicitly exempts commercial real estate from the application of the Rule.

■≡■

## Quicknotes

**COMMON LAW** A body of law developed through the judicial decisions of the courts as opposed to the legislative process.

**LEASE** An agreement or contract which creates a relationship between a landlord and tenant (real property) or lessor and lessee (real or personal property).

**OPTION** A contract pursuant to which a seller agrees that property will be available for the buyer to purchase at a specified price and within a certain time period.

**VESTING** The attaining of the right to pension or other employer-contribution benefits when the employee satisfies the minimum requirements necessary in order to be entitled to the receipt of such benefits in the future.

■≡■

# Concurrent Ownership

## Quick Reference Rules of Law

# In re Estate of Michael

Son of deceased co-tenant (P) v. Remaining co-tenants (D)

Pa. Sup. Ct., 421 Pa. 207, 218 A.2d 338 (1966).

**NATURE OF CASE:** Appeal from decree interpreting deed.

**FACT SUMMARY:** Joyce King deeded farm property to two married couples, and Bertha Michael, one of the four grantees, died.

## 🏛 RULE OF LAW
The right of survivorship in a joint tenancy may only be created where the granting instrument expresses a clear intent that such a right should exist.

**FACTS:** Joyce King deeded the King Farm to Harry and Bertha Michael, and Ford and Helen Michael, two married couples. The deed's pertinent provision stated the property went to "Harry L. Michael and Bertha K. Michael, his wife, tenants by the entireties and Ford W. Michael and Helen M. Michael, his wife by tenants of the entireties, with right of survivorship." Bertha Michael died. Her will gave her interest in the farm to her son, Robert Michael, the appellant. Robert was appointed co-executor of his mother's estate. A dispute arose as to what interest, if any, Bertha Michael had in the farm. A proceeding brought under the Uniform Declaratory Judgment Act ruled that the deed created a joint tenancy with right of survivorship between the two sets of husbands and wives. Robert Michael appealed contending that the deed created a tenancy in common between the two married couples, with each couple holding its undivided one-half interest as tenants by the entireties. The basis for Robert's contention was that there was no unambiguous expression in the deed that the grantor intended to create a joint tenancy with the right of survivorship.

**ISSUE:** Should the right of survivorship in a joint tenancy only be created where the granting instrument expresses a clear intent that such a right should exist?

**HOLDING AND DECISION:** (Jones, J.) Yes. The right of survivorship in a joint tenancy may only be created where the granting instrument expresses a clear intent that such a right should exist. We fail to find a sufficiently clear expression of intent to create a right of survivorship, to overcome the presumption of a tenancy in common. The lower court found that the use of the phrase in the deed "with right of survivorship" was a clear expression of an intended right of survivorship. The difficulty with such an interpretation is that it is purely conjectural and finds certainty in a totally ambiguous phrase. Nowhere in the deed is the term "joint tenants" employed. We find that the deed created a tenancy in common between the two sets of married couples, each couple holding its undivided one-half interest as tenants by the entireties. Decree reversed.

## ▶ ANALYSIS

Early common law presumed that a conveyance to husband and wife created a tenancy by the entirety, even without survivorship language. Despite the modern trend (followed in the principal case) recognizing a presumption for tenancies in common, some states still continue a presumption for tenancies in the entireties. Other states that recognize tenancies by the entirety require that they be expressly declared.

■▬■

## *Quicknotes*

**JOINT TENANCY** An interest in property whereby a single interest is owned by two or more persons and created by a single instrument; joint tenants possess equal interests in the use of the entire property and the last survivor is entitled to absolute ownership.

**RIGHT OF SURVIVORSHIP** Between two or more persons, such as in a joint tenancy relationship, the right to the property of a deceased passes to the survivor.

■▬■

# Jackson v. O'Connell

Four nieces (P) v. Aunt (D)

Ill. Sup. Ct., 23 Ill. 2d 52, 177 N.E.2d 194 (1961).

**NATURE OF CASE:** Appeal in an action for partition of real estate.

**FACT SUMMARY:** Anna Duffy's four nieces (P) claimed that the joint tenancy interest which Anna held with O'Connell (D) had been severed by reason of Anna's having received a conveyance of yet another joint tenant's interest.

## 🏛 RULE OF LAW
Where there are more than two joint tenants, and one of them conveys his interest to another cotenant, that cotenant grantee holds that share as a tenant in common, although he continues to hold his original share in joint tenancy with the remaining cotenants.

**FACTS:** Nellie Duffy, Anna Duffy, and Katherine O'Connell (D), sisters, held property as joint tenants. Nellie quitclaimed her interest to Anna. Anna, now deceased, in turn devised her interest by will to her four nieces, Beatrice Jackson (P), Eileen O'Barski (P), and Catherine Young (P) and Margaret Miller (P). The nieces (P) sued O'Connell (D) to partition the real estate. They claimed that: (1) Nellie's quitclaim deed to Anna had destroyed the joint tenancy since the conveyance to a fellow joint tenant destroys the required unity of interest; (2) as a result, Anna became the owner of an undivided two-thirds interest and O'Connell (D) became an owner of an undivided one-third interest as tenants in common; and (3) the four nieces (P) accordingly each own an undivided one-sixth and O'Connell (D) owns an undivided one-third interest as tenants in common. O'Connell (D) counterclaimed, arguing that: (1) Nellie's quitclaim to Anna only severed the joint tenancy as to Nellie's one-third interest; (2) the joint tenancy between Anna and O'Connell (D) as to the remaining two-thirds continued to exist; and (3) upon Anna's death, O'Connell (D) succeeded to that two-thirds interest as surviving joint tenant, with the four nieces (P) entitled each to only a one-half interest as devises of the one-third interest they received from Anna's tenancy in common derived from Nellie's quitclaim deed. Both the master and the circuit court ruled for O'Connell (D). The nieces (P) appealed.

**ISSUE:** Where there are more than two joint tenants, and one of them conveys his interest to a fellow cotenant, does that grantee cotenant continue to hold his original share in joint tenancy with the remaining cotenants, even though he holds the newly granted share as a tenant in common?

**HOLDING AND DECISION:** (Klingbiel, J.) Yes. Where there are more than two joint tenants, and one of them conveys his interest to another cotenant, that cotenant grantee holds that share as a tenant in common, although he continues to hold his original share in joint tenancy with the remaining cotenants. Four existing unities are necessary for the existence of a joint tenancy: interest, title, time and possession. Any act of a joint tenant which destroys any of these unities severs the joint tenancy and extinguishes the right of survivorship. But the rule is well settled at common law that where there are three joint tenants, and one conveyed his interest to a third party, the joint tenancy was only severed as to the part conveyed. The third party grantee became a tenant in common with the other two joint tenants; but the latter two still held the remaining two-thirds with the right of survivorship. All authors agree that this rule does not change by reason of the fact that the conveyance was made to a fellow joint tenant. The unity of interest is undisturbed since, as joint tenants, their interest is identical. Affirmed.

## ▶ ANALYSIS

A severance of a joint tenancy may be accomplished in a number of ways, including alienation, mortgage, sale, and lease. Both voluntary and involuntary conveyances sever a tenancy. In states following a title view of mortgages, a mortgage by a joint tenant severs the tenancy. In a lien jurisdiction, no severance occurs, and the lien terminates when, by reason of the mortgagor's death, his interest in the tenancy terminates.

■■■

## Quicknotes

**QUITCLAIM** A deed whereby the grantor conveys whatever interest he or she may have in the property without any warranties or covenants as to title.

**RIGHT OF SURVIVORSHIP** Between two or more persons, such as in a joint tenancy relationship, the right to the property of a deceased passes to the survivor.

■■■

# Matter of Estate of Vadney

Son of deceased (P) v. Other heirs (D)

N.Y. Ct. App., 83 N.Y.2d 885, 634 N.E. 2d 976 (1994).

**NATURE OF CASE:** Appeal from grant of petition to reform deed.

**FACT SUMMARY:** Decedent Vadney had intended to execute a deed conveying her house to herself and her son as co-owners, but her attorney neglected to include the right to survivorship in the deed.

## 🏛 RULE OF LAW
A deed creating an unspecified cotenancy may be deemed to have created a right of survivorship if there is manifestation of intent.

**FACTS:** Vadney executed a deed transferring a piece of property to herself and her son as co-owner. The deed did not specify the type of cotenancy created. Upon Vadney's death, the son, now her executor, did not list the property as part of her estate, contending that the property had been held in joint tenancy with a right of survivorship. Vadney's heirs protested, contending that a tenancy in common had been created. The executor filed an action to reform the deed. At trial, the attorney who had drafted the deed testified that Vadney had intended to create a joint tenancy, but he had forgotten to include the requisite survivorship language. The trial court held that the extrinsic evidence of intent could not be considered and denied the petition. The appellate division reversed, and the court of appeals granted review.

**ISSUE:** May a deed creating an unspecified cotenancy be deemed to have created a right of survivorship?

**HOLDING AND DECISION:** [Judge not stated in casebook excerpt.] Yes. A deed creating an unspecified cotenancy may be deemed to have created a right of survivorship if there is manifestation of intent. The presumption is that a cotenancy is a tenancy in common. This presumption may be overcome by clear and convincing evidence, however, and extrinsic evidence is admissible. Here, the executor offered uncontroverted evidence that Vadney had intended to create a joint tenancy and would have done so, but for a scrivener's error. This was sufficient to meet his burden. Affirmed.

## ▶ ANALYSIS

It is an almost universal rule that cotenancies are presumed to be tenancies in common. Jurisdictions vary, however, on what it takes to defeat the presumption. Some states require clear and convincing evidence; others require only a preponderance of evidence.

## Quicknotes

**JOINT TENANCY** An interest in property whereby a single interest is owned by two or more persons and created by a single instrument; joint tenants possess equal interests in the use of the entire property and the last survivor is entitled to absolute ownership.

**REFORMATION** A correction of a written instrument ordered by a court to cause it to reflect the true intentions of the parties.

**TENANTS IN COMMON** Two or more people holding an interest in property, each with equal right to its use and possession; interests may be partitioned, sold, conveyed, or devised.

# Palmer v. Flint

Sister of deceased (P) v. Widow (D)

Me. Sup. Ct., 156 Me. 103, 161 A.2d 837 (1960).

**NATURE OF CASE:** Petition for a declaratory judgment.

**FACT SUMMARY:** Wife (D) sold her interest in property originally deeded to herself and her husband as "joint tenants, and not as tenants in common" with a remainder in the heirs and assigns of the survivor.

## 🏛 RULE OF LAW
If the intention of the parties to create a joint tenancy, clearly expressed in the deed, is in conflict with technical rules of the common law in the construction of deeds, then that intent takes precedence over and overrides those technical rules.

**FACTS:** Bank (D) conveyed property to Nathan Palmer and his wife, Alice (D), as "joint tenants, and not as tenants in common, to them and their assigns and to the survivor, and the heirs and assigns of the survivor forever." Alice (D) and Nathan were divorced and by quitclaim deed Alice (D) conveyed the premises to Nathan. Subsequently, Roxa Palmer (P) acquired the property. Alice (D) then claimed that the conveyance from the bank to herself and Nathan created a joint life estate with a contingent remainder in fee to the survivor, and that the conveyance to Nathan was inoperative to convey to him her contingent remainder.

**ISSUE:** Does the use of the word "heirs" in the phrase "and the heirs of the survivor forever," and in no other part of the granting or habendum clauses of a deed, which otherwise clearly establishes a joint tenancy, preclude a severance of the property and, thus, create a life estate in the grantees with a contingent fee in the survivor?

**HOLDING AND DECISION:** (Siddall, J.) No. Whereas joint tenancies are abolished or disfavored in most states, in this jurisdiction the tenancy is still recognized, but the intent to create such an estate must be clear and convincing. Two rights common to all joint tenancies are the right of survivorship and the right of severance. If one tenant conveys his interest to a stranger, the unity of title is destroyed and the grantee becomes a tenant in common with the other cotenant. Where, therefore, it is clear that two parties wish to create a joint tenancy from the face of the deed, the use of other common-law language will be ignored in the interest of the security of property titles and in accordance with the intention of the parties. Here, had Nathan and Alice Palmer (D) desired to create a life estate, they could have so indicated by using apt language. Bill of complaint sustained and case remanded.

## ▶ ANALYSIS

Because the interest of a joint tenant is not freely alienable by testamentary and inter vivos disposition, and is protected, to a certain extent, against the claims of creditors, joint tenancies are disfavored. A conveyance of property to two persons will be treated as creating a tenancy in common unless there is an unmistakable expression of intent to create a joint tenancy. Usually, the expression "to X and Y in joint tenancy" will suffice unless there is additional confusing language, as in the present case. A tenancy in common does not give rise to a right of survivorship.

■■■■

## Quicknotes

**HABENDUM CLAUSE** A clause contained in a deed that specifies the parties to the transaction and defines the interest in land to be conveyed.

**INTER VIVOS** Between living persons.

■■■■

# People v. Nogarr

Wife (P) v. Parents-in-law (D)

Cal. Dist. Ct. App., 164 Cal. App. 2d 591, 330 P.2d 858 (1958).

**NATURE OF CASE:** Action to determine rights of mortgage holder to condemnation proceeds.

**FACT SUMMARY:** During his lifetime, husband mortgaged property he held in joint tenancy with his wife.

## 🏛 RULE OF LAW
An execution of a mortgage by one joint tenant does not operate to terminate the joint tenancy and sever his interest. The mortgage is a charge of lien upon his interest as a joint tenant only and therefore upon his death, his interest having ceased to exist, the lien of the mortgage terminates.

**FACTS:** Elaine and Calvert Wilson, husband and wife, purchased property as joint tenants. After they separated, husband mortgaged the property to his parents. Elaine did not have knowledge of or give her consent to the execution of this mortgage. Calvert then died, and the State of California commenced an action to condemn the property. The parents claimed that their mortgage should be satisfied from the proceeds of the condemnation award.

**ISSUE:** Is a mortgage upon real property executed by one of two joint tenants enforceable after the death of that joint tenant?

**HOLDING AND DECISION:** (Nourse, J.) No. Since the mortgage did not operate to transfer the legal title, or entitle the mortgagees to possession, the estate in joint tenancy was not severed. Elaine had a right of survivorship, and upon Calvert's death she became the sole owner of the property. Calvert's interest, upon which the mortgage was based, expired upon his death. It is illogical and unjust to allow one joint tenant to mortgage his interest and obtain the value of one-half of the joint tenancy property, and to retain his right to all the property upon his cotenant's death, yet by the same reasoning deny to the cotenant her full right to the property should the mortgagor die first. Reversed.

## ▶ ANALYSIS

The remedy for the parents, the mortgagees here, is to enforce the lien and mortgage by foreclosure and sale prior to the death of the mortgagor and, thus, sever the joint tenancy. In this event, Elaine and Calvert would have become simply tenants in common. A tenant in common does not have a right to survivorship (receiving all the property upon the death of a cotenant) as does a joint tenant.

## Quicknotes

**FORECLOSURE SALE** Termination of an interest in property, usually initiated by a lienholder upon failure to tender mortgage payments, resulting in the sale of the property in order to satisfy the debt.

**MORTGAGE** An interest in land created by a written instrument providing security for the payment of a debt or the performance of a duty.

# Mann v. Bradley

## Children (P) v. Father (D)

Colo. Sup. Ct., 188 Colo. 392, 535 P.2d 213 (1975).

**NATURE OF CASE:** Quiet title action.

**FACT SUMMARY:** Betty and Aaron (D) Mann made a court-approved divorce agreement that their family residence would remain in joint tenancy until certain eventualities occurred.

## 🏛 RULE OF LAW
A joint tenancy may be terminated by mutual agreement, and such an agreement to dissolve a joint tenancy and hold the property as tenants in common may be inferred from the manner in which the parties deal with the property.

**FACTS:** Betty and Aaron (D) Mann held their residence in joint tenancy. When they later divorced, they entered into a court-approved agreement whereby their residence was to be sold and the proceeds divided equally between them if and when any of the following occurred: (1) Betty remarried; (2) their youngest child attained age 21; or (3) they mutually agreed to sell. Betty lived in the residence with her children (P) until her death. Thereupon, Aaron (D) advised the children (P) that, by reason of the joint tenancy survivorship provisions, he now owned the residence. The administratrix (P) and the children (P) successfully quieted title in themselves on the theory that the divorce settlement had the legal effect of converting the joint tenancy into a tenancy in common so that Betty's interest passed to the children (P) upon her death. The court of appeals affirmed. Aaron (D) petitioned for a writ of certiorari. He argued that the property had remained in joint tenancy since none of the three contingencies stipulated in the divorce settlement had occurred.

**ISSUE:** May a joint tenancy be terminated by mutual agreement; and may such an agreement to dissolve a joint tenancy and hold the property as tenants in common be inferred from the manner in which the parties deal with the property?

**HOLDING AND DECISION:** (Hodges, J.) Yes. A joint tenancy may be terminated by mutual agreement, and such an agreement to dissolve a joint tenancy and hold the property as tenants in common may be inferred from the manner in which the parties deal with the property. The modern tendency is not to require the act of the cotenant to be destructive of one of the four essential unities of time, title, possession or interest. Rather, the parties' intent to dissolve is sufficient. Here, the divorce agreement provided for the ultimate sale of the property and the division of the proceeds. As such, it evinced the intent to no longer hold the property in joint tenancy as of the agreement's date. The whole tenor of the agreement's provisions—despite the three eventualities stated—was inconsistent with the continuance of the right to survivorship which is essential to a joint tenancy. Affirmed.

## ▶ ANALYSIS

Whereas there can be no severance of a tenancy by the entireties since both the husband and wife own the whole and not shares, a joint tenancy may be severed because a joint tenant both owns the whole and also his proportionate share. Thus, any joint tenant may sever his interest and defeat the right of the other joint tenant's right of survivorship.

## Quicknotes

**JOINT TENANCY** An interest in property whereby a single interest is owned by two or more persons and created by a single instrument; joint tenants possess equal interests in the use of the entire property and the last survivor is entitled to absolute ownership.

**RIGHT OF SURVIVORSHIP** Between two or more persons, such as in a joint tenancy relationship, the right to the property of a deceased passes to the survivor.

**TENANCY IN COMMON** An interest in property held by two or more people, each with equal right to its use and possession; interests may be partitioned, sold, conveyed, or devised.

# Duncan v. Vassaur

## Father of killer (P) v. Father of victim (D)

Okla. Sup. Ct., 550 P.2d 929 (1976).

**NATURE OF CASE:** Appeal in a quiet title action.

**FACT SUMMARY:** After killing her husband, Betty Vassaur claimed the right of survivorship in their property which had been in joint tenancy.

## 🏛 RULE OF LAW
By the criminal homicide of his fellow cotenant, the guilty party receives no right of survivorship since he has severed the joint tenancy by an act inconsistent with its continued existence.

**FACTS:** Edgar Vassaur, Jr. and Betty Vassaur, spouses, owned property as joint tenants. After being charged with first degree manslaughter of Edgar, Betty conveyed the property to her father, Duncan (P). However, Edgar Vassaur, Sr. (D), the administrator, claimed ownership of one-half of the property, as well as liens on the victim's insurance and the proceeds of a loan. Duncan (P) brought a quiet title action. Edgar, Sr. (D) asserted the above claims in his answer and cross petition. However, the trial court ruled for Duncan (P) who had demurred and moved for judgment on the pleadings. Edgar, Sr. (D) appealed, arguing that the "slayer statute" forbade a killer from claiming his victim's estate, and that by killing Edgar, Jr., Betty had severed the joint tenancy.

**ISSUE:** By the criminal homicide of his fellow cotenant, does the guilty party lose his joint tenancy rights of survivorship?

**HOLDING AND DECISION:** (Davison, J.) Yes. By the criminal homicide of his fellow cotenant, the guilty party receives no right of survivorship since he has severed the joint tenancy by an act inconsistent with its continued existence. A number of states have varying views regarding this issue. They range from entitling the murderer to keep the property, through placing it in a constructive trust for the victim's estate or following our above-stated rule. We are of the opinion that our solution is not only equitable in denying a murderer the fruits of his crime but comports with reason in that one must be a survivor. Accordingly, we reverse and remand with instructions to allow Duncan (P) the opportunity also to prove that he was a bona fide purchaser of the property.

## ▶ ANALYSIS

There is a conflict in the few cases dealing with the murder of one joint tenant by another. While some cases hold that a murderer forfeits all interest to the victim's representatives, others give him the entire interest as the survivor. Many of the statutes designed to deny a murderer his rights in case of succession, do not cover the joint tenancy situation and the cases must, thus, most often be determined on a nonstatutory basis.

■═■

## *Quicknotes*

**JOINT TENANCY** An interest in property whereby a single interest is owned by two or more persons and created by a single instrument; joint tenants possess equal interests in the use of the entire property and the last survivor is entitled to absolute ownership.

**RIGHT OF SURVIVORSHIP** Between two or more persons, such as in a joint tenancy relationship, the right to the property of a deceased passes to the survivor.

**SLAYER STATUTE** Doctrine that a person who feloniously and intentionally kills another individual is prohibited from receiving any property from the decedent's estate either by will or inheritance or from receiving the proceeds of any life insurance policies.

■═■

# Laura v. Christian

Paying co-tenant (P) v. Nonpaying co-tenant (D)

N.M. Sup. Ct., 88 N.M. 127, 537 P.2d 1389 (1975).

**NATURE OF CASE:** Appeal in a quiet title action.

**FACT SUMMARY:** Upon Christian's (D) refusal to pay his proportionate share to avoid foreclosure on properties held in cotenancy with Laura (P), Laura (P) himself made full payment.

🏛 **RULE OF LAW**
When, to preserve concurrently held property from foreclosure, a cotenant pays more than his share of a debt secured by a mortgage or other lien, his derelict cotenants can nevertheless exercise the option of taking advantage of this benefit by reimbursing the paying cotenant within a reasonable time.

**FACTS:** Laura (P) was a tenant in common with Christian (D) and various other cotenants holding a parcel of real property called Fireside Lodge which was subject to a mortgage lien. Christian's (D) interest was one-fourth. When the mortgage payments went unpaid, the mortgagee successfully obtained a foreclosure on August 3, 1971. A sale of the property was ordered for April 11, 1972. On April 10, 1972, Laura (P), in order to save the property, paid the entire mortgage judgment of $17,288.40. Christian (D) and the other cotenants failed to assume any responsibility although they had knowledge of the foreclosure. However, when in July 1972 the value of the property was greatly increased by reason of the exercise of an option to purchase it, Christian (D) then claimed his interest and willingness to pay. Laura (P) brought an action quieting title in himself. Christian (D) appealed, arguing that—subject to his reimbursing Laura (P) within a reasonable time—he had the option of taking advantage of the benefit created by Laura (P) in saving the property.

**ISSUE:** When, in order to preserve concurrently held property from foreclosure, a cotenant pays more than his share of the mortgage debt, may the derelict cotenants, nevertheless, exercise the option of taking advantage of this benefit by reimbursing the paying cotenant within a reasonable time?

**HOLDING AND DECISION:** (Oman, J.) Yes. When, to preserve concurrently held property from foreclosure, a cotenant pays more than his share of the mortgage debt, the derelict cotenants may nevertheless exercise the option of taking advantage of the benefit by reimbursing the paying cotenant within a reasonable time. While we do not applaud Christian (D) for his failure, the fact remains that the legal title to a one-fourth interest remains vested in him in view of his timely contribution. Reversed for a judgment quieting title to three-quarter interest in Laura (P) and one-quarter in Christian (D).

▶ **ANALYSIS**

This problem arises in a variety of situations. In *Andrews v. Andrews*, 155 Fla. 654 (1945), a wife redeemed property held in tenancy by the entireties from a tax sale. Although the parties were divorced, the court allowed the ex-husband to redeem the property for a share as a tenant in common provided he reimbursed the ex-wife for one-half of the amount paid by her.

■■■

## Quicknotes

**FORECLOSURE SALE** Termination of an interest in property, usually initiated by a lienholder upon failure to tender mortgage payments, resulting in the sale of the property in order to satisfy the debt.

**TENANCY IN COMMON** An interest in property held by two or more people, each with equal right to its use and possession; interests may be partitioned, sold, conveyed, or devised.

■■■

# Mercer v. Wayman

## Possessor of property (P) v. Heirs (D)

Ill. Sup. Ct., 9 Ill. 2d 441, 137 N.E. 2d 815 (1956).

**NATURE OF CASE:** Appeal from action setting aside certain oil and gas leases.

**FACT SUMMARY:** Wayman (D), the grandchild of the deceased owner of a parcel of real property, attempted to execute oil and gas leases as a co-tenant in real property.

## 🏛 RULE OF LAW
Adverse possession cannot be established against a cotenant unless the tenant in possession gives actual or constructive notice of the ouster or disseizin.

**FACTS:** After an original property owner's death, his heirs (D) attempted to convey a parcel of real property to Mercer (P). Three of these heirs (D) were minors and their father attempted to convey their interests. Mercer (P) entered into possession. Numerous oil and gas leases were executed by Mercer (P) during his long term of residence on the property. Mercer (P) remained in constant possession of the property, received all rents and profits from the parcel, paid all taxes on it, and executed several mortgages on the property. More than twenty years after the youngest of the three minor children (D), heirs of the original owner, had reached their majority, they attempted to grant an oil and gas lease on the parcel as co-tenants. Mercer (P) claimed that he had fee title to the property, and even if he didn't, the property was his through adverse possession. The trial court sustained Mercer's (P) contentions and ordered the leases canceled. Wayman (D), one of the minor children, appealed.

**ISSUE:** Can adverse possession be established against a cotenant without some affirmative act or notice which warns the cotenant of ouster or disseizin?

**HOLDING AND DECISION:** (Davis, J.) No. First, the conveyance of the minor children's rights was ineffective. It did not constitute color of title because of the defects appearing on the face of the deed showing that their interests had not been conveyed. Therefore, the minors were cotenants of Mercer (P). In order to start the statute of limitations running against a co-tenant, it must be shown that the tenant in possession gave actual notice or committed an act which would constitute notice of ouster disseizin. All presumptions must be found in favor of the owner. Therefore, the party claiming by adverse possession bears the burden of proving that notice or acts put the co-tenant on notice of the ouster or disseizin. Possession, payment of taxes, collection of rents and profits, and execution of mineral leases are not sufficient to prove actual notice. Since there is no evidence that Wayman (D) had such notice, and since he could execute leases as a co-tenant, the trial court must be reversed.

## ▶ ANALYSIS

To meet the open, notorious, and hostile possession requirements of the statutes, acts must be done or notice given which will alert co-owners of the land that the tenant in possession is acting in complete derogation of their rights. Possession by one co-tenant is deemed permissive.

■=■

## Quicknotes

**ACTUAL NOTICE** Direct communication of information that would cause an ordinary person of average prudence to inquire as to its truth.

**ADVERSE POSSESSION** A means of acquiring title to real property by remaining in actual, open, continuous, exclusive possession of property for the statutory period.

**CONSTRUCTIVE NOTICE** Knowledge of a fact that is imputed to an individual who was under a duty to inquire and who could have learned of the fact through the exercise of reasonable prudence.

■=■

# Centex Homes Corp. v. Boag

## Condominium seller (P) v. Condo unit buyer (D)

N.J. Super. Ct., Chancery Div., 128 N.J. Super. 385, 320 A.2d 194 (1974).

**NATURE OF CASE:** Motion for a summary judgment in action for specific performance for breach of contract.

**FACT SUMMARY:** Centex Homes Corp. (P) sued Boag (D) to recover the purchase price for a condominium that Boag (D) had contracted to buy from Centex Homes (P).

## 🏛 RULE OF LAW
The equitable remedy of specific performance will not lie for the enforcement of a contract for the sale of a condominium apartment as it has no unique quality, and damages at law are adequate.

**FACTS:** On September 13, 1972, Boag (D) contracted to purchase a condominium from Centex Homes Corp. (P) for $73,700. Prior to the signing of the contract, Boag (D) had given a $500 deposit to Centex Homes (P) and, subsequent to the signing, had given to Centex Homes (P) a check for $6,870, which together with the deposit equalled 10% of the purchase price. Shortly after, Boag (D) was transferred from New York to Chicago, whereupon he canceled the $6,870 check and advised Centex Homes (P) that he was not going to buy the condominium. Centex Homes (P) sued Boag (D) for specific performance of the purchase agreement or in the alternative for liquidated damages in the amount of $6,870 and moved for summary judgment.

**ISSUE:** Will the remedy of equitable performance lie for the enforcement of a contract for the sale of a condominium apartment?

**HOLDING AND DECISION:** (Gelman, J.) No. The mutuality of remedy concept has been the prop which has supported equitable jurisdiction to grant specific performance in actions by vendors of real estate. It is not essential that the remedy be mutual as the rule is satisfied if the decree of specific performance operates effectively against both parties and gives to each the benefit of a mutual obligation. The effective disappearance of the mutuality of remedy doctrine from our law dictates that specific performance relief should no longer be automatically available to a vendor of real estate, but should be confined to those special instances where a vendor will otherwise suffer an economic injury for which the remedy at law is inadequate. Here, a condominium apartment unit has no unique quality but is one of hundreds of virtually identical units being offered by Centex Homes (P) for sale to the public. The units are sold by sample, in this case model apartments, in much the same manner as items of personal property are sold in the marketplace. Consequently, one must conclude that the damages sustained by a condominium sponsor, in this case Centex Homes (P), resulting from the breach of a sales agreement are readily measurable, and the remedy at law wholly adequate. Centex Homes (P) damages are limited to the retention of the $500 deposit. Complaints dismissed.

## ▶ ANALYSIS

Condominiums are, in a sense, a new type of subdivision—vertical rather than horizontal—and they have the same potential for development that has occurred in subdivision growth generally since the end of the Second World War. All of the states now have condominium statutes governing this form of concurrent ownership, and condominium law represents a rich blend of common-law principles and legislative policy. It also represents a new lucrative area for lawyers to enter.

## Quicknotes

**LIQUIDATED DAMAGES** An amount of money specified in a contract representing the damages owed in the event of breach.

**MUTUALITY OF REMEDY** An equitable doctrine that one party to a contract may not have available an equitable remedy if the other party does not have such remedy available.

**SPECIFIC PERFORMANCE** An equitable remedy whereby the court requires the parties to perform their obligations pursuant to a contract.

# Dutcher v. Owens

## Part-owner of common area (D) v. Owner of burned unit (P)

Tex. Sup. Ct., 647 S.W.2d 948 (1983).

**NATURE OF CASE:** Appeal from award of damages for negligence.

**FACT SUMMARY:** Owens (P) sued Dutcher (D) and a class of co-owners of condominiums for damages resulting from a fire in the common area that spread to Owens's (P) apartment which had been leased from Dutcher (D).

## 🏛 RULE OF LAW
Given the uniqueness of the type of ownership involved in condominiums, the onus of liability for injuries arising from the management of condominium projects should reflect a degree of control exercised by the condominium co-owner and is limited to his pro rata interest.

**FACTS:** Owens (P) leased a condominium apartment from Dutcher (D) which was located in a condominium project. Dutcher's (D) ownership of the apartment included a 1.572% undivided ownership in the common elements of the project. Owens (P) subsequently suffered substantial property loss in a fire which began in an external light fixture in a common area. The trial court rendered judgment against Dutcher (D) on the jury's finding of liability, in the amount of $1,087.04, which represented Dutcher's (D) 1.572% undivided ownership in the common elements of the condominium project. The court of appeals reversed in part and held that Dutcher (D) as a unit owner was a tenant in common with the other unit owners and was, therefore, jointly and severally liable. Dutcher (D) appealed, maintaining that as a condominium co-owner he should be liable only for pro rata interest in the management of a condominium project.

**ISSUE:** Should the onus of liability for injuries arising from the management of condominium projects reflect a degree of control exercised by the condominium co-owner, limited to his pro rata interest?

**HOLDING AND DECISION:** (Ray, J.) Yes. A condominium is an estate in real property together with a separate fee simple interest in another portion of the same parcel. An individual apartment cannot be conveyed separately from the undivided interest in the common interest and vice versa. This is in keeping with the statutory scheme under the Texas Condominium Act. To say that a condominium co-owner had any effective control over the operation of the common areas would be to sacrifice "reality to theoretical formalism" for, in fact, a co-owner has no more control over operations than he would have as a stockholder in a corporation which owned and operated the project. Here, because of the limited control afforded a unit owner by the statutory condominium regime, the creation of the regime effects a re-allocation of tort liability and is limited to his pro rata interest in the regime as a whole, where such liability arises from those areas held in tenancy in common. Court of appeals judgment reversed and trial court judgment affirmed.

## ▶ ANALYSIS

As a system, the term "condominium" means a form of ownership under which separate units of a multi-unit improvement of real property are subject to ownership by different owners, and there is appurtenant to each unit an individual share in the common elements. As applied to the building, the term "condominium" simply refers to the entire building or project and can refer to an individual living unit as well. The condominium form of ownership goes back to at least the Middle Ages, but condominium regimes were seldom created in the United States prior to statutory enactments in the 1960s.

■≡■

## Quicknotes

**PRO RATA** In proportion.

**TENANCY IN COMMON** An interest in property held by two or more people, each with equal right to its use and possession, interests may be partitioned, sold, conveyed, or devised.

**TEXAS CONDOMINIUM ACT** The Texas Legislature defined a condominium as the merger of two estates into one: the fee simple ownership of a unit in a condominium project and a tenancy in common with other co-owners in the common elements.

■≡■

# Aquarian Foundation, Inc. v. Sholom House, Inc.

Condominium buyer (D) v. Board of directors (P)

Fla. Dist. Ct. App., 448 So.2d 1166 (1984).

**NATURE OF CASE:** Appeal from judgment nullifying a conveyance in action for ejectment and damages.

**FACT SUMMARY:** When a condominium owner sold her unit to Aquarian Foundation, Inc. (D) without the consent of Sholom House's (P) board of directors, Sholom House (P) sued to set aside the conveyance.

## 🏛 RULE OF LAW
A clause in a condominium's declaration permitting the association to arbitrarily withhold its consent to transfer a unit constitutes an unreasonable restraint on alienation.

**FACTS:** A provision of the declaration of condominium at Sholom House (P) required the written consent of the condo association's board of directors to any sale, lease, or transfer of a unit owner's interest. In the event of a violation, the fee simple title to the condominium reverted to the association upon payment of the unit's fair value to the owner. The clause stated that the association could "arbitrarily, capriciously, or unreasonably" withhold its consent. Bertha Albares sold her unit to Aquarian Foundation, Inc. (D) without the board's consent. Sholom House (P) sued to set aside the sale. The trial court, having concluded that Albares had violated the declaration of condominium, nullified the sale to Aquarian (D). Aquarian (D) appealed.

**ISSUE:** Does a clause in a condominium's declaration permitting the association to arbitrarily withhold its consent to transfer constitute an unreasonable restraint on alienation?

**HOLDING AND DECISION:** (Pearson, J.) Yes. A clause in a condominium's declaration permitting the association to arbitrarily, capriciously, or unreasonably withhold its consent to transfer a unit constitutes an unreasonable restraint on alienation. By necessity, unit owners give up a certain degree of freedom of choice to ensure the happiness and peace of mind of all the residents who live close together and share the condominium's facilities. Accordingly, restrictions on the right to transfer property within the condominium are generally upheld by the court. They will, however, be invalidated when found to violate some external public policy or constitutional right of the individual. An association may reject perpetually any unit owner's prospective buyer for any or no reason, so long as the association provides another purchaser or purchases the property itself. Here, the reverter clause does not obligate the association to compensate the owner within a reasonable time. In fact, the clause is not even triggered until there is a sale, which would not ordinarily be expected to occur without the association's consent. Thus, the association's accountability to the unit owner is illusory. Therefore, the restraint on alienation is unlawful. Reversed.

## ▶ ANALYSIS

Courts may generally uphold provisions in condominium by-laws prohibiting alienation of units as per se reasonable but will still review the reasonableness of refusals to grant such consent. One court has held that an association's refusal to consent to a time-share arrangement was unreasonable and impermissible. See *Laguna Royale Owners Ass'n v. Darger*, 119 Cal. App. 3d 670 (1981).

■■■

## Quicknotes

**REVERTER** A type of reversionary interest referring to an interest in land that remains in the grantor until the happening of a condition precedent.

**UNREASONABLE RESTRAINT ON ALIENATION** A provision restricting the transferee's ability to convey interests in the conveyed property and which is unenforceable.

■■■

# Non-Freehold Estates: Landlord and Tenant

## *Quick Reference Rules of Law*

# Brown v. Southall Realty Co.

### Lessee (D) v. Fraudulent lessor (P)

D.C. Ct. App., 237 A.2d 834 (1968).

**NATURE OF CASE:** Action to regain possession of leased premises for nonpayment of rent.

**FACT SUMMARY:** Southall Realty Co. (P) leased premises to Brown (D) despite notice from the city of a series of code violations rendering the premises uninhabitable.

## 🏛 RULE OF LAW
As a general rule, an illegal contract, made in violation of statutory prohibitions designed for police or regulatory purposes, is void and confers no right upon the wrongdoer; and, a lease made in violation of housing regulations which imply such prohibitory purposes is just as void as any other contract.

**FACTS:** Brown (D) leased premises from Southall Realty Co. (P). Prior to the lease, Southall Realty (P) had been notified by a Housing Inspector of the District of Columbia of various code violations: (1) an obstructed commode, (2) a broken railing, and (3) insufficient ceiling height in the basement. As a result, Southall Realty (P) gave a sworn statement to the Housing Division that the affected areas would not be occupied until the violations were remedied. Despite this statement, however, Southall Realty (P) leased the premises to Brown (D) on a representation that they were habitable. Brown (D) has subsequently withheld rent because of these conditions. Southall Realty (P) sued to regain legal possession. From a judgment for Southall Realty (P), Brown (D) appeals. Though she has already vacated the premises, she desires to avoid the adjudication of her failure to pay rent as wrongful for res judicata purposes.

**ISSUE:** May a lease be voided by a court because of violations of the housing code?

**HOLDING AND DECISION:** (Quinn, J.) Yes. As a general rule, an illegal contract, made in violation of statutory prohibitions designed for police or regulatory purposes, is void and confers no right upon the wrongdoer; and, a lease made in violation of housing regulations which imply such prohibitory purposes is just as void as any other contract. To determine whether or not an ordinance is "prohibitory," the court must look to the intent of the legislature as manifested in the subject matter involved and the penalty (if any) provided. Here, the District of Columbia has clearly indicated that its prohibitions were intended to insure that all dwellings be "habitable." Further, the provision, as here, of penalties usually implies a prohibition. As such, to uphold the validity of this agreement, in light of the statutorily prohibited defects known to have existed at the time of the lease, would be to flout the purposes for which the Housing Code was instituted. The lease is void. The judgment below is reversed.

## ▶ ANALYSIS

This case points up the clear trend of authority of protecting the tenant's right to habitable premises by finding a lease void which is made in spite of housing code violations. Traditionally, the covenant of quiet enjoyment by the landlord, the covenant to pay rent by the tenant were not mutually dependent. As such, breach of one did not justify the breach of another. So, where premises were found to be so inhabitable as to constitute a constructive eviction, the tenant was held to rent for all the time in occupancy. By applying contract principles to leases, however, inhabitable conditions which violate the housing codes render such leases void, relieving the tenant of his responsibility to pay rent ab initio. This case is actually more important, therefore, for what it does not say: that a lease is a contract as well as the sale of an interest (term) in land.

■══■

## Quicknotes

**AB INITIO** From its inception or beginning.

**RES JUDICATA** The rule of law that a final judgment by a court precludes subsequent litigation between the parties regarding the same cause of action.

■══■

# Jancik v. Department of Housing and Urban Development

Landlord (D) v. Regulatory agency (P)

44 F.3d 553 (7th Cir. 1995).

**NATURE OF CASE:** Petition for review of a HUD decision awarding damages for discrimination.

**FACT SUMMARY:** Jancik's (D) advertisement for an apartment expressed a preference for a "mature person."

## RULE OF LAW
Landlord advertisements expressing a preference based on family status violate the Fair Housing Act.

**FACTS:** Jancik (D) owned a building in a Chicago suburb which he leased to tenants. In 1990, he advertised one of the apartments, expressing a preference for a "mature person." The Leadership Council suspected that Jancik (D) was illegally discriminated and sent two testers to inquire about the apartment. A white tester was asked by Jancik (D) about her race over the phone. A black tester was asked about her race, marital status, and whether she had children. Based on these tests, the Leadership Council filed a complaint with HUD (P) for violation of § 804(c) of the Fair Housing Act, which proscribes advertisements indicating preferences based on race or family status. An administrative law judge ruled against Jancik (D), who appealed.

**ISSUE:** Do landlord advertisements that express a preference based on family status violate the Fair Housing Act?

**HOLDING AND DECISION:** (Rovner, J.) Yes. Landlord advertisements that express a preference based on family status violate the Fair Housing Act. In determining whether an advertisement indicates an illegal preference, an objective ordinary reader standard is applied. Thus, if the ad discourages an ordinary reader of a particular protected group from responding, it violates the Fair Housing Act. A showing of subjective intent to discriminate is not necessary, but evidence of such an intent is relevant to the determination. In the present case, Jancik's (D) advertisement suggested an illegal preference for persons without children, and given the context of his questions to the testers, there was substantial evidence supporting the HUD (P) decision. Affirmed.

## ANALYSIS

The decision also upheld HUD's (P) decision that Jancik (D) was also illegally discriminating based on race, given his questions to the testers. The court found that the fact that Jancik (D) had never rented an apartment to a black tenant bolstered this conclusion. In other cases, advertisements for apartment complexes that show pictures of only white people have been held violative of the Fair Housing Act.

■═■

# Adrian v. Rabinowitz

## Lessee (P) v. Delinquent landlord (D)

N.J. Sup. Ct., 116 N.J.L. 586, 186 A. 29 (1936).

**NATURE OF CASE:** Action for damages for breach of a lease.

**FACT SUMMARY:** Rabinowitz (D) leased a building to Adrian (P) to be used as a shoe store, but the preceding tenant had not vacated when Adrian's (P) lease began.

**RULE OF LAW**
Where the commencement of the lease is in the future, the lessor is under an implied duty to have the leased premises legally and actually open for the lessee's immediate possession.

**FACTS:** On April 30, 1934, Adrian (P) leased a store building from Rabinowitz (D). The lease was to commence on June 15 and was to last six months. The lease provided that the lessee shall and may peaceably and quietly have, hold, and enjoy the premises on June 14. The prior tenant of the premises failed to respond to the lessor's notice to vacate. The lessor immediately brought an action for removal of the holdover. On July 9, Adrian (P) took possession. The trial court held that Adrian (P) did not have to pay any rent for the time period of which he was deprived possession. Adrian (P) was also awarded $500 as the loss sustained when he resold his stock of seasonable shoes.

**ISSUE:** Does a lease impliedly impose on a lessor the duty of putting the lessee in actual and exclusive possession of the premises at the beginning of the term?

**HOLDING AND DECISION:** (Heher, J.) Yes. The English rule is that where the lease is to commence at a point in the future, there is an implied undertaking by the lessor that the premises shall be open to the lessee's actual and legal entry when the time for possession arrives. This rule effectuates the intent of the parties, and the implied duty on the lessor is an essential, if implied, term of the lease. Under the facts, the lessor prosecuted the holdover tenant. The lessor, therefore, interpreted the lease as imposing this duty. The measure of damages for a breach of a lease is, in the absence of special circumstances communicated by one party to the other, the difference between actual rental value and the rent reserved for the period in which the lessee did not have possession. Reversed and a venire de novo awarded.

## ▶ ANALYSIS

A minority of courts follow the American rule which imposes on the lessor merely the obligation to give the lessee the legal right to possession, but not the duty to put the tenant into possession. The rationale is that once the lease commences, the lessee has the right of possession, not the lessor. Therefore, occupancy by another is a wrong toward the lessee only. This rule is based on the general rule that a party to a bargain, himself without fault, is not responsible for the tortious interference of a third party. A covenant for quiet enjoyment, if not expressed in the lease, is, as a general rule, implied in every lease unless the terms of the lease are construed to exclude the implication.

## Quicknotes

**HOLDOVER TENANT** A tenancy that arises upon the expiration of a lawful tenancy and the tenant remains in possession of the property.

**TENANT AT WILL** An individual who holds possession of property by permission of the owner but without a fixed term.

# Commonwealth Building Corp. v. Hirschfield

## Strict landlord (P) v. Tenant (D)

Ill. Ct. App., 307 Ill. App. 533, 30 N.E.2d 790 (1940).

**NATURE OF CASE:** Appeal in a suit for rent.

**FACT SUMMARY:** When Hirschfield (D) was a few hours delinquent in moving from the premises, Commonwealth Building Corp. (P) attempted to charge him as a holdover tenant.

## 🏛 RULE OF LAW
A tenant who holds over involuntarily, due to no fault of his own, may neither be regarded by the landlord as a trespasser nor be held for another similar term.

**FACTS:** Hirschfield's (D) lease with Commonwealth Building Corp. (P) expired on September 30, 1938. The lease contained a clause providing for double rent if the tenant failed to move when the lease expired. Two months before expiration, Hirschfield (D) notified Commonwealth (P) that he intended to move. He employed a professional mover and also enlisted the aid of the building employees. Despite the fact that they worked moving things from September 27th through the 30th, a few household articles remained when the lease expired at midnight on the 30th. However, these final few articles were promptly moved on October 1st. Nevertheless, at 10:00 A.M. on October 1, Commonwealth (P) notified Hirschfield (D) that he was regarded as a holdover tenant for another year and that payment of October rent was due. When Hirschfield (D) refused, Commonwealth (P) sued for $3,300 in rent. The jury gave Commonwealth (P) a $1,100 judgment; the trial court granted Hirschfield (D) a new trial. Commonwealth (P) appealed.

**ISSUE:** May a tenant who holds over involuntarily, due to no fault of his own, either be regarded by the landlord as a trespasser or be held for another similar term?

**HOLDING AND DECISION:** (Matchett, J.) No. A tenant who holds over involuntarily, due to no fault of his own, may neither be regarded by the landlord as a trespasser nor be held for another similar term. Two theories enable the landlord to take such action: (1) that, by the voluntary act of the tenant, the landlord can rightfully assume an intention to create a second tenancy and (2) the tenant's action is such that a quasi-contract can be assumed as a matter of law. However, neither of these theories applies here. Despite a delay of a few hours, Hirschfield (D) vacated the premises with reasonable speed and good faith. There is no evidence whereby a jury could find an intent to continue the lease, nor, especially in view of the lease itself providing for double payment for brief holdover, could a quasi-contract for a new term be found. Reversed.

**CONCURRENCE:** (O'Connor, J.) Under the "rule of reason," not every dereliction, however slight, will give rise to a cause of action. The $3,300 claim by Commonwealth (P) shocks the conscience.

## ▶ ANALYSIS

In *Feiges v. Racine Dry Goods Co.*, 231 Wis. 270 (1939), a tenant was unable to move because its striking employees were picketing the premises. The court denied the landlord's request for treble damages, holding that only a tortious act in the sense of failure to perform an obligation or duty could warrant such a penalty.

■=■

### Quicknotes

**HOLDOVER TENANT** A tenancy that arises upon the expiration of a lawful tenancy and the tenant remains in possession of the property.

**TRESPASS** Unlawful interference with, or damage to, the real or personal property of another.

■=■

# Richard Barton Enterprises, Inc. v. Tsern

Lessee (P) v. Lessor (D)

Utah Sup. Ct., 928 P.2d 368 (1996).

**NATURE OF CASE:** Suit to establish landlord's legal duty to repair premises.

**FACT SUMMARY:** Barton (P) sought a rent abatement when Tsern (D) refused to repair a nonfunctioning elevator on the premises he leased to Barton (P) and which he promised to repair.

## 🏛 RULE OF LAW
Courts may not impose a modification of a lease to which the parties have not agreed and may not do so when the parties have explicitly disagreed as to the lease's essential terms.

**FACTS:** Barton (P) and Tsern (D) entered into a lease agreement whereby Barton (P) agreed to pay $3,000 per month for a one-year lease. When Barton (P) took possession, the elevator was inoperable. Finally it was shut down by a city inspector. Tsern (D) refused to pay for the repairs, believing Barton (P) would exercise an option to purchase the building, and each sent a communication to the other regarding a rent abatement. Barton (P) tendered less than the full amount of the rent and filed a complaint for a declaratory judgment to establish Tsern's (D) legal duty to repair the elevator. The trial court found the elevator had not been repaired to good working order as required by the lease, and that Barton (P) was entitled to have the rent abated to $2,000 a month. It also ruled that Barton's (P) damages plus interest be deducted from the purchase price of the building and awarded attorney's fees of $10,000. Tsern (D) appealed.

**ISSUE:** May courts impose a modification of a lease to which the parties have not agreed and when the parties have explicitly disagreed as to the lease's essential terms?

**HOLDING AND DECISION:** (Stewart, C.J.) No. Courts may not impose a modification of a lease to which the parties have not agreed and may not do so when the parties have explicitly disagreed as to the lease's essential terms. A valid modification requires a "meeting of the minds of the parties" which must be stated with sufficient definiteness. The lessee's covenant to pay rent is dependant on the lessor's performance of covenants that were of a significant inducement to the consummation of the lease or to the purpose for which the lessee entered the lease. Tsern (D) knew that an operable elevator was essential to Barton's (P) use of the property and that his promise to repair the elevator was a significant inducement to enter the lease. A lessee is entitled to a rental abatement equal to the amount by which the property is reduced due to the lessor's breach.

## ▶ ANALYSIS

At common law, the lessee's covenant to pay rent was independent of the lessor's covenants. This rule was mitigated somewhat by the doctrine of constructive eviction, which allowed tenant to stop paying rent if the lesson's failure to perform a covenant was equivalent to an eviction. The breach, however, must be significant in order to abate rent.

■■■

## Quicknotes

**CONSTRUCTIVE EVICTION** An action whereby the landlord renders the property unsuitable for occupancy, either in whole or in part, so that the tenant is forced to leave the premises.

**COVENANT** A written promise to do, or to refrain from doing, a particular activity.

**LEASE** An agreement or contract which creates a relationship between a landlord and tenant (real property) or lessor and lessee (real or personal property).

**MEETING OF THE MINDS** A requirement of a valid contract that the parties possess a mutuality of assent as manifested by the terms of the agreement and not by a hidden intent; enforceability of the contract is limited to those terms to which the parties assented.

■■■

# Town of Telluride v. Lot Thirty-Four Venture, L.L.C.

## Municipality (D) v. Developer (P)

Colo. Sup. Ct., 3 P.3d 30 (2000).

**NATURE OF CASE:** Challenge to municipal ordinance.

**FACT SUMMARY:** Thirty-Four Venture (P) challenged the validity of a local ordinance as an unlawful rent control ordinance.

## 🏛 RULE OF LAW
Rent control is allowable rent capped at a fixed rate with only limited increases.

**FACTS:** In 1994, Thirty-Four Venture (P) acquired lots in the AC-2 zoning district in Telluride. A few months later the town adopted Ordinance 1011 which amended the Land Use Code to add "affordable housing" mitigation requirements, requiring developers to provide affordable housing units for 40% of the number of employees a proposed development generated. Thirty-Four Venture (P) challenged the ordinance arguing such amendment constituted rent control in violation of state law. The trial court granted summary judgment to Telluride (D) on the basis that the ordinance fell outside the scope of rent control, and the court of appeals reversed.

**ISSUE:** Is rent control allowable rent capped at a fixed rate with only limited increases?

**HOLDING AND DECISION:** (Kourlis, J.) Yes. Rent control is allowable rent capped at a fixed rate with only limited increases. Because the ordinance sets a base rental rate per square foot and then strictly limits the growth of the rental rate, the ordinance constitutes rent control. Affirmed.

## ▶ ANALYSIS

The primary effect of rent control is to suppress rental value of property below their fair market values. The court when construing a statute looks to the plain meaning of the language employed and will not resort to legislative history or other rules of statutory construction where the meaning is clear on the statute's face.

■■■

## Quicknotes

**ORDINANCE** Law or statute usually enacted by a municipal government.

**RENT CONTROL** A municipal ordinance limiting the maximum rent that may be lawfully charged for rental property.

■■■

# Piggly Wiggly Southern, Inc. v. Heard

Supermarket tenant (D) v. Other tenants (P)

Ga. Sup. Ct., 261 Ga. 503, 405 S.E.2d 478 (1991).

**NATURE OF CASE:** Appeal from judgment awarding damages for breach of contract.

**FACT SUMMARY:** Piggly Wiggly Southern, Inc. (D) contended that lease language permitting it to use retail property for any lawful purpose prevented the finding of an implied covenant of continuous operations.

## 🏛 RULE OF LAW
An implied covenant of continuous operations will not be read into a lease containing express language to the contrary.

**FACTS:** Heard's (P) predecessor executed a lease of commercial premises to Piggly Wiggly Southern, Inc. (D). The lease provided that Piggly (D) intended to operate a supermarket, but also contained language that the lessee, Piggly (D), could use the premises for "any other lawful business." The lease provided for a base rent plus a percentage of sales. Piggly (D) later closed the supermarket and rejected all sublease offers, choosing instead to leave the premises vacant. Loss of the anchor store adversely affected smaller tenants in the shopping center. Heard (P) brought a breach of contract action, alleging breach of an implied covenant of continuous operation. The court of appeals agreed, finding the clause breached and awarding damages. Piggly (D) appealed.

**ISSUE:** Will an implied covenant of continuous operations be read into a lease containing express language to the contrary?

**HOLDING AND DECISION:** [Judge not stated in casebook excerpt.] No. An implied covenant of continuous operations will not be read into a lease containing express language to the contrary. If the parties did not agree to or bargain for such a covenant, as evidenced by lease terms, a court should not and may not find one. In the lease in question here, language clearly gives Piggly (D) the right to put the premises to any lawful use, which includes nonuse. Also, the presence of a base rent implies that the parties contemplated the possibility of nonuse. Reversed.

**DISSENT:** (Benham, J.) The lease calls for any "lawful business." This implies some sort of business use, not nonuse.

## ▌ *ANALYSIS*

The basic rule in contractual interpretation is that a court should give effect to the parties' intentions. The first and best evidence thereof is the language of the contract. As this case shows, however, what is meant by some provisions may be subject to different interpretations.

---

### *Quicknotes*

**IMPLIED COVENANT** A promise inferred by law from a document as a whole and the circumstances surrounding its implementation.

# Handler v. Horns

## Sister (P) v. Meat-packing brother (D)

N.J. Sup. Ct., 2 N.J. 18, 65 A.2d 523 (1949).

**NATURE OF CASE:** Appeal from ruling including trade fixtures in sale of premises.

**FACT SUMMARY:** In the course of a meat packing business, Horns's (D) father affixed business equipment to a building owned by Handler (P) and Horns's (D) mutual grandparents.

## 🏛 RULE OF LAW
Trade fixtures may be removed by the commercial lessee if their removal will not cause material damage to the real estate.

**FACTS:** Horns's (D) father leased a commercial building from his parents in 1929. Under the first lease, the premises were to be used for a meat packing business and to be returned to lessor in the same condition as existed when used as a warehouse and shop prior to installation of meat packing improvements. The second lease of 1939 explicitly allowed for removal of any trade fixtures that could be removed without material damage to premises. When Horns's (D) father died, he bequeathed the meat business and his share of the interest in the premises to Horns (D). Horns's (D) sister, Handler (P), as granddaughter and one-third heir of the building's original owners, sued for partition. The lower court ordered the sale of the entire premises, including all fixtures, with the proceeds to be split three ways among the surviving grandchildren. Horns (D), also a grandchild of the original owners, claimed title to the trade fixtures in their entirety as the son and heir of the owner of the business who had made the improvements to the commercial premises during a lease.

**ISSUE:** Are trade fixtures removable at the end of a tenancy if the trade fixtures can be removed without material harm to the underlying real estate?

**HOLDING AND DECISION:** (Ackerson, J.) Yes. Trade fixtures may be removed at the end of a commercial lease if they can be removed without material harm to the real estate. Contracts are to be construed strictly in order to encourage trade. To the extent that fixtures are used in a trade or business and can be removed without material harm to the premises as measured at the point in time prior to the initial improvements, the court will enforce the intention of the parties. Reversed and remanded.

maximum flexibility in the use of a nonfreehold estate. Thus, the court creates an exception to the ancient property theory that fixtures become part of the realty and cannot be removed at the end of a tenancy.

■═■

## ▌ *ANALYSIS*

Here, the Supreme Court of New Jersey looks to public policy to justify its decision. Because it is in the public's best interests to encourage commerce, the court favors the

# Walls v. Oxford Management Co.

Sexual assault victim (P) v. Landlord (D)

N.H. Sup. Ct., 137 N.H. 653, 633 A.2d 103 (1993).

**NATURE OF CASE:** Two certified questions to state supreme court in action alleging negligence and breach of warranty of habitability.

**FACT SUMMARY:** Walls (P) was sexually assaulted on property adjacent to the apartment her mother rented from Oxford Management Co. (D).

## 🏛 RULE OF LAW
Unless a landlord has voluntarily assumed a duty to provide security, contractually assumed a duty to provide security, created a defect that foreseeably increases the risk of criminal attack, or has been responsible for such a defect, the landlord will not be liable for criminal attacks committed by third parties.

**FACTS:** Wall (P) resided with her mother in an apartment managed by Oxford (D). The rental contract did not provide for security and the landlord had not instituted any security provisions. Wall (P) was sexually assaulted by a person who did not work for Oxford (D) while sitting in her car, which was parked on the apartment premises managed by Oxford (D).

**ISSUE:** Does the landlord have a duty to secure its tenants against criminal acts of third parties?

**HOLDING AND DECISION:** (Horton, J.) No. Unless a landlord has voluntarily assumed a duty to provide security, contractually assumed a duty to provide security, created a defect that foreseeably increases the risk of criminal attack, or has been responsible for such a defect, the landlord will not be liable for criminal attacks committed by third parties. Liability exists when the duty is voluntarily or contractually assumed; and liability also exists when the landlord has created or is otherwise responsible for a condition that enhances the probability of criminal acts. Oxford (D), the landlord here, has no duty to provide security against the criminal acts of third parties. Remanded.

## ▶ ANALYSIS

The jurisdictions are split on a landlord's general duty when the criminal acts are foreseeable. Wall (P) also argued that a landlord's implied warranty of habitability to provide reasonably safe premises required Oxford (D) to protect her against criminal attack. But the court concluded that the implied warranty of habitability was expressly limited to structural-type physical conditions, and the court refused to expand it to cover security from crime. As crime becomes more prevalent, other courts have been willing to require reasonable protection against foreseeable criminal acts, particularly in common areas under the landlord's management.

■■■

## Quicknotes

**HABITABILITY** A warranty implied by a landlord that the premises are suitable, and will remain suitable, for habitation.

**IMPLIED WARRANTY** An implied promise made by one party to a contract that the other party may rely on a fact, relieving that party from the obligation of determining whether the fact is true and indemnifying the other party from liability if that fact is shown to be false.

■■■

# Foundation Development Corp. v. Loehmann's, Inc.

## Landlord (P) v. Delinquent tenant (D)

Ariz. Sup. Ct., 163 Ariz. 438, 788 P.2d 1189 (1990).

**NATURE OF CASE:** Appeal from judgment ordering forfeiture of lease in breach of contract action.

**FACT SUMMARY:** When Loehmann's (D) was late in paying the common area charges due to its landlord, Foundation Development Corp. (P), Foundation (P) sued, claiming material breach because the lease specified that time was of the essence in all rental payments.

## 🏛 RULE OF LAW
A trivial breach of a commercial lease will give rise only to an action for contract damages and will not justify forfeiture of the tenancy.

**FACTS:** Loehmann's (D) leased a store on a long-term basis in a shopping center owned by Foundation Development Corp. (P). The lease specified that time was of the essence when making rental payments. One month, Loehmann's (D) was late in paying the common area charges. Payment was not received by landlord Foundation (P) until twelve days after Loehmann's (D) received a second notice demanding payment of the late common area rental charges. Foundation (P) sought forfeiture of the tenancy, but the trial court held the breach to be technical and trivial. Hence, the trial court limited Foundation (P) to monetary damages for the breach. Foundation (P) appealed, arguing that the "time of the essence" provision rendered the breach a material one. The appellate court agreed and reversed the trial court's denial of forfeiture. Loehmann's (D) appealed.

**ISSUE:** Will the court countenance forfeiture of a commercial lease where the breach was a trivial one?

**HOLDING AND DECISION:** [Judge not stated in casebook excerpt.] No. A trivial breach of a commercial lease will give rise only to an action for contract damages and will not justify forfeiture of the tenancy. A lease conveys an interest in land. Commercial tenants frequently make substantial outlays for fixtures based on the expectation that they will be able to conduct their businesses for the term of the lease. Because public policy supports the stability of commercial economic relationships, the contractual clause making time of the essence will not be enforced in this case as the breach was technical and trivial. Appeals court decision vacated and trial court decision in favor of Loehmann's (D) affirmed.

of material breach would give the Foundation (P) grounds to end the tenancy. The court opposes that result as it would destabilize long-term tenancies. As the judge noted, the interaction between real property law and contracts law is a matter of compromise.

■===■

## Quicknotes

**TIME IS OF THE ESSENCE** Contract provision specifying that the time period in which performance is rendered constitutes an essential term of the agreement.

■===■

## ▶ *ANALYSIS*

The court here refuses to enforce a bargained-for contract clause even though both parties to the lease were sophisticated businesses. The court does this because a finding

# Edwards v. Habib

Retaliatory landlord (P) v. Tenant (D)

397 F.2d 687 (D.C. Cir. 1968); *cert. denied*, 393 U.S. 1016 (1969).

**NATURE OF CASE:** Appeal from a decision upholding an eviction action.

**FACT SUMMARY:** After Edwards (D) complained to authorities about housing code violations on the property she rented from Habib (P), Habib (P) gave her a 30-day notice to vacate and obtained a judgment for possession of the property.

> **RULE OF LAW**
> A landlord cannot evict a tenant in retaliation for such tenant reporting housing code violations to the authorities, and proof of such a retaliatory motive constitutes a defense to an action of eviction.

**FACTS:** In March 1965, Yvonne Edwards (D) rented housing property from Habib (P) on a month-to-month basis. Subsequently, Edwards (D) complained to the Department of Licenses and Inspections about sanitary code violations which Habib (P) refused to remedy. Thereafter, several code violations were discovered, and Habib (P) was ordered to correct them. Soon afterwards, Habib (P) gave Edwards (D) a 30-day notice to vacate and obtained a default judgment for possession of the rented premises. Thereupon, Edwards (D) moved to reopen the judgment, alleging excusable neglect for the default and, as a defense to eviction, that the notice to quit was given in retaliation for her complaints to housing authorities. The trial court, though, deemed retaliatory motive irrelevant and directed a verdict for Habib (P). After this decision was affirmed, Edwards (D) appealed.

**ISSUE:** Can a landlord evict a tenant in retaliation of such tenant reporting housing code violations to the authorities?

**HOLDING AND DECISION:** (Wright, J.) No. A landlord cannot evict a tenant in retaliation for his reporting housing code violations to the authorities, and proof of such a retaliatory motive constitutes a defense to an action of eviction. It is evident that the effectiveness of housing code regulations (designed to assure minimal standards in housing conditions) would be inhibited if those tenants reporting code violations could be threatened with eviction. Of course, though, a tenant cannot remain in possession forever once he has proven that the landlord has a retaliatory motive for eviction. "If this illegal purpose is dissipated, the landlord can, in the absence of legislation or a binding contract, evict his tenants or raise the rents for economic or other legitimate reasons, or even for no reason at all." Here, even though the housing code of the District of Columbia provides that a tenant may be evicted after a specified notice, such provision does not eliminate defenses to eviction. As such, Edwards (D) should have been allowed to introduce evidence regarding the defense of retaliatory motive on the part of Habib (P). Reversed and remanded.

## ▶ ANALYSIS

This case illustrates the general rule—a landlord cannot evict a tenant for reporting housing code violations. Most states further hold that a landlord cannot raise rents in retaliation for his tenant reporting housing code violations. Note that these rules evolved after many courts recognized that any lease of residential premises contains an implied warranty of fitness (i.e., the landlord has the duty to maintain the premises in a habitable condition). Many courts further recognized that compliance with housing code regulations was necessary under this implied warranty of habitability, and it became necessary to prevent a landlord from evicting any tenant who complained of housing code violations. Note, also, that a tenant, under the implied warranty of habitability, can defend against an eviction for nonpayment of rent on the basis that the premises are uninhabitable.

■■■

## Quicknotes

**IMPLIED WARRANTY OF FITNESS** An implied promise made by a merchant in a contract for the sale of goods that such goods are suitable for the purpose for which they are purchased.

**IMPLIED WARRANTY OF HABITABILITY** A warranty implied by a landlord that the premises are suitable, and will remain suitable, for habitation.

■■■

# United States National Bank of Oregon v. Homeland, Inc.

### Landlord (P) v. Tenant (D)

Or. Sup. Ct., 291 Or. 374, 631 P.2d 761 (1981).

**NATURE OF CASE:** Appeal from an award of damages for breach.

**FACT SUMMARY:** At issue was a claim by National Bank (P), as lessor, against Homeland, Inc. (D), receiver, as tenant, for unpaid rent accruing following Homeland's (D) abandonment of the premises.

## 🏛 RULE OF LAW
Following abandonment of the leased premises, the lessor has a duty to make a reasonable effort to mitigate damages finding a suitable tenant, as the tenant, by abandoning the leased premises, forfeits his estate in the real property but remains liable for damages for breach of contract.

**FACTS:** Homeland, Inc. (D) leased office space from National Bank (P) for a five-year term, April 1, 1971, to March 31, 1976. Homeland (D) vacated the premises on July 31, 1973, with 32 months remaining on the lease and thereafter paid no more rent, which was $1,415 per month. After Homeland's (D) default, National Bank (P) attempted to lease the premises to other tenants on the same terms as other premises in its office building and finally in February leased to another party the same space, said lease to run until January 1977, which was 10 months longer than Homeland's (D) lease, and at a monthly rental of $1,500. Said party defaulted, and National Bank (P) subsequently found a new tenant but not before suing Homeland (D) for the rent owed between August 1, 1973, and July 31, 1975, at a monthly rent of $1,415, less the rent already paid by the subsequent tenant. Homeland (D) argued that the reletting of the premises for a higher rent and for a longer period of time than that called for in the original lease terminated the Homeland (D) lease as a matter of law. The trial court ruled that National Bank's (P) claim was limited to the period from the date that Homeland (D) vacated to February 1, 1974, the date the premises were relet. National Bank (P) appealed.

**ISSUE:** Does a lessor have a duty to mitigate damages by reletting premises that have been abandoned by a tenant?

**HOLDING AND DECISION:** (Peterson, J.) Yes. The lessor has a duty to make a reasonable effort to mitigate damages by finding a suitable tenant. The tenant, by abandoning the leased premises, forfeits his estate in the real property but remains liable for damages for breach of contract. Mere acceptance and reletting from the surrendered premises does not release the tenant from contractual liability for breach of contract. The tenant is in the position of one who has anticipatorily breached a contract for the sale of goods. The tenant remains liable for the entire amount of the rent for the time the lessor is unable to relet or for the difference between the agreed price and the fair rental value of the premises. Furthermore, reletting or attempting to relet at a higher rate does not, as a matter of law, bar the landlord's claim of damages. Here, the lessor reasonably attempted to relet the premises. Homeland (D) must pay for unpaid accrued rent up until July 31, 1975. Reversed and remanded.

## ⯈ ANALYSIS

Abandonment by the tenant has typically given the landlord four remedies. These are as follows: (1) accept a surrender for the leasehold and relieve the tenant of all further liability; (2) retake possession of the premises for the purposes of mitigating damages; (3) do nothing and sue for rent as it comes due; and (4) sue immediately for damages on the basis of anticipatory breach of contract.

### Quicknotes

**ANTICIPATORY BREACH** Breach of a contract subsequent to formation but prior to the time performance is due.

**DUTY TO MITIGATE** The general rule that a person who is wronged must act reasonably to avoid or limit losses or precluded from recovering damages that could reasonably could have been avoided.

# Jaber v. Miller

## Landlord of burned building (D) v. Assignee (P)

Ark. Sup. Ct., 219 Ark. 59, 239 S.W.2d 760 (1951).

**NATURE OF CASE:** Cancellation of promissory notes.

**FACT SUMMARY:** Jaber's (D) lease provided that the lease would terminate if the building were destroyed by fire. The lease was transferred to Miller (P). When the building burned down, Miller (P) contended that his sublease ended when the fire terminated the original lease.

### 🏛 RULE OF LAW
The intention of the parties is to govern in determining whether an instrument is an assignment or a sublease.

**FACTS:** Jaber (D) leased a building. His lease provided that the lease would terminate if the building were destroyed by fire. Jaber (D) transferred his lease to Norber & Sons, who transferred it to Miller (P). The document between Jaber (D) and Norber & Sons was in the form of an assignment rather than a sublease and is entitled "Contract and Assignment." It contained no provision as to fires. Norber & Sons agreed to pay Jaber (D) $700 at four-month intervals and to pay the owner of the building the monthly rent. Jaber (D) reserved the right to take possession if Norber & Sons failed to pay the rent. Miller (P) arranged with Jaber (D) to pay the $700 in monthly installments of $175 each, and, accordingly, the promissory notes now in question were executed. When the building burned down, Miller (P) argued that the transfer from Jaber (D) to Norber & Sons was a sublease and that under the rule that a sublease terminates when the primary lease terminates, his sublease ended when the fire terminated the original lease.

**ISSUE:** Does the intention of the parties govern in determining whether an instrument is an assignment or a sublease?

**HOLDING AND DECISION:** (Smith, J.) Yes. Under English law, if the instrument purports to transfer the lessee's estate for the entire remainder of the term, it is an assignment regardless of its form or the intentions of the parties. Conversely, if the instrument purports to transfer the lessee's estate for less than the entire term, it is a sublease. This archaic and inflexible rule has worked injustices in many cases. Still, it is followed in a majority of jurisdictions. In a minority of jurisdictions the intentions of the parties govern in determining whether a document is an assignment or a sublease. This court adopts the minority rule. Here, it cannot be doubted that the parties intended an assignment rather than a sublease, since the document is so entitled. It is in the language of an assignment, and prom-

issory notes are not normally given when making a lease. Reversed.

### ▶ ANALYSIS

A sublease is not a transfer of the original leasehold but an entirely independent transaction which creates a new landlord-tenant relationship between the original lessee and the sublessee. There is no privity of estate and ordinarily no privity of contract between the original lessor and the sublessee. Hence, the sublessee is not bound by the rent covenant or any covenant in the original lease.

■═■

### *Quicknotes*

**ASSIGNMENT** A transaction in which a party conveys his or her entire interest in property to another.

■═■

# Childs v. Warner Brothers Southern Theatres

Lessor (P) v. Reassigning lessee (D)

N.C. Sup. Ct., 200 N.C. 333, 156 S.E. 923 (1931).

**NATURE OF CASE:** Action for unpaid rent.

**FACT SUMMARY:** The lease between Childs's (P) predecessor in interest and Warner's (D) assignor said that the lessee could not assign the lease without the lessor's consent. Childs's (P) consented to the lessee's assignment to Warner (D). Warner (D) then reassigned the lease without Childs's (P) consent.

> 🏛 **RULE OF LAW**
> Where a reasonable construction of a lease leads to the conclusion that the restriction against assignment and subletting operated upon the heirs and assignees of the lessee, as well as upon the lessee himself, the lessor does not waive that restriction of the lease by consenting to one assignment.

**FACTS:** Berkley leased property to Craver. The lease provided that the lessee could not assign the lease without the lessor's written consent. Thereafter, Berkley conveyed the property to Childs (P), and Childs (P) consented to Craver's assignment of the lease to Warner (D). Warner (D) then notified Childs (P) of its intention to reassign to Carolina. Childs (P) replied that it would continue to recognize Warner (D) as lessee of the property and would expect it to see that payments were made in accordance with the lease. Carolina had not paid $450 in rent.

**ISSUE:** If a lease provides that the lessee shall not assign the lease without the lessor's written consent, and, thereafter, the lessor consents to an assignment of the lease, can the assignee subsequently make a valid reassignment of the lease without the lessor's consent?

**HOLDING AND DECISION:** (Brogden, J.) No. Where a reasonable construction of a lease leads to the conclusion that the restriction against assignment and subletting operated upon the heirs and assignees of the lease, as well as upon the lessee himself, the lessor does not waive that restriction of the lease by consenting to one assignment. Here, the lease's habendum clause (the clause defining the extent of the grantee's ownership in the thing granted) expressly included the lessee and his assignees. Moreover, the lessee and his assignees expressly agreed to pay the rent. Further, when Warner (D) informed Childs (P) of its intention to reassign the lease, Childs (P) gave express notice that he would still hold Warner (D) liable for the rent. Hence, a reasonable construction of the lease leads to the conclusion that the restriction against assignment operated upon the lessee's assignees. Judgment for Childs (P) is affirmed.

> ▶ *ANALYSIS*
>
> The general rule is that by giving his consent to an assignment without any restrictions as to future assignments, a lessor waives altogether a restriction in the lease against assignment without his consent. Hence, the lessee or assignee may reassign without the lessor's consent. The fact that the consent is given to a specified person, or that the lease was assigned with all its covenants, terms, and conditions, has been held not to alter the general rule. Likewise, there is good authority for the view contrary to *Childs*.

---

### Quicknotes

**ASSIGNMENT** A transaction in which a party conveys his or her entire interest in property to another.

# 21 Merchants Row Corp. v. Merchants Row, Inc.

Lessee (P) v. Unreasonably nonconsenting lessor (D)

Mass. Sup. Jud. Ct., 412 Mass. 204, 587 N.E.2d 788 (1992).

**NATURE OF CASE:** Appeal from jury verdict awarding damages for breach of lease and interference with contractual relations.

**FACT SUMMARY:** Lessor Merchants Row, Inc. (D) refused to consent to an assignment of the lease by its lessee, 21 Merchants Row Corp. (P).

### 🏛 RULE OF LAW
In a commercial lease, the lessor has no duty to act reasonably in withholding consent to an assignment by the lessee.

**FACTS:** Under the terms of its rental contract, lessee 21 Merchants Row Corp. (P) could not sublet without the prior written consent of the lessor, Merchants Row (D). The contract was silent as to the conditions under which the landlord's consent could be withheld. Merchants Row (D) agreed to the assignment of the lease to a subsequent purchaser of 21 Corp.'s (P) business, but absolutely refused to consent to an assignment to the bank that was financing the purchase. 21 Corp. (P) sued for breach of lease, contending that Merchants Row (D) had unreasonably withheld consent to the assignment. 21 Corp. (P) was awarded more than $3 million by the trial court. Merchants Row (D) appealed.

**ISSUE:** Does the lessor have a duty to act reasonably in withholding consent to an assignment by the lessee?

**HOLDING AND DECISION:** (Lynch, J.) No. In a commercial lease, the lessor does not have a duty to act reasonably in withholding consent to an assignment of the lease. There is no reason to grant greater protection to commercial tenants than that afforded to residential tenants, whose landlords are not held to a reasonableness requirement. Reversed.

### ▸ *ANALYSIS*

The traditional view as exemplified by this case is that the courts will not inquire into the lessor's motives in refusing to consent to an assignment. However, the more modern trend requires the landlord to have a colorable reason for denying the assignment of the commercial lease. Note also that for residential leases, a majority of jurisdictions subscribe to the rule that a lease provision requiring the landlord's consent to an assignment or sublease permits the landlord to refuse arbitrarily or unreasonably.

## *Quicknotes*

**BREACH** The violation of an obligation imposed pursuant to contract or law, by acting or failing to act.

# Easements, Covenants, Servitudes, and Related Interests

## Quick Reference Rules of Law

# Mitchell v. Castellaw

Grantee (D) v. Holder of easement (P)

Tex. Sup. Ct., 151 Tex. 56, 246 S.W.2d 163 (1952).

**NATURE OF CASE:** Suit to establish an easement by implication.

**FACT SUMMARY:** Castellaw (P) sued Mitchell (D) to establish the validity of an easement claimed to have been created by implication or necessity when a former common owner of both their lots allowed an encroachment on Mitchell's (D) parcel to be created.

## 🏛 RULE OF LAW
An easement by implication due to necessity will be recognized only where there is a strict necessity for its existence and not merely a reasonable necessity.

**FACTS:** The dispute concerns three adjacent lots (arbitrarily numbered 1, 2, and 3) originally owned by Stapp. The middle lot (No. 3) was leased to a service station sometime in the 1930s, which lease is still in effect through renewals. Stapp sold lot No. 1 to Smith and in the deed made reference to a driveway on lot No. 1 that had been used as access to the service station. While the deed stated that the grantee, his heirs, or assigns could not build on the area covered by the driveway, the clause reserving the right to use the driveway did not contain words of inheritance or other words of art. Smith sold the lot to Mitchell (D). In the meantime, Stapp had died, and the service station lot (No. 3) passed by inheritance to Castellaw (P). Castellaw (P) brought suit to establish the validity of the driveway easement as an easement appurtenant of unlimited duration. Stapp had also conveyed the other adjacent lot (No. 2) to her daughter, who had then sold it to Mitchell (D) as well. At the time of the conveyance to the daughter there existed a shed, which was part of the service station, that encroached on lot No. 2 about 2½ feet. No mention of this encroachment was made in any of the deeds conveying lot No. 2. It was assumed that neither Stapp nor any of the grantees, until Mitchell (D), were aware of the actual encroachment although the structure was obvious to the eye. Castellaw (P) sued to validate the encroachment as an easement by implication.

**ISSUE:** Will an easement by implication of necessity be found where the necessity is not strict but merely reasonable?

**HOLDING AND DECISION:** (Garwood, J.) No. There is universal recognition that easements may be created by implied grant or implied reservation where the circumstances surrounding the conveyance indicate that such easement was intended by the parties even though the deed may be silent on the subject. But the law is not quick to grant the existence of implied easements. Since a grantee is favored over a grantor in the law, an implied easement by reservation is more difficult to establish than an implied easement by grant. There is conflict among the authorities as to the standard to be applied in determining whether an implied easement has arisen by reason of necessity. Several courts and the Restatement would approve the finding of an implied easement upon the showing of a reasonable necessity. This court is of the opinion, however, that the better standard in this jurisdiction should be that a strict necessity be shown.

## ▶ ANALYSIS

The majority view on the standard to be employed in a determination of an implied easement will depend on whether the easement is by grant or by reservation. Where the easement is to be found by implied grant, there need only be a showing of reasonable necessity. Where, however, an easement by implied reservation is sought, a showing of strict necessity must be made. This is because an easement by implied reservation is in derogation of the grant made. In both instances, there must have been common ownership of both parcels at some time previous and at that time the use sought to be perpetuated created a "quasi easement" on the commonly owned parcels.

■══■

## Quicknotes

**EASEMENT APPURTENANT** A burden attached to real property that either benefits or burdens the owner's right to utilize that property.

**EASEMENT BY IMPLICATION** An easement that is not expressly stated in a deed, but which is inferred upon conveyance, that a portion of one parcel had been used to benefit the other parcel and that upon sale the buyer of the benefited parcel could reasonably expect such benefits to continue.

**EASEMENT BY NECESSITY** An easement that arises by operation of law without which the owner of the benefited property is deprived of the use and enjoyment of his property.

■══■

# Willard v. First Church Of Christ, Scientist, Pacifica

Grantee (P) v. Easement-holding church (D)

Cal. Sup. Ct., 7 Cal. 3d 473 473, 498 P.2d 987 (1972).

**NATURE OF CASE:** Appeal in a quiet title action.

**FACT SUMMARY:** When Petersen bought a lot from McGuigan, the deed reserved an easement on the lot for the use of the First Church Of Christ, Scientist (D). Petersen then sold the lot to the Willards (P) without the easement.

🏛 **RULE OF LAW**
Contrary to the ancient common-law rule, modernly, a grantor, in deeding property to one person, may effectively reserve and vest an interest in the same property in a third party.

**FACTS:** Having bought lot 19 from McGuigan, Petersen also offered to purchase the abutting lot 20 from her in order to sell both lots to the Willards (P). However, McGuigan, a member of the First Church Of Christ, Scientist (D), had always allowed the Church (D) to use the lot for parking. Accordingly, she had a clause included in the deed to Petersen whereby lot 20 was subject to an easement for Church (D) parking to run with the land as long as used for Church (D) purposes. Peterson bought the lot and recorded the deed. However, Peterson did not include the easement in his deed to the Willards (P). When the Willards (P) became aware of it, they brought this quiet title action. At trial, McGuigan testified that she had originally bought lot 20 to provide Church (D) parking and would not have sold it without the easement. The trial court found that, although McGuigan and Petersen intended to convey an easement, the clause was invalidated under the common-law rule that the grantor, in deeding property to one person, cannot reserve an interest in the same property to a third party. The Church (D) appealed.

**ISSUE:** May a grantor, in deeding property to one person, effectively reserve and vest an interest in the same property in a third party?

**HOLDING AND DECISION:** (Peters, Assoc. J.) Yes. Contrary to the ancient common-law rule, modernly, a grantor, in deeding property to one person, may effectively reserve and vest an interest in the same property in a third party. Today, courts try primarily to give effect to the grantor's intent, whereas the common-law rule would defeat the intent. Also, it must be recognized that, due to the encumbrance on the property, the grantee paid a reduced price for it. Therefore, it would be inequitable to allow him to remove the third party's interest, thereby greatly increasing the property's value. The determination of whether the common-law rule should still be used involves a balancing of equitable and policy considerations. In this case, despite Willard's (P) contrary contentions that the grantees and title insurers relied on the common-law rule, we believe the modern position applies. Reversed.

▶ **ANALYSIS**

Because easements are interests in land, they normally must be in compliance with the Statute of Frauds. However, easements may also exist by implication in those instances where the parties have not expressly reserved or granted them in writing. Since these easements are created by operation of law, no writing under the Statute of Frauds is necessary. However, easements by implication arise only when common title to land is severed.

■■■

**Quicknotes**

**ACTION TO QUIET TITLE** Equitable action to resolve conflicting claims to an interest in real property.

**EASEMENT BY IMPLICATION** An easement that is not expressly stated in a deed, but which is inferred upon conveyance, that a portion of one parcel had been used to benefit the other parcel and that upon sale the buyer of the benefited parcel could reasonably expect such benefits to continue.

■■■

# Stoner v. Zucker

Landowner (P) v. User of ditch (D)

Cal. Sup. Ct., 148 Cal. 516, 83 P. 808 (1906).

**NATURE OF CASE:** Action to enjoin a continuing trespass by a licensee.

**FACT SUMMARY:** Stoner (P) gave Zucker (D) a license to build an irrigation ditch on the former's land, but when Stoner (P) revoked the license, Zucker (D) continued to use the ditch.

### 🏛 RULE OF LAW
Where a licensee enters under a parol license and expends money or equivalent labor in execution of the license, the license becomes irrevocable for as long as the nature of license requires.

**FACTS:** Stoner (P) gave Zucker (D) a license to construct an irrigation ditch across his land so Zucker (D) could irrigate his land. Zucker (D) expended more than £7,000 to build the ditch. One year later, Stoner (P) revoked Zucker's (D) license, but Zucker (D) continued to maintain the ditch and use it. Stoner (P) claimed Zucker (D) was a trespasser and sought to enjoin him from further entering the land.

**ISSUE:** Where a parol license is executed by expenditure of money and by its nature was to be continuous in use, does the license become irrevocable?

**HOLDING AND DECISION:** (Henshaw, J.) Yes. Where a licensee enters under a parol license and has expended money, or its equivalent in labor, in execution of the license, the license becomes irrevocable. The licensee, Zucker (D), has a right of entry upon the licenser's (P) lands to maintain his structures or his rights under the license. Such right continues for as long a time as the nature of the license continues. As Zucker (D) expended a considerable sum of money, it would be unjust to permit revocation without allowing an adequate remedy. Zucker (D) will continue to have a license until such time as he no longer requires water or nature stops the flow. Affirmed.

### ▶ ANALYSIS

An executed parol license is the only type of irrevocable license and could be termed an easement by estoppel. The two actually are indistinguishable as the term "irrevocable license" is self-contradictory. One requirement is that the expenditures on the license be reasonably foreseeable. Also, the licensee must rely upon the licenser's apparent intention to permit the licensee to make substantial improvements on the land under license. Such a license is irrevocable only as long as necessary by its nature. If one has a license to fell trees on certain timberland and no suitable trees remain for that purpose, the license terminates. If, here, the water

Zucker (D) was transferring became so polluted so as to be unusable, the license would terminate. The licensee is limited to maintaining his current improvements to the land and cannot expand them.

## *Quicknotes*

**CONTINUING TRESPASS** Unlawful interference with, or damage to, the real or personal property of another that is permanent.

**IRREVOCABLE LICENSE** A right that is granted to a person allowing him or her to conduct an activity that without such permission he or she could not lawfully do, and which is unassignable and revocable at the will of the licensor.

**RIGHT OF ENTRY** An interest in property reserved in the conveyance of a fee that gives the holder the right to resume possession of property upon the happening of a condition subsequent.

# Finn v. Williams

## Grantee (P) v. Landowner (D)

Ill. Sup. Ct., 376 Ill. 95, 33 N.E.2d 226 (1941).

**NATURE OF CASE:** Appeal from judgment establishing an easement by necessity.

**FACT SUMMARY:** Finn's (P) land was entirely landlocked after its purchase from Williams (D).

## 🏛 RULE OF LAW
Where an owner conveys a portion of his land which has no outlet except over the land of the grantor, or of strangers, an easement by necessity exists over the retained land of the grantor.

**FACTS:** Charles Williams owned 140 acres of land. In 1895, he conveyed 40 acres of his holdings to Bacon, and in 1937, Finn (P) acquired title to those 40 acres. Zelphia Williams (D) inherited the remaining 100 acres from Charles, who was her husband. The 40 acres acquired by Finn (P) were entirely landlocked, but for many years access was gained over private roads of strangers and a road over the Williams land. In 1939, Williams (D) refused Finn (P) any further access over her land. By that time all of the other private roads leading out had been closed. Finn (P) was unable to take his stock and produce to market and had to walk to the highway on a footpath carrying what produce he could.

**ISSUE:** Is an easement by necessity created when an owner conveys a portion of his land which has no outlet except over the retained land of the grantor or over the land of strangers?

**HOLDING AND DECISION:** (Wilson, J.) Yes. If at one time there had been unity of title, the easement by necessity will pass with each transfer as appurtenant to the dominant estate and may be exercised at any time by the holder. It makes no difference that the easement was not used earlier. The easement came into existence when the unity of title was split. Where an owner of land conveys a parcel which has no outlet except over the remaining lands of the grantor or over the land of strangers, a right of way by necessity exists over the remaining lands of the grantor. When permission to go over the land of strangers is denied, the subsequent grantees of the dominant estate may avail themselves of the dominant easement implied in the deed severing the dominant and servient estates. Affirmed.

## ▶ *ANALYSIS*

A landlocked parcel of land was about the only situation that the common-law courts would recognize as creating an easement by necessity. This was the strict necessity view of such easements. In recent years, some American courts have refused to create an easement by necessity even for landlocked parcels. Their reasoning was that to do so would be to sanction a form of private eminent domain. Since only a governmental unit holds the power of eminent domain, it was the obligation of the landlocked owner to prevail upon the appropriate governmental unit to condemn a right of way and build a public road.

■■■

## *Quicknotes*

**DOMINANT ESTATE** Property whose owners benefit from the use of another's property.

**EASEMENT BY NECESSITY** An easement that arises by operation of law without which the owner of the benefited property is deprived of the use and enjoyment of his property.

**LANDLOCKED** Property that is entirely surrounded by property owned by another person or persons and which cannot be accessed without passing through such surrounding property.

■■■

# Granite Properties Limited Partnership v. Manns

Shopping center owner (P) v. Property owner (D)

Ill. Sup. Ct., 117 Ill. 2d 425, 512 N.E.2d 1230 (1987).

**NATURE OF CASE:** Appeal from granting of permanent injunction.

**FACT SUMMARY:** Granite Properties Limited Partnership (P) claimed two easements over driveways existing on the Mannses' (D) property.

## 🏛 RULE OF LAW

Where the prior use of the land supports the inference of the parties' intention to create an implied easement the required extent of the claimed easement's necessity will be less than when necessity is the only circumstance from which the inference of intention will be drawn.

**FACTS:** Granite Properties Limited Partnership (P) owned a shopping center and an apartment complex. Granite (P) previously owned property located between the center and complex which it sold to Mr. and Mrs. Manns (D). The Mannses (D) have not developed this property. Granite (P) sued the Mannses (D), seeking to enjoin the Mannses (D) from interfering with Granite's (P) use of two claimed easements over driveways which exist on Granite's (P) former property. The first claimed easement provides access to the rear of the shopping center. It is used for deliveries, trash storage and removal, and utilities repair. It would be very inconvenient and disruptive to store operations to accommodate deliveries through the front door. The other easement concerns ingress and egress over a driveway which leads into the parking area of Granite's (P) apartment complex. The driveway provides the only direct access from the parking lot to the street. Other potential driveways would be dangerous and impractical. The circuit court entered judgment for the Mannses (D) on both easement claims. Following Granite's (P) post-trial motion, the court granted a permanent injunction as to the claimed apartment complex easement but affirmed its decision as to the shopping center easement. Both parties appealed. The appellate court granted Granite (P) easements by implication over both driveways. The Mannses (D) appealed. Granite (P) contends to this court that the driveways in question are apparent and obvious, permanent and subject to continuous, uninterrupted use by Granite (P) and its predecessors until the time it sold the property to the Mannses (D) and that both driveways are highly convenient and reasonably necessary for the beneficial use and enjoyment of the shopping center and the apartment complex.

**ISSUE:** If the prior use of the land supposes the inference of the parties' intention to create an implied easement, will the required extent of the claimed easement's necessity be less than when necessity is the only circumstance from which the inference of intention may be drawn?

**HOLDING AND DECISION:** (Ryan, J.) Yes. Where the prior use of the land supports the inference of the parties' intention to create an implied easement, the required extent of the claimed easement's necessity will be less than when necessity is the only circumstance from which the inference of intention will be drawn. The inference of intention of the parties to create the easement is implied from the circumstances surrounding the conveyance. The circumstances surrounding the conveyance from Granite (P) to the Mannses (D) show that the driveways were permanent in character, and that the Mannses (D) were aware of Granite's (P) prior uses of the driveways. While some showing of necessity for the continuance of the use must be shown where a prior use has been made, to the extent that the prior use strengthens the implication, the degree of necessity requisite for implication is reduced. Given the strong evidence of Granite's (P) prior use of the driveways before the conveyance, and the Mannses' (D) knowledge of that use, we agree with the appellate court that the necessity requirement is fulfilled. Affirmed and remanded.

## ▶ ANALYSIS

The court ruled in favor of Granite (P) even though it was the former owner and conveyor of the property on which the claimed easements were located and failed to reserve easements in the land it conveyed. Other courts take a stricter approach toward implied reservation of easements than in implied grants and refuse to recognize the former without a showing of strict necessity of the easement to the conveyor.

■■■

## Quicknotes

**IMPLIED EASEMENT** An easement that is not expressly stated in a deed, but which is inferred upon conveyance, that a portion of one parcel had been used to benefit the other parcel and that upon sale the buyer of the benefited parcel could reasonably expect such benefits to continue.

■■■

# Beebe v. DeMarco

Landowner (P) v. Landowner (D)

Or. Ct. App., 157 Or. App. 176, 968 P.2d 396 (1998).

**NATURE OF CASE:** Suit for prescriptive easement.

**FACT SUMMARY:** Plaintiffs claimed a prescriptive easement in a 12-foot wide roadway across defendants' property.

## 🏛 RULE OF LAW
To establish a prescriptive easement, a claimant must show by clear and convincing evidence an open and notorious use of defendant's land adverse to the rights of defendant for a continuous and uninterrupted period of ten years.

**FACTS:** Plaintiff purchased a lot in the River Acres subdivision in 1957, and defendants owned a lot three lots west of plaintiff's lot. In 1958, a new subdivision, Hidden Acres, was built, and a six-foot-wide alley ran behind the rear lots in plaintiff and defendant's block. In 1979, plaintiff built a large shop at the rear of their lot. In 1994, defendants divided their lot into three parcels. They entered into an agreement with DeMarco to build a house on the southernmost parcel, adjacent to the alley. During that construction, defendants erected a high wooden fence blocking plaintiff's path across the rear of lot 14. Plaintiff sued claiming an easement by prescription. The trial court determined plaintiff acquired a prescriptive easement and enjoined defendants from obstructing or hindering its use. Defendants appealed.

**ISSUE:** To establish a prescriptive easement, must a claimant show by clear and convincing evidence an open and notorious use of defendant's land adverse to the rights of defendant for a continuous and uninterrupted period of ten years?

**HOLDING AND DECISION:** (Riggs, J.) Yes. To establish a prescriptive easement, a claimant must show by clear and convincing evidence an open and notorious use of defendant's land adverse to the rights of defendant for a continuous and uninterrupted period of ten years. The record is clear that use of the roadway by plaintiff was sufficiently continuous to satisfy the requirements for a prescriptive easement. Continuous use does not mean constant use; it is only necessary to show the claimant made such use of the land as his needs required. Plaintiff used the roadway only when necessary to gain access to their property; at first during the summers, and later as much as five times a week. They never showed an intent to abandon its use. Affirmed.

## ▶ ANALYSIS

The use of an easement for the statutory period is presumptively adverse. That presumption may be rebutted by a showing that the plaintiffs used the roadway in a manner that did not interfere with defendant's use of the property or by showing that such use was permissive rather than hostile. Defendants here failed to overcome this presumption.

## Quicknotes

**ADVERSE POSSESSION** A means of acquiring title to real property by remaining in actual, open, continuous, exclusive possession of property for the statutory period.

**CLEAR AND CONVINCING EVIDENCE** An evidentiary standard requiring a demonstration that the fact sought to be proven is reasonably certain.

**PRESCRIPTIVE EASEMENT** A manner of acquiring an easement in another's property by continuous and uninterrupted use in satisfaction of the statutory requirements of adverse possession.

**PRESUMPTION** A rule of law requiring the court to presume certain facts to be true based on the existence of other facts, thereby shifting the burden of proof to the party against whom the presumption is asserted to rebut.

# State ex rel. Thornton v. Hay

State (P) v. Oceanfront property owner (D)

Or. Sup. Ct., 254 Or. 584, 462 P.2d 671 (1969).

**NATURE OF CASE:** Action seeking an injunction.

**FACT SUMMARY:** The State (P) sought to enjoin the Hays (D) from constructing fences enclosing the dry-sand area contained within the legal description of their oceanfront property.

## 🏛 RULE OF LAW
On the basis of the custom of the people of the state to use the dry-sand area of the beaches for public recreation, the public has rights in dry-sand areas contained within legal descriptions of oceanfront property, and the state can prevent landowners from enclosing such areas.

**FACTS:** The Hays (D) wanted to construct fences enclosing the dry-sand area of the beach within the legal description of their oceanfront property. They had a motel on their property. The dry-sand area in the State (P) had been used by the general public for recreational purposes since the beginning of the State's (P) political history. In the area around the Hays' (D) property, State (P) and local officers policed the dry sand, and municipal sanitary crews cleaned there. The area could not be conveniently used by the Hays (D) for any other purposes. The State (P) sought to prevent the enclosure.

**ISSUE:** Does the state have the power to prevent landowners from enclosing the dry-sand area contained within the legal description of their oceanfront property?

**HOLDING AND DECISION:** (Goodwin, J.) Yes. Here the public use was long and continuous. There was no suggestion that permission for such use was sought or given. Rather, the public used the land under a claim of right. Hence, the requirements for acquisition by prescription have been met here. However, the best basis for the decision in this case is the English doctrine of custom. This is because prescription applies only to the tract of land before the court, while an established custom can be proven with reference to a larger region. The public's longstanding use of dry-sand areas satisfies the requirement that a custom must be ancient. Secondly, the public's use has been uninterrupted as is required of customs. The third requirement, that the customary use be peaceable and free from dispute, is satisfied by the evidence which related to the second requirement. The requirement of reasonableness is satisfied by the evidence that the public has always used the land in an appropriate manner. The requirement of certainty is satisfied by the visible boundaries of the dry-sand area. The requirement that a custom must be obligatory is satisfied by the showing that no landowner has ever questioned the public's right. Lastly, a custom must not be repugnant or inconsistent with other customs or law. The custom here violates no law and is not repugnant. Hence, this custom should be affirmed as the source of the rule of law that the public has rights to dry-sand areas contained within legal descriptions of oceanfront property, and the state can prevent landowners from enclosing such areas. Affirmed.

**CONCURRENCE:** (Denecke, J.) I would base the public's right on: (1) long usage by the public of the dry-sands area; (2) a universal and long-held belief by the public in the public's right to such use; (3) long and universal acquiescence by the landowners in such public use; and (4) the extreme desirability to the public of the right to use such areas.

## ▶ ANALYSIS

Access to the portions of the beach which the public is entitled to use may be blocked by development of the upland. A California statute requires subdividers of land fronting the ocean to provide reasonable public access to the land below the high-water mark. In *Hudson v. Board of Supervisors*, 3 ERC 1415, a County Board of Supervisors was ordered to comply with this statute.

■■

## Quicknotes

**CLAIM OF RIGHT** Person claiming a right in property is in possession and intends to claim ownership of that property without regard to the record title owner.

**PRESCRIPTIVE EASEMENT** A manner of acquiring an easement in another's property by continuous and uninterrupted use in satisfaction of the statutory requirements of adverse possession.

■■

# S.S. Kresge Co. v. Winkelman Realty Co.

Landowner (P) v. User of alleyway (D)

Wis. Sup. Ct., 260 Wis. 372, 50 N.W.2d 920 (1952).

**NATURE OF CASE:** Suit for injunction.

**FACT SUMMARY:** The owner of an easement created by prescription for ingress and egress was using the easement as a delivery route for several lots adjacent to the original dominant estate.

## RULE OF LAW

A prescriptive easement acquired by a particular use of the servient property will not justify an added use in connection with the dominant property in a manner far different from that employed under the original use.

**FACTS:** Winkelman (D) acquired several adjacent lots fronting on Washington Street from various previous owners. The middle lot had previously been owned by Dern, who had maintained a barbershop and residence on his property. Dern, and his successor, Tisch, had used an alleyway leading from the back of their property out to Jefferson Street directly behind. The alley crossed land owned by Kresge (P). When Kresge (P) had previously attempted to close the alley, a prescriptive easement had been declared in favor of the Tisch-Dern property. When Winkelman (D) acquired this property along with the properties on either side, they remodeled all the existing structures and began using the alley as a delivery route to service all the stores they maintained on their entire holdings. Kresge (P) brought suit to enjoin this additional use, contending that it was an excessive burden on the easement in favor of the one lot.

**ISSUE:** May the owner of a prescriptive easement make use of the easement in a manner far different in nature and scope than the use which created the easement?

**HOLDING AND DECISION:** (Broadfoot, J.) No. An easement can only be used in connection with the estate to which it is appurtenant. A prescriptive easement acquired by a particular use of the servient estate will not justify an added use in connection with the dominant estate in a manner far different from that employed under the original use. This easement was acquired by prescription for the benefit of a lot containing a barbershop and a residence. Winkelman's (D) use of this easement to service not only the original dominant property but the adjacent lots as well, is clearly an added burden on the servient estate. This added burden is enjoinable lest it ripen into a prescriptive right as well. On appeal, Kresge (P) has asked that all use of the alleyway be enjoined since it is very difficult to determine which use is solely assignable to the original dominant estate. Since this request did not form a part of the original pleading, it need not be considered. Affirmed.

## ANALYSIS

A person acquiring a prescriptive easement does not take exclusive possession of the land but merely makes use of it in an adverse manner that is open and notorious for the prescriptive period. The person acquiring a prescriptive easement need not make exclusive use of the land and may, in fact, share the use with others, including the landowner.

## Quicknotes

**DOMINANT ESTATE** Property whose owners benefit from the use of another's property.

**PRESCRIPTIVE EASEMENT** A manner of acquiring an easement in another's property by continuous and uninterrupted use in satisfaction of the statutory requirements of adverse possession.

**SERVIENT ESTATE** Property that is burdened in some aspect for the benefit of a dominant estate.

# Sakansky v. Wein

Holder of dominant estate (P) v. Holder of servient estate (D)

N.H. Sup. Ct., 86 N.H. 337, 169 A. 1 (1933).

**NATURE OF CASE:** Suit for injunction.

**FACT SUMMARY:** The owner of a servient estate planned to erect a building that would obstruct the height clearance over a general access easement but to provide an alternate unobstructed access route to the dominant estate.

## 🏛 RULE OF LAW
The rule of reason as applied to a dispute over the scope of an easement is to be used to interpret general language but may not be used to alter the express terms of the easement.

**FACTS:** Sakansky (P) owned a parcel of land which included an easement for general access over land owned by Wein (D). The easement had been created in a deed in 1849. It was specifically described as to its width and location on Wein's (D) property. Wein (D) proposed to construct a building over the easement leaving a right of way which was restricted to eight feet in height. He also proposed to create a second right of way around the new building which would have no height restriction. Sakansky (P) sought an injunction to prevent any obstruction of the height clearance over the original easement.

**ISSUE:** In determining the scope of a general access easement, may the rule of reason be used to alter the express terms of that easement?

**HOLDING AND DECISION:** (Woodbury, J.) No. The trial court was correct in determining that the rights of both the dominant and servient estate holders were to be determined by the rule of reason. However, this rule may be applied only to interpret general language in the original grant of the easement. It may not be used to alter the express terms of the easement contract. Within that framework, the rule will not be used to give unreasonable rights or impose unreasonable burdens. In this case, the location of the easement is specifically described. The rule of reason may not be applied to alter its location. Sakansky (P) is entitled to the reasonable use of the granted easement. The eight-foot height restriction proposed is an unreasonable restriction. Sakansky (P) cannot be forced to use another route. While Sakansky (P) cannot insist upon an unlimited height clearance, further hearings are needed, if requested, to determine what is reasonable. Case discharged.

## ▶ ANALYSIS

The court also pointed out that the nature of the use of the easement was not to be determined by the facts as they existed at the time of the original grant. The reasonableness of the dominant estate's use was to be judged by current circumstances. Thus, in this case, the fact that the easement was originally granted in horse and buggy days would not prohibit the modern day use of automobiles and trucks.

## Quicknotes

**DOMINANT ESTATE** Property whose owners benefit from the use of another's property.

**SERVIENT ESTATE** Property that is burdened in some aspect for the benefit of a dominant estate.

# Lindsey v. Clark

Servient owner (P) v. Grantor (D)

Va. Sup. Ct. of App., 193 Va. 522, 69 S.E.2d 342 (1952).

**NATURE OF CASE:** Suit for injunction.

**FACT SUMMARY:** Clark (D) had granted a lot adjacent to his own, reserving an easement in the deed. By mistake he had been using a strip other than the reserved easement. Lindsey (P), the owner of the servient property, contended Clark (D) had abandoned the reserved easement by nonuse.

## 🏛 RULE OF LAW
Mere nonuse of an easement created by deed, for a period however long, will not constitute abandonment unless there is also a clear manifestation of intent to abandon by the easement holder.

**FACTS:** Clark (D) had originally owned four contiguous lots facing on the same street. He had built a house on two of the lots for himself and had conveyed the front two-thirds of the other two lots to his son-in-law. In the conveyance to his son-in-law, Clark (D) had reserved an easement along the south side of the lots for access to the rear one-third. He built a rental dwelling on this rear portion. The son-in-law built a house on the lots conveyed to him. Apparently by mistake, Clark had used a strip on the north side of the conveyed lots for the access easement. The son-in-law sold his property by a deed which noted the easement. The land was ultimately sold to Lindsey (P) by a deed which did not mention the easement. The strip actually used for access to the rear property had been used continually as a driveway, and Lindsey (P) had actual notice of this fact. Lindsey (P) finally brought suit to enjoin the use of the driveway, claiming it was not the reserved easement and that the reserved easement had been abandoned by nonuse.

**ISSUE:** May an easement created by deed be abandoned by mere nonuse without a manifested intent to abandon by the easement holder?

**HOLDING AND DECISION:** (Buchanan, J.) No. Abandonment is a question of intention. A person entitled to a right of way or easement in land may abandon and extinguish that right by express instrument. He may also abandon by a cessation of use coupled with acts or circumstances clearly showing an intent to abandon. But mere nonuse of an easement created by deed, for a period however long, will not amount to abandonment. There must also be a clear manifestation of intent to abandon. A right of way will not be extinguished by the habitual use of another convenient way unless there is a clear intent to abandon the prescribed easement. The burden of proof to show abandonment is on the servient estate holder. It is

clear that Clark's (D) use of the wrong right of way was a mistake, and there was no intent to abandon the reserved easement. Because of this mistake, Clark (D) did not object when his son-in-law built over part of the reserved easement. Lindsey (P) had actual notice of the way being used and constructive notice of the reserved easement. Since it would be impractical to tear down part of the house, the right of way that has actually been used will be deemed to be the reserved easement, and a decree so fixing the rights of the parties shall be issued. Affirmed and remanded.

## ▶ ANALYSIS

A recorded easement will always give constructive notice to subsequent purchasers of the servient estate whether the easement is actually observable or not. But when an easement has been created by prescription or implication and is not discoverable by inspection, a subsequent purchaser of the servient estate must have actual notice or the easement may be extinguished. The holder of an implied or prescriptive easement should demand a deed showing the easement and if that is refused should request a court of equity to declare his right.

■■■

## Quicknotes

**IMPLIED EASEMENT** An easement that is not expressly stated in a deed, but which is inferred upon conveyance, that a portion of one parcel had been used to benefit the other parcel and that upon sale the buyer of the benefited parcel could reasonably expect such benefits to continue.

**TERMINATION OF EASEMENT (BY ABANDONMENT)** Conduct on the part of the user of an easement demonstrating an intent to abandon the easement and not to reclaim it.

■■■

# Gallagher v. Bell

Owner of house (D) v. Owner of land (P)

Md. Ct. Spec. App., 69 Md. App. 199, 516 A.2d 1028 (1986).

**NATURE OF CASE:** Appeal from award of damages.

**FACT SUMMARY:** Gallagher (D) owned a house in the middle of land owned by Bell (P) and sold the land.

## 🏛 RULE OF LAW
A covenant will be considered to run with the land if (1) the covenant touches and concerns the land; (2) the original covenanting parties intend the covenant to run; and (3) there is privity of estate.

**FACTS:** In 1960, Gallagher (D) bought a house situated on a half-acre of land. Gallagher's (D) property was located in the middle of land owned by Bell (P). When Bell (P) purchased his land in 1959, the sales contract provided that subsequent purchasers of the house and half-acre tract would agree to dedicate half of the street bounding the tract and share in the cost of installing streets and utilities installed by Bell (P). Gallagher's (D) 1960 contract regarding his purchase of the house and tract referred to his obligation as buyer of the property to make the dedication and pro rata contribution. The contract further agreed that the obligations would be binding on the principals and their respective heirs, successors, and assigns and that its provisions would "survive the execution and delivery of the deed." In 1961, Bell (P) and Gallagher (D) entered into an agreement in which Bell (P) granted Gallagher (D) an easement in exchange for reaffirming his obligations under the 1960 contract. In 1979, Gallagher (D) sold his land to Ms. Camalier, who knew of Bell (P) and Gallagher's (D) 1961 agreement and insisted on indemnity from Gallagher (D). Bell (P) finally started on the roads in the area of the Gallagher/Camalier property and made a demand to Ms. Camalier for her pro rata contribution. She refused payment, relying on her indemnity agreement with Gallagher (D). Then, Bell (P) made the demand on Gallagher (D). When Gallagher (D) refused to pay, Bell (P) sued Gallagher (D). Gallagher (D) defended the action on the basis that his 1961 obligation was a covenant running with the land and that his liability ended when he conveyed the property to Ms. Camalier. The court submitted the issue of a covenant to the jury, and the jury returned a verdict for Bell (P) and awarded Bell (P) damages. Gallagher (D) appealed.

**ISSUE:** Should a covenant be considered to run with the land if (1) the covenant touches and concerns the land; (2) the original covenanting parties intend the covenant to run; and (3) there is privity of estate?

**HOLDING AND DECISION:** (Wilner, J.) Yes. A covenant will be considered to run with the land if (1) the covenant touches and concerns the land; (2) the original covenanting parties intend the covenant to run; and (3) there is privity of estate. For a covenant to run with the land, it must extend to the land so that the obligation to be done will affect the quality, value, and mode of enjoying the estate conveyed and constitute a condition appurtenant to it. There is no doubt that a covenantee such as Ms. Camalier would be benefited by performance of the covenant and that their interest in the land would be more valuable by it. The intent requirement is shown by Gallagher's (D) insertion of the covenant in the 1961 contract and the fact that the obligation was expressly assigned to the assigns and successors of Gallagher (D). The existence of the indemnity agreement shows that Ms. Camalier recognized her obligation, and she tried to obtain recourse from the original covenantor. The modern view is that only vertical privity is required. Vertical privity requires that the person presently being subjected to the burden is a successor to the estate of the original person burdened. Here, it is clear that Ms. Camalier was a successor of Gallagher (D). Therefore, the privity requirement is satisfied. We can conclude that the covenant in question—to pay a pro rata share of the cost of the streets—was one that ran with the land. Because the covenant ran with the land, Gallagher's (D) obligation ended when he severed his relationship to the land by conveying it to Ms. Camalier. Reversed.

## ▶ ANALYSIS

Many traditional elements required for a covenant have been modified or abandoned over time. Most courts have repudiated the in esse doctrine requiring the covenantor to expressly bind his assigns if the covenant dealt with something which was not yet in existence. Nevertheless, the phrase "heirs, successors, and assigns" should be included as evidence that the parties intended the covenant in question to run with the land.

■═■

## Quicknotes

**PRIVITY OF ESTATE** Common or successive relation to the same right in property.

**TOUCH AND CONCERN** The requirement, in order for a covenant to be binding upon successors, that the covenant enhance the use or value of the benefited party.

■═■

# Neponsit Property Owners' Ass'n v. Emigrant Industrial Savings Bank

Property owners (P) v. Bank (D)

N.Y. Ct. of App., 278 N.Y. 248, 15 N.E.2d 793 (1938).

**NATURE OF CASE:** Action to foreclose a lien upon land.

**FACT SUMMARY:** Neponsit Property Owners (P) claimed that Emigrant Bank's (D) deed to certain property conveyed such property subject to a covenant contained in the original deed which provided for the payment by all subsequent purchasers of an annual improvements charge.

## RULE OF LAW

A covenant in a deed subjecting land to an annual charge for improvements to the surrounding residential tract is enforceable by the property owners' association against subsequent purchasers if: (1) grantor and grantee so intended; (2) it appears that the covenant is one touching or concerning the land; and (3) privity of estate is shown between the party claiming benefit of the covenant and the party under the burden of such covenant.

**FACTS:** Neponsit Property Owners' (P) assignor, Neponsit Realty Company, conveyed the land now owned by Emigrant Bank (D) to R. Deyer and wife by deed. That original deed contained a covenant providing: (1) that he conveyed land should be subject to an annual charge or improvements upon the entire residential tract then being developed; (2) that such charge should be a lien; (3) such charge should be payable by all subsequent purchasers to the company or its assigns, including a property owners' association which might thereafter be organized; and (4) such covenant runs with the land. Neponsit Property Owners (P) brought action based upon the above covenant to foreclose a lien upon the land which Emigrant Bank (D) now owns, having purchased it at a judicial sale. Emigrant Bank (D) appealed from an order denying their motion for judgment on the pleadings.

**ISSUE:** Does a covenant in the original deed subjecting land to an annual charge for improvements run with the land and create a lien which is enforceable against subsequent owners by Neponsit Property Owners (P)?

**HOLDING AND DECISION:** (Lehman, J.) Yes. A covenant will run with the land and will be enforceable against a subsequent purchaser if: (1) the grantor and grantee intend that the covenant run with the land; (2) the covenant touches or concerns the land with which it runs; (3) there is privity of estate between the party claiming benefit of the covenant and the party who rests under the burden of the covenant. In the instant case, the grantor and grantee manifested their intent that the covenant run with the land by so stating in the original deed. The covenant touches or concerns the land in substance if not in

form, i.e., the covenant alters the legal rights of ownership for the land, by providing that the burden of paying the cost of maintaining public improvement is inseparably attached to the land which enjoys the benefits of such improvements. The concept of privity of estate between the parties usually requires that the party claiming benefit from the enforcement of a covenant own the property which benefits from such enforcement. Although Neponsit Property Owners (P), the corporation, does not own the property which would benefit from enforcement, the corporation is acting as the agent of property owners and should therefore be considered in privity in substance if not in form. Since the covenant complies with the legal requirements for one which runs with the land and is enforceable against subsequent purchasers, the order which denied Emigrant Bank's (D) option for judgment on the pleadings is affirmed.

## ANALYSIS

It has been suggested that the technical requirements which determine the enforceability of covenants as to future parties, e.g., *Neponsit*, might well be abandoned and that the intention of the covenanting parties be the sole criterion. This suggestion is supported by the following developments: (1) the benefit of a contract may now be assigned or even created initially for the benefit of a third person; (2) recording systems, though imperfect, afford much protection to the purchaser of land against outstanding burdens of which he may be unaware. It should be noted, however, that the unrestricted enforcement of covenants may seriously impair the usefulness of land. A student reading this case should keep in mind that *Neponsit* is not concerned with the enforcement of covenants between original covenanting parties. That question of enforceability is left to the contracts course.

---

### Quicknotes

**PRIVITY OF ESTATE** Common or successive relation to the same right in property.

**"RUN WITH THE LAND"** Covenants that are binding on successor in interest to the property to which they are attached.

**TOUCH AND CONCERN** The requirement, in order for a covenant to be binding upon successors, that the covenant enhance the use or value of the benefited party.

# Tulk v. Moxhay

Fee owner (P) v. Deed purchaser (D)

Ct. of Chancery, 2 Phillips 774, 41 Eng. Rep. 1143 (1848).

**NATURE OF CASE:** Bill for injunction to enforce covenant in deed.

**FACT SUMMARY:** Moxhay (D) indicated an intention to build upon an open ground, even though he was aware of an original, prohibitive covenant passed on by Tulk (P), forty years earlier, which forbade any construction on the ground.

## 🏛 RULE OF LAW
Privity of estate notwithstanding, a person who acquires real property with notice of a restriction placed upon it will not be allowed, in equity, to violate its terms.

**FACTS:** Tulk (P), owner in fee of a piece of ground, as well as adjacent houses, sold the property to Elms. A covenant in the deed of conveyance prohibited Elms and his assigns from ever constructing upon the ground. The piece of land eventually came into the hands of Moxhay (D), whose purchase deed contained no similar covenant, yet Moxhay (D) admitted he knew of the original covenant. When Moxhay (D) indicated he wanted to build on the piece of ground, Tulk (P) successfully obtained an injunction.

**ISSUE:** Can the purchaser of a deed of conveyance containing a restriction violate the restriction if he has notice of the original covenant?

**HOLDING AND DECISION:** (The Lord Chancellor) No. To hold otherwise would make it impossible for an owner of land to sell part of it without running the risk of seeing the part he retained rendered worthless. At issue is not whether a party may violate a contract entered into by his vendor by using the land in an inconsistent manner. If there were a mere agreement and no covenant, a court would enforce it against a party purchasing with notice; so long as an equity is attached by an owner, no one purchasing with notice can stand in a different situation than the original purchaser.

## ▶ ANALYSIS

Notice is the key element of the principle, commonly referred to as "the doctrine of *Tulk v. Moxhay*," enunciated in this case. Notice of the restriction may be either actual, inquiry, or record. The rights and obligations recognized here are variously named but are generally known as "equitable servitudes." The restriction in the transfer of land need not be embodied in a covenant—an informal contract or agreement is sufficient. A party intended to receive the benefit, as well as the original covenantor, can bring the suit in equity. However, proof of notice is essential to the doctrine.

■≡■

## Quicknotes

**EQUITABLE SERVITUDE** Land use restriction enforceable in equity.

■≡■

# London County Council v. Allen

Municipal council (P) v. Landowner (D)

Court of Appeal, 3 K.B. 642, Ann. Cas. 1916C 932 (1914).

**NATURE OF CASE:** Action to enforce covenant against assignee of land.

**FACT SUMMARY:** Landowner Allen (D), after entering into an agreement with the London County Council (P) whereby he promised not to build on certain areas of his land, transferred his interest in the land to his wife (D), who built three structures on the property.

🏛 **RULE OF LAW**
If the benefit of a covenant does not run to a particular piece of property, the covenant cannot be enforced against an assignee of the land burdened.

**FACTS:** Allen (D), a builder and landowner, entered into a covenant with London County Council (P) in which he agreed not to build any structures upon certain portions of his land. The covenant also stated that notice of the covenant would be given upon any conveyance, mortgage, transfer, or lease of the property. He subsequently conveyed the land to his wife, Mrs. Allen (D), and she built three structures on it. London County Council (P) issued a writ claiming a mandatory injunction to knock down the structures. Allen (D) filed a demurrer claiming that since the London County Council (P) were not actual owners of the benefitted property, they could not enforce the covenant, whether Mrs. Allen (D) had notice of its existence or not.

**ISSUE:** Can the benefit of a covenant be asserted against an assignee of the land burdened if the covenant does not run to a specific piece of land?

**HOLDING AND DECISION:** (Scrutton, J.) No. If the benefit of a covenant does not run to a particular piece of property, the covenant cannot be enforced against an assignee of the land burdened. Because the benefit of the covenant in this case did not run to a specific piece of property, the covenant cannot be enforced against Mrs. Allen (D), the assignee. The covenant was in essence a personal one because the London County Council (P) was not the owner of land adjoining Allen's (D) property. Even though Mrs. Allen (D) had notice of the covenant at the time of the transfer of the property, she is not bound by it and the structures may remain. The judgement against Allen (D) stands, however. Mrs. Allen's (D) demurrer is granted; Allen's (D) appeal is dismissed.

▶ **ANALYSIS**

While this rule is still followed by the majority of American courts today, there are a number of jurisdictions that will enforce a covenant against an assignee even when the benefit is not to a piece of land. Particularly when the assignee had notice of the covenant, this result is arguably more fair. Even the court in *London County Council v. Allen* was pained to decide the case in favor of Mrs. Allen (D) and noted in their opinion that they were "not at all favourably impressed with her conduct as a good citizen."

■══■

## Quicknotes

**ASSIGNMENT** A transaction in which a party conveys his or her entire interest in property to another.

**TOUCH AND CONCERN** The requirement, in order for a covenant to be binding upon successors, that the covenant enhance the use or value of the benefited party.

■══■

# Sprague v. Kimball

Grantee (P) v. Grantor of multiple lots (D)

Mass. Sup. Jud. Ct., 213 Mass. 380, 100 N.E. 622 (1913).

**NATURE OF CASE:** Suit for specific performance of deed restrictions.

**FACT SUMMARY:** Kimball (D) conveyed five separate adjacent lots to different grantees. The deeds to all but one lot contained restrictive covenants, and Sprague (P), the owner of one of the restricted lots, sought to have the restrictions enforced against the fifth lot.

## 🏛 RULE OF LAW
Equitable servitudes create an interest enforceable against the land burdened so long as the restrictions sought to be enforced are in writing.

**FACTS:** Kimball (D) owned a tract of land for which he had recorded a plan. The plan outlined five separate lots which were sold at different times to different grantees. While the plan indicated no restrictions on the use of the property, each of the deeds referred to the plan, and the first four contained a restrictive covenant that basically limited the property to residential use with a minimum setback from the street. The covenant, however, did not bind Kimball (D) to restrict the other lots in the tract to the same use. Sprague (P), the owner of one of the restricted lots, sought to have the restriction enforced against the fifth lot which had been sold without the deed restrictions. Sprague (P) alleged that as part of the inducement for his purchase, Kimball (D) had orally promised that all the deeds would contain the restriction.

**ISSUE:** Will an equitable servitude be enforceable against a burdened estate if it has not been reduced to writing?

**HOLDING AND DECISION:** (Braley, J.) No. While the plan contained no reference to the restrictions, the restrictions as expressed in the deeds are uniform, and it is clear that Kimball (D) intended that all the lots would be subject to the same restrictions as they were sold. The lots as they were conveyed were burdened with the restriction and were also vested with a right of enforcement against the other lots. Each grantee was granted an equitable servitude which, when conveyed, must be evidenced by a writing to be enforceable. The plan did not refer to the restrictions, and the individual deeds did not create a right of enforcement against the other lots in the plan. Kimball's (D) oral promise is not sufficient to create an enforceable right. The part performance doctrine will not be invoked to create an interest in land not evidenced by a writing. The suit cannot be maintained, and the bill must be dismissed.

## ▶ ANALYSIS

An equitable servitude is a real property interest. As such it must be conveyed by a written instrument. The writing can be a provision in the deed or other instrument of conveyance. It may also be evidenced by a separate agreement between the landowners involved. More modernly, it can also be shown by a recorded subdivision plot map. This latter method is the most common form for restricting a large number of lots in a given area.

■■■

## Quicknotes

**EQUITABLE SERVITUDE** Land use restriction enforceable in equity.

**RESTRICTIVE COVENANT** A promise contained in a deed to limit the uses to which the property will be made.

**SUBDIVISION PLOT** A parcel of land that is divided into portions to be resold or developed.

■■■

# Sanborn v. McLean

Adjoining landowner (P) v. Gas station builder (D)

Mich. Sup. Ct., 233 Mich. 227, 206 N.W. 496 (1925).

**NATURE OF CASE:** Action to enjoin erection of gasoline filling station.

**FACT SUMMARY:** Sanborn (P) and McLean (D) trace the titles to their adjoining lots to the proprietor of the subdivision. Residences are built on all the surrounding lots. Sanborn (P) objected to McLean's (D) erection of a gas station on her lot.

## 🏛 RULE OF LAW
If the owner of two or more lots, which are situated so as to bear a relation to each other, sells one with restrictions which are of benefit to the land retained, during the period of restraint, the owner of the lot or lots retained can do nothing forbidden to the owner of the lot said. This is the doctrine of reciprocal negative easements.

**FACTS:** On December 28, 1892, McLaughlin, who was then owner of the lots on Collingwood Avenue, deeded four of the lots with the restriction that only residences would be built on the lots. On July 24, 1893, McLaughlin conveyed several more lots with the same restriction. Sanborn (P) traces title to McLaughlin. McLean's (D) title runs back to a deed dated September 7, 1893, which does not contain the restrictions. No buildings other than residences have been erected on any of the lots of the subdivision.

**ISSUE:** (1) If the owner of two or more lots, which are situated so as to bear a relation to each other, sells one with restrictions which are of benefit to the land retained, during the period of restraint, can the owner of the lot or lots retained do anything forbidden to the owner of the lot sold? (2) Is a reciprocal negative easement personal to owners?

**HOLDING AND DECISION:** (Wiest, J.) (1) No. The doctrine of reciprocal negative easements makes restrictions which are of benefit to the land retained mutual so that the owner can do nothing upon the land he has retained that is forbidden to the owner of the lot sold. In this case McLaughlin deeded lots with the restriction that only residences be built on them. Such restrictions were imposed for the benefit of the lands retained by McLaughlin to carry out the scheme of a residential district, and a restrictive negative easement attached to the lots retained. Since his was one of the lots retained in the December 1892 and July 1893 deeds, a reciprocal negative easement attached to the lot which later became McLean's (D). (2) No. Reciprocal negative easements are not personal to owners but are operative upon use of the land by any owner having actual or constructive notice thereof. In this case the reciprocal negative easement attached to McLean's (D) lot may now be enforced by Sanborn (P) provided McLean (D) had constructive knowledge of the easement at the time of purchase. At the time of purchase, McLean (D) had an abstract of title showing the subdivision and that his lot had 97 companion lots. He could not avoid noticing the strictly uniform residential character of the companion lots, and the least inquiry would have revealed the fact that his lot was subject to a reciprocal negative easement. The injunction is granted. Circuit decree affirmed as modified.

## ▶ ANALYSIS

Reciprocal negative easements must start with common owners. They cannot arise and fasten upon one lot by reason of other lot owners conforming to a general plan. Such easements are never retroactive, and as demonstrated here, they pass their benefits and carry their obligations to all purchasers of land provided the purchaser has constructive notice of the easement.

■=■

## Quicknotes

**CONSTRUCTIVE NOTICE** Knowledge of a fact that is imputed to an individual who was under a duty to inquire and who could have learned of the fact through the exercise of reasonable prudence.

**RECIPROCAL NEGATIVE EASEMENTS** An implied covenant that arises when a common grantor conveys property and fails to contain a restriction placed on prior conveyances, pursuant to a general development scheme, to the present one and the grantee has either actual or constructive notice of such restrictions.

■=■

# Snow v. Van Dam

Original lot buyer (P) v. Buyer of new lot (D)

Mass. Sup. Jud. Ct., 291 Mass. 477, 197 N.E. 224 (1935).

**NATURE OF CASE:** Suit for injunction.

**FACT SUMMARY:** A grantor subdivided a large tract by dividing a portion of it into individual lots which were conveyed with building restrictions. When the remaining portion was subsequently subdivided, a buyer of one of the new lots sought to avoid the restrictions as being unenforceable against his lot.

## 🏛 RULE OF LAW
For an equitable servitude to bind subsequent grantees, the benefit of the restriction must be intended to run to an identifiable dominant estate or else it will be considered a personal covenant between the original contracting parties only.

**FACTS:** Shackelford acquired a tract of land in about 1907, which had been recorded with a development plan. The plan showed that a large portion of the tract was to be subdivided into individual lots. The remaining portion was not so subdivided since it was thought to be totally incapable of development. The subdivided lots were sold as individual lots with deed restriction restricting development to single-family residences. While these original lots were still being sold, the undivided portion was sold as a unit, but a revised plan was recorded showing a subdivision of this parcel as well. Van Dam (D) acquired one of the new lots by a deed containing the same restrictions. He built a commercial building on his lot, intending to operate a store. Snow (P), one of the buyers of the original subdivided lots, brought suit to enjoin Van Dam (D) from violating the restrictions.

**ISSUE:** Will the restriction of an equitable servitude run to subsequent grantees if there is no ascertainable dominant estate intended to receive the benefit of the restriction?

**HOLDING AND DECISION:** (Lummus, J.) No. When a restriction is placed upon land by a covenant at time of grant, the restriction must be intended to benefit an ascertainable dominant estate before it will run with the land. The benefit must be appurtenant to the dominant estate. The intent that the benefit shall attach can be shown by the existence of a scheme of restrictions in a particular tract which binds each lot for the benefit of every other lot. Upon the showing of such a scheme, an earlier purchaser can enforce the restrictions against a later purchaser even though this would technically be allowing a stranger to the later conveyance to enforce a benefit in his favor. It is clear that from the beginning this entire tract was intended to be restricted in the same manner. The original plan of

development did not contemplate any use of the area including Van Dam's (D) lot. But the conveyance to Van Dam's (D) grantor contained the restrictions and was a part of the common scheme of development. The scheme having been shown, the restriction is enforceable against Van Dam (D), and he is enjoined from violating it.

## ▶ ANALYSIS

Equitable servitudes as applied to the development of a tract of land into smaller lots were the forerunners of modern zoning plans. Since the essential element at privity of estate was lacking between various purchasers of individual lots in tract development, the restrictions could not be enforced as covenants running at law. By using the common plan or scheme approach to bind all the lots in the tract in favor of each other, the intended nature of the development could be maintained during the intended life of the restrictions.

■=■

## Quicknotes

**EQUITABLE SERVITUDE** Land use restriction enforceable in equity.

■=■

# McMillan v. Iserman

### Deed restriction enforcer (P) v. Land purchaser (D)

Mich. Ct. of App., 120 Mich. App. 785, 327 N.W.2d 559 (1982).

**NATURE OF CASE:** Appeal from summary judgment invalidating a deed restriction.

**FACT SUMMARY:** McMillan (P) attempted to enforce a deed restriction against Iserman (D) to prevent the use of the land as a facility for the mentally handicapped.

## 🏛 RULE OF LAW
Land use restrictions which discriminate against the mentally handicapped are against public policy and unenforceable.

**FACTS:** Iserman (D) purchased land in 1958, which was subject to certain land use restrictions. In 1980, the restrictions were amended to prohibit the use of the land for any use other than private residence. They specifically prohibited the operation of any state-licensed residential care facilities for the mentally handicapped. McMillan (P) sued to enforce the restriction in order to prevent the proposed use. Iserman (D) moved for summary judgment on the basis that the restriction discriminated against the mentally handicapped and, therefore, was against public policy and unenforceable. The trial court granted the motion, and McMillan (P) appealed.

**ISSUE:** Are land use restrictions which discriminate against the mentally handicapped against public policy and unenforceable?

**HOLDING AND DECISION:** (Cavanagh, J.) Yes. Land use restrictions which discriminate against the mentally handicapped are against public policy and unenforceable. The policy permitting the enforcement of land use restrictions is overridden by express Michigan state policy of promoting facilities to care for the mentally handicapped. As a result, the restriction in this case was against public policy and unenforceable. Affirmed.

**DISSENT:** (MacKenzie, J.) Restrictions should rarely be held contrary to public policy. The policy supporting the promotion of facilities for the mentally handicapped is limited in areas specifically zoned for such use. Further, the restriction does not exclusively apply to residential care for the mentally handicapped. It prohibits any use for residential care and, therefore, is not discriminatory.

## ▌ ANALYSIS

In this case the court was called upon to choose between two strong public policies. Land use restrictions are generally upheld as within the prerogative of the grantor in disposing of his property. The power to so restrict land is itself an element of ownership and fundamental to the concept of private property ownership. These restrictions, however, are subject to constitutional scrutiny and will be analyzed in the terms of their discriminatory properties.

■══■

## Quicknotes

**DEED** A signed writing transferring title to real property from one person to another.

■══■

# Joslin v. Pine River Development Corp.

Purchaser of shore property (P) v. Unidentified party (D)

N.H. Sup. Ct., 116 N.H. 814, 367 A.2d 599 (1976).

**NATURE OF CASE:** Appeal in an action for injunctive relief.

**FACT SUMMARY:** Joslin (P) claimed that deed restrictions prevented the Pine River Development Association (D) from using its shore lot as a homeowners' recreational area.

## 🏛 RULE OF LAW
The former policy of disapproval and strict construction of restrictive covenants is no longer operative in view of the modern recognition of the value of such covenants as land use planning devices.

**FACTS:** Joslin (P) purchased shore parcels of land in the Scribner Park Subdivision. The Pine River Development Corp. (D) also purchased a number of lots, including Lot 26, which was one of the 48 share lots available. The Corporation (D) subdivided its land into 161 lots, selling 147 of them to buyers who then formed the Pine River Development Association (D). In order that its members would have access to the water, the Corporation (D) conveyed Lot 26 to the Association (D) which then began clearing the lot for docking, beach, and recreational purposes. Joslin (P) sought to enjoin this use on the basis that it violated restrictions in the deed. The Corporation (D) and Association (D) argued that all such restrictions must be strictly construed to permit free use of land and that no restrictions may be implied from those expressly stated. The trial court granted the injunction. The Corporation (D) appealed.

**ISSUE:** Are restrictive covenants on the use of land disfavored and strictly construed so as to permit free use of land?

**HOLDING AND DECISION:** (Kenison, C.J.) No. The former policy of disapproval and strict construction of restrictive covenants is no longer operative in view of the modern recognition of the value of such covenants as land planning devices. Private land use restrictions are of substantial importance, especially today when the value of one's property largely depends upon maintaining the character of the neighborhood. The intent of the parties when the covenants are created will be given great weight. Here, the obvious restriction was to guarantee that Lot 26 would be only used for residential purposes. Recreational use by hundreds of people was never intended. Defendants' exceptions overruled.

## ▶ ANALYSIS

In *Jones v. The Park Lane for Convalescents, Inc.*, 120 A.2d 535 (1956), the court stated that a covenant that the land shall only be used for private dwellings did not prevent the owner from using a residence for a convalescent home and making interior alterations for that purpose. There the court spoke in terms of disfavor and strict construction of such restrictions as interfering with an owner's free and full use of his property.

■■■

## Quicknotes

**RESTRICTIVE COVENANT** A promise contained in a deed to limit the uses to which the property will be made.

■■■

# Rhue v. Cheyenne Homes, Inc.

House owners (D) v. Housing subdivision (P)

Colo. Sup. Ct., 168 Colo. 6, 449 P.2d 361 (1969).

**NATURE OF CASE:** Appeal in an action for injunctive relief.

**FACT SUMMARY:** Cheyenne Homes, Inc. (P) claimed that the Rhues' (D) moving their 30-year-old home into Cheyenne's (P) subdivision without the prior approval of the architectural committee violated the restrictive covenant.

## RULE OF LAW
Restrictive covenants requiring the prior approval of an architectural committee of prospective housing plans are valid providing any refusal is based on reasonable standards and made in good faith.

**FACTS:** Cheyenne Homes, Inc.'s (P) new housing subdivision was covered by a recorded restrictive covenant which, among other things, provided that no building be placed upon any lot until its plans were approved by the architectural control committee. However, the Rhues (D), without submitting their plans to the committee, proposed to move a 30-year-old Spanish-style house into this subdivision, consisting only of new modern ranch-style or split-level homes. Cheyenne (P) obtained an injunction on the basis that this action breached the restrictive covenant, and that the house, being out of harmony with the neighborhood, would depreciate property therein. The Rhues (D) appealed, arguing that the restriction was unenforceable, since no specific standards were given to guide the committee in their decision.

**ISSUE:** Are restrictive covenants requiring the prior approval of an architectural control committee of prospective housing plans valid when any refusal is based on reasonable standards and made in good faith?

**HOLDING AND DECISION:** (Pringle, J.) Yes. Restrictive covenants requiring the prior approval of an architectural committee of prospective housing plans are valid providing any refusal is based on reasonable standards and made in good faith. Modern legal authority recognizes that today's subdividers use restrictive covenants to guarantee to purchasers that: (1) their houses will be protected from impairment of value by inharmonious adjacent construction and (2) that a general plan of construction will be followed. So long as this intent of the covenant is clear (as it is in this case), it will be upheld even though specific instructions and guidelines to the screening committee may be lacking. The house of the Rhues (D) had a stucco exterior and red tile roof and was completely out of harmony with the other houses. Clearly, the judgment of the committee was reasonable. Affirmed.

## ANALYSIS

The covenant running with the land is a legal fiction whereby the rights of the covenantee and the duties of the covenantor are somehow attached to the land and, therefore, the rights can be enforced by either the covenantee or by someone who assumes a subsequent interest in or title to his land. The need for covenants usually arises out of cases such as the above wherein a developer of many lots and subdivisions wishes to make the development attractive to purchasers.

## Quicknotes

**RECORDATION** The recording of a document in the public record.

**RESTRICTIVE COVENANT** A promise contained in a deed to limit the uses to which the property will be made.

# Cowling v. Colligan

Owner of lot (P) v. Commercial lot developer (D)

Tex. Sup. Ct., 158 Tex. 458, 312 S.W.2d 943 (1958).

**NATURE OF CASE:** Suit for injunction.

**FACT SUMMARY:** The owner of a lot on the border of a subdivision restricted to residential use sought to use his lot for commercial purposes, contending that the conditions just outside the subdivision had changed to such an extent as to defeat the validity of the restriction on his lot.

## 🏛 RULE OF LAW
If the benefits of the original plan for a restricted subdivision can still be realized for the protection of interior lots, the restriction should be enforced against the border lots as well even though such border lots may be made more valuable by lifting the restrictions.

**FACTS:** Post Oak Gardens was a subdivision that had been platted and recorded as a tract limited to residential structures and use. The tract had been divided into 49 lots. Over the years several lots had been purchased by religious organizations and churches erected thereon. Colligan (D) purchased a lot on the outside border of the subdivision. Across both streets bounding his lot, the land was unrestricted and had been heavily developed for commercial use. Colligan (D) proposed to convert his lot to commercial use as well, contending that the commercial development adjacent to the subdivision had resulted in conditions so changed as to render the restrictions unenforceable in equity. Cowling (P) and 17 other lot owners sought to enjoin Colligan's (D) proposed commercial use of his lot.

**ISSUE:** Will a change of conditions immediately outside a restricted subdivision justify a refusal to enforce the restrictions against the border lots of the subdivision?

**HOLDING AND DECISION:** (Calvert, J.) No. The trial court found that the conditions within the subdivision had not changed sufficiently to warrant a refusal to enforce the restrictions against all the other lots in the tract. But the trial court found that the changes external to the tract had removed the justification for enforcing the restriction against Colligan's (D) lot. A court of equity may refuse to enforce restrictions in a subdivision if there have been substantial violations within the tract that amount to a waiver or abandonment of the covenants. A refusal may also be justified where there is a change in circumstance in the surrounding territory so that it is no longer possible to secure the benefits sought to be realized through the restrictions. While the erection of the churches constituted a violation of the covenants, this has been consistently held to be so trivial a deviation that it cannot constitute abandonment or waiver. And the change of external conditions must be substantial and the damage to the tract as a whole substantial before it can justify removal of the restrictions. Removal of the restriction from this one lot is no answer, for then the external boundary has been moved inward and the next adjacent property owner could then claim his restriction should be removed for the same reason and so on until the entire tract is destroyed. The injunction shall issue against Colligan's (D) proposed commercial development. Judgment of the trial court affirmed as reformed.

## ▶ ANALYSIS

The benefit of equitable servitudes may be lost through four basic circumstances. The first is laches when the enforcement of the restriction is delayed for an unreasonable and prejudicial period of time. A waiver may be found where the restrictions have not been enforced against other known violations. A lack of uniform observance by a substantial number of owners may indicate an intent by them to abandon the restrictions. And, finally, changed conditions in the surrounding area, as pointed out in the principal case, will defeat the servitudes only where the benefit sought to be achieved is no longer possible because of the changed external circumstance.

■■■

## Quicknotes

**EQUITABLE SERVITUDE** Land use restriction enforceable in equity.

**SUBDIVISION PLOT** A parcel of land that is divided into portions to be resold or developed.

■■■

# Nuisance and Interests in Natural Resources

## Quick Reference Rules of Law

# Rose v. Chaikin

### Adjacent landowner (P) v. Windmill operator (D)

N.J. Sup. Ct., 187 N.J. Sup. 210, 453 A.2d 1378 (1982).

**NATURE OF CASE:** Action to enjoin the operation of a privately owned windmill.

**FACT SUMMARY:** Rose (P) contended that a windmill operated by Chaikin (D), an adjacent landowner, was a private nuisance and sued to enjoin its operation.

## 🏛 RULE OF LAW
A private nuisance is an unreasonable interference with the use and enjoyment of the land, and the volume, frequency, time, and locality of noise may constitute such an interference.

**FACTS:** Rose (P) and Chaikin (D) were adjacent landowners. In an effort to conserve energy, Chaikin (D) erected a windmill, pursuant to a city ordinance. Rose (P) contended the noise was so loud, frequent, and perpetual as to cause him tension, nervousness, dizziness, loss of sleep, and a general inability to enjoy the peace of his home. He sued, contending the windmill was a private nuisance and sought a permanent injunction. Chaikin (D) filed a counterclaim to enjoin Rose (P) from operating a heat pump which also exceeded permissive noise levels. Chaikin (D) contended it too constituted a private nuisance and caused a distraction during reading and dinner.

**ISSUE:** Can noise of sufficient volume, frequency, and locality constitute a private nuisance?

**HOLDING AND DECISION:** (Gibson, J.) Yes. A private nuisance is an unreasonable interference with the use and enjoyment of land. Noise of sufficient volume, frequency, and locality may so interfere with the use and enjoyment of the land as to constitute a private nuisance. In this case, the symptoms of stress suffered by Rose (P) clearly indicate that the noise unreasonably interfered with his right to peaceful enjoyment. The noise level exceeded acceptable levels, and it was virtually non-stop. Further, the proximity of the property to Rose's (P) land accentuates the interference. As a result the noise clearly constitutes a private nuisance. The operation of the heat pump did not cause the same level of interference and, therefore, was not shown to be a nuisance. Consequently, the operation of the windmill must be enjoined and Rose (P) may continue to operate the heat pump.

## ▶ ANALYSIS

A person is duty bound to use his land in a manner which does not unreasonably interfere with another's use of his property. As is illustrated by this case, an unreasonable use may constitute a nuisance and be enjoined. In determining whether a particular use constitutes a nuisance, courts generally engage in a balancing of interests. This involves determining whether the social utility of the particular use is outweighed by the harm it causes. If it is, it constitutes a nuisance. Another problem involves standing to sue to abate a nuisance. If the harm is so widespread as to affect the public as a whole, only public prosecutorial agencies have standing to sue. Only where the injury is peculiar to a particular party may that party sue to abate the activity as a private nuisance.

■■■

## Quicknotes

**PRIVATE NUISANCE** An unlawful use of property interfering with the enjoyment of the private rights of an individual or a small number of persons.

■■■

# Boomer v. Atlantic Cement Co.

## Landowners (P) v. Plant owner (D)

N.Y. Ct. App., 26 N.Y.2d 219, 257 N.E.2d 870 (1970).

**NATURE OF CASE:** Action to enjoin maintenance of nuisance and for damages.

**FACT SUMMARY:** Trial court refused to issue injunction which would close down the plant, but awarded permanent damages instead.

### 🏛 RULE OF LAW
Although the rule in New York is that a nuisance will be enjoined even when there is a marked disparity shown in economic consequence between the effect of the injunction and the effect of the nuisance, an injunction should not be applied if the result is to close down a plant. Permanent damages may be awarded as an alternative.

**FACTS:** A group of landowners (P), complaining of injury to their property from dirt, smoke, and vibration emanating from a neighboring cement plant (D), brought an action to enjoin the continued operation of the plant and for damages. The trial court held that the plant constituted a nuisance, found substantial damage but, because an injunction would shut down the plant's operation, refused to issue one. Permanent damages of $185,000 were awarded the group of landowners (P) instead.

**ISSUE:** Where the issuance of an injunction to enjoin the maintenance of a business would shut down a business, may permanent damages be issued as an alternative?

**HOLDING AND DECISION:** (Bergan, J.) Yes. Damages may be awarded as an alternative to an injunction in nuisance cases. Another alternative would be to grant the injunction but postpone its effect to a specified future date to give opportunity for technical advances to permit the company (D) to eliminate the nuisance. However, there is no assurance that any significant technical improvement would occur. Moreover, the problem is universal, and can only be solved by an industry-wide effort. Permanent damages would themselves be a spur to conduct more research. Future owners of this land would not be able to recover additional damages, since the award is to the land. Reversed and remanded.

**DISSENT:** (Jasen, J.) The majority approach is licensing a continuing wrong. Furthermore, permanent damages alleviate the need for more research, and decrease incentive.

### ▶ ANALYSIS

The reasoning advanced here has been carried one step further by other courts. In *Pennsylvania Coal Co. v. Sanderson,* 113 Pa. St. 126, 6 A. 453 (1886), a suit for damages was frowned upon by the Supreme Court which said, "To encourage the development of the great natural resources of a country, trifling inconveniences to particular persons must sometimes give way to the necessities of a great community."

### Quicknotes

**INJUNCTION** A remedy imposed by the court ordering a party to cease the conduct of a specific activity.

**NUISANCE** An unlawful use of property that interferes with the lawful use of another's property.

# Spur Industries, Inc. v. Del E. Webb Development Co.

## Cattle feeding operation (D) v. Housing developer (P)

Ariz. Sup. Ct., 108 Ariz. 178, 494 P.2d 700 (1972).

**NATURE OF CASE:** Action seeking an injunction.

**FACT SUMMARY:** Del E. Webb Development Co. (P) developed a new city near Spur Industries, Inc.'s (D) cattle feedlot.

## 🏛 RULE OF LAW
A preexisting lawful enterprise may become a nuisance by reason of the expansion of a city, especially where it presents a health hazard to residents.

**FACTS:** Spur Industries, Inc. (D) set up a cattle feedlot in an unsettled rural area. Del E. Webb Development Co. (P) subsequently developed Sun City, a retirement community a short distance away. As lots were sold, the community spread toward Spur's feedlot. Residents and Webb (P) then filed suit, alleging that the odor and flies constituted a public nuisance and they sought a permanent injunction closing down Spur's (D) operation. Spur (D) appealed the injunction, alleging that the people came to it and should not be allowed to complain.

**ISSUE:** May a preexisting lawful enterprise become a nuisance by reason of the expansion of a city, especially where it presents a health hazard to residents?

**HOLDING AND DECISION:** (Cameron, V.C.J.) Yes. The difference between a public and private nuisance is very close. Because of the large number of people affected and the health hazard present herein, we find that Spur's (D) operation constitutes a public nuisance. A preexisting lawful enterprise may become a nuisance by reason of the expansion of a community, especially where it presents a health hazard. For the public good, private interests may be enjoined. However, where a developer comes to a nuisance, and by his actions creates the situation which causes the issuance of the injunction, he should be required to bear at least a portion of the loss or the cost of relocation. Webb (P) must indemnify Spur (D) for some of its loss. Affirmed in part, reversed in part, and remanded.

## ▶ ANALYSIS

The result of this case accords with the reasoning employed by modern enlightened courts in dealing with nuisance. The operator of a nuisance imposes an externality upon the parties affected thereby. Those parties may simultaneously impose an externality upon the operator of the nuisance by interfering with his lawful enterprise. In such a situation, the most economically efficient solution is one which requires one party to be compensated for his economic loss while permitting the other party to continue his desired conduct, i.e., permanent damages in lieu of an injunction.

■■■

## Quicknotes

**INDEMNITY** The duty of a party to compensate another for damages sustained.

**PRIVATE NUISANCE** An unlawful use of property interfering with the enjoyment of the private rights of an individual or a small number of persons.

**PUBLIC NUISANCE** An activity that unreasonably interferes with a right common to the overall public.

■■■

# Noone v. Price

## Hillside homeowner (P) v. Supporting homeowner (D)

W.Va. Ct. App., 171 W.Va. 185, 298 S.E.2d 218 (1982).

**NATURE OF CASE:** Appeal from grant of summary judgment denying damages for eroding lateral support of land.

**FACT SUMMARY:** Noone (P) contended Price (D) breached her duty to supply lateral support for Noone's (P) hillside home by allowing a retaining wall to fall into disrepair.

## 🏛 RULE OF LAW
An adjacent landowner is strictly liable for acts of omission and commission which withdraw lateral support of his neighbor's land sufficient to support it in its natural state; however, if as a result of the additional weight of a building so much strain is placed on the lateral support that it will not hold, then in the absence of negligence the adjacent landowner is not liable for any resulting damages.

**FACTS:** In 1912, a house was built at the base of a hill, along with a stone and cement wall located at the base of the hillside. In 1928, Union Carbide (P) built a house on the hillside above the wall. After several years, the wall fell into disrepair. In 1955, Price (D) purchased the house at the base of the hill. She made no repairs to the wall. Noone (P) bought the house above on the hillside in 1960. Subsequently, Noone (P) discovered that his house was slipping down the hillside, and sued Price (D), contending the wall was constructed to supply lateral support to his property, and that its disrepair caused the slippage. Price (D) moved for summary judgment, contending Noone (P) was negligent in failing to protect his own property and estopped from suing because he had purchased his house with the knowledge of the wall's deteriorating condition. The trial court agreed and granted summary judgment to Price (D). Noone (P) appealed.

**ISSUE:** Is an adjacent landowner liable only for supplying lateral support to his neighbor's land in its natural state?

**HOLDING AND DECISION:** (Neely, J.) Yes. An adjacent landowner is strictly liable for acts of omission and commission which withdraw lateral support from his neighbor's land sufficient to support it in its natural state. However, if as a result of the additional weight of a building so much strain is placed on the lateral support that it will not hold, then in the absence of negligence, the adjacent landowner is not liable for any resulting damages. At the time the retaining wall was built, there were no structures on Noone's (P) land. Therefore, the wall needed only to support the land in its natural state. The builder was not required to supply support sufficient to withstand the erection of any building on the land. Therefore, Price (D), as the successor in interest, was not obligated to strengthen the wall to support Noone's (P) house. If Noone (P) is to recover, he must do so by proving that the disrepair of the wall would have inevitably led to the subsidence of his land in its natural condition, without the house upon it. Consequently, as this is a factual question, the entry of summary judgment was error. Reversed and remanded.

## ▶ ANALYSIS

This case illustrates the scope of the duty to supply lateral support. The duty is absolute as to the land in its natural state, but to recover for damages to a building, negligence must be shown. A negligent withdrawal of support is actionable even if the land would not have slipped but for the presence of the added weight of a building. In determining whether negligence exists, the type of withdrawal, the nature of the soil, and whether notice of the proposed withdrawal was given are all relevant.

■━■

## *Quicknotes*

**LATERAL SUPPORT** The right of a landowner to have his land supported by adjoining property.

**STRICT LIABILITY** Liability for all injuries proximately caused by a party's conducting of certain inherently dangerous activities without regard to negligence or fault.

■━■

# Armstrong v. Francis Corp.

## Owner of affected land (P) v. Residential developer (D)

N.J. Sup. Ct., 20 N.J. 320, 120 A.2d 4 (1956).

**NATURE OF CASE:** Action in equity to enjoin landowner from artificially discharging waste waters from his land.

**FACT SUMMARY:** Francis Corp. (D) drained off excess water from its land by means of culverts and pipes, thereby causing severe injury to its neighbor's (P) property.

## 🏛 RULE OF LAW
A possessor of land is not privileged to discharge upon adjoining land, by artificial means, large quantities of surface water in a concentrated flow otherwise than through natural drainways, regardless of the means by which the surface water is collected and discharged.

**FACTS:** Francis Corp. (D) wanted to develop a tract of land for residential subdivision. To drain off excess water, Francis (D) constructed a series of underground pipes and culverts. Water from this system emptied into a natural stream which ran across the lands of Armstrong (P) and Klemp (P). Because of the increased flow of water, the stream often flooded and caused considerable erosion or silting on surrounding banks. In addition, the stream, being polluted by Francis's (D) pipes, became discolored and evil-smelling and lost all fish. Armstrong (P) and Klemp (P) sued to have Francis (D), at its own cost, pipe the rest of its water discharge.

**ISSUE:** Does a landowner have an absolute right to rid his property of excess surface waters as he wills?

**HOLDING AND DECISION:** (Brennan, J.) No. Most states adopt the rule that, since surface water is the "common enemy" of necessary development, the landowner has an absolute right to discharge it upon adjoining land regardless of the harm caused his neighbors by the means he employs. However, no state applies this harsh rule literally. Courts will read in a "reasonable use" approach which has the particular virtue of flexibility. The issue of reasonableness includes such factors as the amount of harm caused, the foreseeability of the harm which results, the purpose or motive with which the possessor acted, and other relevant matter. Accordingly, Francis (D) is liable to fix its drainage system. Affirmed.

## ▌ *ANALYSIS*

The competing approach with the "common enemy" rule is the civil law rule, which holds that a possessor has no privilege, under any circumstances, to interfere with the surface water on his land so as to cause it to flow upon adjoining land in a manner or quantity substantially different from its natural flow. Even here, however, courts will read in a "reasonable use" exception to permit minor alterations.

## Quicknotes

**COMMON ENEMY RULE** The right of a landowner to conduct activities on his land so as to ward against the intrusion of surface water without regard to the effect of such activities on other landowners.

**WATER RIGHTS** The right to reduce water naturally flowing to possession for private use.

# Stratton v. Mt. Hermon Boys' School

## Mill owner (P) v. Water diverter (D)

Mass. Sup. Jud. Ct., 216 Mass. 83, 103 N.E. 87 (1913).

**NATURE OF CASE:** Damages for riparian rights.

**FACT SUMMARY:** Mt. Hermon Boys' School (D) diverted water from a stream going through Stratton's (P) and Hermon's (D) property to another stream for the use of Hermon's (D) school.

## 🏛 RULE OF LAW
A proprietor may make any reasonable use of the water of a stream related to his riparian estate and for lawful purposes within the watershed, providing the current is not unreasonably diminished for other riparian owners.

**FACTS:** Mt. Hermon Boys' School (D) owned a tract of land through which flowed a stream. The same stream flowed though Stratton's (P) land on which Stratton (P) operated a mill. Hermon (D) diverted 60,000 gallons of water daily from the stream to another stream for the use of Hermon's (D) school. The diversion caused a substantial diminution in the volume of water flowing to Stratton's (P) land. Stratton (P) sued Hermon (D) for damages. A jury instruction was given that Hermon's (D) right was confined to a reasonable use of water for the benefit of its land adjoining the stream, and did not extend to diverting it for use for other premises not contiguous to the stream; and that if such diversion were found, Hermon (D) would be liable for at least nominal damages. Hermon (D) requested an instruction that its diversion of water to another estate owned by it was not conclusive evidence that it was liable, and the correct question was whether it had diverted an unreasonable quantity of water. The court refused Hermon's (D) instruction. Hermon (D) took exception.

**ISSUE:** May a proprietor make any reasonable use of the water of a stream related to his riparian estate and for lawful purposes within the watershed, if the current is not unreasonably diminished for other riparian owners?

**HOLDING AND DECISION:** (Rugg, C.J.) Yes. A proprietor may make any reasonable use of the water of a stream related to his riparian estate and for lawful purposes within the watershed, providing the current is not unreasonably diminished for other riparian owners. The only question is whether there is actual injury to Stratton's (P) estate for any present or future reasonable use. The diversion alone without such evidence does not warrant recovery of even nominal damages. However, the jury found substantial evidence of such injury. Exceptions overruled.

## ▶ ANALYSIS

Would the holding of the case have been the same if Hermon (D) had owned no riparian land but still diverted the stream water for its own use? The Restatement of Torts 856, Comment on Subsection (1) declares that a nonriparian user has a "privilege" that is to some extent a legally protected interest. "A nonriparian who is making a reasonable and beneficial use of water that causes no harm to a riparian is entitled to protection from intentional or unintentional conduct, other than the exercise of a riparian right, which may constitute a tort."

## *Quicknotes*

**RIPARIAN RIGHT** The right of an owner of real property to the use of water naturally flowing through his land.

# Coffin v. Left Hand Ditch Co.

Owner of irrigated land (P) v. Water diverter (D)

Colo. Sup. Ct., 6 Colo. 443 (1882).

**NATURE OF CASE:** Appeal of damages and injunctive relief in a trespass action.

**FACT SUMMARY:** Left Hand Ditch Co. (D) diverted water for irrigation from a creek near land owned by Coffin (P).

🏛 **RULE OF LAW**
Under the prior appropriation doctrine, the first appropriator of water from a natural stream for a beneficial purpose has a prior, vested right to the extent of such appropriation.

**FACTS:** Coffin (P) owned land near the St. Vrain creek which provided natural irrigation to his land. Left Hand Ditch Co. (D) appropriated water for irrigation purposes from the St. Vrain creek by creating ditches to divert the water onto its land. In 1879, when water was too scarce to meet both Coffin's (P) and Ditch Co.'s (D) requirements, Coffin (P) tore out Ditch Co.'s (D) dam to divert the water to irrigate Coffin's (P) land. At trial, Ditch Co. (D) sued for damages and injunctive relief in a trespass action and successfully sought ownership title to the diverted water under the prior appropriation doctrine. Coffin (P) appealed on the basis that riparian owners have a superior right over prior appropriators to the natural flow of water.

**ISSUE:** Under the prior appropriation doctrine, does the first appropriator of water from a natural stream for a beneficial purpose have a prior, vested right to the extent of such appropriation?

**HOLDING AND DECISION:** (Helm, J.) Yes. Under the prior appropriation doctrine, the first appropriator of water from a natural stream for a beneficial purpose has a prior, vested interest to the extent of such appropriation. This rule is in accord with the national policy of encouraging the diversion and use of water for agricultural purposes and for fertilizing unproductive lands. Thus, the common-law rule giving a riparian owner the right to the flow of water in his lands even in the absence of beneficial use is rejected here. Moreover, the location of the area to where the water is being diverted has no bearing on the prior appropriation doctrine. The necessity for artificial irrigation is sufficient to invoke the applicability of this doctrine. Any other holding would result in sanctioning water waste in sterile lands while preventing profitable cultivation of productive lands. Affirmed.

▌ *ANALYSIS*

The prior appropriation doctrine has been adopted by Mississippi and 17 western states including eight of the most arid regions: Utah, Idaho, Nevada, Arizona, Montana, Wyoming, Colorado, and New Mexico. The common-law riparian rights doctrine has not been adopted in these states because it would discourage investment in irrigation and in other beneficial uses of water. The prior appropriation doctrine arose out of the practice of miners who out of necessity had to divert water, sometimes very far from its source. A notable aspect of this doctrine is that when a water right is confirmed, it is severable from the land and can be sold as an interest independent of the land.

■■■

## Quicknotes

**RIPARIAN RIGHT** The right of an owner of real property to the use of water naturally flowing through his land.

■■■

# Sipriano v. Great Spring Waters of America, Inc.

Landowners (P) v. Bottled water company (D)

Tex. Sup. Ct., 1 S.W.3d 75 (1999).

**NATURE OF CASE:** Suit for negligence.

**FACT SUMMARY:** Relying on the rule of capture, the trial court granted summary judgment against landowners who sued a bottled-water company for negligently draining their water wells.

## 🏛 RULE OF LAW
The law of capture allows a landowner to pump as much groundwater as he chooses, without liability to neighbors who claim the pumping has depleted their wells.

**FACTS:** Landowners (P) sued a bottled-water company (D) for negligently draining their water wells. The trial court granted summary judgment against landowners (P) based on the rule of capture. The court of appeals affirmed and landowners (P) appealed.

**ISSUE:** Does the law of capture allow a landowner to pump as much groundwater as he chooses, without liability to neighbors who claim the pumping has depleted their wells?

**HOLDING AND DECISION:** (Enoch, J.) Yes. The law of capture allows a landowner to pump as much groundwater as he chooses, without liability to neighbors who claim the pumping has depleted their wells. The proposed rule of reasonable use constitutes a sweeping change in the law that is not appropriate at this time. Affirmed.

**CONCURRENCE:** (Hecht, J.) Texas is the only remaining state adhering to the law of capture. The reasons for adopting the rule are no longer valid.

## ▶ ANALYSIS

The rule of reasonable use limits the common-law right of landowners to take water from a common well by imposing liability on those who take "unreasonably" to their neighbors' detriment.

■═■

## Quicknotes

**COMMON LAW** A body of law developed through the judicial decisions of the courts as opposed to the legislative process.

**NEGLIGENCE** Conduct falling below the standard of care that a reasonable person would demonstrate under similar conditions.

■═■

# Orr v. Mortvedt

## Landowner (P) v. Landowner (D)

Iowa Sup. Ct., 735 N.W.2d 610 (2007).

**NATURE OF CASE:** Suit to clarify property rights in a non-navigable lake.

**FACT SUMMARY:** Three deeds granted three separate sets of owners property rights in three parcels of land underlying a non-navigable lake. The landowners disputed, among other things, the extent to which each set of owners could use the lake.

## 🏛 RULE OF LAW
The owner of part of a private lakebed cannot use and enjoy the surface of the entire lake.

**FACTS:** In 1994, the Sevdes (P) bought twenty acres of land that included a portion of a lakebed and land surrounding the lake. In 1996, the Mortvedts (D) bought another portion of the lakebed, and the Orrs (P) bought a third portion of the lakebed in 1998. The Mortvedts (D) eventually used portions of the lake that exceeded the boundaries of portions of the lakebed that were deeded to them. The Orrs (P) and Sevdes (P) sued the Mortvedts (D), contending, among other things, that the Mortvedts (D) could lawfully use only that portion of the lake that covered the portion of the lakebed established by the Mortvedts' (D) deed. The trial court agreed with the Orrs (P) and Sevdes (P), and the Mortvedts (D) appealed.

**ISSUE:** Can the owner of part of a private lakebed use and enjoy the surface of the entire lake?

**HOLDING AND DECISION:** (Hecht, J.) No. The owner of part of a private lakebed cannot use and enjoy the surface of the entire lake. The lake in this case clearly is non-navigable, and therefore subject to private control, because the lake cannot reasonably be "likened to a public highway." In such circumstances, most American jurisdictions follow the rule that an owner may use only that portion of a lake that covers the portion of the lakebed that he owns. A minority of jurisdictions in this country do permit owners such as the Mortvedts (D) to use the entire lake. Contrary to the Mortvedts (D), however, the Iowa legislature has not adopted the minority rule as the law in this State. Despite the many advantages of the minority rule—perhaps chief among them an easing of tensions over boundaries that are difficult to identify—the majority rule should be the law in Iowa because it better accords with real estate law in this State. Affirmed.

**DISSENT:** (Cady, J.) The old notion of owning property "up to the sky and down to the depths" does not logically extend to the surface of a lake that covers ownership rights in a lakebed. The notion is outdated anyway, and its inapplicability appears all the more clearly because of the intrinsic differences between land, water, and air. Furthermore, it is unreasonable to apply the majority rule (what the majority in this case calls the "common law rule") to Iowa. The better rule, what the Scots called the "free access rule" (that is, what the majority in this case calls the "civil law rule"), permits adjoining owners of a lake to use the entire lake regardless of ownership interests in the underlying lakebed. The majority today rejects free access in favor of each landowner's exclusive dominion, even though no true majority rule on this issue exists in this country, and even though differences such as those being decided in this case will seldom be resolved by private agreement. The majority's exclusive-dominion rule is unreasonable also because the rationale fails to account for the nature of a particular property and ignores contemporary norms, which are better served in the twenty-first century by the free access rule.

---

## ▶ ANALYSIS

In Iowa, non-navigable watercourses, such as the lake in *Orr,* are subject to control by private landowners. The "civil law rule" rejected by the majority in *Orr* might well be the better policy choice, as the Court admits, but that rule conflicts with the firmly established legal fiction of property lines extending "up to the sky and down to the depths." The Court chose the more conservative of the two available rules of decision here, but students should note that the Iowa legislature still may adopt the "civil law rule" by statute.

■■■

## Quicknotes

**CIVIL LAW RULE** Rule of law pertaining to an individual's private rights; rule based upon statutory law rather than upon court decisions.

**COMMON LAW RULE** A body of law developed through the judicial decisions of the courts as opposed to the legislative process.

■■■

# Wronski v. Sun Oil Company

## Landowner (P) v. Oil company (D)

Mich. Ct. App., 89 Mich. App. 11, 279 N.W.2d 564 (1979).

**NATURE OF CASE:** Appeal from award of damages for conversion.

**FACT SUMMARY:** Wronski (P), a landowner, accused the Sun Oil Company (D) of illegally over-producing oil from wells drilled on the land adjoining his property in violation of fair share regulations.

## 🏛 RULE OF LAW
A violation of a proration order constitutes conversion of oil from the pool and subjects the violator to liability to all owners of interests in the pool for conversion of the illegally obtained oil.

**FACTS:** Wronski (P) owned 200 acres of land and the attendant mineral rights. Sun Oil Company (D) leased the property adjoining Wronski's (P) land and drilled several wells, all located in compliance with well spacing regulations. Wronski (P) alleged that Sun Oil (D) violated a proration order that limited production of oil to a maximum of 75 barrels per day per well. Wronski (P) brought suit, claiming that Sun Oil (D) overproduced more than 180,000 barrels and that the overproduced oil was drained from beneath his land. The trial court found Sun Oil (D) liable to Wronski (P) for the conversion of 50,000 barrels of oil. Sun Oil (D) appealed.

**ISSUE:** Does a violation of a proration order constitute conversion of oil from the pool and subject the violator to liability to all owners of interests in the pool for conversion of the illegally obtained oil?

**HOLDING AND DECISION:** (Holbrook, J.) Yes. A violation of a proration order constitutes conversion of oil from the pool and subjects the violator to liability to all owners of interests in the pool for conversion of the illegally obtained oil. Because there was a proration regulation in effect here, the rule of capture is limited, and Sun Oil (D) is liable for any amount taken in excess of the allotted amount. There is a recognized right to have a reasonable opportunity to produce one's just and equitable share of oil in a pool. Sun Oil (D) is liable to Wronski (P) because it has deprived him of the opportunity to claim the oil under his property. Any violation under a proration order constitutes conversion of the oil and subjects the violator to liability. Affirmed.

## ▶ ANALYSIS

For reasons of public policy, the state of Michigan, as well as many other states, have modified the harsh rule of capture so that a landowner is entitled only to his equitable share of the oil recovered from wells on his land. Another method of modification has been through a private arrangement called unitization, in which a group of individuals or companies own interest in a reservoir consisting of many wells. No matter which wells produce the oil for the reservoir, the profits are distributed according to pre-arranged percentages.

■≡■

## Quicknotes

**CONVERSION** The act of depriving an owner of his property without permission or justification.

**PRO RATA** In proportion.

■≡■

# United States v. Causby

## Federal government (D) v. Farm owner (P)

328 U.S. 256 (1946).

**NATURE OF CASE:** Suit seeking compensation for an alleged taking of property.

**FACT SUMMARY:** United States (D) planes, using a nearby airport, disturbed the Causbys (P) in their home and forced the discontinuation of their chicken farming business.

> ## 🏛 RULE OF LAW
> The use of a landowner's airspace by low-flying government planes constitutes a partial taking for which, under the Fifth Amendment, the landowner is entitled to be compensated.

**FACTS:** The United States (D), during World War II, leased an airport located near a farm owned by Causby (P) and his wife (P). One of the airport's runways was located less than half a mile from the Causbys' (P) house and barn, and this runway was, from time to time, used by the United States (D) for the landing and taking off of airplanes. These planes sometimes passed over the Causbys' (P) property at altitudes as low as 83 feet, making sleep impossible and causing acute nervousness. The low-flying planes also proved so frightening to the chickens that the Causbys (P) were eventually forced to give up their chicken business. Presented with these facts, the United States Court of Claims ruled that there had been a taking of the Causbys' (P) property through the acquisition by the United States (D) of an easement. The United States (D) was ordered to pay $2,000 in compensation. The United States (D) then petitioned the Supreme Court, which granted certiorari.

**ISSUE:** Is a private landowner entitled to compensation for a reduction in property value which results from the disturbance created by low-flying government aircraft?

**HOLDING AND DECISION:** (Douglas, J.) Yes. The use of a landowner's airspace by low-flying government planes constitutes a partial taking for which, under the Fifth Amendment, the landowner is entitled to compensation. In this day and age, aircraft operators obviously enjoy at least a limited privilege to utilize the airspace above a private landowner's property. But, despite the United States' (D) argument that the path of glide followed by the planes had been approved by the Civil Aeronautics Authority, this is not the standard to be used in evaluating the legality of a plane's altitude. Minimum safe altitudes are prescribed by law, and the flights over the Causbys' (P) land did not comply with the statutory standards. Therefore, the United States (D) did, in effect, usurp an easement in the Causbys' (P) property, and should be required to pay

compensation for this taking. However, since the court of claims failed to make a finding as to the extent and duration of this easement, the case must be remanded to that court so that the propriety of the amount of the compensation award may be determined. Reversed and remanded.

**DISSENT:** (Black, J.) The noise and disturbance caused by modern aircraft will probably cause new problems for the private landowner, but to cast his remedy in constitutional terms is an egregious error. The landowner may sue for damages or seek injunctive relief, but the broad sweep of the majority's opinion will only increase the difficulties to be encountered by those whose expertise qualifies them to seek solutions to the problems created by today's sophisticated planes.

## ▶ ANALYSIS

Courts are inclined to be generous in their treatment of landowners who are disturbed by aircraft flying over their property. Although plane flights are regarded as qualifiedly privileged, abuses are readily found to have occurred. The rule of the *Causby* case has been applied even to flights which were not violative of Civil Aeronautics Authority regulations and were no lower than necessary for landings or take-offs. (*Griggs v. Allegheny County*, 369 U.S. 84, 82 S. Ct. 531, 7 L. Ed. 2d 585 (1962), *reh. den.*, 369 U.S. 857, 82 S. Ct. 931, 8 L. Ed. 2d 16.)

■■■

## Quicknotes

**TAKING** A governmental action that substantially deprives an owner of the use and enjoyment of his or her property, requiring compensation.

■■■

# Prah v. Maretti

## Home owners (P) v. Builder of obstructing home (D)

Wis. Sup. Ct., 108 Wis. 2d 223, 321 N.W.2d 182 (1982).

**NATURE OF CASE:** Appeal from summary judgment denying relief from a proposed obstruction of sunlight.

**FACT SUMMARY:** Prah (P) sued to enjoin Maretti (D) from building on his land so as to block the flow of sunlight to Prah's (P) solar-heated house.

## 🏛 RULE OF LAW
The doctrine of prior appropriation applies to the use of sunlight as a protectable resource.

**FACTS:** In 1978, Prah (P) built a house which was equipped to use solar energy. Subsequently, Maretti (D) proposed to build a house which would have obstructed the free flow of sunlight onto Prah's (P) land, and, therefore interfered with his solar energy system. Prah (P) sued to enjoin the construction, contending he had begun using sunlight as a resource prior to Maretti's (D) plans, and, therefore, under the doctrine of prior appropriation, he had a protectable right in the sunlight. He then asserted that Maretti's (D) construction constituted a private nuisance. The trial court granted Maretti's (D) motion for a summary judgment, holding that prior appropriation doctrine did not apply and no easement in light and air could be recognized. Prah (P) appealed.

**ISSUE:** Does the doctrine of prior appropriation apply to the use of sunlight as a protectable resource?

**HOLDING AND DECISION:** (Abrahamson, J.) Yes. The doctrine of prior appropriation applies to the use of sunlight as a protectable resource. Because of the development of technology allowing the practical use of solar energy, sunlight has taken on an enhanced value. At early American common law, sunlight was valued for aesthetic purposes only, and it was left that an adjacent landowner's ability to use his land as he wished outweighed this aesthetic value, and no easement of light and air was recognized. However, given this new technology, sunlight must be regarded as a valuable resource and the doctrine of prior appropriation applies to protect those who first exploit the resource. Consequently, Prah (P) could maintain an action for nuisance. A factual question is presented whether Prah's (P) use was reasonable; therefore, summary judgment should not have been granted. Reversed and remanded.

**DISSENT:** (Callow, J.) Any recognition of rights in sunlight would be contrary to established law. Therefore, it is a question for legislative resolution. Further, under the facts of this case, no action for nuisance existed. Maretti's (D) use was not an unreasonable interference with Prah's (P) peaceful enjoyment of his property as the use of solar energy is an unusually sensitive use.

## ▶ ANALYSIS

Some states, such as New Mexico, have enacted statutes which create property rights in access to solar energy. Local governments are given the power under statutes to enact zoning regulations concerning solar rights. The New Mexico statute provides regulations protecting access in the absence of local regulations. Also, in order to be protected, solar rights, as other property rights, must be recorded.

■=■

## Quicknotes

**EASEMENT OF 'LIGHTS'** An interest in land granted for the unobstructed passage of light and air; from English common law.

**PRIVATE NUISANCE** An unlawful use of property interfering with the enjoyment of the private rights of an individual or a small number of persons.

■=■

# CHAPTER 18

# Introduction to the Traditional Land Use Controls

## *Quick Reference Rules of Law*

# Village of Euclid v. Ambler Realty Co.

## Municipality (D) v. Realtor (P)

272 U.S. 365 (1926).

**NATURE OF CASE:** Action to enjoin enforcement of a zoning ordinance.

**FACT SUMMARY:** Euclid (D) zoned property of Ambler Realty Co. (P) in a manner which materially reduced its potential value.

## 🏛 RULE OF LAW
A zoning ordinance, as a valid exercise of the police power, will only be declared unconstitutional where its provisions are clearly arbitrary and unreasonable, having no substantial relation to the public health, safety, morals, or general welfare.

**FACTS:** Ambler Realty Co. (P) was the owner of 68 acres in the village of Euclid (D). Though surrounded primarily by residential neighborhoods, the 68 acres also were bounded by a major thoroughfare to the south and a railroad to the north. Euclid (D) instituted zoning ordinances placing use, height, and area restrictions. Restrictions were placed on Ambler Realty's (P) prohibiting (1) apartment houses, hotels, churches, schools, or any other public or semi-public buildings for the first 620 feet from Euclid Avenue, the above-described major thoroughfare, and (2) industry, theatres, banks, shops, etc., for the next 130 feet after that. As a result of this zoning, the value of Ambler Realty's (P) property declined from $10,000 per acre to $2,500 per acre. Ambler Realty (P) brought an action to enjoin Euclid (D) from enforcing the ordinance on the ground that it constituted a violation of Fourteenth Amendment due process. From a decree in favor of Ambler Realty (P), Euclid (D) appealed, contending that the ordinance was a valid exercise of the police power of the state.

**ISSUE:** Is a zoning ordinance unconstitutional as a deprivation of property without due process because it results in a diminution of value in the property zoned?

**HOLDING AND DECISION:** (Sutherland, J.) No. A zoning ordinance, as a valid exercise of the police power, will only be declared unconstitutional where its provisions are clearly arbitrary and unreasonable, having no substantial relation to the public health, safety, morals, or general welfare. Zoning ordinances, and all similar laws and regulations, must find their justification in some aspect of the police power, asserted for the public welfare. Until recent years, urban life was comparatively simple; but with the great increase and concentration of population, problems have developed which require new restrictions on the use and occupation of private lands in urban communities. There is no serious difference of opinion on the state power to avoid the nuisances which industry may cause in a residential area. As for residential regulation, many considerations point toward

their validity. Segregation of residential business and industrial buildings makes it easier to provide appropriate fire apparatus, for example. Further, it is often observed that the construction of one type of building destroys an area for other types. In light of these considerations, the court is not prepared to say that the end of public welfare here is not sufficient to justify the imposition of this ordinance. It clearly cannot be said that it "passes the bounds of reason and assumes the character of a merely arbitrary fiat." The decree must be reversed. No injunction may be had. Reversed.

## ▶ ANALYSIS

Village of *Euclid v. Ambler Realty* is the landmark Supreme Court decision on zoning ordinances as valid exercises of the police power. Essentially, any zoning ordinance which is tied to public health, safety, morals, or welfare will be upheld unless clearly arbitrary and unreasonable. So-called Euclidian Zoning, which resulted from this decision, usually consists in the division of areas into zones, in which building use, height, and area are regulated in a manner designed to guarantee homogeneity of building patterns. All too often, however, zoning operates not so much to protect the public interest as to protect the vested interests in a community. Building restrictions may all too easily be used as an economic sanction by which social segregation is perpetuated. (Barring low-cost housing keeps out economically deprived segments of the population.) Note, however, that *Euclid* did not foreclose the possibility that government land-use regulations may constitute a "taking" which requires compensation. In *Pennsylvania Coal Co. v. Mahon*, 260 U.S. 393 (1922) the U.S. Supreme Court held that an anti-mining restriction, which totally destroyed the interest of the party who owned only the mineral rights, constituted a taking as to that person which had to be compensated for. There, the diminution in value of the party's property was to zero, and this is clearly a "taking."

■━■

## Quicknotes

**POLICE POWERS** The power of a state or local government to regulate private conduct for the health, safety and welfare of the general public.

**TAKING** A governmental action that substantially deprives an owner of the use and enjoyment of his or her property, requiring compensation.

**ZONING ORDINANCE** A statute that divides land into defined areas and which regulates the form and use of buildings and structures within those areas.

■━■

# Nectow v. City of Cambridge

Landowner (P) v. Municipality (D)

277 U.S. 183 (1928).

**NATURE OF CASE:** Action to enjoin the enforcement of a zoning ordinance.

**FACT SUMMARY:** City of Cambridge (D) restricted a portion of Nectow's (P) land for residential use only.

## RULE OF LAW
A zoning ordinance, as applied, must bear a substantial relation to the public health, safety, morals, or general welfare in order to be constitutional.

**FACTS:** Nectow (P) owned a tract of land, part of which was restricted to residential use by a zoning law. The rest of the tract of land was unrestricted. Nectow (P) claimed that the land restricted to residential use was so worthless, because of the restrictions, as to constitute a deprivation of property without due process of law in contravention of the Fourteenth Amendment. The land was separated from other residential land by streets on both sides, while there was a Ford Motor Company auto assembling factory on the south side of the land and other industrial property nearby. Nectow (P) sought an injunction to force the city to allow him to use the land without regard to the zoning ordinance. The case was referred to a Master, who found that enforcing the ordinance as to this property wouldn't benefit the city. At trial, however, the court sustained the ordinance as applied to Nectow (P) and denied the bill.

**ISSUE:** Must a zoning ordinance, as applied, promote the general welfare, safety, and health of a city in order to be held valid?

**HOLDING AND DECISION:** (Sutherland, J.) Yes. The zoning ordinance of Cambridge (D) was not itself being challenged, but rather the manner in which it was being applied. The court held that a zoning ordinance as applied must substantially promote the public health, safety, morals, or general welfare of the city in order to be valid. In this case the ordinance restricted land to residential use only, while the land was practically worthless when restricted in that manner. The land was basically located in an industrial area and restricting the use of the land in this case did not benefit the city. The zoning ordinance as applied deprived Nectow (P) of his property without due process of law and, therefore, as applied in this case, was unconstitutional. The judgment of the lower court was reversed.

## ▶ ANALYSIS

After this case was decided by the Supreme Court, it refused to consider the validity of any zoning ordinance and, therefore, the constitutionality of zoning ordinances is unquestioned. As a result, the Court has left it to the various states to apply the constitutional principle of reasonableness to individual cases as they arise. Today, there is a wide difference in both emphasis and doctrine from state to state.

■=■

## Quicknotes

**ZONING ORDINANCE** A statute that divides land into defined areas and which regulates the form and use of buildings and structures within those areas.

■=■

# Durant v. Town of Dunbarton

Subdivision planner (P) v. Municipality (D)

N.H. Sup. Ct., 121 N.H. 352, 430 A.2d 140 (1981).

**NATURE OF CASE:** Appeal from denial of a subdivision plan.

**FACT SUMMARY:** Durant (P) contended that the subdivision regulations under which her subdivision plan was rejected were invalid due to vagueness.

## 🏛 RULE OF LAW
A municipality has broad powers to consider subdivision plans and its regulations may require such plans to conform to conditions favorable to health, safety, convenience, and welfare.

**FACTS:** Durant (P) petitioned the Dunbarton Planning Board (D) for approval of her subdivision plan. Under its subdivision regulations, half of the Board (D) rejected the plan for three reasons: (1) potential disruption of water flow; (2) sight problems caused by existing driveways onto a state highway; and (3) problems with septic system location. Durant (P) appealed, contending the regulations were too vague to support a denial of her plan on those grounds. The trial court affirmed, holding the Board's (D) decision was reasonable. Durant (P) appealed.

**ISSUE:** Does a municipality exercise broad power in determining whether to approve a subdivision plan?

**HOLDING AND DECISION:** (Douglas, J.) Yes. A municipality has broad powers to consider subdivision plans, and its regulations need not state specifically each ground upon which a plan may be rejected. It is sufficient that the regulations allow rejection in order to promote conditions favorable to health, safety, convenience, and welfare. In this case, each express ground for rejecting Durant's (P) plan falls under the promotion of these conditions. Therefore, the rejection was reasonable. Affirmed.

## ▶ ANALYSIS

In *Kaufman & Gold Construction Co. v. Planning and Zoning Commission of the City of Fairmont*, 298 S.E.2d 148 (1982), a planning board's rejection of a subdivision plan was overturned. The court held that if the developer conforms to all applicable statutes and ordinances, the act of approving a plan is ministerial and no discretion exists to reject it.

■≡■

## Quicknotes

**SUBDIVISION PLOT** A parcel of land that is divided into portions to be resold or developed.

■≡■

# Village of Valatie v. Smith

## Municipality (P) v. Mobile home inheritor (D)

N.Y. Ct. App., 83 N.Y.2d 396, 632 N.E.2d 1264 (1994).

**NATURE OF CASE:** Appeal of grant of cross-motion for summary judgment authorizing continued nonconforming land usage.

**FACT SUMMARY:** After Smith (D) inherited a mobile home, the Village of Valatie (P) sought to enforce a law that terminated any nonconforming land use at the time of ownership transfer.

🏛 **RULE OF LAW**
An amortization period that uses transfer of a property to fix duration does not violate due process rights.

**FACTS:** The Village of Valatie (P) enacted chapter 85 of its Village Code to prohibit placement of mobile homes outside of mobile home parks. Under the law, a mobile home outside a park could remain as a nonconforming use until the ownership of either the land or the home changed hands. Six mobile homes fell within the nonconforming use exception. Smith (D) inherited the home from her father. The Village (P) brought suit to have the law enforced. Both the Village (P) and Smith (D) moved for summary judgement. The court granted Smith's (D) motion and denied the Village's (P). The Village (P) appealed.

**ISSUE:** Will an amortization period using the transfer of a property to set its duration violate due process rights?

**HOLDING AND DECISION:** (Simons, J.) No. An amortization period using the transfer of a property to set its duration will not violate due process rights. To pass due process scrutiny, an amortization period must be reasonably related to some legitimate government interest in land use planning. The government body must balance the need for the individual to recoup an investment with the interests of the public in having orderly land use. Here, the Village (P) designed an amortization scheme which meets the balancing goal by giving the owner the power to determine how long the nonconforming use will continue. And in this case, the Village (P) went one step further. The Village (P) also considered the individual's desire not to be displaced involuntarily, adding greater weight to the concerns of the individual. Appellate decision modified by denying Smith's (D) cross-motion for summary judgment. Affirmed as modified.

▶ *ANALYSIS*

The law of amortization periods is unsettled. In *Pennsylvania*, for example, the courts have generally banned all amortization schemes for nonconforming uses. And other municipalities have approached nonconforming use control by

designating a zoning board of appeals to authorize or deny nonconforming land use, as opposed to an amortization period.

■══■

## *Quicknotes*

**AMORTIZATION** Period of time permitted property owner to comply with zoning ordinance.

**NONCONFORMING USE** The use of a structure which is rendered unlawful by the promulgation or revision of a zoning ordinance.

■══■

# Stone v. City of Wilton

Property buyer (P) v. City (D)

Iowa Sup. Ct., 331 N.W.2d 398 (1983).

**NATURE OF CASE:** Appeal of relief sought in a zoning dispute.

**FACT SUMMARY:** Stone (P) purchased property for a multi-family housing project which was later rezoned as a single-family residential area.

## 🏛 RULE OF LAW
A substantial investment in actual construction on land prior to rezoning creates a vested right in the original zoning classification.

**FACTS:** In June 1979, Stone (P) bought six acres of land to build a low-income, federally funded housing development. Three-fourths was zoned as single-family residential. In December 1979, after Stone (P) had submitted a preliminary plan with the city clerk, a rezoning recommendation to single-family residential was made by the planning and zoning commission of the City of Wilton (D) to the city council. In May 1980, when Stone's (P) application was denied pending the rezoning proposal, Stone (P) sought a temporary injunction to prohibit the rezoning. The injunction was denied and the area was rezoned to a single-family residential classification. Stone's (P) application was thereafter approved, but only for single-family residential housing projects. Stone (P) appealed on the basis that the rezoning classification effectuated a taking of his vested right, and, thus, the new zoning classification was inapplicable to him. He sued for declaratory judgment and injunctions to invalidate any rezoning and, in the alternative, $570,000 damages for money expended, future lost profits, and decrease in land value.

**ISSUE:** Does a substantial investment in actual construction on land prior to rezoning create a vested right in the original zoning classification?

**HOLDING AND DECISION:** (McGiverin, J.) Yes. A substantial investment in actual construction on land prior to rezoning creates a vested right in the original zoning classification. The factors which determine whether a substantial investment was made "depends on the type of project, its location, ultimate cost, and principally the amount accomplished under conformity." *Board of Supervisors of Scott County v. Paaske*, 250 Iowa 1293, 98 N.W.2d 827 (1959). In *Paaske*, the plaintiff had excavated five basements of four houses, built an underground septic tank, laid concrete basements for two houses, entered building contracts for five houses, and placed construction materials on the property before rezoning occurred. Here, although Stone (P) expended $7,900, secured funding, and hired architects and engineers to draw up plans and plats, those were only preliminary steps toward construction. No contracts or construction bids were ever made, no construction materials were on site, and no construction was actually started. Thus, Stone (P) made no substantial investment on his land prior to rezoning. Affirmed.

## ▶ ANALYSIS

A minority of jurisdictions have created two exceptions to the "substantial investment" requirement. The first exception is that of detrimental reliance, and the second is where the aim of rezoning is to hinder the proposed development project. This minority approach is hailed as being more administratively feasible as well as more equitable because it provides more uniformity in outcome. See *Smith v. Winhall Planning Commission*, 140 Vt. 178, 436 A.2d 760 (1981).

■■■

### Quicknotes

**VESTED RIGHT** Rights in pension or other retirement benefits that are attained when the employee satisfies the minimum requirements necessary in order to be entitled to the receipt of such benefits in the future.

**ZONING VARIANCE** Exemption from the application of zoning laws.

■■■

# Land Use Planning: Eminent Domain and Regulatory Takings

## *Quick Reference Rules of Law*

# Kelo v. City of New London

Landowners (P) v. Municipality (D)

545 U.S. 469 (2005).

**NATURE OF CASE:** Suit challenging a city's proposed taking of private properties to promote the city's planned economic revitalization.

**FACT SUMMARY:** A city adopted a development plan designed to revitalize the local economy. To implement its plan, the city sought to condemn fifteen properties owned by nine private landowners who refused to sell their properties to the city.

🏛 **RULE OF LAW**
A city's proposed taking of private property for general economic development qualifies as a public use consistent with the Takings Clause of the Fifth Amendment to the U.S. Constitution.

**FACTS:** In 1990, a Connecticut state agency officially designated the City of New London ("the City" or "New London") (D) as a "distressed municipality." New London's (D) economy worsened in 1996 when the federal government closed a facility that employed 1,500 people. The City's (D) unemployment rate almost doubled that for the rest of the state, and its population had dwindled to its lowest level in almost eighty years. State and local officials therefore targeted New London (D) for economic revitalization. Eventually a development plan focused on a 90-acre area known as Fort Trumbull as the center of the City's (D) revitalization efforts. The drafters designed the development plan to coincide with the expected arrival of a major company, Pfizer Inc., and to rejuvenate the local economy with jobs, tax revenue, and a generalized momentum for future growth and recreational activities. Most landowners in the Fort Trumbull area agreed to sell their properties to the City (D). Nine owners, however, refused to sell their fifteen properties. The City (D) condemned the fifteen properties purely because they were within the area designated for development; the City (D) never alleged that the properties were in any degree of substandard condition. [Susette Kelo (P) and the other eight resisting owners sued the City (D) in state court, where the trial judge permanently enjoined the City (D) from taking eleven of the contested properties but permitted the taking of the other four properties. Both sides appealed to the Connecticut Supreme Court, which held that all fifteen properties could properly be taken by New London (D). Applying state statute, the state's highest court held that the proposed taking was for a public use that satisfied both state and federal constitutional requirements. Kelo (P) and her fellow landowners petitioned the U.S. Supreme Court for further review.]

**ISSUE:** Does a city's proposed taking of private property for general economic development qualify as a public use consistent with the Takings Clause of the Fifth Amendment to the U.S. Constitution?

**HOLDING AND DECISION:** (Stevens, J.) Yes. A city's proposed taking of private property for general economic development qualifies as a public use consistent with the Takings Clause of the Fifth Amendment to the U.S. Constitution. A government may not take private property merely to transfer it to another private owner; conversely, private property may be taken if the taking is legitimately for "use by the public." Neither of these general propositions controls this case, though, because the question here narrows to whether a proposed taking for general economic development serves a "public purpose," which is the broader reading of "public use" that this Court has consistently used for more than a century. The Court upheld the redevelopment plan at issue in *Berman v. Parker*, 348 U.S. 26 (1954), because creating a "better balanced, more attractive community" was a valid public purpose. Similarly, in Hawaii Housing *Authority v. Midkiff*, 467 U.S. 229 (1984), the Court upheld a state statute that took fee title from lessors and vested title in lessees to more broadly distribute land ownership in the affected area. Thus, under the appropriately deferential standard of review, New London's (D) proposed takings here do meet the public use requirement imposed by the Takings Clause. Kelo's (P) objection that economic development confuses the distinction between public and private use contradicts precedent; public use often benefits specific private owners, too. Finally, Kelo's (P) objection that nothing would stop a city from transferring land from one private owner to another specific private owner for a public purpose presents issues that are not before the Court in this case. Accordingly, this Court's takings jurisprudence provides no basis for preventing the City of New London (D) from taking the fifteen properties in the Fort Trumbull area. Affirmed.

**CONCURRENCE:** (Kennedy, J.) Rational basis review under the Public Use Clause should invalidate a taking clearly designed primarily to favor a specific private party where only minor or pretextual benefits will accrue to the public. Some cases might justify a higher standard of review to justify takings, but this is not such a case, given the City's several safeguards in formulating its proposed development plan.

*Continued on next page.*

**DISSENT:** (O'Connor, J.) The Court has abandoned one of the Constitution's most basic restraints on governments by removing any distinction between public and private uses. To define the proper distinction, this Court's role is to decide the matter for itself instead of blindly deferring to legislative determinations, as the majority does today. Properly considered under judicial standards, takings for economic development are not consistent with the Takings Clause. The takings in *Berman* and *Midkiff* differed from the takings here because those takings directly benefited the public by immediately removing harmful uses. In sharp contrast, the uses of the homes by Kelo (P) and the other landowners here are not inherently harmful. The definition of public use, then, now means much more than it has ever meant in earlier cases. The Takings Clause's requirement that takings be "for public use" is effectively meaningless now because the phrase no longer reasonably excludes any takings. In these circumstances, the City's deliberative process is irrelevant because the new standard of wholesale deference to legislative bodies means that takings resulting from less-stringent processes must also be upheld. These conditions will benefit citizens who already have more resources and more political influence—a situation that flouts what was supposed to be the American commitment to just, impartial government.

**DISSENT:** (Thomas, J.) The text of the Constitution permits takings of private property for public use, not for public necessity. Justice O'Connor therefore correctly argues that this Court cannot abridge specifically enumerated constitutional liberties guaranteed by the Takings Clause. But the majority's error today is far more fundamental: as originally understood, and as this Court long ago forgot, the Takings Clause imposes real restraints on the power of eminent domain. The Court certainly does not owe effectively complete deference to legislative determinations of public use, just as such deference is not appropriate when reviewing legislative definitions of other constitutional provisions. This deferential standard is particularly inappropriate when compared to the searching review extended to, for example, grants of welfare benefits or warrants for mere searches of homes. Such a standard of review only ensures that those who already have more resources will more easily victimize the weak, which in most cases will regrettably equate with the black landowners most often affected by urban renewal projects.

## ▌*ANALYSIS*

Despite the public outcry that greeted the *Kelo* decision, the majority opinion has too much support in precedent, specifically in *Berman* and *Midkiff*, to fit naïve definitions of judicial activism. At the same time, Justice O'Connor's distinction between the inherently harmful uses in *Berman* and *Midkiff* and what she sees as the inherently harmless uses in *Kelo* seems to impose something like the higher standard hinted at in Justice Kennedy's concurrence. For

Justice O'Connor, New London's (D) chronic and deepening economic demise does not qualify as a harm caused by the affected private ownership itself that would, for her, justify a taking.

■≡■

## *Quicknotes*

**EMINENT DOMAIN** The governmental power to take private property for public use so long as just compensation is paid therefore.

**PUBLIC USE** Basis for governmental taking of property pursuant to its power of eminent domain so that property taken may be utilized for the benefit of the public at large.

**TAKINGS CLAUSE** Provision of the Fifth Amendment to the United States Constitution prohibiting the government from taking private property for public use without providing just compensation therefor.

■≡■

# Loretto v. Teleprompter Manhattan CATV Corp.

Landlord (P) v. Cable company (D)

458 U.S. 419 (1982).

**NATURE OF CASE:** Appeal from enforcement of state statute.

**FACT SUMMARY:** Loretto (P) contended that a New York law requiring apartment house owners to allow for the installation of cable television equipment allowed a taking of property without just compensation.

## 🏛 RULE OF LAW
Any permanent physical occupation of an owner's property which is governmentally authorized constitutes a taking of property for which just compensation must be paid.

**FACTS:** New York enacted a statute which required apartment house owners to provide tenants with access to cable television reception. Loretto (P) brought a class action against Teleprompter Manhattan CATV Corp. (D), contending its placement of its cable television installation equipment constituted trespass and that the statute allowed for a taking of her property without just compensation. The trial court granted summary judgment for Teleprompter (D), upholding the constitutionality of the statute. The appellate court affirmed, and Loretto (P) appealed to the U.S. Supreme Court.

**ISSUE:** Is any permanent physical occupation of an owner's property which is authorized by the government a taking of property which requires the payment of just compensation?

**HOLDING AND DECISION:** (Marshall, J.) Yes. Any permanent physical occupation of an owner's property which is authorized by the government constitutes a taking of property which requires a payment of just compensation. Any occupation, no matter how slight, impacts on the owner's right to exclusive possession of his property. In this case, the equipment occupied a very small area of the property. Yet its presence constituted a physical occupation and thus necessarily must be classified as a taking of property within the meaning of the Fifth Amendment. Therefore, just compensation must be paid. Reversed.

**DISSENT:** (Blackmun, J.) The Court goes against established precedent by recognizing a per se "taking" rule. It has previously been held on many occasions that each taking case must be considered on its peculiar facts. A rigid per se rule finding a taking in every physical encroachment will require compensation in situations not justified under previous interpretations of the taking clause.

## ▶ ANALYSIS

The Court recognizes the fundamental inconsistency with the elements of private ownership presented by any physical invasion of the property by a stranger. When such an invasion is authorized by the government, a compensable taking occurs. The amount of money necessary to constitute just compensation will vary with the case. The Court declined to rule on whether the $1 per unit payment was sufficient in this case.

## Quicknotes

**CLASS ACTION** A suit commenced by a representative on behalf of an ascertainable group that is too large to appear in court, who shares a commonality of interests and who will benefit from a successful result.

**JUST COMPENSATION** The right guaranteed by the Fifth Amendment to the United States Constitution of a person, when his property is taken for public use by the state, to receive adequate compensation in order to restore him to the position he enjoyed prior to the appropriation.

**SUMMARY JUDGMENT** Judgment rendered by a court in response to a motion by one of the parties, claiming that the lack of a question of material fact in respect to an issue warrants disposition of the issue without consideration by the jury.

**TAKING** A governmental action that substantially deprives an owner of the use and enjoyment of his or her property, requiring compensation.

**TRESPASS** Unlawful interference with, or damage to, the real or personal property of another.

# Pennsylvania Coal Co. v. Mahon

Coal company (D) v. Property owner (P)

260 U.S. 393 (1922).

**NATURE OF CASE:** Review of judgment granting an injunction against the exercise of contractual rights.

**FACT SUMMARY:** Mahon (P) sought to prevent coal mining under his property by enforcing the Kohler Act, after contractually leaving subterranean rights in the hands of Pennsylvania Coal Co. (D).

## 🏛 RULE OF LAW
While property may be regulated to a certain degree, if that regulation goes too far, then the regulation will be seen as a taking under the Fifth and Fourteenth Amendments.

**FACTS:** Pennsylvania Coal Co. (D) conveyed by deed the surface rights of a property to Mahon (P), but explicitly retained, in a valid contract, the right to remove coal under the same property. Subsequently, Pennsylvania passed the Kohler Act, which forbade, in part, the mining of coal in such a way as to cause subsidence of any residence. Mahon (P) sought an injunction to prevent Pennsylvania Coal Co. (D) from mining and damaging his property.

**ISSUE:** Will an intrusive regulation of property by government, at some degree, be deemed a taking under the Fifth and Fourteenth Amendments?

**HOLDING AND DECISION:** (Holmes, J.) Yes. While property may be regulated to a certain degree, if that regulation goes too far, then the regulation will be seen as a taking under the Fifth and Fourteenth Amendments. An intrusive regulation of property by government, at some degree, is deemed to be a taking under the Fifth and Fourteenth Amendments. To some degree, nearly every government action affects property values. But, at some magnitude, the intrusion is so great as to require the exercise of eminent domain to compensate the property owner. Thus it becomes a case-by-case analysis depending upon the facts at hand. Here, Mahon's (P) property interest touches little on the public interest. The danger of subsidence is uncommon and could be avoided by a simple warning or notice requirement. And the regulatory intrusion is extreme, eliminating an estate in land and destroying a freely bargained contract. The Kohler Act cannot be sustained as a valid exercise of the police power; otherwise, individuals would inure to rights greater than they purchased. Reversed.

**DISSENT:** (Brandeis, J.) All regulations deprive the owner of some property use. But restrictions to protect health and safety are not takings. Incidental benefit to Mahon (P) should not vitiate a valid purpose of public safety.

## ▶ ANALYSIS

This landmark case is often cited for the proposition that government may execute laws or programs that adversely affect recognized economic values without compensating those affected. Taking challenges have since been held to be without merit in a wide variety of situations, including zoning, when the government action prohibited a beneficial use, causing substantial individualized harm. Justices Holmes and Brandeis represent the two perspectives of the continuing conflict between the obligation of government to provide for the general welfare and the right of citizens to privately own property.

■■■

## Quicknotes

**EMINENT DOMAIN** The governmental power to take private property for public use so long as just compensation is paid therefore.

**POLICE POWERS** The power of a state or local government to regulate private conduct for the health, safety and welfare of the general public.

**TAKING** A governmental action that substantially deprives an owner of the use and enjoyment of his or her property, requiring compensation.

■■■

# First English Evangelical Lutheran Church of Glendale v. County of Los Angeles

Church (P) v. County (D)

482 U.S. 304 (1987).

**NATURE OF CASE:** Review of appeal denying a claim for damages originating in the Just Compenstation Clause of the Fifth Amendment.

**FACT SUMMARY:** After a flood destroyed properties, including those held by the First English Evangelical Lutheran Church of Glendale (P), the County of Los Angeles (D) enacted an ordinance that prohibited construction in a flood control zone that encompased the Church (P) property.

## 🏛 RULE OF LAW
When a regulation is eventually determined to be a taking under the Fifth and Fourteenth Amendments, a landowner is entitled to recover damages accruing before such a determination is made.

**FACTS:** The First English Evangelical Lutheran Church of Glendale (P) purchased land in a canyon along a creek. The Church (P) placed structures on the land and ran a campground. After a forest fire damaged the upstream watershed, a flood destroyed the buildings on the Church (P) land. The County of Los Angeles (D), in an effort to preserve the public health and safety, defined a flood control zone that encompassed all the flat areas of the Church's (P) land. Construction was prohibited in the flood control zone. The Church (P) then filed a complaint in superior court, alleging a regulatory taking. The court of appeals ruled that the Church (P) could not receive compensation for the amount of time it was temporarily deprived of the use of its land before the ordinance was invalidated. The Church (P) appealed.

**ISSUE:** If a regulation is eventually determined to be a taking under the Fifth and Fourteenth Amendments, is a landowner entitled to recover damages accruing before such a determination is made?

**HOLDING AND DECISION:** (Rehnquist, C.J.) Yes. If a regulation is eventually determined to be a taking under the Fifth and Fourteenth Amendments, a landowner is entitled to recover damages accruing before such a determination is made. Any government action that works as a taking activates the constitutional obligation to pay just compensation. In cases where the government has only temporarily exercised its right to use private property, the issue was never whether compensation was required, but how such compensation should be measured. In this case, the County of Los Angeles (D) ordinance denied all use of the Church (P) property for a period of years. Invalidation of the ordinance alone, without payment of compensation, would be a constitutionally insufficient remedy. Reversed and remanded.

**DISSENT:** (Stevens, J.) A regulatory scheme that diminishes property value does not constitute a taking unless it destroys a major portion of the property's value. Scope, severity, and duration of regulations must all be analyzed to determine the extent by which property value is reduced. This decision will make officials overly cautious, and much important regulation will never be enacted.

## ▶ ANALYSIS

This case raised a question as to whether moratoria on land development pending impact studies are constitutional. Another question still unsettled is the method by which temporary takings should be compensated. Courts are divided on this issue, but many have used rental income during the regulated period as a measure of damages.

■═■

## Quicknotes

**MORATORIUM** Suspension of legal remedies or proceedings.

**TAKING** A governmental action that substantially deprives an owner of the use and enjoyment of his or her property, requiring compensation.

■═■

# Penn Central Transportation Co. v. City of New York

## Railroad (P) v. City (D)

438 U.S. 104 (1978).

**NATURE OF CASE:** Appeal from an action seeking an injunction and a declaratory judgment.

**FACT SUMMARY:** Penn Central Transportation Co. (Penn Central) (P), owner and proposed developer of the air rights above Grand Central Terminal, brought this action seeking a declaration that a landmark regulation as applied to the terminal property was unconstitutional.

### 🏛 RULE OF LAW
Although governmental regulation is invalid if it denies a property owner all reasonable return on his property, there is no constitutional imperative that the return embrace all attributes or contributing external factors derived from the social complex in which the property rests.

**FACTS:** Penn Central Transportation Co. (Penn Central) (P), owner and proposed developer of the air rights above Grand Central Terminal, brought this action against the City of New York (D) seeking a declaratory judgment that the landmark preservation provisions as applied to the terminal property were unconstitutional. Penn Central (P) also sought to enjoin the City of New York (D) from enforcing the landmark regulation against the subject property. Penn Central (P) desired to construct an office building atop the terminal and contended that the landmark regulation deprived it from realizing a reasonable return on the property in violation of the due process clause of the Constitution. Trial term granted the requested relief, but the appellate division reversed. Penn Central (P) appealed.

**ISSUE:** Is a government regulation invalid if it denies a property owner of all reasonable return on his property?

**HOLDING AND DECISION:** (Brennan, J.) Yes. Although government regulation is invalid if it denies a property owner all reasonable return, there is no constitutional imperative that the return embrace all attributes or contributing external factors derived from the social complex in which the property rests. So many of these attributes are not the result of private effort or investment, but of opportunities for the utilization or exploitation which an organized society offers to any private enterprise, especially to a public utility, favored by government and the public. It is enough, for the limited purposes of a landmarking statute, that the privately created ingredient of property receive a reasonable return. All else is society's contribution. Moreover, in this case, the challenged regulation provides Penn Central (P) with transferable above-the-surface development rights which, because they may be attached to specific parcels of property, some already owned by Penn Central (P), may be considered as part of the owner's return on the terminal property. Thus, the regulation does not deprive Penn Central (P) of property without due process of law, and should be upheld as a valid exercise of the police power. Absent past heavy public governmental investment in the terminal, the railroads, and connecting transportation, it is indisputable that the terminal property would be worth but a fraction of its current economic value. Penn Central (P) may not now frustrate legitimate and important social objectives by complaining, in essence, that government regulation deprives them of a return on so much of the investment made not by private interests but by the people of the city and state through their government. Affirmed.

**DISSENT:** (Rehnquist, J.) Not every destruction or injury to property by the government is a taking. Examining the two exceptions where the destruction of property does not constitute a taking shows that a compensable taking has occurred here. The first is that there is no taking where the government is prohibiting a nuisance, which it is not here. The second, which applies to broad land use controls such as zoning, is where a prohibition applies over a broad cross section of land and thereby secures an average reciprocity of advantage. That, however, is not the case at hand. Here, a multimillion dollar loss has been imposed, but it is not offset by any benefits flowing from the preservation of less than one-tenth of one percent of other "landmarks" in New York City. Although the public may benefit, it is exactly this imposition of general costs on a few individuals at which the "taking" protection is directed.

### ▶ ANALYSIS

Landmark regulation is not a zoning problem. Restrictions on alteration of individual landmarks are not designed to further a general community plan, but to prevent the alteration or demolition of a single piece of property. To this extent, such restrictions resemble discriminatory zoning restrictions. There is, however, a significant difference. Discriminatory zoning is condemned because there is no acceptable reason for singling out one particular parcel for different and less favorable treatment. When landmark regulation is involved, there is such a reason: the cultural, architectural, historical, or social significance attached to the property.

■=■

*Continued on next page.*

## *Quicknotes*

**POLICE POWERS** The power of a state or local government to regulate private conduct for the health, safety and welfare of the general public.

**TAKING** A governmental action that substantially deprives an owner of the use and enjoyment of his or her property, requiring compensation.

# Lucas v. South Carolina Coastal Council

## Lot purchaser (P) v. Regulatory agency (D)

505 U.S. 1003 (1992).

**NATURE OF CASE:** Appeal of the denial of a taking claim in action for compensation of property value.

**FACT SUMMARY:** South Carolina's (D) Beachfront Management Act barred Lucas (P) from erecting homes on two parcels of land near the ocean.

### 🏛 RULE OF LAW
The state must compensate a landowner when a regulatory action denies the owner economically viable use of the land, unless the prohibited use constitutes a nuisance.

**FACTS:** In 1986, Lucas (P) bought two residential lots near the ocean for $975,000. In 1988, South Carolina (D) enacted the Beachfront Management Act, which sought to counteract coastal erosion. The law restricted new development of beachfront areas and barred Lucas (P) from building homes on his lots as he intended. Lucas (P) brought suit contending that the Act was an unconstitutional taking of his property. The trial court ruled that the Act deprived Lucas (P) of any reasonable economic use of the land and was an uncompensated taking. The South Carolina Supreme Court reversed, holding that the regulation was designed to prevent serious public harm and did not constitute a taking. Lucas (P) appealed, and the Supreme Court granted review.

**ISSUE:** Must the state compensate a landowner when a regulatory action denies an owner economically viable use of the land?

**HOLDING AND DECISION:** (Scalia, J.) Yes. The state must compensate a landowner when a regulatory action denies an owner economically viable use of his land, unless the prohibited use constitutes a nuisance. Physical intrusions on property must always be compensated. A regulation that denies all economically beneficial and productive uses of land is the equivalent of physical appropriation and must also be compensated under the Takings Clause. The Court has previously acknowledged that regulations that restrict nuisance-like uses of land may provide an exception to the general rule on takings. The court of appeals attempted to distinguish laws that prevented harmful use from those regulations that confer benefits on the public. This distinction should not provide the basis for our determinations because it is impossible to objectively distinguish the two rationales. The better rule is that the government may only restrict uses that are already unlawful under existing nuisance and property laws. South Carolina's (D) Beachfront Management Act deprived Lucas's (P) land of all economically beneficial use and restricted uses which were previously permissible. Therefore, it was an unconstitutional taking. Reversed and remanded.

**CONCURRENCE:** (Kennedy, J.) The trial court's finding that Lucas's (P) land had been deprived of all beneficial use is highly questionable. Furthermore, the nuisance exception should not be the sole justification for severe restrictions when the state's unique concerns for fragile land systems are involved.

**DISSENT:** (Blackmun, J.) Lucas (P) may continue to use his land for recreation and camping and retains the right to alienate the land. Therefore, the trial court's ruling is certainly erroneous.

**DISSENT:** (Stevens, J.) The rule stated by the court in this case is wholly arbitrary; a landowner who loses 95% recovers nothing while one whose property declines 100% recovers the full land value. Courts will define property broadly to avoid finding takings, and developers will design small, specialized estates that will be more likely to suffer complete diminution of value in order to effect a total taking.

### ▶ ANALYSIS

Justice Souter wrote separately to indicate that he felt the writ of certiorari was improvidently granted because he also thought that the trial court's conclusion as to the value of Lucas's (P) land after the regulation was highly questionable. Souter also indicated that, contrary to Scalia's conclusion, nuisance law should not be the basis of regulatory takings because it focuses on conduct and not on the character of the property.

■══■

### Quicknotes

**NUISANCE** An unlawful use of property that interferes with the lawful use of another's property.

**TAKING** A governmental action that substantially deprives an owner of the use and enjoyment of his or her property, requiring compensation.

■══■

# Nollan v. California Coastal Commission

Beachfront property owner (P) v. Regulatory agency (D)

483 U.S. 825 (1987).

**NATURE OF CASE:** Review of court order upholding conditional land-use permit.

**FACT SUMMARY:** The California Coastal Commission (D) conditioned a building permit on the owners' granting of a public beach access easement.

## 🏛 RULE OF LAW
A state may not condition a property use permit on an act not addressing the problem caused by the permitted use.

**FACTS:** The Nollans (P) owned certain beachfront property. They applied for a permit to build a residence upon it. The California Coastal Commission (D), finding that such a use would impede public viewing of the beach, conditioned the permit upon the Nollans' (P) granting of a public easement permitting lateral movement along the Nollans' (P) property to adjacent public beaches. The Nollans (P) challenged this as a deprivation of property rights without due process. The trial court agreed and enjoined the condition. The California Court of Appeals reversed. The Supreme Court accepted review.

**ISSUE:** May a state condition a property use permit on an act not addressing the problem caused by the permitted use?

**HOLDING AND DECISION:** (Scalia, J.) No. A state may not condition a property use permit on an act not addressing the problem caused by the permitted use. A land-use regulation does not effect a taking if it substantially advances legitimate state interests and does not deny an owner economically viable use of his land. Thus, when a state finds a public interest and does not leave the owner with useless property, no taking occurs when a land use is prohibited. However, this constitutional propriety disappears when the condition substituted for outright prohibition fails to further the end advanced as the justification for the prohibition. When this occurs, the prohibition no longer becomes a vehicle for advancing a state interest, but rather a manner of extorting a property right without paying just compensation. Here, the recognized public interest was preventing the blockage of the beach from public view. The condition, providing an easement for lateral public access along the beach, does nothing to alleviate this perceived problem. The conditional use, therefore, fails to advance a state interest and therefore constitutes a taking. Reversed.

**DISSENT:** (Brennan, J.) The imposition made by the Commission's (D) condition is so minimal as to not constitute a taking. Further, no investment-backed expectations exist here.

## ▶ ANALYSIS

The Court was far from clear as to what sort of nexus must exist between a condition and the interest advanced by the original prohibition. At one point, the opinion notes that a taking will occur if there is "utterly" no connection, which implies only a slight relationship as being necessary. On the other hand, language in the opinion speaks of a "substantial relationship" as being necessary.

■■■

## Quicknotes

**EASEMENT** The right to utilize a portion of another's real property for a specific use.

**TAKING** A governmental action that substantially deprives an owner of the use and enjoyment of his or her property, requiring compensation.

■■■

# Dolan v. City of Tigard

Businessowner (P) v. City (D)

512 U.S. 374, 114 S. Ct. 2309 (1994).

**NATURE OF CASE:** Review of appeal upholding the denial of a variance to local zoning provisions.

**FACT SUMMARY:** The City of Tigard (D) required an easement for a public bike path and flood control area as a condition to issuing a permit to Dolan (P) for property redevelopment.

## 🏛 RULE OF LAW

For a conditioned grant of a building permit to be constitutional, a reasonable relationship must exist between the exactions demanded by the city's permit and a legitimate state interest.

**FACTS:** Dolan (P) owned a business near a creek, and she wanted to expand the business on her property. The City of Tigard (D) required that 15% of land on each parcel be left as open space, and that any development in or near the 100-year creek floodplain be accompanied by a land dedication sufficient to develop a vegetation greenway in the floodplain to minimize flood damage. The City (D) also required that new developments dedicate a pedestrian/bike path to promote alternative transportation. The City (D) made certain findings that the bike path might reduce traffic congestion. Dolan (P) sought a variance to the required dedications of a greenway and bike path along the creek and was denied. She appealed to the Land Use Board of Appeals, which upheld the Commission findings. The court of appeals affirmed the Supreme Court granted certiorari.

**ISSUE:** For a conditioned grant of a building permit to be constitutional, must a reasonable relationship exist between the exactions demanded by the city's permit and a legitimate state interest?

**HOLDING AND DECISION:** (Rehnquist, C.J.) Yes. For a conditioned grant of a building permit to be constitutional, a reasonable relationship must exist between the exactions demanded by the city's permit and a legitimate state interest. If a city is going to exact dedications of property as a condition to issuing a building permit for a development, then the exaction must show the required relationship to the impact of the development. Here, it is hard to see how recreational visitors using a floodplain easement are sufficiently related to the City's (D) legitimate interest in reducing flooding problems. Furthermore, the City (D) has not offered or explored less invasive alternatives to minimize flood damage. And as to the bicycle path, the City (D) has made no showing of how much traffic will be reduced by the required exaction of such a path; no math is necessary, but the City (D) made no effort at all to

form a basis for the exaction. To Dolan (P), the loss is the ability to control access to her property. Reversed and remanded.

**DISSENT:** (Stevens, J.) The Court has added a new hurdle to land use conditions. In addition to showing that the conditions have some rational nexus to the public purpose, now the City (D) must also show that the harm caused by the new land use is in "rough proportionality" to the benefit obtained by the condition.

**DISSENT:** (Souter, J.) In *Nollan v. California Coastal Commision*, 483 U.S. 825 (1987), this Court declared the need for a nexus between an exaction of a land interest and the nature of the government interest. Here, the Court adds another question: the degree of connection between an exaction and the adverse effects of development. The easement will help with flood control, and any other use is inconsequential.

## ▶ ANALYSIS

Many cities require "impact" fees to be paid for new developments. After *Dolan*, the Supreme Court remanded a case in which the California Supreme Court had upheld fees that were arguably no more closely related to the governmental purpose than the exactions in *Dolan*. On remand, the California Supreme Court concluded that exactions of physical interest in private property were the most invasive, thus requiring "heightened scrutiny," but that monetary exactions required only a "rational relationship" standard of review. See *Ehrlich v. Culver City*, 512 U.S. 1231 (1994).

■══■

### Quicknotes

**TAKING** A governmental action that substantially deprives an owner of the use and enjoyment of his or her property, requiring compensation.

**ZONING VARIANCE** Exemption from the application of zoning laws.

■══■

# Palazzolo v. Rhode Island

Developer (P) v. State (D)

533 U.S. 606 (2001).

**NATURE OF CASE:** Inverse condemnation action.

**FACT SUMMARY:** Palazzolo (P) brought an inverse condemnation suit against the State (D) after his development proposals for a parcel of waterfront property were rejected.

## RULE OF LAW

A purchaser or successive title holder is not barred from bringing a takings claim by the mere fact that the title was acquired after the effective date of the state regulation.

**FACTS:** Palazzolo (P) owned a waterfront parcel of land, almost all of which was designated as coastal wetlands. After his development proposals were rejected, he filed suit in state court claiming the State's (D) application of its wetlands regulations constituted a taking in violation of the Fifth Amendment. The state supreme court rejected the claim that Palazzolo (P) was denied all economically beneficial use of the property since the regulation predated his ownership of the property. Palazzolo (P) appealed.

**ISSUE:** Is a purchaser or successive title holder barred from bringing a takings claim by the mere fact that the title was acquired after the effective date of the state regulation?

**HOLDING AND DECISION:** (Kennedy, J.) No. A purchaser or successive title holder is not barred from bringing a takings claim by the mere fact that the title was acquired after the effective date of the state regulation. We agree with the court's decision that all economically viable use of the property was not deprived since the uplands portion of the property could still be developed. Affirmed in part, reversed in part, and remanded.

**CONCURRENCE:** (O'Connor, J.) *Penn Central* still controls. Under that analysis interference with investment-backed expectations is one of a number of factors that a court must examine. The regulatory scheme at the time the property is acquired also shapes the reasonableness of the claimant's expectations.

**CONCURRENCE:** (Scalia, J.) The investment-backed expectations the law will take into account on remand do not include the assumed validity of a restriction that in fact deprives property of so much of its value that it is an unconstitutional taking.

**CONCURRENCE IN PART, DISSENT IN PART:** (Stevens, J.) Palazzolo (P) is the wrong person to be bringing this action; if anyone is to be compensated it is the owner of the property at the time the regulations were adopted.

**DISSENT:** (Ginsburg, J.) The Rhode Island Supreme Court was correct in finding that the claim was not ripe for several reasons including that Palazzolo (P) had not sought permission for development of the upland portion of the property only.

## ▶ ANALYSIS

The court here did away with the prior rule under *Lucas* and *Penn Central* that a purchaser or successive title holder was deemed to have notice of an earlier-enacted restriction and was barred from bringing a takings claim. The court also held that a state does not avoid the duty to compensate based on a "token interest." So long as a landowner is permitted to build a substantial residence on the parcel, then it is not deemed to constitute a deprivation of all economic value.

■■■

### Quicknotes

**FIFTH AMENDMENT** Provides that no person shall be compelled to serve as a witness against himself, or be subject to trial for the same offense twice, or be deprived of life, liberty, or property without due process of law.

**NOTICE** Communication of information to a person by an authorized person or an otherwise proper source.

**TAKING** A governmental action that substantially deprives an owner of the use and enjoyment of his or her property, requiring compensation.

■■■

# CHAPTER 20

# Exclusionary Zoning

## Quick Reference Rules of Law

# Village of Arlington Heights v. Metropolitan Housing Development Corp.

## Municipality (D) v. Developer (P)

429 U.S. 252 (1977).

**NATURE OF CASE:** Review of appeal reversing bench trial for declaratory and injunctive relief.

**FACT SUMMARY:** The Village of Arlington Heights (D), zoned predominantly for single-family homes, denied a rezoning request to develop a lot for multi-family homes.

### 🏛 RULE OF LAW
To show discrimination was a motivating factor in official action, and thus a violation of the Equal Protection Clause, a plaintiff must establish intent, because racially disproportionate impact alone is insufficient.

**FACTS:** The Village of Arlington Heights (D), a suburb of Chicago, was predominantly zoned for single-family, detached homes. A religious order holding an eighty-acre parcel decided to devote a portion of that land to low and moderate income housing. The order contacted the Metropolitan Housing Development Corp. (MHDC) (P), a developer experienced in securing federal assistance money. After working with the Village (D) for some time, MHDC (P) was finally denied a rezoning request. MHDC (P) and three potential residents of the housing development then filed suit, contending that the denial was racially discriminatory and violated the Fourteenth Amendment. The court of appeals agreed, and the Village (D) petitioned for Supreme Court review.

**ISSUE:** To show discrimination was a motivating factor in official action, and thus a violation of the Equal Protection Clause, must a plaintiff establish intent, rather than racially dispropotionate impact alone?

**HOLDING AND DECISION:** (Powell, J.) Yes. To show discrimination was a motivating factor in official action, and thus a violation of the Equal Protection Clause, a plaintiff must establish intent, because racially disproportionate impact alone is insufficient. Rarely can a legislative body be found that makes a decision motivated by a single concern. But when there is proof that a discriminatory purpose has been a motivating factor, then the decision must be overturned as unconstitutional. However, proving the discriminatory purpose is difficult. Many factors, such as historical background, departures from normal procedure sequences, and contemporary statements of officials must be analyzed to find an intent. Disproportionate impact alone, though, will not define a discriminatory intent. Turning to this case, nothing in evidence suggests that the Village's (D) decision was based on anything but a consistently applied zoning ordinance. The MHDC (P) has not

carried its burden of showing discriminatory intent. Reversed and remanded.

## ▶ ANALYSIS

The Fair Housing Act has been treated differently than the Equal Protection argument. Disparate effects between races has been held to be prima facie evidence of a violation of the Act. The burden is then on the local government to show its actions furthered a legitimate government interest and that no alternative to meet that interest exists that is less discriminatory in effect.

■══■

## Quicknotes

**EQUAL PROTECTION** A constitutional guarantee that no person shall be denied the same protection of the laws enjoyed by other persons in life circumstances.

**INTENT** The existence of a particular state of mind whereby an individual seeks to achieve a particular result by his action.

■══■

# Village of Belle Terre v. Boraas

Municipality (D) v. Co-lessee of house (P)

416 U.S. 1 (1974).

**NATURE OF CASE:** Appeal from an action seeking a declaratory judgment and an injunction.

**FACT SUMMARY:** Boraas (P) and other co-lessees of a house in the Village of Belle Terre (D) brought this action for an injunction and a judgment declaring an ordinance restricting land use to one-family dwellings unconstitutional.

## 🏛 RULE OF LAW
Zoning legislation does not violate the Equal Protection Clause if it is reasonable, not arbitrary, and bears a rational relationship to a permissible state objective.

**FACTS:** The Village of Belle Terre (D) had restricted land use to one-family dwellings. The word "family" as used in the ordinance meant one or more persons related by blood or a number of persons not exceeding two living together as a single housekeeping unit though not related by blood. The Dickmans (P), owners of a house in the Village of Belle Terre (D), leased it to two single males, a single female, and three others, Boraas (P) among them. The Village (D) served the Dickmans (P) with an "Order To Remedy Violations" of the ordinance. Thereupon, Boraas (P) and two of the other tenants, as well as the Dickmans (P), brought this action seeking an injunction and a judgment declaring the ordinance unconstitutional as violative of the Equal Protection Clause. The district court held the ordinance constitutional and the court of appeals reversed. The Village (D) appealed to the Supreme Court.

**ISSUE:** Does zoning legislation violate the equal protection clause if it is reasonable and bears a rational relationship to a permissible state objective?

**HOLDING AND DECISION:** (Douglas, J.) No. The ordinance now before the court does not discriminate against unmarried couples in violation of the Equal Protection Clause. The ordinance is not aimed at transients so as to interfere with a person's right to travel. It involves no procedural disparity inflicted on some but not on others. It involves no fundamental right guaranteed by the constitution. Economic and social legislation does not violate the Equal Protection Clause if the law be reasonable, not arbitrary, and bears a rational relationship to a permissible state objective. Boraas (P) argues that if two unmarried people can constitute a family under the ordinance, there is no reason why three or four may not. But every line drawn by a legislature leaves some out that might well have been included. That exercise of discretion, however, is a legisla-

tive, not a judicial, function. A quiet place where yards are wide, people few, and motor vehicles restricted are legitimate guidelines in a land-use project addressed to family needs. This goal is a permissible one. The police power is not confined to elimination of filth, stench, and unhealthy places. It is ample to lay out zones where family values make the area a sanctuary for people. Therefore, the decision of the court of appeals is reversed.

**DISSENT:** (Marshall, J.) The disputed classification burdens the tenants' fundamental rights of association and privacy guaranteed by the First and Fourteenth Amendments. Therefore, strict equal protection scrutiny should be applied. The First Amendment provides some limitation on zoning laws which, for example, seek to restrict occupancy to individuals adhering to particular religious, political, or scientific beliefs. Zoning officials properly concern themselves with the uses of land and can restrict the number of persons who reside in certain dwellings. But they cannot validly consider who those persons are or how they choose to live.

## ▶ ANALYSIS

The freedom of association is often inextricably entwined with the constitutionally guaranteed right of privacy. In *Meyer v. Nebraska*, 262 U.S. 390 (1923), the Supreme Court held that the right to establish a home is an essential part of the liberty guaranteed by the Fourteenth Amendment. In *Stanley v. Georgia*, 394 U.S. 557, in the concurring opinion, Justice Goldberg stated that the Constitution secures to an individual a freedom to satisfy his intellectual and emotional needs in the privacy of his own home. Both of these cases were used in the dissent to support the argument of discrimination.

■■■

### Quicknotes

**FREEDOM OF ASSOCIATION** The right to peaceably assemble.

**FUNDAMENTAL RIGHT** A liberty that is either expressly or implicitly provided for in the United States Constitution, the deprivation or burdening of which is subject to a heightened standard of review.

■■■

# Moore v. City of East Cleveland

Extended family (D) v. City (P)

431 U.S. 494 (1977).

**NATURE OF CASE:** Appeal from an action challenging the constitutionality of a housing ordinance.

**FACT SUMMARY:** Inez Moore (D), who lived with her own son and two grandsons, first cousins to each other, was directed to remove her grandson John from her home in compliance with a housing ordinance of Cleveland (P).

🏛 **RULE OF LAW**
Freedom of personal choice in matters of marriage and family life is one of the liberties protected by the Due Process Clause of the Fourteenth Amendment and any zoning ordinance infringing on these freedoms is subject to strict scrutiny.

**FACTS:** Inez Moore (D) lived in her Cleveland home together with her son and her two grandsons. The two boys were first cousins. Moore (D) received a notice of violation of a housing ordinance from the City of Cleveland (P) stating that John, her grandson, was an illegal occupant and directing her to comply with the ordinance. Cleveland's (P) housing ordinance limited occupancy of a dwelling unit to members of a single family, but contained an unusual and complicated definitional section that recognized as a family only a few categories of related individuals. Moore's (D) family did not fit into any of these categories. When Moore (D) failed to remove her grandson from her home, Cleveland (P) filed a criminal charge. Moore (D) moved to dismiss, claiming that the ordinance was constitutionally invalid on its face. The motion was overruled, and, upon conviction, Moore (D) was sentenced to five days in jail and a fine. The Ohio Court of Appeals affirmed and the Ohio Supreme Court refused review. Moore (D) appealed to the United States Supreme Court.

**ISSUE:** Is any zoning ordinance which infringes on a person's freedom of choice in matters of marriage and family life subject to the strict scrutiny of the Due Process Clause?

**HOLDING AND DECISION:** (Powell, J.) Yes. This Court has long recognized that freedom of personal choice in matters of marriage and family life is one of the liberties protected by the due process clause of the Fourteenth Amendment. When government intrudes on choices concerning family living arrangements, this Court must scrutinize carefully the importance of the governmental interests advanced and the extent to which they are served by the challenged regulation. When thus examined, the Cleveland ordinance cannot survive. The City (P) sought to justify it as a means of preventing overcrowding, minimizing traffic and parking congestion, and avoiding an undue financial burden on the school system. Although these are legitimate goals, the ordinance serves them marginally at best. For example, the ordinance permits any family consisting only of husband, wife, and unmarried children to live together, even if the family contains a half-dozen licensed drivers, each with his own car. At the same time, it forbids an adult brother and sister to share a household, even if both faithfully use public transportation. The ordinance would permit a grandmother to live with a single dependent son and children, even if his school-age children number a dozen, yet it forces Moore (D) to find another dwelling for her grandson, simply because of the presence of his uncle and cousin in the same household. The decision of the Ohio Court of Appeals is, therefore, reversed.

**DISSENT:** (Stewart, J.) To suggest that the biological fact of common ancestry necessarily gives related persons constitutional rights of association superior to those of unrelated persons is to misunderstand the nature of the associational freedoms that the Constitution protects. Freedom of association has been constitutionally recognized because it is often indispensable to effectuation of explicit First Amendment guarantees. The association in this case is not for any purpose relating to the promotion of speech, assembly, the press, or religion.

▶ **ANALYSIS**

The Supreme Court relied on the *Pierce* case, 268 U.S. 535, to support its decision here. *Pierce* struck down an Oregon law requiring all children to attend the state's public schools, holding that the Constitution excludes any general power of the state to standardize its children by forcing them to accept instruction from public teachers only. The Court, in *Moore*, reasoned that by the same token the Constitution prevents East Cleveland (P) from standardizing its children and its adults by forcing all to live in certain narrowly defined family patterns.

■==■

*Quicknotes*

**FREEDOM OF ASSOCIATION** The right to peaceably assemble.

**TAKING** A governmental action that substantially deprives an owner of the use and enjoyment of his or her property, requiring compensation.

■==■

# City of Cleburne v. Cleburne Living Center, Inc.

## Municipality (D) v. Group home for the mentally disabled (P)

473 U.S. 432 (1985).

**NATURE OF CASE:** Appeal of order enjoining enforcement of zoning ordinance.

**FACT SUMMARY:** In reviewing a local ordinance that regulated group housing of the feeble-minded, the court of appeals imposed a heightened-scrutiny standard of review and found the ordinance to deny equal protection.

## 🏛 RULE OF LAW

Mental retardation is not a suspect or quasi-suspect classification requiring heightened judicial scrutiny.

**FACTS:** The City of Cleburne, Texas (D), had zoned certain portions of the city to permit group housing. Certain types of such housing required a special use permit. One such use was group housing of the "insane" or "feeble-minded." The Cleburne Living Center, Inc. (P) applied for such a use. Citing neighbors' fears and concerns about occupants' interactions with an adjacent junior high school, the permit was denied. The Center (P) sued, contending that the ordinance denied equal protection. The district court entered judgment in favor of the City (D). The Fifth Circuit reversed, finding retardation to be a quasi-suspect class and that the City (D) therefore had to justify the ordinance under a heightened-scrutiny standard of review. The City (D) obtained review in the Supreme Court.

**ISSUE:** Is mental retardation a suspect or quasi-suspect classification requiring heightened judicial scrutiny?

**HOLDING AND DECISION:** (White, J.) No. Mental retardation is not a suspect or quasi-suspect classification requiring heightened judicial scrutiny. Generally speaking, governmental regulation is presumptively valid, and must only be shown to be rationally related to a legitimate governmental objective to be valid. Certain classifications, such as race or national origin, are presumed to bear no relation to legitimate governmental interests, so strict scrutiny requiring the showing of a compelling interest will be imposed. Gender is a classification that does sometimes further governmental interests but usually does not, and an intermediate level of scrutiny, which requires substantial relation to important governmental interests, is required. Here, the court of appeals placed mental retardation into this latter category. This was improper. Mental retardation has several characteristics that make it appropriate for governmental regulation. First, persons so affected do have a reduced ability to cope with and function in the world. Second, the retarded do have differing ability levels. As a consequence of this, regulating how they are treated is a legitimate governmental activity. In light of this, heightened scrutiny is not appropriate. [The Court went on to hold that, under the rational basis standard of review, the regulation was not valid. The Court ruled that differing treatment accorded the retarded in this case from other group living arrangements in the City (D) was based on irrational fear and prejudice, not legitimate policy considerations.] Affirmed in part, vacated in part, and remanded.

**CONCURRENCE AND DISSENT:** (Marshall, J.) The Court says it imposes only a rational basis test. However, under traditional rational basis scrutiny, the regulation would certainly have been valid. The Court has in fact imposed heightened scrutiny, but has failed to so articulate.

## ▶ ANALYSIS

The Court's equal protection analysis has become more complicated in recent years. Formerly, a strict dichotomy existed: strict scrutiny and rational basis. In 1973, the Court adopted intermediate review to apply to gender. Further complicating matters is the present case. In years past, a regulation would always survive rational basis review; here it did not. The Court appears to have toughened its rational basis review, without so stating.

---

## Quicknotes

**HEIGHTENED SCRUTINY** A purposefully vague judicial description of all levels of scrutiny more exacting than minimal scrutiny.

**STRICT SCRUTINY** Method by which courts determine the constitutionality of a law, when a law affects a fundamental right. Under the test, the legislature must have had a compelling interest to enact the law and measures prescribed by the law must be the least restrictive means possible to accomplish its goal.

**ZONING ORDINANCE** A statute that divides land into defined areas and which regulates the form and use of buildings and structures within those areas.

# Britton v. Town of Chester

Developer (P) v. Municipality (D)

N.H. Sup. Ct., 134 N.H. 434, 595 A.2d 492 (1991).

**NATURE OF CASE:** Appeal of ruling by Superior Court Master for declaratory and injunctive relief.

**FACT SUMMARY:** Britton (P) attempted, and was denied permission to build a medium-density housing tract in the Town of Chester (D), which effectively zoned only 1.73% of town land for such uses.

## ▥ RULE OF LAW
When a municipality adopts zoning regulations, it must consider the impact beyond the boundaries of the municipality.

**FACTS:** The Town of Chester (D) was a small residential community outside the larger city of Manchester. Almost all housing in the Town of Chester (D) was single-family homes; only a scant 1.73% was multi-family approved, and much of that land was undesirable hilly terrain and wetlands. The zoning ordinance in the Town (D) contained numerous oppressive restrictions allowing the town planning board substantial subjective standards for reviewing development requests. Remillard (P) sought to develop a twenty-three-acre parcel into multi-family low- and moderate-income housing. He was not permitted to develop the site. Britton (P) and other potential residents of the development filed suit, and a Court Master was appointed to evaluate the zoning ordinance of the Town of Chester (D).

**ISSUE:** When a municipality adopts zoning regulations, must it consider the impact beyond the boundaries of the municipality?

**HOLDING AND DECISION:** (Batchelder, J.) Yes. When a municipality adopts zoning regulations, it must consider the impact beyond the boundaries of the municipality. Municipalities are not isolated enclaves and may not refuse to confront the future by building a moat around themselves and pulling up the drawbridge. Rather, they must promote the general welfare both within and without their political boundaries. Where a zoning-enabling statute requires that the general welfare of the community be considered, the municipality must consider the broader community impacted outside its borders. In this case, the Town of Chester (D) has all but precluded any development that is not single-family homes. Only a small portion is zoned for other than single-family lots, and much of that small portion is undesirable land. The Town of Chester (D) has not borne its fair share of low- and moderate-income housing needs in the greater community. The court will give the legislative body reasonable time to correct the deficiencies of the zoning ordinance, and thus

the Master's recommendation to set aside the ordinance is for the time being reversed. Affirmed in part and reversed in part.

## ▶ ANALYSIS

Had the court relied on the Equal Protection Clause, then the outcome of this case would likely have been different. Wealth is not a suspect classification, and housing is not a fundamental right.

■■■

### Quicknotes

**SUSPECT CLASSIFICATION** A class of persons who have historically been subject to discriminatory treatment; statutes drawing a distinction between persons based on a suspect classification, i.e., race, nationality or alienage, are subject to a strict scrutiny standard of review.

**ZONING VARIANCE** Exemption from the application of zoning laws.

■■■

## Quick Reference Rules of Law

**24. Risk of Loss.**   In a contract to convey real property, equitable conversion by the   *196*
purchaser does not take place until the seller has fulfilled all conditions and is entitled
to enforce specific performance, and the parties, by their contract, intend that title shall pass
to the buyer upon the signing of the contract of purchase. As a result, since the buyer does
not have equitable title until all of the above conditions are met, he may not claim under
the seller's insurance policy for recovering damage to the property by an act of God.
(Sanford v. Breidenbach)

**25. Risk of Loss.**   When a land purchase contract requires the buyer to keep the property   *197*
insured against fire and there is a fire loss before performance of the contract is completed,
any such insurance received by the seller is to be applied on any remaining balance of
the purchase price. (Raplee v. Piper)

# Shaughnessy v. Eidsmo

Holders of option (P) v. Lessor (D)

Minn. Sup. Ct., 222 Minn. 141, 23 N.W.2d 362 (1946).

**NATURE OF CASE:** Appeal from trial court's decision granting specific performance.

**FACT SUMMARY:** Eidsmo (D) allegedly entered into an oral contract to lease his property for one year with an option to buy.

### 🏛 RULE OF LAW
Cases are taken out of the purview of the Statute of Frauds by part performance. Part performance may be shown by possession and part payment plus evidence that the dominant intent of the parties was to effect a sale.

**FACTS:** On April 5, 1943, the Shaughnessys (P) entered into an oral agreement with Eidsmo (D) to lease a house for one year with an option to buy at a specified price and with credit allowed for previous rental payments. Prior to the expiration of the lease, Shaughnessy (P) notified Eidsmo (D) that they intended to exercise their option. Eidsmo (D) claimed no option to purchase was ever given. The Shaughnessys (P) sued for specific performance. Eidsmo (D) raised the Statute of Frauds, but the trial court found for the Shaughnessys (P). Eidsmo (D) appealed.

**ISSUE:** Is an option to purchase land within the Statute of Frauds and, if so, can the statute be satisfied through the doctrine of part performance?

**HOLDING AND DECISION:** (Matson, J.) Yes as to both issues. An option agreement is a unilateral contract which, until exercised, is not within the Statute of Frauds. When the option is exercised, a new contract to purchase real property comes into existence and is within the purview of the Statute of Frauds. Therefore, the Statute is a valid affirmative defense to the oral contract unless taken therefrom by the doctrine of part performance. This court now adopts the Restatement of Contracts principle to the effect that the taking of possession, coupled with part payment and an unequivocal reference to a vendor-vendee relationship, is sufficient to remove the transaction from the Statute. Since land is unique, and damages can never recompense one adequately for its loss, specific performance is an appropriate remedy. Since the triers of fact found that a vendor-vendee relationship existed, the Shaughnessys (P) were in possession and had made payments on the land. Affirmed.

## ▌ ANALYSIS

Many eminent jurists feel that no exceptions should be made to the Statute of Frauds. It was enacted to prevent fraud and perjury. Exceptions tend to weaken it. The requirement that contracts be written is not onerous and is one that any prudent person should insist upon. There are five modern views as to what constitutes part performance. These are: (1) possession alone; (2) possession and payments; (3) possession plus lasting and valuable improvements; (4) possession, change of position, and irreparable injury; and (5) part performance is not recognized.

■==■

## Quicknotes

**PART PERFORMANCE** Partial perfomance of a contract, promise or obligation.

**SPECIFIC PERFORMANCE** An equitable remedy whereby the court requires the parties to perform their obligations pursuant to a contract.

■==■

# Burns v. McCormick

Caretakers (P) v. Executor of estate (D)

N.Y. Ct. of App., 233 N.Y. 230, 135 N.E. 273 (1922).

**NATURE OF CASE:** Appeal from decision denying specific performance.

**FACT SUMMARY:** Burns (P) agreed to take care of Halsey (now deceased) for life in exchange for Halsey's house and furnishings after his death.

## 🏛 RULE OF LAW
To establish the doctrine of part performance, the performance must unequivocally refer to the agreement, and must not be reasonably susceptible of other possible meanings.

**FACTS:** Halsey told the Burnses (P) that if they would board and care for him during his life, he would give them his house and furniture at his death. Halsey died without will, deed, or memorandum of the alleged transfer. The Burnses (P) sued for specific performance of the oral contract, and other parties in interest raised the Statute of Frauds. McCormick (D) was successful and the trial court denied specific performance. The Burnses (P) appealed.

**ISSUE:** Is performance which is susceptible to several different interpretations sufficient to remove an oral contract from the Statute of Frauds?

**HOLDING AND DECISION:** (Cardozo, J.) No. Not every act of part performance will move a court of equity to grant specific performance, even though legal remedies are deemed inadequate. The performance must be unequivocally referable to the agreement. An act which admits of explanation without reference to the alleged oral contract will not generally be deemed to have satisfied the Statute of Frauds. The performance must be such that the actions alone and without the alleged words of promise would be unintelligible, or at least extraordinary if no incidents of ownership were involved. Here, the Burnses' (P) board and care of Halsey could have been in exchange for the partial use of his house, i.e., rent. Since the Burnses' (P) actions could be otherwise explained, their performance will not satisfy the Statute. Since no fraud is alleged or involved, the decision of the trial court must be upheld. Reversed.

## ▶ ANALYSIS

Hardship, estoppel, and numerous casual remarks by a decedent may be recognized in various jurisdictions as proving the existence of the alleged oral contract to pass property after death. Some jurisdictions, notably California, have held that hardship alone may remove an oral contract from the Statute through estoppel. However, a majority of courts still strictly construe the Statute of Frauds and the doctrine of part performance.

## Quicknotes

**INCIDENTS OF OWNERSHIP** The retention of control over a life insurance policy.

**LEGAL REMEDY** Compensation for violation of a right or injuries sustained that is available in a court of law, as opposed to in equity.

**STATUTE OF FRAUDS** A statute that requires specified types of contracts to be in writing in order to be binding.

# Hickey v. Green

## Buyer of land (P) v. Seller (D)

Mass. App. Ct., 14 Mass. App. 671, 442 N.E.2d 37 (1982).

**NATURE OF CASE:** Appeal from grant of specific performance of a real estate contract.

**FACT SUMMARY:** Green (D) contended that the real estate sales contract she orally entered into with Hickey (P) was unenforceable based on the Statute of Frauds.

## 🏛 RULE OF LAW
An oral contract for the transfer of interest in land may be specifically enforced despite the Statute of Frauds if the party seeking performance changed his position in reasonable reliance on the contract and injustice can be avoided only through specific performance.

**FACTS:** Green (D) orally agreed to sell a parcel to Hickey (P), and accepted a check as a deposit. In reliance on the contract, Hickey (P) accepted a deposit on his home from a purchaser, intending to build a new home on the land he purchased from Green (D). Subsequently, Green (D), knowing Hickey (P) sold his house in reliance on the contract, refused to sell the land to Hickey (P). Hickey (P) sued for specific performance, and Green (D) defended, contending the contract was unenforceable under the Statute of Frauds. The trial court granted specific performance, and Green (D) appealed.

**ISSUE:** Can an oral contract for the sale of real estate be specifically enforced if the party seeking enforcement changed his position in reasonable reliance upon the contract?

**HOLDING AND DECISION:** (Cutter, J.) Yes. An oral contract for the transfer of an interest in land may be specifically enforced, despite the Statute of Frauds requirement of a writing, if the party seeking enforcement changed his position in reasonable reliance on the contract and injustice can be avoided only through specific performance. In this case, Hickey (P) clearly changed his position in reliance on the contract by selling his house in anticipation of occupying another on Green's (D) land. The reliance was reasonable, and Green (D) was fully aware of this change in position when she refused to honor the contract. As a result, it would be manifestly unjust to refuse specific performance in this case. Therefore, it must be ordered. Remanded.

## ▶ ANALYSIS

This case could have been decided on different grounds. Some commentators, spurred by dicta in the opinion, contend that the check which Hickey (P) gave Green (D) as a deposit on the land constituted an adequate memorandum to satisfy the requirements of the Statute of Frauds.

## Quicknotes

**RELIANCE** Dependence on a fact that causes a party to act or refrain from acting.

**SPECIFIC PERFORMANCE** An equitable remedy whereby the court requires the parties to perform their obligations pursuant to a contract.

**STATUTE OF FRAUDS** A statute that requires specified types of contracts to be in writing in order to be binding.

# Ward v. Mattuschek

### Ranch purchaser (P) v. Seller (D)

Mont. Sup. Ct., 134 Mont. 307, 330 P.2d 971 (1958).

**NATURE OF CASE:** Action for specific performance.

**FACT SUMMARY:** Mattuschek (D) signed a written agreement to permit Carnell, a real estate broker, to sell his ranch. Ward (P) signed a written agreement to purchase the ranch in accordance with the terms of the agreement between Cornell and Mattuschek (D). It was accompanied by a check as a down payment.

## 🏛 RULE OF LAW
Where a property owner entered into a written agreement with a real estate agent giving the latter permission to sell certain property and stating the terms of the sale, and the purchaser's unqualified acceptance was in writing and was accompanied by a check, such writings are sufficient to take the case out of the Statute of Frauds.

**FACTS:** Mattuschek (D) unqualifiedly and exclusively agreed in writing to permit Carnell to sell his ranch for $30,000 for which Carnell would receive a commission of $1,000. The terms were stated: "Cash to seller. Possession Dec. 1, 1953, seller retain 5% land-owner, royalty. Seller pay 1953 taxes. Seller transfers all lease land to buyer." Ward (P) signed a written agreement to purchase the ranch in accordance with the terms of the agreement between Mattuschek (D) and Carnell. It was accompanied by a check as a down payment. When Mattuschek (D) refused to convey the ranch to Ward (P), Ward (P) brought this action for specific performance.

**ISSUE:** Is a written agreement with a real estate broker giving him permission to sell certain property and specifying the price, the broker's commission, and the terms of the sale together with an unqualified acceptance in writing, accompanied by a check, sufficient to take the case out of the Statute of Frauds?

**HOLDING AND DECISION:** (Fall, J.) Yes. To take a lease out of the Statute of Frauds, the note of memorandum must name the parties and must contain all the essentials of the contract. It may consist of several writings. The writings in this case contain the names of the parties, and all the essential terms of the contract. "It is difficult to conceive of a more clear-cut offer and acceptance in writing" than is shown here. Hence, the writings are sufficient to take the case out of the Statute. It's true that ordinarily both parties to a written agreement execute it, and here Ward (P) did not sign the contract executed by Mattuschek (D). However, mutuality does not require that both parties sign the contract, and if a contract signed by one party is acted upon by the other party, a binding agreement may result. Hence, Ward (P) is entitled to specific performance.

**DISSENT:** (Adair, J.) The Mattuschek's (D) listing agreement was with Carnell, not with any prospective purchaser. Hence, Ward (P), as a prospective purchaser, has no cause of action against Mattuschek (D) for specific performance.

## ▶ ANALYSIS

In most states, the Statute of Frauds applies to real estate brokerage contracts and many of the same problems that arise in real estate contracts arise in the broker's agreement. These include the necessity for a proper signature, proper identification of the parties, and adequate description of the land. In some states, the Statute does not apply to real estate brokerage contracts and the broker's agreement may be oral, although the contract between the vendor and purchaser remains subject to the provisions of the Statute.

■■■

### Quicknotes

**LEASE** An agreement or contract which creates a relationship between a landlord and tenant (real property) or lessor and lessee (real or personal property).

**STATUTE OF FRAUDS** A statute that requires specified types of contracts to be in writing in order to be binding.

■■■

# King v. Wenger

Purchaser of real property (P) v. Tenants-in-common (D)

Kan. Sup. Ct., 219 Kan. 668, 549 P.2d 986 (1976).

**NATURE OF CASE:** Action for specific performance.

**FACT SUMMARY:** King (P) and one of the three co-tenants of real property entered into an informal agreement to transfer the property, a formal contract to be drawn up embodying all of the terms.

## 🏛 RULE OF LAW
**Where circumstances show that the parties did not intend to be bound until a formal contract had been executed, a temporary informal agreement does not create legally enforceable rights.**

**FACTS:** Wenger (D) and her two daughters, Loraine Wenger (D) and Lorene Ralston (D), owned real property as tenants-in-common. While Wenger (D) was in the hospital, King (P) agreed to purchase the real property. The three co-tenants agreed, but only Loraine (D) signed an informal agreement on behalf of herself and her mother, Wenger (D). The agreement stated the basic terms of the sale. The parties then went to King's (P) attorney to have a formal contract drawn up with all of the terms of the sale included. The attorney could not take the time to draw up the contract and suggested that he would prepare a formal contract and mail it to the parties for their signatures. The $1,000 down payment called for in the informal agreement was left with the attorney at his suggestion. A formal contract was prepared, but it did not comport with the terms of the informal agreement and was rejected by the cotenants (D). They then sold the property to a third party. King (P) then brought an action for specific performance. Wenger (D) alleged that the informal contract was not binding, since a formal contract was intended.

**ISSUE:** Is an informal agreement not binding where all of the circumstances establish that the parties did not intend to be bound until a formal agreement had been executed?

**HOLDING AND DECISION:** (Fromme, J.) Yes. As a normal rule, informal agreements remain binding even if the parties intend to subsequently execute a formal contract. To avoid being bound by the informal agreement, the defendant must establish that, based on all of the facts and circumstances, the parties did not intend to be bound until a formal contract was signed. Here, only one of the three co-tenants signed the contract. Loraine (D) did not have written authority to sign on behalf of her mother (D). The $1,000 down payment called for by the agreement was never paid. The parties immediately went to King's (P) attorney to have a formal contract prepared and many important terms had not been agreed upon at that time. All of these factors, plus the fact that the formal contact changed some of the terms of the informal one, indicate that the parties did not intend to be bound until a formal contract was executed. Affirmed.

## ▶ ANALYSIS

The memo must contain sufficient terms to constitute a valid contract. Missing terms may be implied by the court. For example, a court will imply a reasonable time for performance, payment of the purchase price in cash, and even that a reasonable price will be paid if none is specified. Courts will not infer the number of acres to be transferred if not specified. See generally *Hanlon v. Hayes.*

■▬■

## Quicknotes

**SPECIFIC PERFORMANCE** An equitable remedy whereby the court requires the parties to perform their obligations pursuant to a contract.

**TENANTS-IN-COMMON** Two or more people holding an interest in property, each with equal right to its use and possession; interests may be partitioned, sold, conveyed, or devised.

■▬■

# Niernberg v. Feld

Seller of real property (D) v. Purchaser (P)

Colo. Sup. Ct., 131 Colo. 508, 283 P.2d 640 (1955).

**NATURE OF CASE:** Appeal from decision requiring vendor to return down payment received on a real estate contract.

**FACT SUMMARY:** When the Felds (P) backed out of a real estate sales contract with Niernberg (D), an oral agreement was made to return the Felds' (P) down payment if the property was later sold for the contract price or more.

## 🏛 RULE OF LAW
An oral contract is sufficient to rescind an executory contract for the purchase of real property.

**FACTS:** The Felds (P) gave Niernberg (D) a $1,500 down payment on the purchase of real property. The written contract contained a clause stating that the down payment was to be considered liquidated damages if the Felds (P) backed out of the deal. The Felds (P) decided not to complete the contract. Mr. Feld (P), his attorney, and Mr. Niernberg (D) met and orally agreed to rescind the contract. It was further agreed that Niernberg (D) would return the $1,500 if he later sold the land for an amount equal to or greater than the amount offered him by the Felds (P). He later sold the land for more than the original contract price, but refused to return the $1,500. The Felds (P) brought suit and Niernberg (D) claimed that he had never agreed to return the money. Niernberg (D) also alleged the following: (1) a written real estate contract cannot be modified or rescinded orally because of the Statute of Frauds; (2) the modification was void for lack of consideration; and (3) the modification was void because Niernberg's (D) wife was not a party to it and was a party to the written contract. The jury found for the Felds (P) and Niernberg (D) appealed.

**ISSUE:** Is an oral rescission or modification of a written real estate contract violative of the Statute of Frauds?

**HOLDING AND DECISION:** (Holland, J.) No. An executory contract involving title to, or an interest in, lands may be rescinded by an agreement resting in parol. The triers of fact determined that the rescission and modification had been entered into by the parties. The consideration was founded upon a promise for a promise. The Felds (P) were to receive their down payment upon the happening of a future contingency and the Niernbergs (D) were released from further performance. Finally, to dispose of Mr. Niernberg's (D) final argument, his wife has been released from this case, and it would be inequitable to allow him to escape from the consequences of his own actions. The decision of the trial court is sustained.

## ▶ ANALYSIS

Most American cases agree with the holding in *Niernberg*. However, a sizable minority have held that where the contract is required to be in writing, a modification canceling the contract must also be written. Almost all jurisdictions require that modifications to a contract which is to be completed by the parties must be in writing if the statute of frauds requires that the underlying contract be written.

■☰■

## Quicknotes

**LIQUIDATED DAMAGES** An amount of money specified in a contract representing the damages owed in the event of breach.

**PAROLE EVIDENCE RULE** Doctrine precluding parties to an agreement from introducing evidence of prior or contemporaneous agreements in order to repudiate or alter the terms of a written contract.

■☰■

# Kasten Construction Co. v. Maple Ridge Construction Co.

Seller of land (D) v. Buyer of land (P)

Md. Ct. App., 245 Md. 373, 226 A.2d 341 (1967).

**NATURE OF CASE:** Appeal from award of specific performance of real estate sales contract.

**FACT SUMMARY:** Maple Ridge Construction Co. (P) sued to compel specific performance of a land sale contract with Kasten Construction Co. (D) although Maple Ridge (P) had delayed making payment until after the settlement date.

## 🏛 RULE OF LAW
A land sale contract is enforceable in equity after the date of performance has passed if performance is offered within a reasonable time afterward and time is not of the essence.

**FACTS:** Maple Ridge Construction Co. (P) contracted to purchase a tract of land from Kasten Construction Co. (D) on December 4, 1964. When Maple Ridge (P) encountered financing problems, the settlement date was extended until on or before March 19, 1965. Neither the original contract nor the extension contract stated that time was of the essence. Maple Ridge (P) requested and was subsequently refused additional extensions. When Karsten (D) notified Maple Ridge (P) that the contract of sale had expired and was thus null and void, Maple Ridge (P) sued for specific performance. At the hearing, the chancellor found that Maple Ridge (P) had tendered full performance although it had been dilatory in making financial arrangements and making a title examination. The chancellor also found that Kasten (D) was lackadaisical in its performance as it had not provided "finished" lots and that Kasten (D) had suffered no loss that could not be compensated by the payment of interest. Maple Ridge (P) was awarded specific performance. Kasten (D) appealed.

**ISSUE:** Is a land sale contract enforceable in equity after the date of performance has passed if performance is offered within a reasonable time afterward and time is not of the essence?

**HOLDING AND DECISION:** (Horney, J.) Yes. A land sale contract is enforceable in equity after the date of performance has passed if performance is offered within a reasonable time afterward and time is not of the essence. Time is not of the essence in a land sale contract unless it is stated in the contract or the parties' conduct and circumstances indicate that this is their intention. Although in this case a closing date was indicated in the contract, equity dictates that this date was a formality rather than an essential term. Affirmed.

## ▶ ANALYSIS

Litigation frequently results when one party desires promptness and the other needs more time to close the deal. When parties do not specify that time is of the essence, courts will often allow a reasonable time. A reasonable delay in performance may be a breach of contract at law; however, it is a nonmaterial breach in equity. Thus, it is not sufficient merely to allow the other party to rescind the contract.

## Quicknotes

**MATERIAL BREACH** Breach of a contract's terms by one party that is so substantial as to relieve the other party from its obligations pursuant thereto.

**SPECIFIC PERFORMANCE** An equitable remedy whereby the court requires the parties to perform their obligations pursuant to a contract.

# Doctorman v. Schroeder

## Purchaser of land (P) v. Seller (D)

N.J. Ct. Err. and App., 92 N.J. Eq. 676, 114 A. 810 (1921).

**NATURE OF CASE:** Action in equity to reform a contract.

**FACT SUMMARY:** Doctorman (P) failed to meet an express condition in a land sale contract and so forfeited the prior payments he made.

## 🏛 RULE OF LAW
Where the parties to a land sale contract have specifically agreed that time is of the essence, equity will not prevent a forfeiture when the purchaser has violated this condition.

**FACTS:** Schroeder (D) was the owner of land. Doctorman (P) contracted to buy Schroeder's (D) land. Five hundred dollars was paid as a down payment and $1,500 was due on December 19. In the contract, the parties specifically stated that unless the $1,500 was paid on December 19, then all moneys previously paid would be forfeited and the agreement would be null and void. It was further stated that time was of the essence in the contract. On December 19, Doctorman (P) was unable to raise the full amount. Schroeder (D) accepted $500 and executed another agreement to the effect that the $500 was received upon condition that Doctorman (P) pay $1,000 to Schroeder (D) at a specific location on December 20 at no later than 2:30 P.M. It was further stated that time was of the essence and that the acceptance of the $500 did not waive Schroeder's (D) rights under the contract. Doctorman (P) appeared at the specified place with the cash but was 30 minutes late. Schroeder (D) refused the payment and informed Doctorman (P) that the contract was void and that all moneys were forfeited. There was evidence that Schroeder (D) wished to be rid of Doctorman (P) as a prospective purchaser.

**ISSUE:** May a court of equity reform a land sale contract to relieve a purchaser from forfeiture where the purchaser has failed to comply with the strict and explicit conditions of the contract?

**HOLDING AND DECISION:** (Leaming, V. Chan.) No. A court of equity is powerless to aid a purchaser who has failed to pay at the appointed time where the contract explicitly stated that time was of the essence. A default causes substantial damage to the purchaser in that he loses his chance to buy the property as well as forfeiting past payments, but the parties specifically contracted that time was of the essence. The supplemental agreement giving an extension was even more explicit on this issue. There is no difference that a specific time was set rather than a specific date, and the rule is the same. There can be a waiver of this condition when there is repeated acceptance of late payments, but there is no waiver when a seller accepts a late payment with notice that he will thereafter insist on strict performance. There was no waiver here merely because Schroeder (D) waited around thirty minutes until Doctorman (P) finally arrived. It is irrelevant that Schroeder (D) was dissatisfied with Doctorman (P) and wished to get a new buyer, and so availed himself of the chance to void the contract. Affirmed per curiam based on Vice Chancellor Leaming's opinion.

## ▶ ANALYSIS

This court took an incredibly limited view of its own equitable powers. As a general rule, equity abhors a forfeiture and will do anything legally possible to prevent it. But contract rules are quite strict when the parties specifically agree on a specific time for payment and state that time is of the essence. Generally, time is not of the essence in a land sale contract unless specifically stated or where there is a rise or depreciation in the property value.

■══■

## Quicknotes

**COURT OF EQUITY** A court that determines matters before it consistent with principles of fairness and not in strict compliance with rules of law.

**FORFEITURE** The loss of a right or interest as a penalty for failing to fulfill an obligation.

**REFORMATION OF CONTRACT** An equitable remedy whereby the written terms of an agreement are altered in order to reflect the true intent of the parties; reformation requires a demonstration by clear and convincing evidence of mutual mistake by the parties to the contract.

■══■

# Gerruth Realty Co. v. Pire

### Seller of land (P) v. Purchaser (D)

Wis. Sup. Ct., 17 Wis. 2d 89, 115 N.W.2d 557 (1962).

**NATURE OF CASE:** Action on a promissory note.

**FACT SUMMARY:** A land sale contract included a subject-to-financing clause, and when Pire (D) could not get financing, he refused to pay a promissory note.

### 🏛 RULE OF LAW
A land sale contract or an offer to purchase containing a subject-to-financing clause, but which does not indicate a standard by which the proper amount of financing can be judged, is void for indefiniteness.

**FACTS:** Pire (D) signed an offer to purchase land from Gerruth Realty Co. (P). The offer was conditioned on Pire's (D) being able to buy an adjacent piece of land and was also conditioned on Pire's (D) obtaining sufficient financing to cover the $70,000 purchase price for both properties. The offer to purchase was void unless the purchaser, Pire (D), obtained the proper amount of financing. There was nothing else in the contract or in the negotiations concerning financing. Pire (D) signed a promissory note for $5,000 to cover the down payment. Pire (D) attempted to get financing from his bank but was informed that he could not get the amount he needed. Gerruth (P) then offered $75,000 to finance part of the price, but Pire (D) refused. Gerruth (P) sued to have Pire (D) pay on the promissory note, but Pire (D) defended on the ground that the subject-to-financing clause gave Pire (D) the option to determine the proper amount of financing needed.

**ISSUE:** Are there sufficient facts from which a court could ascertain the intent of the parties so as to be able to construe the subject-to-financing clause?

**HOLDING AND DECISION:** (Hallows, J.) No. It is impossible to ascertain the parties' intent and the contract is void for indefiniteness. Pire (D) is not allowed to determine the meaning of the clause, for that would make the contract illusory. The clause must be construed by the terms of the contract and in light of all the circumstances. There is no evidence as to what either party meant by the clause, its limitations, or whether either party even knew what it meant. Financing is a crucial element, and neither party gave it much thought. There is no evidence that the parties contracted in light of the current community financing practices. Whatever either party had in mind, it was not communicated to the other, and the contract is void for indefiniteness and is a bar to collection of the note. Affirmed.

### ▶ ANALYSIS

The financing of a land sale is of essential importance to the transaction. The rule in construing a subject-to-financing clause is that the court will infer the intent of the parties in light of the contract itself and all the circumstances surrounding the making of the contract, including customary community practices. To do this, the parties must have in some way expressed their intent or given some standard by which the intent could be ascertained. Where the contract and circumstances are silent, this indicates that there was no meeting of the minds and no contract was made.

### Quicknotes

**ILLUSORY CONTRACT** A contract that is unenforceable for lack of consideration because a promise by one of the parties to perform is completely within his discretion.

**MEETING OF THE MINDS** A requirement of a valid contract that the parties possess a mutuality of assent as manifested by the terms of the agreement and not by a hidden intent; enforceability of the contract is limited to those terms to which the parties assented.

# Skendzel v. Marshall

## Seller of real property (P) v. Purchaser (D)

Ind. Sup. Ct., 261 Ind. 226, 301 N.E.2d 641 (1973), *cert. denied*, 415 U.S. 921 (1974).

**NATURE OF CASE:** Action to enforce terms of a contract and to obtain possession of real property.

**FACT SUMMARY:** Burkowski (P) sold real property to Marshall (D), the sales contract containing a clause that if the contract were breached, Burkowski (P) could retain all payments made as liquidated damages and also recover the property.

## 🏛 RULE OF LAW
Before a liquidated damage forfeiture provision will be upheld, it must be shown that actual damages cannot be reasonably ascertained and the damage provision is a reasonable attempt to fix the damages actually suffered by the vendor.

**FACTS:** Burkowski (P) sold real property to the Marshalls (D) through a land sale contract. The contract called for payments of $2,500 on or before January 15 of each year until the sum of $36,000 was paid. No interest was charged and the vendor was obligated to accept prepayments. If a payment was more than 30 days late, the vendor could, without notice or demand, retain all payments made as liquidated damages and could recover the property. The Marshalls (D) prepaid, through erratic payments, a total of $21,000 of the purchase price. Payments were subsequently missed. Skendzel (P), an heir of Burkowski (P), was assigned the contract under her will. Skendzel (P) brought an action on the contract to enforce the forfeiture provision and to recover possession of the property. Marshall (D) alleged that acceptance of the irregular payments constituted a waiver of the provision and that the forfeiture clause was a penalty, which was not related to the damages suffered in the event of default, and should not be enforced. The trial court held that no waiver was made because Burkowski (P) was required by the contract terms to accept prepayments. However, it denied Skendzel (P) relief, holding the liquidated damages clause to be a penalty.

**ISSUE:** Will a court enforce a forfeiture provision where the liquidated damages bear no relation to the loss suffered and exact damages may be easily calculated?

**HOLDING AND DECISION:** (Hunter, J.) No. The law abhors forfeitures. Equity will interfere where it determines that such clauses are penalties. The test is whether compensation can or cannot be adequately made for a breach of the obligation. If a liquidated damage provision bears no relationship to the loss suffered and the amount of damages can be easily calculated, it is a penalty clause which will not be enforced. Merely because a party stipulates to such an unfair clause does not automatically bind him. The parties are contracting to accomplish an act and the failure to so perform should not cause a wholly disproportionate loss to the party. Here, the Marshalls (D) have paid $21,000 on a $36,000 debt. Under the liquidated damage provision, Skendzel (P) would be entitled to the payments plus possession of the property. While reasonable liquidated damage provisions will be enforced, the clause herein is really a penalty wholly unrelated to actual damages suffered from the default. A land sale contract leaves the vendor with bare legal title and vests the buyer with equitable title and possession. It is a present sale with legal title as security for repayment of the debt. Judicial foreclosure is the proper remedy on default and certain rights, i.e., redemption and appraisal, are given the vendee. To allow the forfeiture provision herein to be utilized would achieve an unconscionable result. Skendzel (P) must utilize the judicial foreclosure procedure required by statute and his recovery is limited to the balance due on the contract plus interest from the date of this judgment. Although no waiver occurred here, since the vendor was required to accept all prepayments under the contract, Skendzel (P) should not have been denied all equitable relief. Because the trial court failed to exercise its discretionary power under the mistaken belief it lacked such power in this case, the case must be remanded with instructions to enter a judgment of foreclosure on the vendors' lien and an order for payment of unpaid principal balance due with 8% interest from the date of judgment. Reversed and remanded.

**CONCURRENCE:** (Prentice, J.) If the vendee has little or no equity in the property, such forfeiture provisions should be enforced. It is only where enforcement would be unjust that equity should deny it.

## ▶ *ANALYSIS*

There must be a shocking unfairness to the forfeiture provision before many jurisdictions will refuse to enforce it. *Bishop v. Beecher*, 355 P.2d 277 (1960). Many courts will refuse enforcement of such clauses even if the default is blatant, e.g., no payments for one year, and time is made "of the essence." However, such courts normally require payment of the entire purchase price plus interest. *State v. Superior Court for King County*, 57 Wash. 2d 571 (1961).

■■■■

*Continued on next page.*

## *Quicknotes*

**FORFEITURE**   The loss of a right or interest as a penalty for failing to fulfill an obligation.

**LIQUIDATED DAMAGES**   An amount of money specified in a contract representing the damages owed in the event of breach.

■━━■

# Union Bond & Trust Co. v. Blue Creek Redwood Co.

### Purchaser of timberland (P) v. Seller (D)

128 F. Supp. 709 (N.D. Cal. 1955); *aff'd*, 243 F.2d 476 (9th Cir. 1957).

**NATURE OF CASE:** Action for specific performance and cross-complaint for damages for default of contract and quiet title.

**FACT SUMMARY:** Upon a willful breach of an installment sales contract, the vendor sought forfeiture and the vendee sought the right to complete performance of the contract.

> ## 🏛 RULE OF LAW
> If a vendee has breached an installment sales contract and faces a forfeiture, the vendee has the right to complete the contract by paying the purchase price, if he was able to do so and if he had made substantial part performance or substantial improvements.

**FACTS:** The vendee, the assignor of Union Bond & Trust Co. (P), agreed to purchase timberland from the vendor, the assignor of Blue Creek Redwood Co. (D). There was an installment sales contract for a total price of $750,000 to be paid in installments. Vendees had paid $585,000 when they willfully defaulted on the contract. Vendor gave a 60-day notice and then notified vendee that, by the terms of the contract, all moneys were forfeited and the contract was canceled. The contract stated that time was of the essence. Union Bond (P) sued requesting that the land be conveyed to them upon full payment of the purchase price plus any damages. Blue Creek (D) argued that a willful default allows only restitution of any payments in excess of the damages to the vendor.

**ISSUE:** Under California law, may a willful defaulter of an installment sales contract be allowed to complete the contract upon a showing of substantial part performance or substantial improvements?

**HOLDING AND DECISION:** (Goodman, J.) Yes. If there has been substantial part performance or substantial improvement, to permit the vendor to terminate the contract and keep the installments would result in the harshest sort of forfeiture. If the vendee were willing and able to do so, he should be allowed to pay off the remaining price plus any damages to the vendor caused by the breach. To deny the vendee this right merely because the breach was willful would be to incorporate a form of punitive damages or a form of liquidated damages into a contract merely because the vendee partially performed before he breached. To require the vendee to accept restitution of all moneys paid less damages to the vendor would leave the vendee without the property and perhaps without any of the installments if the damages were great. The vendee has this option if he wishes, but is not required to exercise it. The determination of the relief will not be conditioned by a purpose to penalize the vendee.

## ▶ ANALYSIS

The issue in this case revolved around the element of willful breach. Had there been no willful breach, the applicable California statute would clearly have applied to allow the vendee to complete the contract. The court analogized punitive damages for contract breach to a forfeiture because of willful breach, and held that if the former is not allowed, then neither would the latter. In essence, the forfeiture or penalty would be allowed only because the vendee partially performed before the breach rather than having not performed before breaching.

---

## Quicknotes

**INSTALLMENT CONTRACT** A contract pursuant to which the parties are to render performance or payment in periodic intervals.

**LIQUIDATED DAMAGES** An amount of money specified in a contract representing the damages owed in the event of breach.

**PART PERFORMANCE** Partial performance of a contract, promise or obligation.

**SUBSTANTIAL PERFORMANCE** Performance of all the essential obligations pursuant to an agreement.

# Wallach v. Riverside Bank

Buyer of land (P) v. Seller (D)

N.Y. Ct. App., 206 N.Y. 434, 100 N.E. 50 (1912).

**NATURE OF CASE:** Action to recover down payment plus expenses.

**FACT SUMMARY:** The vendee agreed to accept a quitclaim deed and the vendor tendered unmarketable title.

## 🏛 RULE OF LAW
When a vendor contracts to sell land, the law imputes to him a covenant that he will convey a marketable title free of encumbrances unless the vendee stipulates to accept less than marketable title.

**FACTS:** Wallach (P) contracted to buy land from Riverside Bank (D) subject to any existing leases or restrictions of record. Riverside (D) agreed to convey a quitclaim deed upon receipt of the payment from Wallach (P). On the law day, Riverside (D) tendered a quitclaim deed and demanded payment. Wallach (P) refused to accept the deed on the ground that the title was clouded by an outstanding inchoate right of dower in the wife of a former grantor. Wallach (P) stated that he would make payment only upon condition that Riverside (D) could give a marketable title to the property. Riverside (D) refused to meet this condition and Wallach (P) sued to recover his down payment and for additional expenses incurred in examining title.

**ISSUE:** If a vendee agrees to accept a quitclaim deed, does this waive his right to demand marketable title from the vendor?

**HOLDING AND DECISION:** (Vann, J.) No. The law implies in all executory land sale contracts a covenant by the vendor to convey marketable title free from encumbrances, unless the vendee specifically agrees to accept less than marketable title. The mere agreement by the vendee to accept a quitclaim deed does not waive the covenant of marketable title, Also, the fact that Wallach (P) agreed to take the land subject to any outstanding restrictions of record was not a waiver of his right to good title. Here, the fact that there was an outstanding dower right in the property made it impossible for Riverside (D) to convey all the land it had promised to convey because the dower right could, in the future, be asserted to claim possession of the land. Even if the vendee knows of the defect in title when the land sale contract was made, he still has the right to demand marketable title, free from encumbrances, on the day set for delivery of the deed. Affirmed.

## ▶ ANALYSIS

Marketable or merchantable title is defined as a title which is free from "reasonable doubt." Although it does not require perfect title, it must be title that a reasonably prudent buyer would be willing to accept because it is free from the threat of possible future litigation over the title. A marketable title is one that a court of equity would force an unwilling purchaser to accept in a suit for specific performance.

■═■

## Quicknotes

**MARKETABLE TITLE** Title that, although not perfect, would be acceptable to a reasonably well-informed buyer exercising ordinary business prudence.

**QUITCLAIM DEED** A deed whereby the grantor conveys whatever interest he or she may have in the property without any warranties or covenants as to title.

■═■

# Bartos v. Czerwinski

### Buyer of land (P) v. Owner-seller (D)

Mich. Sup. Ct., 323 Mich. 87, 34 N.W.2d 566 (1948).

**NATURE OF CASE:** Action for specific performance.

**FACT SUMMARY:** The vendor could not convey marketable title because there was an outstanding interest in the property, and suit for specific performance of the contract to convey marketable title was brought by the vendee.

### 🏛 RULE OF LAW
A title is unmarketable if a reasonable, prudent person would not accept it because there is such doubt or uncertainty as to its status as may reasonably result in litigation, regardless of the probable outcome of the litigation.

**FACTS:** In 1945, Bartos (P) signed an offer to buy land owned by Czerwinski (D). The contract called for marketable title. Bartos's (P) attorney concluded from an examination of the title to the land that Czerwinski (D) could not convey marketable title, based on the following facts: In 1922, the land had been conveyed to Hickey and Eppinga and was recorded. In 1923, these two grantees conveyed the land to Peoples State Bank who recorded. On December 28, 1927, Eppinga gave a quitclaim deed to the land to Hickey and it was recorded January 7, 1928. On December 29, 1927, the Peoples State Bank gave a quitclaim deed to the land to both Hickey and Eppinga, and this was recorded on January 10, 1928. Bartos's (P) attorney determined that there was a serious question as to whether Eppinga still had an outstanding interest in the land which Czerwinski (D) had contracted to convey, and Eppinga refused to sign a quitclaim deed to the property. Bartos (P) sued for specific performance of the contract to convey the land with marketable title.

**ISSUE:** Was there sufficient doubt as to the status of this title so that the vendee could reasonably assume that there would be litigation over it?

**HOLDING AND DECISION:** (Carr, J.) Yes. While it cannot be conclusively determined, Eppinga could reasonably be said to have a possible interest in the land. The vendee, Bartos (P), is not required to accept a conveyance of the title in such a condition that he may be required to defend litigation challenging his possession and interest. The title need not actually be bad, there need be only reasonable doubt about it. However, the remedy of specific performance to compel Czerwinski (D) to convey marketable title is improper because there can be no assurance that he could obtain the proper release or conveyance from Eppinga. A court of equity is loathe to impose and supervise the performance of contracts containing contingencies or uncertainties. Bartos (P), therefore, must seek a legal, not an equitable, remedy. Judgment of the trial court affirmed as modified.

---

### ▶ *ANALYSIS*

The doubt as to title refers to possible litigation as to both fact and law. The doubt raised by the possible existence of third-party claims would not be resolved in a marketable title suit between vendor and vendee because a judgment on such a suit would not be res judicata on potential third-party claimants.

■=■

### *Quicknotes*

**MARKETABLE TITLE**  Title that, although not perfect, would be acceptable to a reasonably well-informed buyer exercising ordinary business prudence.

**QUITCLAIM DEED**  A deed whereby the grantor conveys whatever interest he or she may have in the property without any warranties or covenants as to title.

■=■

# Luette v. Bank of Italy National Trust & Savings Ass'n

Purchaser of land (P) v. Seller of land (D)

42 F.2d 9 (9th Cir. 1930).

**NATURE OF CASE:** Action for rescission of contract.

**FACT SUMMARY:** Luette (P) and Bank of Italy National Trust & Saving Ass'n (D) entered into an installment contract for the sale and purchase of land. Luette (P) learned of an adverse claim against Bank of Italy (D) and sought to have the contract rescinded.

## RULE OF LAW
There can be no rescission by a vendee of an executory contract of sale merely because of lack of title in the vendor prior to the date when performance is due.

**FACTS:** Luette (P) entered into a contract to purchase land from Bank of Italy National Trust & Savings Ass'n's (D) predecessors in interest. Luette (P) paid a deposit and was to pay monthly installments for seven years. Bank of Italy (D) was to convey the deed upon completion of the payments. Luette (P) made the payments for two years. Luette (P) alleged that an adverse claim had been asserted, the outcome of which was uncertain. Luette (P) asked that Bank of Italy (D) be enjoined from canceling Luette's (P) contract and that they be relieved of having to make payments pending the outcome of the claim. Luette (P) asked that if the court could not grant the injunction, the contract be rescinded.

**ISSUE:** Can there be a rescission by a vendee of an executory contract of sale because of lack of title in the vendor prior to the date when performance is due?

**HOLDING AND DECISION:** (Kerrigan, J.) No. The court will not issue an injunction since Luette (P) makes no pleading of any equities to justify such relief. Secondly, there can be no rescission by a vendee of an executory contract of sale merely because of lack of title in the vendor prior to the date when performance is due. In this case, there is no showing that Bank of Italy (D) is in default, since under the contract the deed would not be conveyed for three more years. Assuming a defect does exist, Bank of Italy (D) still has three years in which to perfect its title. Affirmed.

## ANALYSIS

An installment land contract is used as an instrumentality for the long-range financing of the purchase of land. As demonstrated in this case, under such an arrangement, the purchaser goes into possession immediately and is obligated to pay specified installments. The vendor will deliver the deed upon completion of the payments. The vendor's security is the right to retake the land if the purchaser defaults in making payments. The more common method of financing the purchase of land is the mortgage.

## Quicknotes

**INSTALLMENT CONTRACT** A contract pursuant to which the parties are to render performance or payment in periodic intervals.

**RESCISSION** The canceling of an agreement and the return of the parties to their positions prior to the formation of the contract.

# Cohen v. Kranz

Buyer of land (P) v. Seller (D)

N.Y. Ct. App., 12 N.Y.2d 242, 189 N.E.2d 473 (1963).

**NATURE OF CASE:** Action for return of down payment.

**FACT SUMMARY:** The vendee, Cohen (P), failed to notify the vendor, Kranz (D), of claimed defects in title and failed to make a proper tender of performance.

## 🏛 RULE OF LAW
While a vendee can recover money paid on the contract from a vendor who defaults on law day without a showing of tender, or even of willingness and ability to perform, where the vendor's title is incurably defective, a tender and demand are required to put the vendor in default where his title could be cleared without difficulty and in a reasonable time.

**FACTS:** Cohen (P) contracted to buy Kranz's (D) house, paying $4,000 down with the balance due on the date set for delivery of the deed, November 15. Cohen (P) asked to have the date for delivery postponed until December 15 and Kranz (D) agreed to the time extension. On November 30, Cohen's (P) attorney sent a letter to Kranz (D) stating that the title to the property was unmarketable due to building defects and demanded return of the down payment. The letter rejecting title did not specify the defects which Cohen (P) claimed made the title unmarketable. It was later shown that the only ways in which Kranz's (D) house was unmarketable was that there was no certificate of occupancy for the swimming pool and a fence projected beyond the front line of the dwelling. Although these defects violated a protective covenant in the title, they could have been easily cured by Kranz (D) on timely notice and demand from Cohen (P). When Kranz refused to return the down payment, Cohen (P) sued for return of his down payment and the cost of title search, and Kranz (D) counterclaimed for damages for breach of contract.

**ISSUE:** Is a vendee barred from recovering the down payment from a vendor whose title defects are curable and whose performance was not demanded on law day?

**HOLDING AND DECISION:** (Burke, J.) Yes. A tender and demand of performance of the contract are required to put the vendor in default where his title could be cleared without difficulty and in a reasonable time. The certificate of occupancy and removal of the fence could have been easily done had the vendor been put on notice of the nature of the defects. The failure of tender and demand prevented the vendor's title defect from amounting to a default. Had the defects been incurable, the vendor would have automatically been in default and no tender and demand would have been necessary, though a showing of willingness and ability to perform on the part of the vendee would have been necessary. The failure to specify the defects made it impossible for the vendor to cure them. Cohen's (P) advance rejection of title and demand for immediate return of the down payment were unjustified and amounted to anticipatory breach of contract. Affirmed.

## ▶ ANALYSIS
The vendor is only obligated to tender a good and marketable title on the date when the conveyance is to be executed. A purchaser may not rescind a land sale contract before the time for performance unless it can be shown that it would be virtually impossible for the vendor to clear title by law day. Where the defect is curable, a vendor is entitled to a reasonable time beyond law day to make his title good. The remedies for absence of marketable title include suit for damages for breach, rescission, specific performance, or quiet title.

■■■

## Quicknotes

**ANTICIPATORY BREACH** Breach of a contract subsequent to formation but prior to the time performance is due.

**MARKETABLE TITLE** Title that, although not perfect, would be acceptable to a reasonably well-informed buyer exercising ordinary business prudence.

■■■

# Handzel v. Bassi

## Purchaser of land (P) v. Seller (D)

III. App. Ct., 343 III. App. 281, 99 N.E.2d 23 (1951).

**NATURE OF CASE:** Action for an injunction.

**FACT SUMMARY:** A land sale contract contained a provision for forfeiture if the vendee assigned the contract prior to full payment, and the vendee later contracted to sell the property to a third person.

## 🏛 RULE OF LAW
A provision against assignment in a land sale contract is designed merely to secure performance, and when the vendor has received the purchase price, he has received all that the provision against assignment was intended to secure and a forfeiture will, therefore, not be allowed.

**FACTS:** Handzel (P) contracted to buy Bassi's (D) land. There was a $5,000 down payment with the balance to be paid in installments on October 1 of the years 1949 to 1953. When half of the price had been paid, on October 1, 1950, then Bassi (D) would convey the property and Handzel (P) would deliver a purchase money mortgage for the balance. The contract provided that any assignment of the agreement or an interest would void the contract and would result in a forfeiture of all money paid to Bassi (D). In February 1950, Handzel (P) contracted to sell the property to a third party. After notifying Handzel (P), Bassi (D) declared the contract void in May, 1950. In June 1950, and again in September, Handzel (P) tendered the October payment and offered to execute a purchase money mortgage on the unpaid balance in exchange for the deed. Bassi (D) refused and Handzel (P) brought an action to enjoin Bassi (D) from forfeiting the contract.

**ISSUE:** Is a provision against assignment of a land sale contract merely a security device to assure payment not giving the vendor the right to forfeit the contract where the vendee has tendered full performance?

**HOLDING AND DECISION:** (Dove, J.) Yes. Equity abhors a forfeiture and the policy of the law is to strictly construe restraints on alienation. Bassi's (D) basic right was to receive the purchase price. The provision against assignment was meant merely to secure that right. It is collateral to the main purpose of the contract and is not an integral covenant. Where the object of that security device, the full payment, has been achieved, the vendor cannot use the provision as an excuse for not conveying and for a forfeiture. Handzel's (P) contract with the third party in no way released him from the duty under the contract. Even if it did, Handzel (P) has offered and is able to perform fully on the contract. The object of the

provision against assignment was accomplished upon the tender of the payment and the mortgage. Affirmed.

## ▶ ANALYSIS

The modern bias in favor of free assignment is very strong. Mere covenants not to assign do not destroy the power to assign, but do withdraw the right to assign. Thus, the assignment will stand, but the assignor is liable for breach of the covenant. Covenants which explicitly state that a purported assignment is void destroy both the power and the right to assign. In either case, the provision will be construed as strongly as possible in favor of upholding an assignment. In the present case, there was no real assignment because Handzel's (P) duties to Bassi (D) were unaffected. The court looked at the full performance by Handzel (P) as a more determinative factor than the existence of the covenant not to assign.

■=■

## Quicknotes

**ASSIGNMENT** A transaction in which a party conveys his or her entire interest in property to another.

**PURCHASE MONEY MORTGAGE** A mortgage or other security in property taken in order to ensure the performance of a duty undertaken pursuant to the purchase of such property.

**RESTRAINT AGAINST ALIENATION** A provision restricting the transferee's ability to convey interests in the conveyed property.

■=■

# Kramer v. Mobley

Purchaser of land (D) v. Second purchaser (P)

Ky. Ct. App., 309 Ky. 143, 216 S.W.2d 930 (1949).

**NATURE OF CASE:** Action for breach of contract.

**FACT SUMMARY:** The vendor wanted to sue later on a title dispute and indemnify the vendee for any damages, but the vendee wanted him to immediately pay off the disputed claim.

## 🏛 RULE OF LAW
If a land sale contract fails by reason of a defect in vendor's title and the vendor is not guilty of any bad faith or fraud, then the measure of the vendee's damages for breach of contract is the consideration he has paid, plus interest, and any legitimate expenses incurred.

**FACTS:** Kramer (D) bought land from Gordon, paying off all but $2,000. Kramer (D) later offered to sell the land to Mobley (P), and Mobley (P) signed the contract. When the time for conveying the deed came, Mobley (P) learned of Gordon's possible $2,000 interest in the land. Kramer (D) offered to pay Mobley (P) $3,000 to indemnify him against Gordon's claim and promised he would later sue Gordon to clear title. Mobley (P) refused and stated he would not accept the deed until Kramer (D) paid off Gordon's claim and obtained a release. Kramer (D) refused, stating that Gordon's claim was false. The contract fell through and Kramer (D) returned the down payment, and Mobley (P) sued for breach of contract. The trial court awarded Mobley (P) the difference between the contract and the market price of the land.

**ISSUE:** Where a land sale contract fails because of a title defect and the vendor was not guilty of fraud or bad faith, was the difference between the contract and the market price of the land the proper measure of damages?

**HOLDING AND DECISION:** (Rees, J.) No. The measure of damages will be the difference between the market price and the contract price of the land only where the vendor refuses to deliver the property or where the vendor willfully refuses to deliver a good and marketable title. Where the sale fails because of title defect, and the vendor shows no bad faith or fraud, the measure is the consideration paid by the vendee and any legitimate expenses incurred by him. Here, Kramer (D) was unable to convey good title but was guilty of no fraud or bad faith; his refusal to pay off Gordon did not constitute any fraud. The vendor is not required to make a substantial sacrifice by paying off a disputed claim and Kramer (D) made a fair offer to indemnify Mobley (P). Reversed for further proceedings.

## ▶ ANALYSIS

This rule is known as the English rule on the "out of pocket" measure of damages, and is followed by about half the states. The American rule allows the difference between market price and contract price for any breach of contract by the vendor, the "benefit of the bargain." Various reasons given for the English rule include the difficulty inherent in a vendor's determination that he has good title, the oscillating property market price, and the desire to keep landowners at the status quo so that land development will not be hampered.

## Quicknotes

**FRAUD** A false representation of facts with the intent that another will rely on the misrepresentation to his detriment.

**INDEMNITY** The duty of a party to compensate another for damages sustained.

# Smith v. Warr

### Buyer of real property (P) v. Seller (D)

Utah Sup. Ct., 564 P.2d 771 (1977).

**NATURE OF CASE:** Action for breach of land sale contract.

**FACT SUMMARY:** Smith (P) purchased real property from Warr (D), which was lost because a third-party adverse possessor eventually obtained title to it.

## 🏛 RULE OF LAW
The proper measure of damages for breach of a land sale contract by the vendor is the benefit of the bargain.

**FACTS:** Smith (P) purchased real property from Warr (D) on a land sale contract. A third-party adverse possessor then filed suit and obtained a judgment awarding him title to the property. Smith (P), who had cross-claimed for breach of contract, was awarded his out-of-pocket losses. Smith (P) appealed, alleging that the proper measure of damages was for the benefit of the bargain. Warr (D) alleged that such damages were awarded only where there was bad faith.

**ISSUE:** Is the proper measure of damages for breach of a land sale contract by the vendor the benefit of the bargain?

**HOLDING AND DECISION:** (Wilkins, J.) Yes. While there is a split in jurisdictions, we find that in this state benefit of the bargain damages are awarded whenever a vendor breaches a land sale contract. Good faith is immaterial. Under benefit of the bargain damages, the vendee is entitled to the difference between the market value at the time of breach and the unpaid balance on the property under the contract. The court improperly awarded only out-of-pocket expenses. Reversed and remanded.

## ▶ ANALYSIS

The so-called English Rule, followed by approximately one-half of the states, grants out-of-pocket expenses only in the absence of bad faith. It is justified on the basis of the intricacies of titles and complicated real estate practices which might lead a seller to believe that he really had good title. Absent bad faith, a return to the status quo causes no injury to the purchaser. *Crenshaw v. Williams*, 231 S.W. 45 (1921).

■≡■

## Quicknotes

**ADVERSE POSSESSION** A means of acquiring title to real property by remaining in actual, open, continuous, exclusive possession of property for the statutory period.

**CROSS-CLAIM** A claim asserted by a plaintiff or defendant to an action against a co-plaintiff or co-defendant, and not against an opposing party, arising out of the same transaction or occurrence as the subject matter of the action.

**GOOD FAITH** An honest intention to abstain from any unconscientious advantage of another.

■≡■

# Clay v. Landreth

## Property owner (P) v. Purchaser (D)

Va. Ct. App., 187 Va. 169, 45 S.E.2d 875 (1948).

**NATURE OF CASE:** Action for specific performance.

**FACT SUMMARY:** Landreth (D) made a contract to buy Clay's (P) property for a specific business use but a supervening change in the zoning laws rendered that use illegal, so Landreth (D) refused to perform the contract.

## 🏛 RULE OF LAW
In a specifically enforceable land sale contract, equity treats the vendee as the real owner with a real property interest and will order specific enforcement of the contract so long as nothing has intervened which equity determines is sufficient to prevent performance, such as the change of zoning laws, precluding buyer from using the land as he planned.

**FACTS:** Landreth (D) contracted to buy Clay's (P) land. The known purpose was to build on the land a storage plant for ice cream and fruit. When the contract was made, the zoning laws did not prohibit such a use. Between the time the contract was made and delivery of the deed was to be made, the zoning laws were changed so that the land could be used only for residence purposes. The rezoning caused a substantial depreciation in value. There was no fraud, misrepresentation, unfair dealing, or inequitable conduct by either party. Landreth (D) refused to perform the contract.

**ISSUE:** Should a land sale contract be specifically enforced when the agreed purpose for which the land was purchased was defeated by a subsequent, unanticipated zoning change from business to residential use?

**HOLDING AND DECISION:** (Gregory, J.) No. The doctrine of equitable conversion holds that when there is a specifically enforceable land sale contract, equity views that as done which should be done, and, therefore, treats the vendee as the real owner and the vendor as a trustee. But the doctrine will not be applied where it would defeat the intent and purpose of the parties with resulting hardship to the vendee. It is not applied where there has been a change of circumstances which has intervened after the contract was made and which was not contemplated by the parties. Equitable conversion is based on the presumed intent of the parties. Where a zoning change precludes the known, intended use of the land, specific performance will not be granted. Affirmed.

## ▶ ANALYSIS

Equitable conversion can be conceptualized in the sense that the interests owned by the parties prior to the contract becoming specifically enforceable reverse after the contract becomes specifically enforceable. What the seller had before that point in time now belongs to the buyer. While the buyer has equitable title, possession follows legal title. A court of equity may find a title unmarketable and, thus, refuse specific performance if zoning regulations which frustrate the buyer's plans are adopted after the execution of the contract but before the closing date. The vendor can still sue for damages if the vendee does not perform, and the vendee cannot get rescission.

---

## Quicknotes

**EQUITABLE CONVERSION** Doctrine pursuant to which once property is sold pursuant to a land sale contract, equitable title passes to the buyer and legal title remains in the seller as security until the remainder of the purchase price is tendered.

**TRUSTEE** A person who is entrusted to keep or administer something.

# Shay v. Penrose

Husband of property owner (P) v. Sister of wife (D)

Ill. Sup. Ct., 25 Ill. 2d 447, 185 N.E.2d 218 (1962).

**NATURE OF CASE:** Suit for partition of real property.

**FACT SUMMARY:** During her life, Shay's (P) wife had sold four parcels of property by land contract of sale. At her death, none of the parcels had been completely paid for and Penrose (D), the wife's sister, asserted her claim to one-half interest in each parcel as a surviving heir.

## ▥ RULE OF LAW
At the moment a valid contract for the sale of land is executed, an equitable conversion occurs which vests the equitable title to the land in the buyer, leaving the seller holding bare legal title in trust for the buyer who holds the balance of the purchase price in trust for the seller.

**FACTS:** Shay's (P) wife had acquired six parcels of land during her lifetime and had sold four of them. The sales were by contract for deed (land contracts of sale) which provided for installment payment by the buyers. Until the final payment was made, the legal title to the land remained in the name of Shay's (P) wife. Upon her death, Shay (P) filed an action for partition for the remaining two parcels since the intestate succession statute provided that all real property held by the decedent should be split between a surviving spouse and any surviving brothers or sisters. Penrose (D) was the wife's sister and was, therefore, entitled to one-half of the real property. Penrose (D) filed an answer and cross-complaint seeking partition of the four sold parcels as well, claiming they were real property forming a part of the decedent's estate.

**ISSUE:** Upon the execution of a valid contract for the sale of land, does the seller retain a real property interest in the land sold?

**HOLDING AND DECISION:** (House, J.) No. At the moment a valid contract for the sale of land is executed, an equitable conversion occurs which vests the equitable title in the buyer. The seller retains bare legal title to the land, but in trust for the buyer. The buyer holds the balance of the purchase price in trust for the seller. The concept of equitable conversion converts the seller's interest in the land to personalty. If, prior to the completion of the terms of the contract, the seller dies, the interest in the balance of the purchase price passes to those entitled to receive the decedent's personal property and not to those entitled to the real property. Shay (P), as his wife's personal representative, succeeded to the full rights in these contracts and only the unsold parcels are subject to partition. Affirmed.

## ▶ ANALYSIS

The doctrine of equitable conversion has lost its importance due to statutory changes in the laws of intestate succession in most jurisdictions. At one time, there was an important distinction made between those persons who would take the decedent's personal property and those who would take his real property. The statute in this case provided that a surviving spouse would take all personalty but must divide the realty with surviving brothers and sisters.

■■■

## Quicknotes

**EQUITABLE TITLE** Interest in property that is not recognized in a court of law but that is protected in equity.

**LEGAL TITLE** Title such that is recognized by a court of law.

■■■

# Clapp v. Tower

### Holder of real estate (P) v. Claimants to ownership (D)

N.D. Sup. Ct., 11 N.D. 556, 93 N.W. 862 (1903).

**NATURE OF CASE:** Action to quiet title to land.

**FACT SUMMARY:** Executors of Hadley's estate, treating certain real estate as personal property, sold the land to Clapp (P).

## 🏛 RULE OF LAW
Subsequent to entering into a contract for the sale of real estate, the seller's interest in equity is in the unpaid purchase price, and is treated as personal property; the buyer's interest is in the land, and is realty. Upon the death of the seller, his interest passes to the executors of his estate as personal property. If the buyer then defaults in his payments, the executors may regain the land, and reconvey it. The title so conveyed is good as against the heirs of the decedent.

**FACTS:** Tower sold some real estate to Hadley upon a contract which provided that the deed would not be delivered until Hadley, the buyer, completed all his payments. Tower died before Hadley had paid in full. When Hadley then defaulted in making payments, the executors of Tower's estate foreclosed on the real estate and reconveyed it to Clapp (P). Tower's heirs (D) claimed that the real estate, as real property, should have devolved to them under the laws of succession.

**ISSUE:** Is real estate which is sold by executory contract treated as personal property?

**HOLDING AND DECISION:** (Young, J.) Yes. Under state law, the heirs (D) can only lay claim to real property. Personal property, upon the death of the seller, may be disposed of as the seller's executors see fit. Therefore, it is necessary to determine what Tower's interest in the real estate was prior to his death. A seller of land under an executory contract still holds the legal title, but only as a trustee: his interest is in the purchase price, while the buyer's interest is in the land contracted to be conveyed. Courts of equity will regard as done that which ought to be done. Under the doctrine of equitable conversion, the seller has exchanged his interest in real estate for an interest in personal property. Hence, the interest of the executors, after the seller's death, is in personal property. The heirs have no claim to the land, for it can no longer be regarded as real property for purposes of administering the estate. Affirmed.

## ▶ ANALYSIS

Here, the doctrine of equitable conversion is easily applied for the contract of sale was made after the will. A different problem arises, however, when the contract precedes a will in which the seller leaves the property to a third party, but bequeaths all his personal property to yet another person. One court has held that, so long as the contract was still executory (unfulfilled) at the time of the seller's death, the sale proceeds still went to the recipient of the property under the will on the theory that such must be presumed the seller's intent.

---

## Quicknotes

**EQUITABLE CONVERSION** Doctrine pursuant to which once property is sold pursuant to a land sale contract, equitable title passes to the buyer and legal title remains in the seller as security until the remainder of the purchase price is tendered.

**LEGAL TITLE** Title such that is recognized by a court of law.

# Eddington v. Turner

## Holder of option to purchase (P) v. Sister (D)

Del. Sup. Ct., 27 Del. Ch. 411, 38 A.2d 738, 155 A.L.R. 562 (1944).

**NATURE OF CASE:** Action for specific performance of a land contract.

**FACT SUMMARY:** Thomas Turner, subsequent to making a will in which he left some land to his sister (D), gave an option to purchase the land to Eddington (P), and then died before the option could be exercised.

## 🏛 RULE OF LAW
The granting of an option to purchase realty, made after the execution of a will disposing of the same realty, does not operate as an equitable conversion of the property relating back to the date of the option so as to give the proceeds of the sale to the decedent's estate rather than to the named recipient of the land under the will.

**FACTS:** Thomas Turner made a will in which he left some land to his sister, Sallie (D). Turner then gave an option to Eddington (P) to purchase the land. The option was to run for 60 days. Within the period, Turner died. Within the life of the option, Eddington (P) elected to exercise his option. In a suit for specific performance, Eddington (P) prevailed and the court, sitting in equity, ordered that the proceeds of the sale be paid to Sallie (D). The executors of Turner's estate objected on the ground that, according to the doctrine of equitable conversion, the proceeds were personal property which must go into the estate.

**ISSUE:** Where an option is exercised after the death of the seller, does the equitable conversion relate back to the date the option was extended, and not to the date of its exercise, so as to make the proceeds of sale personal property, and thereby passing to the decedent's estate rather than to specifically named recipients of the land in the decedent's will?

**HOLDING AND DECISION:** (Rodney, J.) No. If there be any equitable conversion at all it could not occur prior to the exercise of the option, for until then, no duty rested on anyone in connection with the land. Furthermore, since the land had not been transferred during Turner's lifetime, he could not have claimed the purchase price while living. As a result, neither could the executors of his estate once Turner died. Sallie (D) took the land subject to the exercise of the option. At the time of the option, the land was converted into money and, as Sallie (D) had a life interest in the land, she was similarly entitled to a life interest in the proceeds of the sale. Affirmed.

## ▶ ANALYSIS

In cases involving death of the vendor prior to the exercise of an option, the majority approach holds that equitable conversion takes place only when the option is actually exercised and not just executed. A minority of courts hold that conversion relates back to the time of execution. As a result, the seller retains only a personal property interest in the land, and his death is immaterial, so long as the option is exercised in the agreed-upon period.

■■■■

## Quicknotes

**WILL** An instrument setting forth the distribution to be made of an individual's estate upon his death; since a will is not effective until the death of its maker, it is revocable during his life.

■■■■

# Bleckley v. Langston

Buyers of land (P) v. Sellers (D)

Ga. Ct. App., 112 Ga. App. 63, 143 S.E.2d 671 (1965).

**NATURE OF CASE:** Appeal from judgment granting plaintiffs' motion for summary judgment in action for rescission of land sale contract and recovery of earnest money.

**FACT SUMMARY:** After buyer (P) signed a land sale contract, an ice storm destroyed pecan trees on the property, which reduced the fair market value of the land.

## 🏛 RULE OF LAW
Under the doctrine of equitable conversion, when real property is destroyed through no fault of the seller before a buyer takes possession, risk of loss falls upon the buyer.

**FACTS:** On December 23, 1963, the parties entered into a land sale contract whereby the buyers (P) agreed to purchase the sellers' (D) land for $120,000 and made a deposit of $10,000. On New Year's Eve and New Year's Day, an ice storm damaged the pecan trees on the property, which reduced the land's fair market value. The sellers (D) still possessed the land and had not yet closed the sale by tendering a deed to the buyers (P). The contract made no provision for who would bear the risk of loss. Prior to February 1, 1964, the buyers (P) notified the sellers (D) of their intention to rescind the contract and demanded the return of their deposit. The sellers (D) responded to the buyers (P) that they were willing and able to perform the contract; they requested plaintiffs to perform, and they refused to return the deposit. The trial court granted the buyers' (P) motion for summary judgment, thereby rescinding the contract and restoring the buyers' (P) deposit. The sellers (D) appealed.

**ISSUE:** When real property is destroyed through no fault of the seller before the buyer takes possession, does the buyer bear the risk of loss?

**HOLDING AND DECISION:** (Hall, J.) Yes. Under the doctrine of equitable conversion, risk of loss falls upon the buyer, who is in substance the owner of the property. Actual possession of the property is not material with respect to either legal or equitable title to land. Since the parties here have entered into a binding contract that the sellers (D) were willing and able to consummate, the loss should fall on the buyers (P). Reversed.

## ▎ ANALYSIS

The doctrine of equitable conversion is the majority position. It rests on the premise that the buyer has equitable title during the time between the contract date and closing date and therefore buyer should assume the risk of loss.

A minority of states have adopted the Massachusetts rule, which states that risk of loss falls upon the seller due to failure of consideration when land is destroyed through no one's fault during the executory period.

■══■

## *Quicknotes*

**EQUITABLE CONVERSION** Doctrine pursuant to which once property is sold pursuant to a land sale contract, equitable title passes to the buyer and legal title remains in the seller as security until the remainder of the purchase price is tendered.

**RISK OF LOSS** Liability for damage to or loss of property that is the subject matter of a contract for sale.

■══■

# Sanford v. Breidenbach

Seller of house (P) v. Buyer (D)

Ohio Ct. App., 111 Ohio App. 474, 173 N.E.2d 702 (1960).

**NATURE OF CASE:** Action for specific performance of land sale contract.

**FACT SUMMARY:** Following a fire which destroyed the contracted-for house, buyer (D) sought to hold the seller's (P) insurance company liable for the damage.

## 🏛 RULE OF LAW
In a contract to convey real property, equitable conversion by the purchaser does not take place until the seller has fulfilled all conditions and is entitled to enforce specific performance, and the parties, by their contract, intend that title shall pass to the buyer upon the signing of the contract of purchase. As a result, since the buyer does not have equitable title until all of the above conditions are met, he may not claim under the seller's insurance policy for recovering damage to the property by an act of God.

**FACTS:** Sanford (P), as seller, contracted with Breidenbach (D), as buyer, for the sale of a house, possession of which was to be delivered on transfer of title. A material part of the agreement was that Sanford (P) would furnish the house with a septic tank easement. Both Sanford (P) and Breidenbach (D) took out fire insurance policies on the house. The house burned down. At the time the house burned down, Sanford (P) had not provided for the easement. Breidenbach (D) thereupon refused to go through with the deal. When Sanford (P) brought an action for specific performance, Breidenbach (D) argued that both his and Sanford's (P) insurance companies were mutually obligated to pay the purchase price.

**ISSUE:** Under the doctrine of equitable conversion, may an out-of-possession buyer shift the loss of the property to the seller who is in such default at the time as to be unable to enforce the contract?

**HOLDING AND DECISION:** (Hunsicker, J.) Yes. Because Sanford (P) had not fully complied with the terms of the contract to provide an easement, equity will not allow him to seek specific performance. Absent any intention in the contract that the risk of loss should be on Breidenbach (D) when the contract was executed by the parties, there is no equitable conversion and Sanford (P) must bear the loss, being the owner of the property at the time it was destroyed. However, since Breidenbach (D) did not go through with the deal, he cannot claim Sanford's (P) insurance proceeds. By refusing to go through with escrow, all of his money has been returned. Furthermore, he is not required to perform his contract. Accordingly,

since Breidenbach (D) has suffered no indemnifiable loss, he has no interest in Sanford's (P) policy.

## ▶ ANALYSIS

Breidenbach (D) could have maintained his interest by waiving the defect in title caused by Sanford's (P) failure to provide an easement and insisting on a delivery of the deed. Of course, the subject matter of the contract having been destroyed, Breidenbach (D) probably felt that the property, absent the house, was not worth the transaction.

═

## Quicknotes

**EQUITABLE CONVERSION** Doctrine pursuant to which once property is sold pursuant to a land sale contract, equitable title passes to the buyer and legal title remains in the seller as security until the remainder of the purchase price is tendered.

**EQUITABLE TITLE** Interest in property that is not recognized in a court of law but that is protected in equity.

**INDEMNITY** The duty of a party to compensate another for damages sustained.

═

# Raplee v. Piper

Seller of real property (D) v. Buyer (P)

N.Y. Ct. App., 3 N.Y.2d 179, 143 N.E.2d 919 (1957).

**NATURE OF CASE:** Action for specific performance of land sale contract.

**FACT SUMMARY:** By terms of contract, buyer (P) took out fire insurance in seller's (D) name.

### 🏛 RULE OF LAW
When a land purchase contract requires the buyer to keep the property insured against fire and there is a fire loss before performance of the contract is completed, any such insurance received by the seller is to be applied on any remaining balance of the purchase price.

**FACTS:** Piper (P), as buyer, and Raplee (D), as seller, entered into a contract for the purchase of some real property. They agreed that Piper (P) was to take out fire insurance on the property in Raplee's (D) name to be effective until the transaction was completed. While Piper (P) was in possession, and before performance of the contract was completed, a fire occurred. Raplee (D), under the policy, received $4,650 for the loss. Piper (P) offset this amount from the remaining balance on the purchase price.

**ISSUE:** Where a land sale contract requires the buyer to pay insurance premiums on a policy in the seller's name only, and a fire occurs between execution of the contract and passing of title while buyer was in possession, is the buyer entitled to have the insurance proceeds applied in reduction of the purchase price, even though there was no specific agreement?

**HOLDING AND DECISION:** (Desmond, J.) Yes. A different conclusion would obtain if the seller had taken out the policy himself at his own cost. However, here, it would be unjust to not permit Piper (P) some benefit from the insurance. Otherwise, Raplee (D) would get the full purchase price plus the insurance proceeds while Piper (P) would not even get the house he bargained for. Affirmed.

**DISSENT:** (Burke, J.) The majority is, in effect, describing the insurance proceeds as something other than a trust fund by saying that the contract was insured for the benefit of all the parties concerned. However, insurance runs to the individual insured and not with the land. Piper (P) could have protected his own interest by taking out two policies, one in his own name.

### ▶ *ANALYSIS*

Although the court here did not specifically tag the policy as a trust fund, most American courts maintain that so long as the risk of loss is on the buyer, the seller acts as a

trustee for the buyer in receiving the insurance proceeds. The theory behind this is simply that it is unjust enrichment for the seller to get a windfall in addition to the purchase price.

▪▬▪

### *Quicknotes*

**RISK OF LOSS** Liability for damage to or loss of property that is the subject matter of a contract for sale.

**TRUSTEE** A person who is entrusted to keep or administer something.

▪▬▪

# The Deed

## Quick Reference Rules of Law

# French v. French

Grantor-son (D) v. Grantee-father (P)

N.H. Sup. Ct., 3 N.H. 234 (1825).

**NATURE OF CASE:** Writ of entry brought by Andrew French (P) against George French (D).

**FACT SUMMARY:** George French (D) executed a deed granting property to his father, Andrew French (P). He contended that the deed was inoperative because it was only signed by one witness and the statute of 1791 required that deeds be signed by two or more witnesses.

## 🏛 RULE OF LAW
Though a deed is not valid to pass real estate under the 1791 statute unless signed by two or more witnesses, it may operate as a covenant to stand seized, or as a bargain and sale, and thus pass the estate.

**FACTS:** George French (D) executed a deed granting his father, Andrew French (P), the use and improvement of certain property during his (Andrew's [P]) natural life. The deed was signed by only one witness. Under the statute of 1791, nothing will pass by a deed unless it is signed by two or more witnesses.

**ISSUE:** Is every deed which is not a valid conveyance under the 1791 statute wholly inoperative?

**HOLDING AND DECISION:** (Richardson, C.J.) No. Bargains and sales and covenants to stand seized are two modes of conveyance at common law. The colonial laws recognize both of these modes of conveyance. George (D) claims that the 1791 statute abolished all former modes of conveying real estate, and the only mode remaining is by deed as prescribed by the statute. However, affirmative words in a statute do not take away the common law, or former statutes, unless the words contain a negative. The 1791 statute declares what will constitute a valid conveyance, but it contains no negatives. Hence, though a deed is not valid to pass real estate under the 1791 statute unless signed by two or more witnesses, it may operate as a covenant to stand seized, or as a bargain and sale, and thus pass the estate. The deed in question here may be construed as a covenant to stand seized and pass the land without the aid of the statute. Judgment for Andrew (P), the demandant.

## ▶ ANALYSIS

At common law the ceremony necessary to transfer title was known as livery of seisin which took place on the land itself. The statute of uses, enacted in 1535, brought into almost universal use modes of conveyance which did not require livery of seisin. Bargain and sales and covenants to stand seized were two modes of conveyance which resulted from the statute of uses. The former is the transferring of property from one to another upon valuable consideration by way of a sale. The latter is a covenant by one conveying property to his wife, child, or kin in consideration of his natural love and affection. The statute of uses executed the contract in both cases, and thus the grantee acquired title and possession of the property as though there had been a livery of seisin. Covenants to stand seized are now practically obsolete.

■═■

## Quicknotes

**COVENANT OF SEISIN** A promise that the conveyor of property has the lawful right to convey the interest he is attempting to transfer.

**DEED** A signed writing transferring title to real property from one person to another.

■═■

# First National Bank of Oregon v. Townsend

Executor (P) v. Decedent/Grantor (D)

Or. Ct. App., 27 Or. App. 103, 555 P.2d 477 (1976).

**NATURE OF CASE:** Action to ascertain the interest conveyed by a deed.

**FACT SUMMARY:** A deed between Miller (D) and Townsend (P) could be read as conveying either a mineral and timber interest in real property or a fee simple.

## 🏛 RULE OF LAW
When a deed is so ambiguous that it supports two or more possible interpretations and no outside facts or circumstances clarify the ambiguity, the deed should be interpreted as conveying the greater possible estate.

**FACTS:** When Miller (D) died, his executor, First National Bank of Oregon (P), found a deed which could have been construed as either granting a fee simple interest in land to Miller (D) or merely a mineral and timber interest. Townsend (D), the grantor, was dead and had no relatives. The State (D), based on its escheat rights, maintained that the deed conveyed an interest only in the timber and mineral rights. This was the title to the deed and one of the clauses gave Miller (D) the right to enter onto the land. The granting clause, however, conveyed fee simple title to Miller (D) and obligated him to pay taxes. No extrinsic evidence was available to explain the ambiguities. The court found that the deed was so ambiguous that it could have conveyed either interest and it was impossible to determine the real intent of the parties. In such cases, the court concluded that the greater interest should be deemed conveyed. It found that Miller (D) had fee simple title to the property.

**ISSUE:** Where a deed is so ambiguous as to support an equal inference as to what type of title was conveyed, should the courts find that the greater title was transferred?

**HOLDING AND DECISION:** (Tanzer, J.) Yes. As a general rule of construction, where a deed is so ambiguous as to support an equal inference that two possible estates were conveyed, the courts should find that the greater one was intended. The court may consider the words of the deed itself and extrinsic evidence to explain the ambiguities. Here, no extrinsic evidence is available and the deed equally supports both possible estates. We find that a fee simple was transferred. Also, when there is a conflict between the granting clause and other parts of the deed, the granting clause is given priority. The judgment is affirmed.

## ▶ ANALYSIS

A court may ignore the title of an instrument in determining the true intent of the parties. Many instruments are poorly drafted, especially if done by laymen. Thus, in *Hinchliffe v. Fischer*, 750 S.W.2d 737 (1968), the court found that a document titled a "Private Annuity Contract" was actually a deed of real property transferring land in exchange for annuity payments made to the grantor.

■■■

## Quicknotes

**DEED** A signed writing transferring title to real property from one person to another.

**FEE SIMPLE** An estate in land characterized by ownership of the entire property for an unlimited duration and by absolute power over distribution.

■■■

# Grayson v. Holloway

### Heir (P) v. Wife of decedent (D)

Tenn. Sup. Ct., 203 Tenn. 464, 313 S.W.2d 555 (1958).

**NATURE OF CASE:** Action to determine the proper construction of a deed.

**FACT SUMMARY:** The granting clause of a deed executed by A. Holloway and M. Holloway conveyed property to G. Holloway in consideration for his taking care of them. The deed's habendum clause conveyed the land to G. Holloway and his wife, M. Holloway (D). G. Holloway's heir, Grayson (P), contested M. Holloway's (D) interest in the property.

**RULE OF LAW**
The rule of construction of a deed is to ascertain the intention of the grantor, if possible, by giving to every word of the deed its appropriate meaning, and to enforce that intention regardless of the mere formal divisions of the instrument.

**FACTS:** A. Holloway and Manervy Holloway executed a deed. Its granting clause purported to convey certain land to G. Holloway, "the consideration being G. Holloway is to take care of A. Holloway and Manervy Holloway as long as they live." The deed's habendum clause conveyed the land to G. Holloway and his wife, M. Holloway (D). A deed's habendum clause usually followed its granting clause and defined the extent of the ownership in the thing granted. Grayson (P), G. Holloway's heir, contended that he, rather than M. Holloway (D), was entitled to the land.

**ISSUE:** Where a granting clause and a habendum clause are in conflict, must the granting clause control?

**HOLDING AND DECISION:** (Neil, C.J.) No. The modern rules of construction make it the duty of courts to ascertain the intention of the grantor by giving to every word of the deed its appropriate meaning and to enforce that intention regardless of the mere formal or technical parts of the instrument. The technical rules of the common law as to the division of deeds into formal parts have long been disregarded. When the granting and habendum clauses of Holloway's deed are examined to determine their intention, this court holds that the deed vested in G. Holloway and M. Holloway (D) an estate by the entireties. The deed shows on its face that the Holloways (grantors) contemplated that both of the grantees (G. Holloway and M. Holloway [D]) would render services. It certainly was not contemplated that G. Holloway would do any washing, ironing, cooking, or making beds or perform other household duties which usually devolve upon the wife. Hence, a joint undertaking must have been intended by the grantors.

## ANALYSIS

In situations where there is a conflict between the habendum and the granting clause, the rule applied most frequently is that the real intention of the parties, if ascertainable from the deed as a whole, will prevail. This is known as the modern rule. The alternative rule is the older, more technical one, that in cases of conflict between the clauses, the granting clause will prevail. However, a granting clause which is general in form or indefinite will be controlled by a specific habendum.

## Quicknotes

**DEED** A signed writing transferring title to real property from one person to another.

**HABENDUM CLAUSE** A clause contained in a deed that specifies the parties to the transaction and defines the interest in land to be conveyed.

# Womack v. Stegner

Holder of deed (P) v. Prospective grantee (D)

Tex. Ct. Civ. App., 293 S.W.2d 124 (1956).

**NATURE OF CASE:** Suit in trespass to try title.

**FACT SUMMARY:** Womack's (P) brother executed and delivered a deed to him for the property involved. The name of the grantee was not filled in, but Womack's (P) brother authorized Womack (P) to fill in his name or any name he desired.

## 🏛 RULE OF LAW
When a deed with the name of the grantee in blank is delivered by the grantor with the intention that title shall vest in the person to whom the deed is delivered, and that person is expressly authorized to fill in his own or any other name as grantee, title passes with that delivery.

**FACTS:** Womack (P) claimed title to certain premises in a deed executed and delivered to him by his brother. The deed was complete except that the name of the grantee was not filled in. There was testimony that at the time of delivery, Womack's (P) brother authorized him to fill in his or any other name as grantee. There was no consideration for the deed, and Womack's (P) brother died before Womack (P) filled in his name.

**ISSUE:** Where there has been a failure to fill in the name of the grantee in a deed, but a person has been authorized to fill in his or any other name, is the instrument coupled with that authority sufficient to vest title in such person?

**HOLDING AND DECISION:** (Hamilton, C.J.) Yes. When a deed with the name of the grantee in blank is delivered by the grantor with the intention that the title shall vest in the person to whom the deed is delivered, and that person is expressly authorized at the time of delivery to insert his own or any other name as grantee, title passes with the delivery. The effect of such a transaction is to vest an irrevocable power coupled with an interest in the person to whom the deed is delivered. This does not terminate with the grantor's death. Hence, the fact that Womack's (P) brother died before Womack (P) filled his name in is immaterial. Nor does a deed have to be supported by consideration to be a valid deed. Hence, the fact that there was no consideration for this deed does not invalidate it. Reversed and remanded.

## ▌ ANALYSIS

As a general rule, an instrument purporting to be a deed, and in which a blank has been left for the name of the grantee, is no deed, and is inoperative as a conveyance so long as the blank remains unfilled. Nevertheless, a grantee

to whom the deed is delivered in pursuance of a contract of sale and purchase assumes contractual liability under the deed. The omission of the name of the grantee on delivery is not necessarily destructive of the conveyance. The general rule is not applicable where the grantee's name appears fully and clearly elsewhere on the deed. Also, equitable title passes by delivery of a deed executed in blank as to the grantee's name. Finally, a deed with the grantee's name in blank may be completed and validated by later insertion of the grantee's name by the grantor or his duly authorized agent.

◼══◼

## Quicknotes

**EQUITABLE TITLE** Interest in property that is not recognized in a court of law but that is protected in equity.

◼══◼

# Clevenger v. Moore

Grantor (P) v. Grantee (D)

Okla. Sup. Ct., 126 Okla. 246, 259 P. 219 (1927).

**NATURE OF CASE:** Action for possession and for cancellation of two deeds.

**FACT SUMMARY:** A deed placed in escrow by Clevenger (P), the grantor, was delivered to Simmons (D), the grantee, without the fulfillment of the conditions. Simmons (D) then deeded the property to Moore (D).

## 🏛 RULE OF LAW
Where a deed is delivered to a grantee by the escrow holder without the performance of the conditions for delivery, and the grantee transfers the property to a third person, such purchaser obtains no title to the property as against the first grantor.

**FACTS:** Clevenger (P), who owned a building, was asked if he would trade it for a building owned by Simmons (D). She executed a deed to Simmons (D) which she gave to a third person pending her inspection of Simmons' (D) building. If she was not satisfied with the building, the deed was to be returned to her. After he inspected the building, she asked that the deed be returned to her. This was not done. Simmons (D) recorded the deed and executed a deed to Moore (D), who claimed to be an innocent purchaser.

**ISSUE:** Where a deed is placed in escrow and then delivered to the grantee without performance of the conditions for delivery, is such deed absolutely void so that it passes no title to either the grantee or an innocent purchaser?

**HOLDING AND DECISION:** (Diffendaffer, J.) Yes. Where a grantee obtains possession of a deed placed in escrow without performance of the conditions for delivery, no title passes. Likewise, where the grantee of such a deed transfers the property to a third person, such purchaser obtains no title to the property as against the grantor. Here, Simmons (D) obtained possession of the deed prior to the condition for delivery, Clevenger's (P) satisfaction with the property. Hence, title did not pass to him, and could not pass to his grantee, Moore (D). While some cases protect third persons claiming to be innocent purchasers, the weight of authority follows the rule enunciated here. The trial court committed error in sustaining Moore's (D) demurrer. The case is reversed and remanded for a new trial.

## ▶ ANALYSIS

The view of *Clevenger* was affirmed in *Blakeney v. Home Owners' Loan Corp.*, 135 P. 2d 339 (1943). There, the purchaser, without paying the full price, obtained the deed, recorded it, and mortgaged the land to a bona fide purchaser. In the absence of ratification or estoppel the vendor's title was held not subject to the mortgage lien. One commentator argues that there are strong considerations to support the view that the bona fide purchaser should be protected. The first is that when a loss has occurred which must fall on one of two innocent persons, it should be borne by him who is the occasion of the loss. Second, if a purchaser could acquire title only at his peril, the merchantability of real estate generally would be impaired.

---

## Quicknotes

**BONA FIDE PURCHASER** A party who purchases property in good faith and for valuable consideration without notice of a defect in title.

**DELIVERY** The transfer of title or possession of property.

**ESCROW** A written contract held by a third party until the conditions therein are satisfied, at which time it is delivered to the obligee.

# Bybee v. Hageman

Holder of junior mortgage (P) v. Holder of senior mortgage (D)

Ill. Sup. Ct., 66 Ill. 519 (1873).

**NATURE OF CASE:** Action to foreclose a mortgage.

**FACT SUMMARY:** Bybee (P), who had the second mortgage on Ewald's property, contested the validity of Hageman's (D) prior mortgage on the property. The description in Hageman's (D) mortgage specified neither the township nor the range.

🏛 **RULE OF LAW**
Where an ambiguity in a description of land in a deed is latent, parol evidence is admissible to aid in the description.

**FACTS:** Ewald executed a mortgage to Hageman (D). He then executed a second mortgage to Manly, who assigned it to Bybee (P). Both Hageman (D) and Bybee (P) sought to foreclose their mortgages. The description in the first mortgage stated, "One acre and a half in the northwest corner of Section 5, together with the brewery, malthouse, all buildings thereon." Bybee (P) claimed that the description was void since it did not specify township or range.

**ISSUE:** Is parol evidence admissible to explain a latent ambiguity in a description of land in a deed?

**HOLDING AND DECISION:** (Lawrence, C.J.) Yes. Parol evidence is admissible to explain a latent ambiguity in a description of land in a deed. Here, if there had been only one Section 5 in the county, the description would have been perfectly certain. The ambiguity arises from the fact that there are several sections bearing that number. Hence, the ambiguity is a latent one (since it does not arise from the face of the instrument, and it may be explained). Here, it was proved that when Ewald made the mortgage he was living in the northwest corner of Section 5 in Township Six North and Range One West, and that he had there a house, brewery, and malthouse. This proof is sufficient to remove the latent ambiguity. Hence, Hageman's (D) mortgage is valid. Affirmed.

▌ *ANALYSIS*

Many older decisions followed the rule that the admissibility of parol evidence to aid in the description of property conveyed by a deed depended on whether the ambiguity was a patent or latent one. A patent ambiguity in the description is such an uncertainty appearing on the face of the deed that the court reading the language in light of all the facts and circumstances referred to in the instrument is unable to determine the intention of the parties as to what land was to be conveyed. A latent ambiguity exists where no doubt or uncertainty exists on the face of the deed, but the language is shown to be applicable to two or more tracts. The decisions held that patent ambiguities could not be removed by parol, while latent ambiguities could be. This distinction is gradually disappearing, in accordance with the modern tendency to allow a liberal interpretation of the description of lands and to uphold the validity of the deed if in any way it is possible to arrive at the intention of the parties.

■■■

## *Quicknotes*

**FORECLOSURE SALE** Termination of an interest in property, usually initiated by a lienholder upon failure to tender mortgage payments, resulting in the sale of the property in order to satisfy the debt.

**MORTGAGE** An interest in land created by a written instrument providing security for the payment of a debt or the performance of a duty.

■■■

# Walters v. Tucker

Owner of property (P) v. Adjacent owner (D)

Mo. Sup. Ct., 281 S.W.2d 843 (1955).

**NATURE OF CASE:** Action to quiet title.

**FACT SUMMARY:** Walters's (P) deed described his property as the "West 50 feet of Lot 13." The trial court decided that the description did not reveal which of two possible surveying methods was to be used, and that an ambiguity existed that justified hearing parol evidence.

## 🏛 RULE OF LAW
When there is no inconsistency on the face of a deed and, on application of the description to the ground, no inconsistency appears, parol evidence is not admissible to show that the parties intended to convey either more or less or different ground from that described.

**FACTS:** Walters (P) and Tucker (D) owned adjoining property. The common source of title was Wolf, who acquired Lot 13 and in 1924 conveyed "the West 50 feet of Lot 13" to Walters's (P) predecessor in title. In 1925, Wolf built a house on the portion of Lot 13 that he retained. Tucker (D) was the last grantee to the remaining part of Lot 13. The trial court found that the description did not reveal whether the property conveyed was to be 50 feet along the street (which ran in a northeast-southwest direction) or fifty feet measured eastwardly at right angles from the west line of the property. If the property was measured by the second method, the property line came within one or two feet of the house on Tucker's (D) property. If it was measured by the first method, the east-west width of Walters's (P) tract was 42 feet.

**ISSUE:** Can parol evidence be introduced to show that the grantor of real property did not intend to convey all the land described in a deed where the description is definite and certain?

**HOLDING AND DECISION:** (Hollingsworth, J.) No. When there is no inconsistency on the face of a deed and, on application of the description to the ground, no inconsistency appears, parol evidence is not admissible to show that the parties intended to convey either more or less or different ground from that described. No ambiguity arises here when the description in Walters's (P) deed is applied to Lot 13. When the deed was made the remaining part of Lot 13 was vacant. The fact that Wolf thereafter built a house within a few feet of the property line cannot be construed as evidence of an ambiguity in the description. Extrinsic evidence should not be allowed. The deed clearly conveys the west 50 feet of Lot 13 to Walters (P). Reversed and remanded.

## ▶ ANALYSIS

Some ambiguity is necessary in order for parol evidence to be introduced. If the description is made definite by another deed or instrument to which reference is made in the deed in question, parol evidence is not admissible to vary such construction. Nor is a document referred to explainable by extrinsic evidence any further than it would be if actually inserted in the deed.

## Quicknotes

**DEED** A signed writing transferring title to real property from one person to another.

**EXTRINSIC EVIDENCE** Evidence that is not contained within the text of a document or contract, but which is derived from the parties' statements or the circumstances under which the agreement was made.

**PAROL EVIDENCE** Evidence given verbally; extraneous evidence.

# Pritchard v. Rebori

Builder (P) v. Conveyer of property (D)

Tenn. Sup. Ct., 135 Tenn. 328, 186 S.W. 121 (1916).

**NATURE OF CASE:** Action to recover for breach of a covenant in a deed.

**FACT SUMMARY:** Pritchard (P) was informed that he was building within limits of a railroad's right-of-way. The edge of the right-of-way was not marked, and Pritchard (P) and Rebori (D), who conveyed the property to Pritchard (P), both believed that the right-of-way did not extend as far as it did.

## 🏛 RULE OF LAW
The rule that in determining boundaries resort is to be had first to natural objects or landmarks, next to artificial monuments, then to boundary lines of adjacent owners, and then to courses and distances, is not an inflexible or absolute rule and is to be used to discover the intention of the parties.

**FACTS:** A railroad owned a right-of-way extending 50 feet west of its track. At one point, 15 feet west of its track, it constructed a fence to hold back dirt that might slide down a slope located there. Rebori (D) conveyed property adjacent to the right-of-way to Pritchard (P). The deed described the property as running to the fence. When Pritchard (P) began building on the property, the railroad informed him of his invasion of their right-of-way. Pritchard (P) sought damages from Rebori (D). Rebori (D) claimed that the land conveyed must stop at the real or record line of the right-of-way, and that in so stopping, the deed did not convey any land within the right-of-way and hence there was no encumbrance.

**ISSUE:** Is the rule that in determining boundaries resort is to be had first to natural objects, next to artificial monuments, then to boundary lines of adjacent owners, and then to courses and distances, an absolute rule?

**HOLDING AND DECISION:** (Williams, J.) No. The rule that in determining boundaries resort is to be had first to natural objects or landmarks, next to artificial monuments, then to boundary lines of adjacent owners, and then to courses and distances is not an inflexible or absolute rule, and it is to be used to discover the intention of the parties. Here, the outer limit of the real right-of-way was not marked in any way, and the parcel was small enough to see at a glance. The outer limit lacked the element of open or manifest definiteness and fixity to constitute a boundary line that ought to be held to override the call of courses and distances. Both Rebori (D) and Pritchard (P) assumed the property went to the fence and acted on that assumption. Judgment of damages for Pritchard (P) is affirmed.

## ▶ ANALYSIS

Courts that have had to determine between conflicting calls have generally agreed upon a gradation of calls by which their relative importance and weight are to be determined, as described in *Pritchard*. The rule is subject to numerous exceptions, and courses and distances will prevail if following a call for natural or artificial monuments would not effectuate the real intention of the parties or would lead to an absurd result or if the call for distance is shown to be the most reliable call.

■═■

## *Quicknotes*

**COVENANT** A written promise to do, or to refrain from doing, a particular activity.

**RIGHT-OF-WAY** The right of a party to pass over the property of another.

■═■

# Parr v. Worley

## Transferor of property (P) v. Transferee (D)

N.M. Sup. Ct., 93 N.M. 229, 599 P.2d 382 (1979).

**NATURE OF CASE:** Appeal from summary judgment granting mineral rights.

**FACT SUMMARY:** Parr (P) contended the deed he executed transferring land to Worley (D) "lying east of the highway" referred to land measured only from the eastern edge of the highway and not from the center of the highway.

> 🏛 **RULE OF LAW**
> It is presumed that a conveyance of land abutting a highway runs from the center of the highway, and this presumption is rebutted only by express language in the deed manifesting a contrary intent.

**FACTS:** Parr (P) conveyed a portion of land to Worley (D) described in the deed as "lying east of the highway, containing 25 acres more or less." The area of the land was 25.8 acres if measured from the eastern edge of the highway, and 31.57 acres if measured from the center of the highway. Parr (P) sued to quiet title in the mineral rights on the land and contended the land should be measured only from the eastern edge, and the specification in the deed that the land was 25 acres rebutted the presumption that the land should be measured from its center. The trial court entered judgment for Parr (P), and Worley (D) appealed.

**ISSUE:** Is the presumption that a conveyance of land abutting a highway runs down the center of the highway rebutted only by the express language in the deed manifesting a contrary intent?

**HOLDING AND DECISION:** (Easley, J.) Yes. It is presumed that a conveyance of land abutting a highway runs from the center of the highway, and this presumption is rebutted only by express language in the deed manifesting a contrary intent. There is an order of preference used in considering statements in a deed to determine the measurement of land conveyed. Monuments are considered before statements of distance. A reference in a deed to a highway shows an intent to use the highway as a monument and the general rule is that boundaries run from the center of a monument. As a result, the statement in the deed purporting to quantify the land did not express a contrary intent to measuring from the center of the highway. Therefore, Worley (D) must receive the land based on the greater measurement. Reversed and remanded.

---

## ▶ *ANALYSIS*

Even though this case illustrates a generally accepted rule, it cannot be blindly applied in every case. Because of the diversity in municipal ordinances and state statutes concerning highways and roadways, the application of a universal rule is impossible. Therefore, each case must be considered on its own unique fact pattern.

■▬■

## *Quicknotes*

**CONVEYANCE** The transfer of property, or title to property, from one party to another party.

**SUMMARY JUDGMENT** Judgment rendered by a court in response to a motion made by one of the parties, claiming that the lack of a question of material fact in respect to an issue warrants disposition of the issue without consideration by the jury.

■▬■

# Systems for Recording Property Transfers

## Quick Reference Rules of Law

# Mountain States Telephone & Telegraph Co. v. Kelton

## Holder of easement (P) v. Digging contractor (D)

Ariz. Sup. Ct., 79 Ariz. 126, 285 P.2d 168 (1955).

**NATURE OF CASE:** Appeal from denial of damages for injuries to an underground telephone cable.

**FACT SUMMARY:** Mountain States Telephone & Telegraph Co. (Telephone Co.) (P) contended that because its easement for the placement of its underground cable was duly recorded, Kelton (D) had constructive notice of the cable and was, therefore, liable for damages caused by its digging equipment.

## 🏛 RULE OF LAW

The recordation of an interest in land is constructive notice of such interest only to those who are under a duty to search for it.

**FACTS:** Kelton (D), a contractor, damaged an underground cable owned by Mountain States Telephone & Telegraph Co. (Telephone Co.) (P) when it used some heavy digging equipment on the land of another. Kelton (D) had no actual notice of the cable, and its existence was not apparent upon visual inspection of the land. The Telephone Co. (P) sued, contending that because its easement over the land allowing it to maintain the cable was duly recorded, Kelton (D) had constructive notice of its existence and was liable for the damages caused. The trial court found Kelton (D) exercised due care and, therefore, was not liable for failing to discover the cable. The Telephone Co. (P) appealed.

**ISSUE:** Does the recordation of an interest in land constitute constructive notice of its existence to the world?

**HOLDING AND DECISION:** (Udall, J.) No. The recordation of an interest in land constitutes constructive notice of such interest only to those who are under a duty to search for it. In this case, Kelton (D) had no interest in the title to the land; it was merely performing a service on it. Therefore, it had no duty to discover the state of the title and no duty to search for encumbrances. Consequently, it will not be deemed to have constructive notice of easement and cannot be held liable for damage to the cable. Affirmed in part and reversed in part with directions.

## ▶ ANALYSIS

The purpose of the recording system is to provide a registry of interests in real property so as to notify interested parties of the state of the title to a particular parcel. It is the duty of the holder of the interest to record such to protect himself from claims of subsequent takers. This case shows that a party who has no duty to search the title of a parcel will not be held to have constructive notice of another's interest in property. A person who has such an interest,

such as a subsequent purchaser, will be deemed to have notice of all recorded interests and will take the property subject to these interests.

■══■

## Quicknotes

**CONSTRUCTIVE NOTICE** Knowledge of a fact that is imputed to an individual who was under a duty to inquire and who could have learned of the fact through the exercise of reasonable prudence.

**EASEMENT** The right to utilize a portion of another's real property for a specific use.

■══■

# Stone v. French

Purchaser of land (D) v. Seller of void deed (P)

Kan. Sup. Ct., 37 Kan. 145, 14 P. 530, 1 Am. St. Rep. 237 (1887).

**NATURE OF CASE:** Action for partition of land.

**FACT SUMMARY:** Stone (D) purchased land from Dudley French without knowing that Dudley had acquired his deed under circumstances that made the deed void. Luther French (P), Dudley's brother, brought a partition action against Stone (D) claiming he (P) and his six brothers were each entitled to a one-half interest in the property through inheritance.

> ## 🏛 RULE OF LAW
> The recordation of a void deed cannot be used to validate an invalid transfer of title evidenced by that deed.

**FACTS:** Prior to his death, Francis French executed a deed to a piece of property in favor of his brother Dudley. The deed was acknowledged before a justice of the peace and contained a recital of delivery. In fact, the deed was never delivered and was not discovered until Francis died. Dudley, upon learning of the deed, promptly recorded it and took possession of the land. He subsequently sold the land to Stone (D) for consideration. Stone (D) took title without knowledge of the circumstances under which Dudley had acquired title. Luther French (P), a brother, brought suit for partition of the land against Stone (D) alleging the deed from Francis to Dudley was void and, therefore, Francis retained title at his death. The suit sought to have the land partitioned into seven equal parts, one for each brother. The trial court ordered the partition but gave Dudley's share to Stone (D) on the basis the Dudley had conveyed his interest to Stone (D).

**ISSUE:** May the recordation of an invalid deed be used to validate the invalid transfer of title evidenced by that deed?

**HOLDING AND DECISION:** (Valentine, J.) No. It is clear that Francis did not intend delivery of the deed to Dudley prior to his death. He retained the right to sell the land and Dudley was not to take title until after Francis' death. The lack of delivery made the deed a void instrument, and no act thereafter undertaken could alter its status. The recordation of a void deal cannot affect its lack of legal validity. Only valid instruments can be legally recorded. Even a bona fide purchaser cannot acquire any form of title under a void deed. The judgment of the trial court in ordering partition was correct and is affirmed.

## ▶ ANALYSIS

The court distinguished between a void deed and a voidable deed. The court pointed out that a bona fide purchaser could acquire enforceable title from a voidable deed if he took it without notice of its defects. Since recording such a deed would create at least an inference of validity, recordation could be used by the bona fide purchaser as evidence he took without notice of any defect. But recordation, in itself, cannot validate an otherwise invalid deed. A grantor and a grantee are bound by a deed whether it is recorded or not. Recordation affords protection only to a third-party bona fide purchaser who can use the recordation as evidence of his lack of notice.

■=■

## Quicknotes

**DELIVERY** The transfer of title or possession of property.

**RECORDING ACT** Statute determining priority of interests in real property.

■=■

# Earle v. Fiske

### Recorder of deed (P) v. Holder of property (D)

Mass. Sup. Jud. Ct., 103 Mass. 491 (1870).

**NATURE OF CASE:** Writ of entry to recover land.

**FACT SUMMARY:** N. Fiske conveyed land to B. Fiske (D) and E. Fiske for their lives, and, subject to their life estate, to M. Fiske. The deeds were not recorded. After N. Fiske died, B. Fiske (D), as her sole heir, conveyed the land to Earl (P). That deed was recorded.

🏛 **RULE OF LAW**
Although an unrecorded deed is binding upon the grantor, his heirs and devisees, and also upon all persons having actual notice of it, it is not valid and effectual as against any other persons.

**FACTS:** N. Fiske conveyed certain property to B. and E. Fiske (D) for their lives, and, subject to their life estate, to M. Fiske. The deeds were dated 1864, but were not recorded until 1867. N. Fiske died in 1865, leaving her son B. Fiske (D) as her sole heir. In 1866, he executed and delivered to Earle (P) a deed of the property. This deed was recorded in 1866. B. and E. Fiske (D) contended that since N. Fiske had given the deed dated 1864, nothing passed from her to B. Fiske (D) so as to allow him to convey the land to Earle (P).

**ISSUE:** Does an unrecorded deed have any force or effect as to a purchaser without notice?

**HOLDING AND DECISION:** (Ames, J.) No. An unrecorded deed is sufficient, as between the original parties to it, to transfer the whole title. However, for the protection of creditors and purchasers, the rule has been established that while an unrecorded deed is binding upon the grantor, his heirs and devisees, and all persons having actual notice of it, it is not binding as against any other persons. As to others, the person who appears on record to be the owner is to be taken as the true and actual owner, and his apparent ownership is not divested or affected by an unknown and unrecorded deed that he may have made. The purpose of the recording system is that a purchaser of land has a right to rely upon the information furnished by the registry of deeds, and he is justified in taking that information as true and acting upon it accordingly. As a purchaser without notice, the unrecorded deeds have no effect as to Earle (P). As against his claim, N. Fiske's unrecorded deeds have no binding force or effect. Plaintiff's exceptions sustained.

▶ **ANALYSIS**

This case demonstrates the importance of recording in determining conflicting claims to real property. The only instances where recording plays a significant part in the field of personal property is in connection with chattel mortgages and conditional-sales agreements. However, as demonstrated here, recording is quite pertinent to real property. Generally, the various recording acts are the basis of deciding conflicting claims to real property. The extent to which a subsequent purchaser is protected against a prior unrecorded deed depends on the type of statute in the local jurisdiction. There are four distinct types of statutes: notice statutes, race-notice statutes, period-of-grace statutes, and race statutes.

■══■

## *Quicknotes*

**ACTUAL NOTICE** Direct communication of information that would cause an ordinary person of average prudence to inquire as to its truth.

**BONA FIDE PURCHASER** A party who purchases property in good faith and for valuable consideration without notice of a defect in title.

■══■

# Mugaas v. Smith

Adverse possessor (P) v. Bona fide purchaser (D)

Wash. Sup. Ct., 33 Wash. 2d 429, 206 P.2d 332, 9 A.L.R.2d 846 (1949).

**NATURE OF CASE:** Action to quiet title.

**FACT SUMMARY:** Mugaas (P) gained title by adverse possession but failed to record his title, and Smith (D) was a bona fide purchaser of the same land who recorded his deed.

## 🏛 RULE OF LAW
Where title to real property has been effectuated by adverse possession, that title cannot be divested by a subsequent bona fide purchaser who records.

**FACTS:** Mugaas (P) acquired title to a strip of land adjoining her property by adverse possession. There was a fence marking where that strip of land ended and which indicated that Mugaas (P) owned the property. Smith (D) purchased the adjoining property. The fence had disintegrated by the time Smith (D) bought the property. Smith's (D) deed included the strip of land adversely possessed by Mugaas (P). Smith (D) recorded his deed. Mugaas (P) never recorded the title gained by adverse possession. Smith (D) put buildings on his lot which encroached on the strip. Mugaas (P) brought an action to quiet title to the strip and to force the removal of any encroachments.

**ISSUE:** Does recordation of a deed protect a bona fide purchaser for value against interests in land arising by adverse possession?

**HOLDING AND DECISION:** (Hill, J.) No. Title gained by operation of law, such as property acquired by adverse possession, cannot be divested by a subsequent conveyance of that property to a bona fide purchaser. It makes no difference that the adverse possessor failed to record or that the subsequent purchaser did record. The recording statutes do not apply to a transfer of title by adverse possession. Once the statute of limitations has run on an adverse possession, that title will stand regardless of any subsequent conveyance. Affirmed.

## ▶ ANALYSIS

Recordation does not protect a subsequent purchaser against interests which arise by operation of law, such as dower rights, prescriptive and implied easements, and title by adverse possession. Since there is no instrument to record in order to perfect such interests, the recording acts do not apply, and subsequent purchasers will take subject to such interests. If the recording act is inapplicable, the common-law rules apply, which, in nearly all cases, give priority to the first grantee in time. An exception to this priority rule is that a subsequent legal claim prevails over a prior equitable claim if the legal taker was a bona fide purchaser.

---

## Quicknotes

**ADVERSE POSSESSION** A means of acquiring title to real property by remaining in actual, open, continuous, exclusive possession of property for the statutory period.

**STATUTE OF LIMITATIONS** A law prescribing the period in which a legal action may be commenced.

# Mortensen v. Lingo

Tenant (P) v. Subsequent grantee (D)

99 F. Supp. 585 (D. Alaska 1951).

**NATURE OF CASE:** Action for breach of covenants of title.

**FACT SUMMARY:** A deed was recorded but not indexed and a subsequent bona fide purchaser took title to the same land.

## RULE OF LAW
Where an instrument was properly recorded but not indexed, the instrument does not impart sufficient constructive notice to protect a prior grantee from a subsequent bona fide purchaser.

**FACTS:** In 1941, McCain conveyed real property to Anglin. This deed was recorded, but was not indexed as the statute directed. In 1947, McCain conveyed the same property to Lingo (D). In 1948, Lingo (D) conveyed the same land by warranty deed to Mortensen (P). Mortensen (P) alleged that Anglin, the prior grantee, threatened to evict him. Lingo (D) did not have actual notice of the conveyance from McCain to Anglin.

**ISSUE:** Does a deed which is recorded but not indexed impart sufficient constructive notice to prevent a subsequent grantee from being a bona fide purchaser without notice?

**HOLDING AND DECISION:** (Folta, J.) No. Recordation and indexing constitute a system of registration which must be construed in its entirety. Only when all of the prescribed steps, including indexing, are performed can the record constitute constructive notice to subsequent grantees. The only practical way to impart notice is through the index rather than to search each volume of records. Also, the index is required by statute and must be construed as part of the recordation process. The recording of the deed to Anglin without indexing was insufficient to give constructive notice to Lingo (D), and Mortensen's (P) cause of action for breach of covenants of title must fail.

## ANALYSIS

A deed is recorded in its entirety and then an index is kept to provide for easy reference to the deed. There is a grantor-grantee index, arranged by reference to the parties, or a tract index, arranged by reference to blocks or lots. Some courts hold that when the deed is delivered for recordation, the grantee has done all he could to give notice and, therefore, the grantee is protected; the failure to index is the fault of the clerk, so the grantee should not be penalized. The *Mortensen* case represents the better view because, as a practical matter, until an instrument has been properly filed and indexed, there is no reasonable

way for a subsequent grantee to locate it. Also, the prior grantee could have prevented any harm by making sure the deed was properly recorded and indexed.

## Quicknotes

**ACTUAL NOTICE** Direct communication of information that would cause an ordinary person of average prudence to inquire as to its truth.

**CONSTRUCTIVE NOTICE** Knowledge of a fact that is imputed to an individual who was under a duty to inquire and who could have learned of the fact through the exercise of reasonable prudence.

**WARRANTY DEED** A deed that guarantees that the conveyor possesses the title that he purports to convey.

# Simmons v. Stum

Lender of purchase funds (P) v. Bona fide purchaser (D)

Ill. Sup. Ct., 101 Ill. 454 (1882).

**NATURE OF CASE:** Action to foreclose a mortgage.

**FACT SUMMARY:** A subsequent purchaser failed to prove that she had recorded her deed prior to the recordation of an earlier mortgage.

## 🏛 RULE OF LAW
Under a race-notice recording statute, a subsequent bona fide purchaser must prove that he recorded his instrument before the prior purchaser recorded his interest in the land.

**FACTS:** Stum (P) loaned McHenry funds to purchase land. McHenry executed a mortgage on the land he bought with these funds to secure the repayment of the loan. The mortgage payment was due on March 1, 1879, but the mortgage was not recorded until March 15, 1879. Prior to that date, on November 7, 1878, McHenry conveyed the previously mortgaged land to Cochran and Strong. These grantees had actual knowledge of the existence of the mortgage on the land they purchased. On March 13, 1879, two days before the mortgage was recorded, Cochran and Strong conveyed the land to Simmons (D). Simmons (D) claimed that she had no knowledge of the prior mortgage and that she was an innocent purchaser.

**ISSUE:** In order to prevail in a title contest in a race-notice jurisdiction, must the subsequent bona fide purchaser prove that he recorded his deed before the recordation of the prior purchaser's deed?

**HOLDING AND DECISION:** (Craig, C.J.) Yes. The record contains no proof of when Simmons' (D) deed was recorded. The deed was executed on March 13, two days prior to the recording of the mortgage, and the deed was subsequently recorded, but there is no evidence of the date on which it was recorded. Assuming that Simmons (D) took innocently and without notice, her deed would be subordinated to the prior mortgage in the absence of proof that it was recorded prior to the recordation of the mortgage. Affirmed.

## ▶ ANALYSIS

There are three basic types of recording statutes. First, under a race statute, whoever records first prevails and actual notice of the existence of the prior deed is irrelevant. This is the rarest type of recording statute. Second, under a notice statute, a subsequent bona fide purchaser for value prevails over a prior grantee. The subsequent purchaser must have no actual or constructive notice at the time of the conveyance, which could happen only if the prior grantee failed to record before the date of the subsequent

purchase. Third, under a race-notice statute, as discussed in this case, a subsequent bona fide purchaser is protected only if he records before the prior grantee. In the present case, the court construed a statute which was ostensibly a notice statute to be a race-notice statute in its application.

## Quicknotes

**BONA FIDE PURCHASER** A party who purchases property in good faith and for valuable consideration without notice of a defect in title.

**RACE NOTICE RECORDING STATUTE** Statute determining priority of interests in real property whereby a person who records first has a preference over others receiving an interest in the property from the same source only if the party received no notice of the prior unrecorded conveyance.

# Eastwood v. Shedd

## Grantee of real property (D) v. Subsequent grantee (P)

Colo. Sup. Ct., 166 Colo. 136, 442 P.2d 423 (1968).

**NATURE OF CASE:** Action to quiet title.

**FACT SUMMARY:** A subsequent donative conveyance was recorded before the prior donative conveyance in a jurisdiction which had a race-notice statute which did not specifically limit its protection to bona fide purchasers for value.

## 🏛 RULE OF LAW
As a general rule, a grantee of real property must be a bona fide purchaser for value in order to be protected by a recording statute.

**FACTS:** On December 2, 1958, Cleo Alexander deeded her property to Eastwood (D). Eastwood (D) did not record the instrument until October 16, 1964. On October 15, 1963, Alexander deeded the same property to Shedd (P), who recorded the instrument on October 23, 1963. Shedd (P) had no actual or constructive notice of the deed to Eastwood (D). Both conveyances were gifts and no value was given for the property. Colorado had a race-notice recording statute which held that a recorded instrument shall be valid as against any class of persons with any kind of rights.

**ISSUE:** Shall the Colorado recording statute be construed so as to protect a donee of real property who has duly recorded the instrument of conveyance?

**HOLDING AND DECISION:** (Day, J.) Yes. The legislature changed the wording of the statute, deleting the former wording that the recording act shall take effect only as to subsequent bona fide purchasers for value, and substituted the words that the act shall be valid as against any class of persons with any kind of rights. The statute was changed for a purpose. It is irrelevant, as far as construing this statute, that every other state limits the protection of their recording statutes to bona fide purchasers for value who are without notice. This is true even where the statute does not specifically so limit the protection. In Colorado, the legislature specifically removed the limitation of purchase from the statute and substituted a broader protection. Affirmed.

## ▶ ANALYSIS

The universal rule is that only bona fide purchasers are entitled to protection under notice and race-notice statutes. To attain this protected status, a person must satisfy the statute's requirements. He must be a purchaser, or perhaps a mortgagee or creditor. He must take without notice of any kind, be it actual, constructive, or inquiry of the prior instrument. And, he must pay valuable consideration of a substantial pecuniary nature, though not necessarily adequate value or the real market value.

## Quicknotes

**ACTUAL NOTICE** Direct communication of information that would cause an ordinary person of average prudence to inquire as to its truth.

**CONSTRUCTIVE NOTICE** Knowledge of a fact that is imputed to an individual who was under a duty to inquire and who could have learned of the fact through the exercise of reasonable prudence.

# Strong v. Whybark

Holder of recorded title (P) v. Holder of unrecorded title (D)

Mo. Sup. Ct., 204 Mo. 341, 102 S.W. 968 (1907).

**NATURE OF CASE:** Bill in equity to have title quieted in certain property.

**FACT SUMMARY:** Both Strong (P) and Boyden (D) claimed an interest in certain property. Strong's (P) title was derived through the vendee of a recorded deed who paid five dollars for the property. Boyden's (D) title was derived through the vendee of a prior unrecorded deed who paid $640.

> **RULE OF LAW**
> A quitclaim deed made in consideration of five dollars paid by the grantee to the grantor was based on a valuable consideration sufficient to entitle the grantee to the rights of a bona fide purchaser for value.

**FACTS:** S. Hayden, by warranty deed and for a consideration of $640, conveyed certain land to Moore on March 6, 1861. On August 26, 1863, S. Hayden conveyed the same land by quitclaim deed for a recited consideration of "natural love and affection and five dollars" to J. Hayden. That deed was recorded in 1868. The Moore deed was recorded in 1874. Strong's (P) title was derived through conveyances by J. Hayden. Boyden's (D) title was derived through conveyances by Moore.

**ISSUE:** Is a quitclaim deed made in consideration of five dollars based on a valuable consideration sufficient to entitle the grantee to the rights of a bona fide purchaser?

**HOLDING AND DECISION:** (Woodson, J.) Yes. A valuable consideration is defined as money or something that is worth money. It is not necessary that the consideration should be adequate in point of value. Five dollars or any other sum in excess of one cent, or dime, or dollar, which are the technical words used to express nominal considerations, is a valuable consideration within the meaning of the law of conveyancing. The courts, upon principles of equity and justice, have repeatedly held that if the subsequent purchaser either had notice of the unrecorded deed or was a purchaser without having paid a good and valuable consideration for the land he would take nothing by his purchase. In this case there is no evidence that J. Hayden knew of the prior unrecorded deed to Moore. Since she paid a valuable consideration, she is entitled to the right of bona fide purchaser. Judgment for Boyden (D) is reversed and a new trial is granted.

---

**▶ ANALYSIS**

Without the consideration question in this case, there would have been no question as to J. Hayden's title since her deed had been recorded and Moore's had not, and there was no evidence that she had knowledge of the prior deed. Technically speaking, a purchaser is one who acquires real property in any other manner than by descent. "Purchase" has been said to mean (1) to obtain property by paying an equivalent in money; (2) the acquisition of property by one's own act or agreement as distinguished from the act or mere operation of law; or (3) the transmission of property from one person to another by their voluntary agreement (valuable consideration).

■=■

## Quicknotes

**NOMINAL CONSIDERATION** Consideration that is so insignificant that it does not represent the actual value received from the agreement.

**QUITCLAIM DEED** A deed whereby the grantor conveys whatever interest he or she may have in the property without any warranties or covenants as to title.

■=■

# Gabel v. Drewrys Limited, U. S. A., Inc.

## Mortgager (D) v. Creditor (P)

Fla. Sup. Ct., 68 So. 2d 372 (1953).

**NATURE OF CASE:** Action to foreclose a mortgage.

**FACT SUMMARY:** To secure a pre-existing debt, Drewrys Limited, U. S. A., Inc. (P) accepted a mortgage on the debtor's property without any new agreement other than a forbearance to sue for the time being.

## 🏛 RULE OF LAW
If a mortgage is given to secure a pre-existing debt, and no new contemporaneous consideration passes, either of benefit to the mortgagor, or detriment to the mortgagee, then the mortgagee does not become a purchaser and, therefore, is not entitled to the protection of the recording acts.

**FACTS:** McCaffrey was a beer distributor who was in financial difficulty. On March 14, 1950, Gabel (D) loaned McCaffrey money secured by a mortgage on property. This mortgage was not recorded until after June 30, 1950. McCaffrey also became indebted to Drewrys Limited, U. S. A., Inc. (P), who had received several bad checks from McCaffrey and so had stopped beer delivery to McCaffrey. An agreement was reached whereby Drewrys (P) accepted a note for the full amount owed in exchange for a mortgage on the same property covered by the prior mortgage to Gabel (D). Drewrys (P) agreed to forbear for the time being any action to enforce the collection of the debt. There was no specific date or element of time fixed for forbearance in filing a suit. Drewrys's (P) mortgage was recorded before Gabel (D) recorded his prior mortgage, and Drewrys (P) had no notice of the prior mortgage. Drewrys (P) sued to foreclose the mortgage. Gabel (D) was joined as a party and he cross-claimed.

**ISSUE:** Is the receiving of a mortgage as security for a pre-existing debt valuable consideration so as to afford the mortgagee the protection of the recording acts?

**HOLDING AND DECISION:** (Drew, J.) No. It is the rule that to be a purchaser for value, a mortgagee must have parted with something valuable, surrendered an existing right, incurred a fixed liability, or submitted to a loss or detriment, contemporaneously with the execution of, or agreement to execute, the mortgage. If the mortgage merely secures a pre-existing debt, and no new contemporaneous consideration passes which either benefits the mortgagor or is to the detriment of the mortgagee, then the mortgagee is not a purchaser. A definite, enforceable time extension would be sufficient consideration, regardless of how short it might be. The facts establish that there was no specific, definite, enforceable time limit given, but only a general forbearance to sue for the time being. Drewrys (P), the mortgagee, was benefited, and McCaffrey, the mortgagor, was in a more detrimental position. Therefore, Drewrys (P) was not entitled to the protection of the recording acts because it was not a purchaser for value, and Gabel's (D) prior mortgage was not superseded. Reversed.

## ▶ ANALYSIS

If a person claims to be a bona fide purchaser, it must be proven that real consideration, not merely nominal consideration, was paid. The test for consideration is different from that in contract law. The consideration must be of a substantial pecuniary value, but it need not be adequate, nor the full market value. An antecedent debt may be sufficient consideration where the creditor has acted in some way to worsen his position, or where the debtor conveys property in satisfaction of prior debt because suit cannot thereafter be brought on the debt. In the present case, the creditor did not worsen his position, but strengthened it by receiving a mortgage.

## Quicknotes

**CONSIDERATION** Value given by one party in exchange for performance, or a promise to perform, by another party.

**FORBEARANCE** Refraining from doing something that one has the legal right to do.

**MORTGAGE** Conveyance of an interest in real property by a debtor to a creditor in order to secure the payment of a debt.

# Osin v. Johnson

Seller of property (P) v. Buyer (D)

243 F.2d 653 (D.C. Cir. 1957).

**NATURE OF CASE:** Foreclosure action.

**FACT SUMMARY:** Osin (P) sold real property to Johnson (D) in exchange for a deed of trust which Johnson (D) fraudulently failed to record.

## 🏛 RULE OF LAW
An earlier equitable lien not capable of being recorded is superior to the lien of a creditor unless the creditor relied on the state of the record title in incurring the obligation.

**FACTS:** Osin (P) sold Johnson (D) real property. The deed was delivered and recorded. Johnson (D) was supposed to record a deed of trust in favor of Osin (P) as a lien on the property. Johnson (D) fraudulently failed to record the trust. Johnson (D) then obtained a first and second mortgage on the property from lenders who were unaware of Osin's (P) lien. Several lien creditors filed liens on the property and foreclosure proceedings were begun. Osin (P) intervened, alleging the earlier interest of her unrecorded deed of trust. The court found that under the recording statute a bona fide purchaser without notice took a superior position to an unrecorded prior lien. Mortgagees occupied the status of bona fide purchasers under the statute. Creditors having valid liens on the property were also given preference over earlier equitable liens not capable of being recorded and unrecorded legal liens. Osin (P) was subordinated to both mortgagees and creditors. Osin (P) alleged that equity could have imposed a constructive trust which would have been incapable of being recorded and, hence, at least with respect to creditors, she should be given a preference.

**ISSUE:** Should a constructive trust, not capable of being recorded, be given priority over lien creditors who have not relied on the nonexistence of the unrecorded lien in making their lending decision?

**HOLDING AND DECISION:** (Burger, J.) Yes. We find that Johnson's (D) fraudulent conduct may have given rise to a constructive trust (i.e., a trust imposed by operation of law to avoid an unconscionable result where traditional remedies are unavailable). We further find that a constructive trust is an equitable lien within the meaning of the recording statute. If Osin (P) is not found guilty of laches or other equitable defenses, and the court below finds that a constructive trust should be imposed, the trust will be given preference to all creditor liens, except insofar as the debt was created in reliance upon the alleged unencumbered state of the property. Affirmed in part, reversed in part, and remanded.

## ▶ ANALYSIS

A judgment creditor does not occupy the same status as a bona fide purchaser. He has parted with nothing and has not changed his position in reliance on the record title. *Holden v. Garrett*, 23 Kan. 98 (1879). Many statutes, however, may grant judgment creditors the same status as a bona fide purchaser. In such jurisdictions, they would take priority over an unrecorded deed holder depending on the state's recording statute.

---

## Quicknotes

**CONSTRUCTIVE TRUST** A trust that arises by operation of law whereby the court imposes a trust upon property lawfully held by one party for the benefit of another, as a result of some wrongdoing by the party in possession so as to avoid unjust enrichment.

**LACHES** An equitable defense against the enforcement of rights that have been neglected for a long period of time.

# Wineberg v. Moore

Buyer of land (P) v. Subsequent purchaser (D)

194 F. Supp. 12 (N.D. Cal. 1961), *aff'd*, 349 F.2d 685 (9th Cir. 1965).

**NATURE OF CASE:** Action to quiet title.

**FACT SUMMARY:** A prior deed was not recorded until after two subsequent deeds were recorded, but the prior grantee's acts gave the subsequent grantees actual and inquiry notice of the prior deed.

## RULE OF LAW
A purchaser is charged with notice and knowledge of whatever an inspection of the property would have disclosed, and if it would have disclosed a possession, the purchaser is put on constructive notice of the possession and what would have been discovered from inquiry of the possessor.

**FACTS:** In 1948, Barker sold his land to Wineberg (P) who failed to record his deed until 1951. In the interim period, Barker sold his land to Moore (D) and Construction Engineers, who recorded their deeds in 1951, prior to Wineberg's (P) recordation. The land was suited for both logging operations and recreation. When Wineberg (P) bought the land, there was a house and a garage, and a fence around part of the property. Wineberg (P) locked the gate and placed a "no trespassing" sign on it with his own name and address on it. Wineberg (P) paid taxes on the property. Wineberg (P) and his friends used the house for occasional recreation, and Wineberg (P) kept his personal property in the house. The dwelling, the road, and various places on the property had "no trespassing" signs identifying Wineberg (P) as the owner.

**ISSUE:** Can subsequent grantees be said to be bona fide purchasers in good faith and without notice when an inspection and inquiry of the land would have put a reasonable person on notice of an adverse claim?

**HOLDING AND DECISION:** (Carter, J.) No. A grantee of real property where a third person is in possession is presumed to purchase with full notice of all rights in the land of the possessing third person and insubordination to these rights. This presumption can be overcome only by clear and convincing proof that the grantee made a diligent and unavailing effort to discover actual notice of the rights of the possessor and failed. Possession of land is notice to the world of the possessor's rights. Possession puts all persons on inquiry as to the nature of the occupant's claims. The subsequent purchasers are charged with all information that could be gained by an actual inspection of the premises. The possessor must do acts of dominion which are adapted to the land, its condition, locality, and appropriate use; Wineberg's (P) acts were sufficient since the land was suitable for recreational purposes.

## ANALYSIS

This case represents the majority view of inquiry notice from possession. There are a number of minority views imposing a lesser inquiry burden on the purchaser. One view is that the purchaser must make inquiry of the possessor only if the purchaser actually knows that a third person is in possession. Another view is that if the possession is consistent with record title, there need be no inquiry. A third view is that there need not even be inquiry of the possessor.

## Quicknotes

**ACTUAL NOTICE** Direct communication of information that would cause an ordinary person of average prudence to inquire as to its truth.

**INQUIRY NOTICE** The communication of information that would cause an ordinary person of average prudence to inquire as to its truth.

# Sabo v. Horvath

Recorder of quitclaim deed (D) v. Prior purchaser (P)

Alaska Sup. Ct., 559 P.2d 1038 (1976).

**NATURE OF CASE:** Action to determine title to real property.

**FACT SUMMARY:** Horvath (P) recorded his deed prior to a patent being granted the seller so that the recorded deed was outside the chain of title.

## 🏛 RULE OF LAW
A deed outside the chain of title is not constructive notice and a subsequently recorded deed will take priority.

**FACTS:** Lowery filed for a federal land patent on real property he was homesteading in Alaska. Prior to the issuance of the patent, Lowery conveyed his interest in the land to Horvath (P) by quitclaim deed. Horvath (P) recorded the deed, which was then outside the chain of record title since Lowery had not yet obtained patent title to the land. After patent title was obtained, Horvath (P) did not re-record the deed. Lowery subsequently "sold" the land a second time to Sabo (D) by quitclaim deed. Sabo (D) recorded his deed. Sabo (D) had no notice of the earlier conveyance. Horvath (P) brought a quiet title action. Sabo (D) alleged that a deed recorded out of chain of title was not constructive notice and that under the state's notice recording law he had no notice of the earlier sale and should be given preference.

**ISSUE:** Is a deed recorded outside the chain of title given preference to a subsequent bona fide purchaser without actual notice?

**HOLDING AND DECISION:** (Boochever, C.J.) No. The purpose of our recording statute is to protect innocent purchasers without notice of an earlier unrecorded sale. Normally, a recordation gives the subsequent purchaser constructive notice of the earlier conveyance. However, we hold that a deed recorded outside the chain of title is not constructive notice to an innocent purchaser for value without actual notice. It is less burdensome for one recording outside the chain of title to re-record than to force purchasers to check all conveyances outside the chain of the title. Quitclaim deedholders are entitled to protection under the recording statutes (the majority rule). While Horvath (P) originally received Lowrey's equitable interest in the land, his failure to re-record after the patent was granted requires us to find for Sabo (D). Reversed.

## ▶ ANALYSIS

*Sabo* would be useful only where the jurisdiction does not use a tract index system. Under a tract index system, every document affecting land is recorded. Some jurisdictions

hold that the grantee of a quitclaim deed is not a bona fide purchaser. In *Crossly v. Campion Mining Co.*, 1 Alaska 391 (1901), a quitclaim grantee with knowledge of a superior unrecorded claim was held not to be in good faith.

■═■

## Quicknotes

**ACTUAL NOTICE** Direct communication of information that would cause an ordinary person of average prudence to inquire as to its truth.

**BONA FIDE PURCHASER** A party who purchases property in good faith and for valuable consideration without notice of a defect in title.

**CHAIN OF TITLE** Successive transfers of particular property.

**QUITCLAIM DEED** A deed whereby the grantor conveys whatever interest he or she may have in the property without any warranties or covenants as to title.

■═■

# Title Assurance and Other Protections for the Grantee

## Quick Reference Rules of Law

# Petersen v. Hubschman Construction Co., Inc.

### Buyer of house (P) v. Seller (D)

Ill. Sup. Ct., 76 Ill. 2d 31, 389 N.E.2d 1154 (1979).

**NATURE OF CASE:** Appeal from judgment ordering the return of a deposit on real estate.

**FACT SUMMARY:** Hubschman (D) contended that since the house he constructed for Petersen (P) was fit for habitation, it fulfilled the implied warranty of habitability, and, thus, the trial court erred in ordering him to return Petersen's (P) deposit.

### 🏛 RULE OF LAW
The implied warranty of habitability provides that when a house is constructed and sold, it is reasonably suited for its intended use.

**FACTS:** Petersen (P) contracted to purchase land from Hubschman (D), upon which Hubschman (D) was to construct a house. Petersen (P) paid $10,000 in earnest money prior to construction. Upon completion, Petersen (P) became dissatisfied with the house due to certain defects such as improperly pitched floor, improperly installed siding, and a defective front door and frame. After Hubschman (D) failed to repair these defects, Petersen (P) sued to recover his deposit. Hubschman (D) defended on the grounds that Petersen (P) was protected by an implied warranty of habitability, and that, because the house, as constructed, was fit for habitation, the warranty had been fulfilled. He further argued that because the warranty was met he had substantially performed his contractual duty requiring Petersen's (P) reciprocal performance. The trial court found Hubschman (D) had not substantially performed and ordered the return of the deposit. Hubschman (D) appealed.

**ISSUE:** Does the implied warranty of habitability provide that when a house is constructed and sold it be reasonably suited for its intended purpose, and not merely fit for habitation?

**HOLDING AND DECISION:** (Ryan, J.) Yes. The implied warranty of habitability provides that when a house is constructed and sold it be reasonably fit for its intended use. In this case, Petersen (P) contracted to pay for a house reasonably fit for use as a home, not one with substantial defects plus damages. Requiring him to purchase the house and sue for damages would be manifestly unfair. Hubschman (D) failed to substantially perform his contractual duty by breaching the implied warranty of habitability. The substantial performance of the builder is a condition precedent to Petersen's (P) duty to perform. Therefore, Petersen (P) effectively repudiated the contract and Hubschman (D) was bound to return the deposit. Affirmed.

## ▶ ANALYSIS

In this case, the court placed great reliance on the fact that Hubschman (D) could still sell the house and land. He, therefore, was not totally deprived of the value of his labor. The implied warranty of habitability was first recognized in England in the case of *Miller v. Cannon Hill Estates Limited*, 2 K.B. 113 (1931), yet it was not applied in the United States until 1957 in the case of *Vanderschrier v. Aaron*, 103 Ohio App. 340 (1957). It did not gain immediate acceptance in all American jurisdictions as was shown by an Alabama case, *Druid Homes, Inc. v. Cooper*, 131 So. 2d 884 (1961). The court there held that all warranties concerning the sale of real property had to appear in written contractual form.

---

## Quicknotes

**IMPLIED WARRANTY OF HABITABILITY** A warranty implied by a landlord that the premises are suitable, and will remain suitable, for habitation.

**SUBSTANTIAL PERFORMANCE** Performance of all the essential obligations pursuant to an agreement.

# G-W-L, Inc. v. Robichaux

Home builder (D) v. Purchaser (P)

Tex. Sup. Ct., 643 S.W.2d 392 (1982).

**NATURE OF CASE:** Appeal from award of damages for breach of warranty.

**FACT SUMMARY:** Goldstar (D) contended Robichaux (P) waived any implied warranty of fitness for the house Robichaux (P) contracted to purchase, and, therefore, he could not recover for any defects in the construction not warranted expressly in the contract.

## 🏛 RULE OF LAW
Language in construction contracts waiving an implied warranty must be clear and unambiguous.

**FACTS:** Robichaux (P) contracted with G-W-L, Inc. (D), doing business as Goldstar (D), for the construction of a house. The contract included a clause stating the writing was the entire agreement between the parties, and that no warranties, express or implied, existed outside the writing. Upon completion, the roof on the house had a substantial sag in it and Robichaux (P) sued for damages. The trial court entered judgment for Robichaux (P), and Goldstar (D) appealed.

**ISSUE:** Must language in a construction contract waiving an implied warranty be clear and unambiguous to be valid?

**HOLDING AND DECISION:** (Sondock, J.) Yes. Language in a construction contract waiving an implied warranty must be clear and unambiguous. Although the court of appeals in this case stated the correct rule of law, it erred in finding the language in this contract insufficient to constitute a waiver. The language of waiver could not be clearer and, in the absence of fraud, Robichaux (P) cannot escape being bound to an agreement he knowingly and voluntarily entered into. As a result the warranty was waived, and Goldstar (D) was not liable. Reversed.

**DISSENT:** (Spears, J.) To be valid, language of waiver must clearly name the specific warranty being disclaimed. As a result, the contractual language in this case was insufficient to constitute a valid waiver.

## ▶ ANALYSIS

Implied warranties of fitness and habitability were established to grant buyers relief from the harsh effect of the application of the doctrine of caveat emptor in the sale of houses and other structures. The evolution of these implied warranties led to the use of disclaimers by vendor-builders. As this case illustrates, such waivers may be valid depending on the clarity of expression provided by the contractual language.

## Quicknotes

**IMPLIED WARRANTY OF HABITABILITY** A warranty implied by a landlord that the premises are suitable, and will remain suitable, for habitation.

**WAIVER** The intentional or voluntary forfeiture of a recognized right.

■■■

# Brown v. Lober

Grantee (P) v. Executor of estate (D)

Ill. Sup. Ct., 75 Ill. 2d 547, 389 N.E.2d 1188 (1979).

**NATURE OF CASE:** Appeal from dismissal of action for breach of covenant.

**FACT SUMMARY:** Brown (P) contended that because he did not, in fact, own what the warranty deed from the grantor purported to convey, he was unable to sell an interest in the land, and, therefore, he was constructively evicted, allowing him to sue for breach of the covenant of quiet enjoyment of the land.

> 🏛 **RULE OF LAW**
> Unless a grantee is actually prevented from possessing or occupying the land, there is no breach of the covenant of quiet enjoyment.

**FACTS:** Brown (P) obtained land from Bost through a warranty deed. Subsequently, he conveyed an option for the coal rights to the land to a coal company for $6,000. He then learned that a prior grantor had reversed a two-thirds interest in the coal rights to the land. Brown (P) was thereby forced to renegotiate the option to the effect that only one-third coal interest could be granted at a price of $2,000. Brown (P) then sued Lober (D), the executor of Bost's estate, contending that because he did not, in fact, own what the warranty deed purported to convey he was constructively evicted from the interest, and, therefore, he had cause of action for breach of the covenant of quiet enjoyment. The trial court dismissed the complaint, holding the action was barred by the limitations. The court of appeals reversed, and Lober (D) appealed.

**ISSUE:** Is there no breach of covenant of quiet enjoyment unless a grantee is actually prevented from possessing or occupying the land?

**HOLDING AND DECISION:** (Underwood, J.) Yes. Unless a grantee is actually prevented from possessing or occupying his interest in the land, there is no breach of the covenant of quiet enjoyment. The covenant of quiet enjoyment is prospective in nature and is breached not at delivery of the deed, but when an eviction, actual or constructive, occurs. Consequently, because no other party had undertaken to remove coal from the land, or manifested a clear intent to exclusively possess the mineral rights, Brown (P) could at any time have taken peaceful possession of it. Therefore, he was never prevented from the enjoyment of the land and no breach occurred. No breach will occur until the paramount title holder asserts his interest. As a result, although the action was not barred, it had no substantive merit, and the dismissal was proper. Reversed.

▶ **ANALYSIS**

At the trial level, Brown (P) asserted a cause of action for breach of the covenant of seisin which was deemed barred by the statute of limitations. One difference between the two covenants is that the covenant of seisin, which warrants that the grantor is seized of an indefeasible estate of the size and duration which he is purporting to convey, arises upon delivery of the deed. If the grantor is not so seized, at that time, the covenant is breached and the limitations period begins to run. The covenant of quiet enjoyment, however, is prospective, as pointed out in this case.

■■■

## Quicknotes

**COVENANT OF QUIET ENJOYMENT**  A promise contained in a lease or a deed that the tenant or grantee will enjoy unimpaired use of the property.

**WARRANTY DEED**  A deed that guarantees that the conveyor possesses the title that he purports to convey.

■■■

# Leach v. Gunnarson

Grantee (D) v. Holding licensee (P)

Or. Sup. Ct., 290 Or. 31, 619 P.2d 263 (1980).

**NATURE OF CASE:** Appeal from judgment denying recovery in action for breach of covenant against encumbrances.

**FACT SUMMARY:** Gunnarson (D) contended that the existence of an irrevocable license to use a spring on the land he received constituted a breach of his grantor's covenant against encumbrances, even though its use by Leach (P) was open and visible.

## RULE OF LAW
A grantor's covenant against encumbrances protects the grantee against all encumbrances existing at the time of the delivery of the deed, including those of which the grantee had knowledge.

**FACTS:** Gunnarson (D) received a parcel of land from his grantor by way of a warranty deed. Gunnarson (D) knew that Leach (P) used a spring on the land, yet he was assured by his grantor that they had no enforceable right to do so. Leach (P) subsequently sued Gunnarson (D) to enforce his irrevocable license to use the spring which had been granted by Gunnarson's (D) grantor. Gunnarson (D) brought a third-party action against his grantor contending the license constituted a breach of covenant against encumbrances. His grantor contended that the covenant was not breached because Gunnarson (D) knew of the use, which was open, notorious, and visible, and, therefore, he took subject to it. The jury found for the grantor, and Gunnarson (D) appealed.

**ISSUE:** Does a grantor's covenant against encumbrances protect the grantee against all encumbrances existing at the time of the delivery of the deed, including those of which the grantee had knowledge?

**HOLDING AND DECISION:** (Howell, J.) Yes. A grantor's covenant against encumbrances included in his warranty deed protects the grantee from all encumbrances existing at the time of the delivery of the deed, including those of which the grantee had knowledge. Only where there is a known easement for a public highway or railroad right-of-way will the grantee be held to take the property without protection from a known encumbrance. An irrevocable license to use a spring is clearly not this type of open, notorious, and visible encumbrance to come within this exception to the general rule. Therefore, it was no defense to the action for breach of covenant to assert the knowledge of Gunnarson (D) of the encumbrance, and a breach did occur. Reversed and remanded.

## ANALYSIS

In *Merchandizing Corp. v. Marine National Exchange Bank*, 106 N.W.2d 317 (1960), a Wisconsin court held that where an easement was open, obvious, and notorious it does not constitute a defect on the vendor's title nor a breach of covenant against encumbrances. Although jurisdictions easily deal with the effect of such a major encumbrance as an easement, it is more difficult to determine the effect of a less intrusive interference such as a use restriction. Such restrictions are technically not encumbrances, yet their violation prior to the sale may constitute a breach of warranty.

## Quicknotes

**COVENANT AGAINST ENCUMBRANCES** A guarantee in a contract that the interest in property being conveyed is unencumbered.

**LICENSE** A right that is granted to a person allowing him or her to conduct an activity that without such permission he or she could not lawfully do, and which is unassignable and revocable at the will of the licensor.

**WARRANTY DEED** A deed that guarantees that the conveyor possesses the title that he purports to convey.

# Davis v. Smith

## Heirs of transferee (P) v. Estate administrator (D)

Ga. Sup. Ct., 5 Ga. 274, 48 Am. Dec. 279 (1848).

**NATURE OF CASE:** Bill in equity filed by administrator of an estate seeking directions for the payment of debts.

**FACT SUMMARY:** Harris (D) conveyed property to Laney (P), and when the title proved totally defective, Laney's (P) heirs sued for breach of a covenant of warranty in the deed.

## 🏛 RULE OF LAW

When a buyer of real property brings an action against the seller for breach of a covenant of warranty (the buyer is evicted or disturbed in possession), his damages are limited to the purchase price plus interest which is the only measure of the seller's liability, and not the value of the property at the time the buyer is ousted or disturbed.

**FACTS:** The administrator (D) of Harris's estate sought directions from the court on how to pay out claims on the estate. Among the debts was a claim by the heirs (P) of Laney that Harris (D) had conveyed a piece of property to Laney (P) by means of a deed containing a covenant of warranty, that the title was defective, and that Harris (D) had thereby breached the covenant.

**ISSUE:** May a purchaser of land who is disturbed in his possession of property, or is ousted therefrom by one claiming superior title, recover damages against the conveyor of a covenant of warranty equivalent to the value of the property plus interest at the time of the eviction?

**HOLDING AND DECISION:** (Nesbet, J.) No. While courts are divided, the majority rule follows the common law in limiting damages to the purchase price. This rule is easy of comprehension and of proof, and, most importantly, it is a criterion of recovery and liability which the parties may always establish for themselves. All that the seller here covenanted was that the buyer would be undisturbed in his title: he did not undertake to be liable for future chances of loss or disturbance. The buyer must be aware of the risk at the time he contracts, and should calculate possible loss in the negotiations over the amount he is willing to pay for the title.

## ▶ ANALYSIS

The minority approach, in placing the potential of loss through eviction on the seller, awards to the injured buyer damages equivalent to the value of the land at the time of eviction plus its natural appreciation, if any. A third suggested method is to allow recovery in the amount of the land's value plus the cost of any improvements placed upon it.

---

## Quicknotes

**OUSTER** The unlawful dispossession of a party lawfully entitled to possession of real property.

# Madrid v. Spears

Holders of forged deed (D) v. Owner of land (P)

250 F.2d 51 (10th Cir. 1957).

**NATURE OF CASE:** Diversity action to cancel a deed and to quiet title.

**FACT SUMMARY:** In an ejectment action brought by the owner, Spears (P), the occupants (D) claimed a right to be reimbursed for the amount their good-faith improvements enhanced the value of the property.

## 🏛 RULE OF LAW

(1) Where the cost of improvements made on land in good faith by the occupants is greatly less than the resulting enhanced value, the occupants are only entitled to recover the actual value of the improvements.

(2) However, the owner is not entitled to a setoff for mesne (accruing between two given times) profits derived from the premises during occupancy in absence of proof as to rental value of the land in its raw state.

**FACTS:** The Madrids (D) acquired land belonging to Spears (P) by way of a forged deed. In the suit to cancel the deed, the Madrids (D) claimed that they had made valuable good faith improvements on the property. Spears (P) sought an accounting for large profits made from the land over a 4-year period. The trial court, finding no evidence of the rental value of the land without the improvements, held that Spears (P) was not entitled to share in the profits although it held the Madrids (D) to the actual value of their improvements.

**ISSUE:**

(1) May occupiers of land, who claim the value of improvements made in good faith under color of title, recover, in ejectment proceedings, an amount equivalent to the enhanced value of the land?

(2) In the absence of evidence of the land's rental value, may the true owner share in profits the occupiers earned?

**HOLDING AND DECISION:** (Murrah, J.)

(1) No. The test of recovery is not how much the owner is enriched by the improvements, but how much he is unjustly enriched. The owner is not unjustly enriched more than the improver's cost. Where enhancement exceeds cost, unjust enrichment equals cost. The Restatement has endorsed this view by limiting the good-faith improver to the reasonable value of his labor and materials except where the enhanced value of the land is less.

(2) No. Modern statutes have modified the common-law rule which considered the innocent improver an interloper without legal remedy. Rather, the equities between the owner and the occupier must be balanced. Hence, in the absence of the value of the land in its raw state without its improvements, Spears (P) could not recover the profits realized by the Madrids (D). Trial court's judgment affirmed.

## ▶ ANALYSIS

Other courts have adopted the contrary position by applying a "betterment" standard. Under this approach, the good-faith occupier's compensation is measured by the amount by which the owner is benefited. In short, the occupier may recover the enhanced value of the land, and is not limited to cost or the actual value of the improvements.

■━■

### Quicknotes

**EJECTMENT** An action to oust someone in possession of real property unlawfully and to restore possession to the party lawfully entitled to it.

**MESNE ASSIGNMENT** An intermediate assignment made between that by the original assignor and that by the final assignee.

■━■

# Robben v. Obering

Purchaser (P) v. Transferee of lease (D)

279 F.2d 381 (7th Cir. 1960).

**NATURE OF CASE:** Diversity declaratory judgment action to determine who holds title to oil and gas lease.

**FACT SUMMARY:** Meirink conveyed a lease to Obering (D) by means of a warranty deed, and when Meirink discovered he had not owned all of the land, acquired the rest, but almost immediately resold it to his brother.

## 🏛 RULE OF LAW
Where a grantor conveys an estate in land by warranty deed which he does not then own, but subsequently acquires the property, his after-acquired title immediately goes to the grantee under the deed.

**FACTS:** Meirink conveyed an oil and gas lease to Obering (D) by way of a warranty deed. When Meirink discovered that he had not owned all of the property, he attempted to acquire the remainder from his brother and sister. Receiving a quitclaim deed from his brother, Meirink, unable to acquire the other portion from his sister, immediately reconveyed the property to his brother. The brother thereupon sold his interest to Robben (P).

**ISSUE:** Where a grantor conveys property by way of warranty deed, and only thereafter acquires title to the property, is the after-acquired property considered part of the original grant so as to entitle the grantee to immediate ownership?

**HOLDING AND DECISION:** (Castle, J.) Yes. Under the doctrine of estoppel by deed, Meirink and his successors in title, his brother and Robben (P), are estopped from claiming that Meirink did not have title at the time he conveyed the property to Obering (D). Obering's (D) interest will be treated as vested at the time of the conveyance's execution. The doctrine applies to conveyances of fee simple not accompanied by a warranty deed, and to lesser estates which are warranted. Reversed and remanded.

## ▶ ANALYSIS

Although the basis for the estopped-by deed doctrine has been characterized by courts as resting on deceit and misrepresentation, the simpler rationale is that the grantor warranted his conveyance, and the grantee should, therefore, be entitled to the benefit of the bargain. The doctrine, with some exceptions, also extends to gift conveyances.

## Quicknotes

**ESTOPPEL** An equitable doctrine precluding a party from asserting a right to the detriment of another who justifiably relied on the conduct.

**QUITCLAIM DEED** A deed whereby the grantor conveys whatever interest he or she may have in the property without any warranties or covenants as to title.

**WARRANTY DEED** A deed that guarantees that the conveyor possesses the title that he purports to convey.

# First American Title Insurance Company, Inc. v. First Title Service Company of the Florida Keys, Inc.

Insurance company (P) v. Title company (D)

Fla. Sup. Ct., 457 So. 2d 467 (1984).

**NATURE OF CASE:** Appeal of dismissal of action for damages for negligent preparation of title.

**FACT SUMMARY:** First Title Service Company of the Florida Keys, Inc. (D) prepared abstracts that failed to note a pending judgment for which First American Title Insurance Company, Inc. (P) had to pay.

🏛 **RULE OF LAW**
Where an abstract company knowingly and reasonably expects and induces third persons to rely on its abstracts, those third persons have a valid cause of action.

**FACTS:** First Title Service Company of the Florida Keys, Inc. (D) prepared abstracts for sellers of two lots, to whom First American Title Insurance Company, Inc. (P) had issued insurance policies. The abstracts had failed to include the fact that judgments were pending against the former owner of the lots in the amount of $75,000. Pursuant to its insurance policies, First American Title Insurance Co. (P) had to pay the judgment, and thus sued First Title Service Co. (D) for negligent preparation of the abstract. The trial court dismissed the complaint for failure to state a cause of action and the appellate court affirmed. First Title Insurance Co. (D) appealed.

**ISSUE:** Where an abstract company knowingly and reasonably expects and induces third persons to rely on its abstracts, do those third-party beneficiaries of the abstract have a valid cause of action against the abstract company?

**HOLDING AND DECISION:** (Boyd, J.) Yes. Where an abstract company knowingly and reasonably expects and induces third persons to rely on its abstracts, those third-party beneficiaries of the abstract have a valid cause of action against the abstract company. *Ultramares Corp. v. Touche*, 255 N.Y. 170 (1931). The approach of *Williams v. Polgar*, 391 Mich. 6 (1974), which held abstractors liable in tort for foreseeable and known reliances upon abstracts on the bases that a duty of diligence is owed to contracting parties and that a general duty exists to act with reasonable care to nonparties, is rejected here. The basis for rejecting these cases is for the policy reason that such holdings could expose abstractors to infinite liability and thereby adversely affect business conduct. Thus, an abstractor's duty to perform diligently runs only to contractual parties and to those third parties which the abstractor knew or reasonably should have known would rely on its negligently prepared abstracts. Here, First American Title

Insurance Co.'s (P) claim that it is such an intended and known beneficiary of the contract for abstract service and may thus recover for First Title Service Co.'s (D) negligent conduct is sufficient to support a valid cause of action. However, knowledge and negligence on the abstractor's part must still be proved. Reversed and remanded.

▶ **ANALYSIS**

Courts generally impose upon abstract companies a high standard of conduct in preparation of abstracts. For example, in *Ford v. Guarantee Abstract & Title Co., Inc.*, dictum stated that an abstract company could be liable to persons who rely on its abstracts in purchasing or investing in land. Moreover, punitive damages were allowed because of the abstractor's "reckless indifference" for the plaintiff's rights. 220 Kan. 244 (1976). In another case, an abstractor was found negligent for relying solely on a court clerk's erroneous judgment docket and for failing to rely on the judgment itself. *Wichita Great Empire Broadcasting, Inc. v. Gingrich*, 4 Kan. App. 2d 223 (1979).

■■■

***Quicknotes***

**ABSTRACT** Summary of the history of a title to property.

**THIRD-PARTY BENEFICIARY** A party who benefits from a promise made pursuant to a contract although he is not a party to the agreement.

■■■

# United States v. Ryan

## Federal government (P) v. Bank (D)

124 F. Supp. 1 (D. Minn. 1954); *rev'd*, 253 F.2d 944 (8th Cir. 1958).

**NATURE OF CASE:** Action to establish and enforce certain liens and claims.

**FACT SUMMARY:** In a Torrens System state, the U.S. government failed to have a new certificate of registration issued in its name so as to perfect a lien.

## 🏛 RULE OF LAW
Because federal law requires the United States government to comply with the notice requirements of state law, it has failed to perfect a federal tax lien if, in a state which follows the Torrens System of land registration, the United States fails to apply for a new certificate of title registered in its name.

**FACTS:** The United States Government (P) had a tax claim against some property in Minnesota. To perfect a lien on the property, the U.S. (P), obligated by federal law to comply with state notice requirements, filed a notice of a tax lien, by name only, in the office of a Minnesota registrar of deeds. Minnesota law, however, which followed the Torrens System of land registration in lieu of the recording act system, required that a party seeking to perfect a lien— an involuntary transfer—must first get a court order directing the registrar to issue a new certificate of title indicating the lien. When a bank (D) foreclosed against the property, the United States (P) sued to have its lien given priority over the bank (D) and the subsequent purchasers (D).

**ISSUE:** Is the United States exempt from complying with the Torrens System of land registration?

**HOLDING AND DECISION:** (Bell, J.) No. The Torrens System is built upon a firm, reasonable policy. The System makes land ownership conclusively evidenced by certificate and thereby makes land title determinable and transferable quickly, cheaply, and safely. The purpose behind the judicial proceeding is to allow those who could possibly have an adverse interest to come forth, or forever be barred from doing so. Because of this procedure, the system does not violate the due process rights of anyone. Dismissal for the defendants granted and summary judgment for the plaintiff denied.

## ▶ ANALYSIS

The motivating theory behind the Torrens System is that a certification of registration is not just evidence of title; it is title. As against a subsequent bona fide purchaser, any claims not indicated on the certificate are invalid.

## Quicknotes

**TORRENS SYSTEM** Method of registering title to land upon application to a court and the court's issuance of a certificate.

■━■

# White v. Western Title Insurance Co.

## Purchaser of lots (P) v. Insurance company (D)

Cal. Sup. Ct., 40 Cal. 3d 870, 710 P.2d 309 (1985).

**NATURE OF CASE:** Appeal of award of damages in a title insurance dispute.

**FACT SUMMARY:** Western Title Insurance Co. (D) provided title reports and insurance to White (P) that failed to mention and cover an existing water easement.

## 🏛 RULE OF LAW
Title insurance companies owe a duty to meet all reasonable expectations of its insureds, to diligently perform title searches, and to exercise good faith and fair dealing.

**FACTS:** White (P) purchased two lots from Longhurst without the knowledge that Longhurst had conveyed water easements on those lots to River Estates Mutual Water Corporation. Western Title Insurance Co. (D) failed to mention the recorded water easement in its title report prepared for White (P) and also provided title insurance to White (P) that excluded coverage for "water rights, claims or title to water." White (P) found out about the easement when River Estates attempted to exercise its easement rights. River Estates later decided not to enforce its easement, but White (P) sought recovery of $62,947 from Western Title (D) for potential loss of groundwater, which Western Title (D) refused to pay. White (P) then sued for breach of contract, negligence, and breach of implied covenants of good faith and fair dealing, and rejected all compromise offers made by Western Title (D). A jury awarded White (P) $8,400 for breach of contract and negligence plus $20,000 for breach of good faith. Western Title (D) appealed.

**ISSUE:** Do title insurance companies owe a duty to meet all reasonable expectations of its insureds, to diligently perform title searches, and to exercise good faith and fair dealing?

**HOLDING AND DECISION:** (Broussard, J.) Yes. Title insurance companies owe a duty to meet all reasonable expectations of their insureds, to diligently perform title searches, and to exercise good faith and fair dealing. As to the first duty, any ambiguity in an insurance policy is interpreted against the insurer in order to protect the insured's reasonable expectations of coverage. Here, White (P) had a reasonable expectation that Western Title (D) would discover and reveal the existence of the recorded water easement, and thus Western Title's (D) attempt to exclude such coverage fails here. As to the second duty, a title insurer is liable for its negligence in failing to conduct a diligent title search of any recorded encumbrances upon land titles. Here, Western Title's (D) failure to include the water easement in its title report to

White (P) constituted prima facie negligence, from which it cannot exculpate itself. Further, a contributory negligence defense is not applicable here because only Western Title (D), and not White (P), had the duty to investigate. As to the third duty, a covenant of good faith and fair dealing is implied in all title insurance contracts. *Gruenberg v. Aetna Ins. Co.*, 9 Cal. 3d 566 (1973). Mere institution of litigation by an insured against an insurer does not terminate this duty of good faith. Such a holding would disserve the public interest by encouraging insurers to induce the early filing of suits in order to avoid the good faith duty. Here, although Western Title's (D) compromise offers were inadmissible to prove liability for breach of contract and negligence, they were admissible to prove liability for breach of good faith and fair dealing. Finally, as to damages for breach of good faith, White (P) is entitled to recover attorney fees and other litigation expenses as the result of Western Title's (D) bad-faith conduct. Affirmed.

**CONCURRENCE AND DISSENT:** (Lucas, J.) The majority's holding as to the good faith issue will only subject insurers to damages for their conduct during litigation, and the admissibility of an insurer's compromise offers will only be interpreted by jurors as an admission of liability.

## ▶ *ANALYSIS*

*White* illustrates the California courts' willingness to enlarge a title insurer's tort liability. Other courts are not as expansive. For example, in *Brown's Tie & Lumber Co. v. Chicago Title Co. of Idaho*, where the title company failed to note a recorded trust deed, the court dismissed the plaintiff's tort claims on the basis that only direct and voluntary duties taken on by the insurer in addition to the contract to insure title will subject the insurer to negligence liability. 115 Idaho 56, 764 P.2d 423 (1988).

■■■■

## *Quicknotes*

**EASEMENT** The right to utilize a portion of another's real property for a specific use.

**FIDUCIARY DUTY** A legal obligation to act for the benefit of another, including subordinating one's personal interests to that of the other person.

**IMPLIED COVENANT** A promise inferred by law from a document as a whole and the circumstances surrounding its implementation.

■■■■

# Transamerica Title Insurance Co. v. Johnson

Insurance company (P) v. Corporation (D)

Wash. Sup. Ct., 103 Wash. 2d 409, 693 P.2d 697 (1985).

**NATURE OF CASE:** Appeal of summary judgment awarding damages under a subrogation agreement.

**FACT SUMMARY:** Transamerica Title Insurance Co. (P) failed to exclude coverage of sewer assessment liens in its policies and sought to recover its payments of the liens against Johnson (D).

## 🏛 RULE OF LAW
A title insurer is liable to a noninsured for breach of duty to search and disclose where the noninsured has foreseeably relied upon the insurer's representations.

**FACTS:** Transamerica Title Insurance Co. (P) issued insurance policies for three parcels of land in which it failed to exclude coverage for sewer assessment liens. Johnson (D), a corporation, was the seller-grantor of the land and had knowledge of the sewer assessments when it originally purchased the land. When Johnson (D) listed the lands for sale, it ensured in its listing agreements that the titles were free from encumbrances. However, the assessments were never disclosed to the current purchasers by Johnson (D) nor by Transamerica (P) when it issued the insurance policies. Transamerica (P) paid the assessments and sought to enforce its subrogation policy against Johnson (D). The trial court granted Transamerica (P) a summary judgment, which was affirmed at the appellate level. Johnson (D) appealed.

**ISSUE:** Is a title insurer liable to a noninsured for breach of duty to search and disclose where the noninsured has foreseeably relied upon the insurer's representations?

**HOLDING AND DECISION:** (Brachtenbach, J.) Yes. A title insurer is liable to a noninsured for breach of duty to search and disclose where the noninsured has foreseeably relied upon the insurer's representations. Because a noninsured has no contractual relationship with an insurer, the only basis of liability exists in tort. However, even if an insurer is negligent in failing to disclose information, no liability can be imposed where no duty is owed. In addition to proving that duty is owed, the noninsured must prove that his reliance upon the nondisclosure was foreseeable. Here, because Johnson (D) knew of the sewer assessments even before Transamerica (P) issued its insurance policies and represented the property to its purchasers as free from encumbrances, no reliance exists. Had Johnson (D) disclosed the assessments, he would have had to pay them from closing costs. Finally, Johnson (D) has no alternative remedy under the Consumer Protection Act, RCW 19.86, because he was an uninsured claimant and because no reliance on his part can be established. Affirmed.

## ▶ ANALYSIS

The modern trend of courts is to impose higher standards of conduct upon title insurance companies. For example, in *L. Smirlock Realty Corp. v. Title Guarantee Co.*, an insured was not held to be duty-bound to disclose information regarding condemnation proceedings to an insurer because such information was available from public records. Even an intentional failure to disclose such facts would not be a basis for revocation of title insurance. However, intentional failure to disclose relevant facts that are not available in public records will void the insurance policy. 52 N.Y.2d 179 (1981).

■▬■

## Quicknotes

**PRIVITY OF CONTRACT**  A relationship between the parties to a contract that is required in order to bring an action for breach.

**RELIANCE**  Dependence on a fact that causes a party to act or refrain from acting.

■▬■

# Short v. Texaco, Inc.

## State (D) v. Oil company (P)

Ind. Sup. Ct., 273 Ind. 518, 406 N.E.2d 625 (1980); *aff'd*, 454 U.S. 516 (1982).

**NATURE OF CASE:** Appeal from decision holding a mineral rights termination statute unconstitutional.

**FACT SUMMARY:** The trial court held an Indiana statute, which terminated interests in coal, oil, gas, and other minerals which had not been used for 20 years, unconstitutional as a denial of due process, equal protection, and just compensation.

### 🏛 RULE OF LAW
Statutes which limit the amount of time within which an owner may assert his interest in land are not per se unconstitutional as a denial of due process, equal protection, or just compensation.

**FACTS:** Texaco, Inc. (P) challenged an Indiana statute which terminated mineral rights which had not been used for 20 years. The statute was enacted to prevent state and abandoned property interests which lead to confusion over title, and to promote maximum use of natural resources. The statute was self-executing and did not require prior notice and hearing before rights were terminated. Texaco (P) contended the statute constituted a denial of due process of law, a violation of equal protection, and a denial of just compensation. The trial court held the statute unconstitutional, and the State (D) appealed.

**ISSUE:** Are statutes which limit the amount of time within which an owner may assert his interest in the land per se unconstitutional?

**HOLDING AND DECISION:** (DeBruler, J.) No. Statutes which limit the amount of time within which an owner may assert his interest in land are not per se unconstitutional as a denial of due process, equal protection, or just compensation. The act in this case is analogous to a statute of limitations. Although mineral rights are as protectable as fee interests, they do not enjoy a greater level of protection. Fee interests are subject to forfeiture through adverse possession, and this is not a deprivation of due process. Further, the state interests in avoiding uncertainty in titles to property, and in exploiting mineral resources, are sufficiently compelling to support the classification made by the statute. Therefore, it does not violate equal protection. Finally, the statute does not involve injury to private property through government conduct in exercise of the power on eminent domain. Rather, it merely declares certain rights will lapse in the event of specified circumstances. Therefore, no compensation need be paid. As a result, the statute was unconstitutional. Reversed and remanded.

### ▶ *ANALYSIS*

In *Texaco, Inc. v. Short*, 454 U.S. 516 (1982), the Supreme Court affirmed the decision of the Indiana Supreme Court in this case. Justice Brennan wrote a strong dissent to the 5-4 majority opinion in which he argued that the State had acted arbitrarily in depriving owners of their mineral rights in violation of the Fourteenth Amendment due process clause. The use of statutes of limitation is common, but they do not generally apply to governmental actions. The remedy in such a case is the invocation of the equitable doctrine of laches.

■=■

### *Quicknotes*

**EMINENT DOMAIN** The governmental power to take private property for public use so long as just compensation is paid therefor.

**STATUTE OF LIMITATIONS** A law prescribing the period in which a legal action may be commenced.

■=■

# H & F Land, Inc. v. Panama City-Bay County Airport and Industrial District

Parties not identified.

Fla. Sup. Ct., 736 So. 2d 1167 (1999).

**NATURE OF CASE:** Suit to assert the right to a way of necessity.

**FACT SUMMARY:** H & F Land, Inc. (P) brought suit asserting the right to a way of necessity for access to a water and landlocked parcel of land.

## 🏛 RULE OF LAW
The Marketable Record Title Act operates to extinguish an otherwise valid claim of a common law way of necessity when such claim was not asserted within thirty years.

**FACTS:** Coastal, once owner of all the land now at issue, conveyed 390 acres to Bay County, which in turn conveyed it to Panama City (D). As a result of the transfer, a small piece of land retained by Coastal became both water- and landlocked. The parties agree a common law way of necessity was created, but no claim was ever filed or asserted by use. Fifty-six years later, H & F Land, Inc. (P) filed suit asserting the right to such way. Panama City (D) filed a motion for summary judgment claiming such way had been extinguished. The trial court granted the motion and the district court affirmed, but certified the question as to whether the MRTA applied to ways of necessity.

**ISSUE:** Does the Marketable Record Title Act operate to extinguish an otherwise valid claim of a common law way of necessity when such claim was not asserted within thirty years?

**HOLDING AND DECISION:** (Anstead, J.) Yes. The Marketable Record Title Act operates to extinguish an otherwise valid claim of a common law way of necessity when such claim was not asserted within thirty years. A way of necessity is an easement that arises from an implied grant or reservation of an interest in land. The MRTA refers to "all claims," and its clear policy is to apply to all claims to an interest in property unless clearly excepted. The MRTA mandates that such claims or interests be publicly asserted and recorded, to serve the underlying goal of stability in property law. Those claiming an interest in land must publicly assert such interest so that they may be a matter of public record. Because H & F's (P) predecessor failed to record or publicly assert its way of necessity, the MRTA mandates its extinguishments.

## ▶ ANALYSIS

The MRTA provided two exceptions to the recording requirement. The first is for interests and defects "inherent in the muniments of title on which an estate is based beginning with the root of title." Such defects must be found on the face of the title, not from the surrounding circumstances. The second is for proper filing with notice within the statutory period of 30 years. The deed here did not disclose the way on its face, nor did H & F's (P) predecessor in interest record the title within the proscribed period.

■═■

## Quicknotes

**TITLE** The right of possession over property.

■═■

# Glossary

*Common Latin Words and Phrases Encountered in the Law*

**A FORTIORI:** Because one fact exists or has been proven, therefore a second fact that is related to the first fact must also exist.

**A PRIORI:** From the cause to the effect. A term of logic used to denote that when one generally accepted truth is shown to be a cause, another particular effect must necessarily follow.

**AB INITIO:** From the beginning; a condition which has existed throughout, as in a marriage which was void ab initio.

**ACTUS REUS:** The wrongful act; in criminal law, such action sufficient to trigger criminal liability.

**AD VALOREM:** According to value; an ad valorem tax is imposed upon an item located within the taxing jurisdiction calculated by the value of such item.

**AMICUS CURIAE:** Friend of the court. Its most common usage takes the form of an amicus curiae brief, filed by a person who is not a party to an action but is nonetheless allowed to offer an argument supporting his legal interests.

**ARGUENDO:** In arguing. A statement, possibly hypothetical, made for the purpose of argument, is one made arguendo.

**BILL QUIA TIMET:** A bill to quiet title (establish ownership) to real property.

**BONA FIDE:** True, honest, or genuine. May refer to a person's legal position based on good faith or lacking notice of fraud (such as a bona fide purchaser for value) or to the authenticity of a particular document (such as a bona fide last will and testament).

**CAUSA MORTIS:** With approaching death in mind. A gift causa mortis is a gift given by a party who feels certain that death is imminent.

**CAVEAT EMPTOR:** Let the buyer beware. This maxim is reflected in the rule of law that a buyer purchases at his own risk because it is his responsibility to examine, judge, test, and otherwise inspect what he is buying.

**CERTIORARI:** A writ of review. Petitions for review of a case by the United States Supreme Court are most often done by means of a writ of certiorari.

**CONTRA:** On the other hand. Opposite. Contrary to.

**CORAM NOBIS:** Before us; writs of error directed to the court that originally rendered the judgment.

**CORAM VOBIS:** Before you; writs of error directed by an appellate court to a lower court to correct a factual error.

**CORPUS DELICTI:** The body of the crime; the requisite elements of a crime amounting to objective proof that a crime has been committed.

**CUM TESTAMENTO ANNEXO, ADMINISTRATOR (ADMINISTRATOR C.T.A.):** With will annexed; an administrator c.t.a. settles an estate pursuant to a will in which he is not appointed.

**DE BONIS NON, ADMINISTRATOR (ADMINISTRATOR D.B.N.):** Of goods not administered; an administrator d.b.n. settles a partially settled estate.

**DE FACTO:** In fact; in reality; actually. Existing in fact but not officially approved or engendered.

**DE JURE:** By right; lawful. Describes a condition that is legitimate "as a matter of law," in contrast to the term "de facto," which connotes something existing in fact but not legally sanctioned or authorized. For example, de facto segregation refers to segregation brought about by housing patterns, etc., whereas de jure segregation refers to segregation created by law.

**DE MINIMIS:** Of minimal importance; insignificant; a trifle; not worth bothering about.

**DE NOVO:** Anew; a second time; afresh. A trial de novo is a new trial held at the appellate level as if the case originated there and the trial at a lower level had not taken place.

**DICTA:** Generally used as an abbreviated form of obiter dicta, a term describing those portions of a judicial opinion incidental or not necessary to resolution of the specific question before the court. Such nonessential statements and remarks are not considered to be binding precedent.

**DUCES TECUM:** Refers to a particular type of writ or subpoena requesting a party or organization to produce certain documents in their possession.

**EN BANC:** Full bench. Where a court sits with all justices present rather than the usual quorum.

**EX PARTE:** For one side or one party only. An ex parte proceeding is one undertaken for the benefit of only one party, without notice to, or an appearance by, an adverse party.

**EX POST FACTO:** After the fact. An ex post facto law is a law that retroactively changes the consequences of a prior act.

**EX REL.:** Abbreviated form of the term ex relatione, meaning upon relation or information. When the state brings an action in which it has no interest against an individual at the instigation of one who has a private interest in the matter.

**FORUM NON CONVENIENS:** Inconvenient forum. Although a court may have jurisdiction over the case, the action should be tried in a more conveniently located court, one to which parties and witnesses may more easily travel, for example.

**GUARDIAN AD LITEM:** A guardian of an infant as to litigation, appointed to represent the infant and pursue his/her rights.

**HABEAS CORPUS:** You have the body. The modern writ of habeas corpus is a writ directing that a person (body) being detained (such as a prisoner) be brought before the court so that the legality of his detention can be judicially ascertained.

**IN CAMERA:** In private, in chambers. When a hearing is held before a judge in his chambers or when all spectators are excluded from the courtroom.

**IN FORMA PAUPERIS:** In the manner of a pauper. A party who proceeds in forma pauperis because of his poverty is one who is allowed to bring suit without liability for costs.

**INFRA:** Below, under. A word referring the reader to a later part of a book. (The opposite of supra.)

**IN LOCO PARENTIS:** In the place of a parent.

**IN PARI DELICTO:** Equally wrong; a court of equity will not grant requested relief to an applicant who is in pari delicto, or as much at fault in the transactions giving rise to the controversy as is the opponent of the applicant.

**IN PARI MATERIA:** On like subject matter or upon the same matter. Statutes relating to the same person or things are said to be in pari materia. It is a general rule of statutory construction that such statutes should be construed together, i.e., looked at as if they together constituted one law.

**IN PERSONAM:** Against the person. Jurisdiction over the person of an individual.

**IN RE:** In the matter of. Used to designate a proceeding involving an estate or other property.

**IN REM:** A term that signifies an action against the res, or thing. An action in rem is basically one that is taken directly against property, as distinguished from an action in personam, i.e., against the person.

**INTER ALIA:** Among other things. Used to show that the whole of a statement, pleading, list, statute, etc., has not been set forth in its entirety.

**INTER PARTES:** Between the parties. May refer to contracts, conveyances or other transactions having legal significance.

**INTER VIVOS:** Between the living. An inter vivos gift is a gift made by a living grantor, as distinguished from bequests contained in a will, which pass upon the death of the testator.

**IPSO FACTO:** By the mere fact itself.

**JUS:** Law or the entire body of law.

**LEX LOCI:** The law of the place; the notion that the rights of parties to a legal proceeding are governed by the law of the place where those rights arose.

**MALUM IN SE:** Evil or wrong in and of itself; inherently wrong. This term describes an act that is wrong by its very nature, as opposed to one which would not be wrong but for the fact that there is a specific legal prohibition against it (malum prohibitum).

**MALUM PROHIBITUM:** Wrong because prohibited, but not inherently evil. Used to describe something that is wrong because it is expressly forbidden by law but that is not in and of itself evil, e.g., speeding.

**MANDAMUS:** We command. A writ directing an official to take a certain action.

**MENS REA:** A guilty mind; a criminal intent. A term used to signify the mental state that accompanies a crime or other prohibited act. Some crimes require only a general mens rea (general intent to do the prohibited act), but others, like assault with intent to murder, require the existence of a specific mens rea.

**MODUS OPERANDI:** Method of operating; generally refers to the manner or style of a criminal in committing crimes, admissible in appropriate cases as evidence of the identity of a defendant.

**NEXUS:** A connection to.

**NISI PRIUS:** A court of first impression. A nisi prius court is one where issues of fact are tried before a judge or jury.

**N.O.V. (NON OBSTANTE VEREDICTO):** Notwithstanding the verdict. A judgment n.o.v. is a judgment given in favor of one party despite the fact that a verdict was returned in favor of the other party, the justification being that the verdict either had no reasonable support in fact or was contrary to law.

**NUNC PRO TUNC:** Now for then. This phrase refers to actions that may be taken and will then have full retroactive effect.

**PENDENTE LITE:** Pending the suit; pending litigation underway.

**PER CAPITA:** By head; beneficiaries of an estate, if they take in equal shares, take per capita.

**PER CURIAM:** By the court; signifies an opinion ostensibly written "by the whole court" and with no identified author.

**PER SE:** By itself, in itself; inherently.

**PER STIRPES:** By representation. Used primarily in the law of wills to describe the method of distribution where a person, generally because of death, is unable to take that which is left to him by the will of another, and therefore his heirs divide such property between them rather than take under the will individually.

**PRIMA FACIE:** On its face, at first sight. A prima facie case is one that is sufficient on its face, meaning that the evidence supporting it is adequate to establish the case until contradicted or overcome by other evidence.

**PRO TANTO:** For so much; as far as it goes. Often used in eminent domain cases when a property owner receives partial payment for his land without prejudice to his right to bring suit for the full amount he claims his land to be worth.

**QUANTUM MERUIT:** As much as he deserves. Refers to recovery based on the doctrine of unjust enrichment in those cases in which a party has rendered valuable services or furnished materials that were accepted and enjoyed by another under circumstances that would reasonably notify the recipient that the rendering party expected to be paid. In essence, the law implies a contract to pay the reasonable value of the services or materials furnished.

**QUASI:** Almost like; as if; nearly. This term is essentially used to signify that one subject or thing is almost analogous to another but that material differences between them do exist. For example, a quasi-criminal proceeding is one that is not strictly criminal but shares enough of the same characteristics to require some of the same safeguards (e.g., procedural due process must be followed in a parole hearing).

**QUID PRO QUO:** Something for something. In contract law, the consideration, something of value, passed between the parties to render the contract binding.

**RES GESTAE:** Things done; in evidence law, this principle justifies the admission of a statement that would otherwise be hearsay when it is made so closely to the event in question as to be said to be a part of it, or with such spontaneity as not to have the possibility of falsehood.

**RES IPSA LOQUITUR:** The thing speaks for itself. This doctrine gives rise to a rebuttable presumption of negligence when the instrumentality causing the injury was within the exclusive control of the defendant, and the injury was one that does not normally occur unless a person has been negligent.

**RES JUDICATA:** A matter adjudged. Doctrine which provides that once a court of competent jurisdiction has rendered a final judgment or decree on the merits, that judgment or decree is conclusive upon the parties to the case and prevents them from engaging in any other litigation on the points and issues determined therein.

**RESPONDEAT SUPERIOR:** Let the master reply. This doctrine holds the master liable for the wrongful acts of his servant (or the principal for his agent) in those cases in which the servant (or agent) was acting within the scope of his authority at the time of the injury.

**STARE DECISIS:** To stand by or adhere to that which has been decided. The common law doctrine of stare decisis attempts to give security and certainty to the law by following the policy that once a principle of law as applicable to a certain set of facts has been set forth in a decision, it forms a precedent which will subsequently be followed, even though a different decision might be made were it the first time the question had arisen. Of course, stare decisis is not an inviolable principle and is departed from in instances where there is good cause (e.g., considerations of public policy led the Supreme Court to disregard prior decisions sanctioning segregation).

**SUPRA:** Above. A word referring a reader to an earlier part of a book.

**ULTRA VIRES:** Beyond the power. This phrase is most commonly used to refer to actions taken by a corporation that are beyond the power or legal authority of the corporation.

## Addendum of French Derivatives

**IN PAIS:** Not pursuant to legal proceedings.

**CHATTEL:** Tangible personal property.

**CY PRES:** Doctrine permitting courts to apply trust funds to purposes not expressed in the trust but necessary to carry out the settlor's intent.

**PER AUTRE VIE:** For another's life; during another's life. In property law, an estate may be granted that will terminate upon the death of someone other than the grantee.

**PROFIT A PRENDRE:** A license to remove minerals or other produce from land.

**VOIR DIRE:** Process of questioning jurors as to their predispositions about the case or parties to a proceeding in order to identify those jurors displaying bias or prejudice.

# Casenote Legal Briefs

Life Estate: a Possessory Interest in Land Measured By the Life of the grantee, or other Person (estate).

Fee Simple Absolute: Land owned in a Fee Simple absolute is owned completely without any limitations or conditions.

See P. 253

Outline

#8. a. Life estate
b. remainder interest
9. possibility of Reverter

9.
?    G: no interest/possibility of Reverting
a. fee Simple

Fee Simple determinable

10. G. Life Possibility of Reverter
A. life
B. no interest
&
B.heirs — Remainder

* 11. G- Reversion
A- estate Per autre via (life estate Measured by another)
B- R.I no interest
C- remainder

12. G-

15, A- life estate
B- remainder of
G- possible Reversion/reverter

CPSIA information can be obtained at www.ICGtesting.com
Printed in the USA
LVOW11s1651120114

369096LV00001B/184/P